A Century of
Rugby
Greats

In association with

RECORD-KEEPING in rugby has been of a rather piecemeal and unsatisfactory nature in the past. Generally, this has not been a reflection on the game's statisticians, but rather a reflection on the muddled, and sometimes even arrogant thinking of administrators charged with deciding what constitutes a 'test' match.

Different countries recognise some matches as official tests while others do not. For instance, South Africa awarded caps for its 'tests' against the New Zealand Cavaliers in 1986, but New Zealand did not (and, in fact, does not recognise these matches as first-class). On the other hand, New Zealand awarded caps for matches against a World XV in 1992, but players appearing for the World team were not credited with caps. This situation has been repeated countless times, especially in matches involving countries like Italy, Romania and Argentina as they emerged from rugby obscurity.

I have endeavoured to be as inclusive as possible in my record-keeping. You will note in Hugo Porta's section that I have included his test matches for Argentina and South America, and therefore his points total in this book is considerably higher than that listed in some publications. My logic is that if all Gareth Edwards' internationals for Wales and the British Isles are to be listed as 'tests', the same rules should apply to Porta.

At the back of the book is my full list of current world records and my criteria. I hope that as rugby continues to become a major world sport, those charged with administering the game will ensure that there is more standardisation in record-keeping. It is too important a part of a sport's history to be treated in anything but a thorough and professional manner.

The records listed throughout this book are as complete as I can make them, and take in all performances to the end of the 1999 Five Nations Championship.

On the matter of style, different countries tend to refer to certain positions by different names. I have done the same. Therefore, while Cliff Morgan is referred to as a flyhalf, Grant Fox is a first five-eighth. Similarly, Joost van der Westhuizen is a scrumhalf, Sid Going is a halfback.

When describing height and weight, some countries use the metric system and others use imperial measurements. For clarity, I have included both.

A Century of
Rugby
Greats

By Keith Quinn

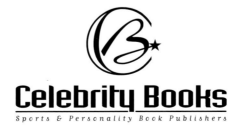

Celebrity Books
Sports & Personality Book Publishers

ACKNOWLEDGEMENTS

While this book has my name on it as author, there are several people whose assistance enabled it to be written.

Joseph Romanos, an industrious worker if ever there was one, helped me to crystallise the concept and has been closely involved throughout the project. He has debated my choices with me, edited my writing and added his own touches, and I thank him sincerely for his contribution. Many of our discussions have taken place over a cup of coffee and a cake, which while doing nothing for our figures, has considerably added to the profits of many of the patisseries and coffee bars in our neighbourhood.

Geoff Miller, one of New Zealand's leading rugby statisticians, responded enthusiastically to my initial plea for help with the various boxes that accompany each profile, then found himself being leaned on more heavily for further information, some of it historical and relatively obscure. He invariably came up with the goods.

The photographs in this book come from two main sources. Andrew Cornaga and his Photosport agency supplied most of the photos of the rugby greats of recent years. Their quality is obvious to anyone with even a passing interest in rugby. Peter Bush, the doyen of New Zealand sports photography, has been covering international rugby for more than 40 years and from his vast collection I was able to illustrate many of the profiles of players who predate PhotoSport. I have included one picture taken during the International Rugby Hall of Fame launch in London in 1997 and thank Fofosport of England for its use. The remaining photos have been culled from a variety of sources. I have endeavoured to trace the owners of the copyright of every photo, but in a few cases this has not been possible, and I apologise for any omissions. It was not through lack of trying.

Several other people supplied me (or Joseph Romanos or Geoff Miller) with specific information when requested and in no particular order, I would therefore also like to thank Andrew Slack, Gordon Bray, Chris Thau, Vittorio Munari, Robyn Murray, Giampaolo Tassinari, John Griffiths, John Lea, Laurie Tempelhoff, Pablo Mamone and Nicolas Sennegon.

I am most grateful to Colin Meads for his generous words in the foreword he has written, and to Bill Honeybone, Paul Neazor and Dallas Bennett for their work on this book.

ISBN No 0-9583729-8-5
Published in 1999 by: Celebrity Books
46A Taharoto Road, Takapuna
Auckland 10, New Zealand.

©1999 Copyright: Keith Quinn and Joseph Romanos
Layout/design by Benefitz Graphics Ltd, Takapuna, Auckland.
Typeset by Benefitz Graphics Ltd.
Cover Art by Dallas Bennett.
Printed in China through Colorcraft Ltd, Hong Kong.
Celebrity Books is the imprint of The Celebrity Book Company Limited,
P.O. Box 331630, Takapuna, Auckland, New Zealand.

CONTENTS

DEDICATION

In my career I have mostly been a TV rugby commentator. I dedicate this book to the two great broadcasters who influenced me the most.

The late Winston McCarthy once said to me: "It doesn't matter what they say about you, sonny, as long as they spell your name right."

Bill McLaren told me: "The secret of good commentating is never to neglect your homework."

I think those two principles have got me through.

FOREWORD

HAVING KNOWN KEITH QUINN for a good many years now, I am delighted that he has asked me to provide the foreword for this fine book.

During his 30 years of broadcasting, Keith has become very much the voice of rugby in New Zealand. In country areas, where people aren't able to so often attend major matches, Keith really is Mr Rugby. He has been broadcasting so long now, and at such a high level, that his reputation has spread internationally and he is truly a world-renowned rugby personality. His commentaries are fair and informative and the amount of knowledge he has about sport in general is staggering.

I have a special affinity with Keith. He comes from Bennydale in the King Country. I moved to Te Kuiti, just along the road from Bennydale, on my seventh birthday. So whenever we get together we always have a bit of a chat about life and rugby in the King Country.

Keith's chosen 100 - a list which is sure to cause some good-natured debate - certainly brings back many memories for me. I see that some of my fiercest rivals in test rugby, players like Frik du Preez, Willie John McBride, Walter Spanghero and Benoit Dauga, are included. I can vouch first hand for their right to be on Keith's list.

Looking through the names of those included, I estimate I played test rugby with or against 27 of the 100. They range from the brilliant French back Jo Maso to that hungry pair of South African flankers, Piet Greyling and Jan Ellis, from the brilliant Welsh backs who helped the Lions win the series against the All Blacks in 1971, to Wallaby forwards of the 1960s Greg Davis and John Thornett, both fine players and respected leaders.

It's nice to see some of my All Black mates included. I doubt anyone ever dominated the game worldwide more than Don Clarke, and taking their place beside him are Ken Gray, as fine a prop forward and a man as you could wish to find, plus Bryan Williams and Sid Going, team-mates later in my test career. Naturally I'd like to have seen more members of the great team of the 1960s included, but I don't envy Keith having to restrict his list to 100, and I applaud his ability to look beyond New Zealand to ensure his book was genuinely representative of world rugby through the century.

Besides those I played with and against, I have been fortunate enough to get to know many others included in this book, either because of my involvement with the New Zealand side as a selector then manager, or just generally because the world rugby fraternity is a close one. For example, I have read with interest Keith's profile on Danie Craven, who figured so largely in New Zealanders' thoughts for so many years, and I found myself nodding in agreement when I read his assessment of Francois Pienaar, who led South Africa so superbly during the 1995 World Cup.

On a personal note, it is an honour to be listed as one of Keith's 100. Looking back on my test career, I do feel I was very fortunate to play under the captaincy of Wilson Whineray, then Brian Lochore. They were two great players and outstanding leaders and helped me immensely. I note Wilson, Brian and my old mate Kel Tremain have missed out on Keith's 100. New Zealanders will also be surprised Ian Kirkpatrick is not included. As I say, Keith set himself a near-impossible task in limiting his choice to 100 and the fact that such undeniably great players can't find a place shows what a high-quality list it is.

I do like the chatty, personal way the stories are written. Keith has the knack of telling a story that encapsulates the personality of a player. I must admit to a wry grin when I read his story of my mother berating Stan and me for fighting in a King Country trial game in the late 1950s and then not speaking the next day. This is typical of Keith. If he hears a story that is off-beat or humorous, he has an uncanny ability to recall it.

There are many such stories in this book. The best I can do is suggest you sit down and read them. At the end you will have been well entertained and will know a tremendous amount more about rugby in the 20th century.

Colin Meads
April, 1999

INTRODUCTION

IT WILL PROBABLY SEEM A BIT STRANGE to some people that a book which purports to celebrate the great rugby players of this century begins by making reference to an American Television sit-com. But a line taken from one such show has been the basic guiding principal behind the selection of the 100 players who are profiled in these pages. In the hit 1980s TV show *Cheers*, a line spoken by the main character caught my attention. He was a laconic Boston barman called Sam Malone. In one episode he auditioned for and won a temporary role as a local television sports presenter - some might say there is a direct link between the two employments! At the end of each of his TV newscasts, Sam would say, "There it is folks. But remember, this is only one man's opinion."

That line has stuck with me. Having your own viewpoint is the basis of all sporting discussion in whatever game you follow. And it certainly is the primary principle of this book. What I have attempted to do here is present just one man's view of the most influential, talented, charismatic, prominent and significant rugby players of this century.

In the pages which follow you will read of great men, how they played, and how they made their mark. My period of choice and judgement covers the world rugby scene from 1900 to 1999 - a century of players in a century of achievement.

You could say the writer of such a book as this one dares to be operates from a totally arrogant base. I might agree with you on that point. After all, you will not find this author's name in any almanack or annual listing the game's great and glorious players. More likely he might make the list of those who were average to awful.

It is very true that I never played the game to a high level and I certainly have not been around for 100 years to observe all of the candidates chosen in these pages. But using the Sam Malone principle - here I go with my choices anyway!

Mind you, I can offer some credentials of justification for my selections. My brothers insist that as a family we travelled from our home near Te Kuiti, in the North Island of New Zealand, over to Hamilton to see the 1950 British Isles rugby team play. I cannot recall this though I can remember crawling through the legs of men standing watching the game! I will be honest and say that does not give me the best credentials to judge how great Jackie Kyle and Bleddyn Williams were. They were both in that Lions team and they both make my book here as great men of our century. I have other ways of drawing conclusions about players from before my time.

I played the game to Senior B level in Wellington in the mid-1960s as a lanky lock forward. At the time, like all young New Zealand males, I thought the modest standard I had attained was just a preliminary to the logical path of rising to become an All Black. But eventually I gave up playing, telling my friends it was only poor eyesight which was holding me back from greater things. In reality I knew I was not tough enough for the physical side of rugby. Plus, there was a glimmer of an opportunity to become a sports broadcaster with Wellington's local radio and TV set-up.

That career choice turned out to be the right one for me because I can now look back on 35 years in broadcasting, mainly following the wonderful sport of rugby union. Writing in 1999 I can say (I hope with some modesty) that I have seen more All Black rugby than anyone else on this planet, and what a splendid privilege that has been. I have commentated for Television New Zealand on the finals of all three Rugby World Cups (and will do No 4 in 1999) and have travelled outside New Zealand on 26 All Black tours, and have been at nearly 150 of their test matches (the highest-capped All Black player is Sean Fitzpatrick with 92). I have written eight books, (including my personal magnum opus *The Encyclopedia of World Rugby*), and have this year undertaken a world tour with a film crew making a six-hour documentary series on the history of the All Blacks. I have commentated at six Hong Kong Sevens tournaments and also at the World Classics in Bermuda. I commentated the first rugby international played by the People's Republic of China, and also the final of the first Commonwealth Games Sevens tournament. Apart from all the 'usual' rugby locations of the 'major' rugby nations which are offered by New Zealand, Australia, South Africa, Britain, Ireland and France, my voice has also been heard from the commentary box in such far-spread rugby places as San Diego, Singapore, Vancouver, Madrid, Osaka, Suva and Kuala Lumpur. I have stood on the playing fields of Rugby School in England, where I doubt very much that William Webb Ellis' run with the ball in 1823 actually started the game. But in case it did, I have also been to Menton in France to pay homage at his graveside.

In 1997, I was honoured to be the MC for the International Rugby Hall of Fame's inaugural induction ceremony, held at the London Hilton Hotel. Of the First XV inducted into the Hall of Fame, two - Danie Craven and George Nepia - had died. I am pictured here with the remaining thirteen. They are, back row (from left): JPR Williams, Mark Ella, Serge Blanco, Mike Gibson, Willie John McBride, Cliff Morgan, Tony O'Reilly, the author. Front row (from left): Hugo Porta, Barry John, Colin Meads, Gareth Edwards, Jean-Pierre Rives, Frik du Preez.

You get the picture? I love this game to bits. No more, no less. The quote that BBC commentator Jim Neilly gave the *Daily Telegraph* a few years ago sums up my life, too. Jim told the *Telegraph:* "Those who can play, play. Those who can't play, coach. Those who can't coach, write. And those who can't write...become commentators!"

So all of the above is me, nothing more or less than a proud rugby man. And never prouder or more affected by the advantages the game has offered me than when I stood alongside 77-year-old George Nepia, the peerless All Black fullback of the 1920s, when he was in the crowd at Swansea in Wales in 1982. The ovation the 30,000 gave him that day spontaneously acknowledged his presence. The crowd showed their complete understanding of the role George had played at the same ground 58 years before when he was the masterful fullback for the 'Invincible' New Zealand team when they beat the Welsh of that year. That moment in 1982 brought tears to my eyes and to many others who were there. Proud to be a New Zealander and proud to be a rugby man.

In terms of honours, when I was asked by my friend Matt Patterson to be the Master of Ceremonies at the glitzy International Rugby Hall of Fame Dinner at the London's Hilton on Park Lane Hotel in December 1997, I was over the moon with delight. A panel of 40 leading world rugby writers and broadcasters had chosen 15 players for induction into the Hall. By then two of them, the beloved Nepia and South Africa's 'Mr Rugby', Danie Craven, had passed away, but the other 13 turned up to be honoured.

It goes without saying I regarded it as a singular distinction just to stand alongside and mingle with Messrs. Meads, Morgan, Edwards, John, O'Reilly, du Preez, Porta, Ella, Rives, Blanco, J P R Williams, Gibson and McBride. What names! It was truly an experience I will never forget.

From the 750 diners you could have picked another top line-up. Gavin Hastings, Sean Fitzpatrick, Andy Irvine, Ronnie Dawson and Nick Farr-Jones were some who were chosen to hand over the induction trophies to the great ones. Among others in the audience I also saw Bleddyn Williams, Jack Matthews and Peter Jackson, making it a true rugby night of the highest order.

This book is really an expansion of that evening. Obviously I have chosen to honour 100 famous players because it rounds off a connection with the 100 years of this century. Twenty-three of my chosen 100 have passed on. They are sadly missed, but not forgotten.

Some of those who are living I know very well, some of the others I know only slightly and some others might pick up this book and say, "Who is the bloke who has written this?" Never mind, I say. Sam Malone at least would approve of what I'm doing.

A very important tenet in compiling my final list was not to make it top-heavy as a New Zealand production. Of course, I am a Kiwi to my bootstraps, but I have found places for only 20 All Blacks. Only 20? This is, I sense, going to cause a degree of consternation among my friends at home, but no matter - maybe they watched *Cheers* that night too. Also on my list are 17 Springboks, 14 Australians, 13 Welshmen, 12 Frenchmen, 10 Englishmen, 7 Irishmen and, may my Scottish friends and forebears forgive me, only four Scots. I also have one each from Argentina, Italy and Fiji. As to the list's final composition, I can say only that it was reached after much thought and hours of discussion with learned colleagues, not all of whom were New Zealanders! It involved much crossing out, great anxiety and the shocking realisation that my 'absolutely final' list of 'musts' needed to be pruned by another dozen.

As I scan my chosen 100, I can only shudder. No Wilson Whineray, Kel Tremain, Kevin Skinner, Brian Lochore or Ian Kirkpatrick. New Zealand rugby followers will be appalled. But then there's no Ken Scotland or Craig Chalmers, no Jonathan Davies or Phil Bennett, no Willie Duggan or Tom Kiernan, no David Duckham or Fran Cotton, no Amedee Domenech or Pierre Berbizier. So there'll be mutters in Europe, too. Not to forget Gary Teichmann and John Gainsford of South Africa, Peter Johnson and Charlie Eastes of Australia. Or Gareth Rees of Canada, or Stefano Bettarello of Italy. Great players, all of them. And they are all from the post-second World War era. There are dozens of other strong candidates from the first 40 years of this century as well. But when all is said and done, 100 **is** 100.

Each profile you will find has a written piece, containing my opinions of their role in the game, perhaps my personal memories of meeting them or watching them play. There will be statistical references for each as well as highlighted 'boxes' containing additional information. I hope that by way of these boxes, I have been able to extend my scope beyond the elite 100 and acknowledge the many other wonderful players of this century. I have been conscious of ensuring that great teams are well represented. Thus the Welsh team of the 1970s has four in my top 100. The All Blacks of the late 1980s are similarly well-represented. England had a super team in the 1920s and three players from that period are included. The best players from the winning sides of each of the World Cups gain inclusion. The project has caused me hours of pondering and debating, but in the end has been a great deal of fun to work on.

For players from those years and decades before I was watching the game from better positions than between spectators' legs, I can say only I have made judgements based on a lifetime of reading about the game, not to mention talking and listening over the years to the delightful company of learned and deep-thinking rugby writers and broadcasters. Men like Sir Terence McLean, JBG (Bryn) Thomas, Clem Thomas, Barry Glasspool, John Reason, Peter Bush, Alun Williams, Trevor Allan, Carwyn James, Winston McCarthy, Bill McLaren, Fred Cogley, Grant Harding, Ian Robertson, Chris Rea, Alex Veysey, Peter Sellers, Greg Growden, Ron Palenski, Andrew Slack, Peter Jenkins, Gordon Bray, Nigel Starmer-Smith, Joseph Romanos, Robyn Murray, Cyril Delaney, Paul Dobson, Grant Nisbett, John McBeth, Muff Scobie, Spiro Zavos, Peter FitzSimons, Ned van Esbeck, Ray Cairns, Donald Cameron, Sean Diffley, Hugh Bladen, Gerard Viviers, Bob Howitt, Lindsay Knight, Terry O'Connor and my good friend Chris Thau. Some of these men have passed away, but from all of them I learned a lot about players in their eras and their countries. You could say I have shamelessly lifted from them and added a thousand conversations into the mix of my own views.

Having said all that it's tempting to pick a World XV of the Century and offer it up for discussion. Of course, this is an exercise fraught with dilemma and danger. How does one judge a player from one generation against that of another? Who can make such choices?

Well, we all can of course. So, based on everything I know and especially from the observations in this book, here is my World XV of the Century;

Fullback	George Nepia	New Zealand
Wingers	Jonah Lomu	New Zealand
	David Campese	Australia
Centres	Bleddyn Williams	Wales
	Jo Maso	France
Flyhalf	Mark Ella	Australia
Scrumhalf/halfback	Gareth Edwards	Wales
Number 8	Morne du Plessis	South Africa
Flankers	Michael Jones	New Zealand
	Piet Greyling	South Africa
Locks	Colin Meads	New Zealand
	Frik du Preez	South Africa
Props	Boy Louw	South Africa
	Ken Gray	New Zealand
Hooker	Sean Fitzpatrick	New Zealand

As I scan through my World XV of the Century, a perverse thought strikes me. Great as they undeniably were, most of them were dropped or overlooked by their national selectors at some point in their careers, often more than once. Only Ken Gray, Boy Louw, Piet Greyling and Gareth Edwards never felt the sharp blade of the selectorial axe. This may say more about the people picking the teams than the players who were being dropped.

If my dream team hasn't got you reaching for your shotgun, let me add this: while my favourite international personality is the loveable, unique and delightful Cliff Morgan of Wales and the Lions, the star player of any team playing this century, for me, would quite clearly be the mighty Jonah Lomu of New Zealand. No other player has made such a world impact. Certainly he was assisted greatly by coming to the fore in the television and satellite era of the 1990s, but his explosive, monumental presence and talent wherever he played was greater than any other person the game has known.

If you cannot agree with that and you want to judge me as a complete rugby no-hoper please remember the principle by which I have written this book. Everything in these pages is only 'one man's opinion'!

Keith Quinn
April, 1999

PIERRE ALBALADEJO

The Original Monsieur le Drop

FRENCHMAN Pierre Albaladejo is proof of the wisdom of the expression, 'If at first you don't succeed, try and try again.' Albaladejo, just 20, was the French fullback for two tests in 1954 and played splendidly. He was then cast into selection isolation, not reappearing on the international scene for six years, by which time France had played a further 36 tests and Albaladejo had turned himself into a flyhalf. Despite this daunting start to his test career, he became a world-renowned player and one of the most identifiable sports figures in France.

Albaladejo's father was Spanish (hence the Spanish surname) and his mother a Basque. Bala, as he was known, was marked as a potential test player while still in his teens. Tall and strongly built - 1.80m (5ft 11in) and 82kg (12st 12lb), he had good hands, was a masterful kicker and read a game cleverly.

He first test was against England in 1954, under the great Jean Prat, and he hardly put a foot wrong. France swept to an 11-3 victory to share the Five Nations Championship. A fortnight later Albaladejo again did all that was asked of him when French whipped Italy 39-12 in Rome. Then, for some curious reason, he was consigned to the 'Never Required Again In Test Rugby' file. Albaladejo, talented and ambitious, could only watch as Michel Vannier made the test fullback spot his own.

In 1958, after four years in the wilderness, Albaladejo knew something drastic would be required, so he transformed himself into a flyhalf. The position suited him well. Though taller than the average flyhalf, he had good vision, was an elegant, effective runner and, critically, could kick well with either foot. His specialty was the drop kick.

Two more years passed before he aroused the interest of the French selectors. When regular flyhalf Roger Martine was injured, Albaladejo was recalled to the national team. It was the beginning of a fairytale second test career.

Once he got his hands on the French jersey again, Albaladejo made the most of his chances. He played masterfully to steer France to a 16-8 win over Wales at Cardiff and was retained for the next match, against Ireland. He broke Irish hearts by dropping three goals in a 23-6 win. This feat, which earned him The tag of 'Monsieur le Drop', one of the best-known nicknames in world rugby (and one which seems to get handed down to each generation

Pierre Albaladejo
Flyhalf
Born: Dax, February 13, 1933
Test debut: France v England, Paris, April 10, 1954
Test career: 1954-64 (30 matches)
Test points: 104 (16 conversions, 12 penalties, 12 drop goals)
* When he retired he was France's most capped flyhalf
* The first player to drop three goals in one test

Typical Albaladejo - another drop kick on the way during a French Five Nations Championship match.

of French flyhalf), has since been equalled but not bettered in a test. Soon after he potted four drop goals in an important club match. There were two more in his next test, against Italy, and his reputation as a drop goal king was sealed.

Suddenly he was indispensable. The following season he played all France's internationals and took on more place-kicking responsibilities as well.

Albaladejo was one of the stars of France's 1961 tour of New Zealand. The *New Zealand Rugby Almanack* named him as one of its Players of the Year, describing him as 'a clever flyhalf with twinkling feet and good tactical ability'. He played eight tour matches and was equal top points-scorer. The first two tests were closely fought, but when Albaladejo missed the third through injury, France were thrashed, 32-3. Albaladejo lived up to his billing, dropping three goals on tour, including two in the first test at Auckland.

Loose forward Michel Celaya and Albaladejo proved a popular pair, especially whenever they staged their mock bullfight, with Albaladejo as matador, Celaya as bull and their team-mates shouting 'Ole' at every pass. Albaladejo proved a relaxed, engaging person with a light-hearted attitude towards life, but not rugby.

Ironically Albaladejo, who had fought so hard to return to test rugby, found it hard to get out in the end. He was part of three successive French Five Nations champion sides, then announced before the test against Ireland in Paris in 1964 that he was to retire.

A few months later he reluctantly responded to pleas to tour South Africa. This was the first year when backs had to stay 10 yards back from a lineout, giving Albaladejo extra space and time. He used it to control the one test in South Africa, at Springs, where France upset the strong Springbok side 8-6.

France's next test was against Fiji in October and the flyhalf again agreed to play. However, the match was overshadowed by a tragedy some weeks earlier when Albaladejo's older brother Raymond (a wing who went close to test selection and represented Dax for a decade) and two other players were killed in a car crash while returning from a night match. There was much public debate about whether Albaladejo should play against Fiji. Eventually he did and France won 21-3, but it was a sad farewell to international rugby.

Albaladejo played in four national club finals for Dax, the last in 1966. Though he had long departed the test scene, he was still an effective flyhalf. In that last final Dax, heavy underdogs, were edged out 9-8 by defending Agenais.

Even in retirement Albaladejo was a French rugby celebrity. He was a typographer, but then moved into the restaurant and hotel trade. His rugby prowess, plus his instantly recognisable nickname, raised his profile and he became a successful businessman. I recall doing a television interview with him at his *Bela Bar* in Dax. He was, as ever, modest and personable, but there was no doubting his standing in his home town.

He remained involved with rugby by turning to radio and television work. His TV commentaries with Roger Couderc, and later Pierre Salviac, which took him all over the world, including several trips to New Zealand, were unique. Albaladejo and his co-commentator seemed to spend the entire match speaking at the same time so that to someone like me, struggling to get by with my rather rudimentary School Certificate French, the whole thing became incomprehensible. Albaladejo was also the long-serving editor of *Le Livre d'or du Rugby*, an authoritative French rugby almanack.

He became a member of the Dax Chamber of Commerce and founding president of the Dax-Ocean radio station. In 1988 he was elected president of the Dax Union of Sports Clubs. For many years he was also the director of a children's summer camp in Dax.

The French Rugby Federation issued Albaladejo with a silver medal in 1963 and he was also awarded the gold medal of youth and sport, a national medal of merit, and a national medal for sportsmanship. 🏉

> **Given his distinctive nickname for his expertise in this sometimes crucial part of rugby, Albaladejo was the first player to successfully kick three drop goals in one test. Since then the feat has been matched, but not beaten. Those who have kicked three drop goals in one test are:**
>
> Pierre Albaladejo, France v Ireland, Paris 1960
> Phil Hawthorne, Australia v England, Twickenham 1967
> Hugo Porta, Argentina v Australia, Buenos Aires, 1979
> Naas Botha, South Africa v South America, Durban 1980
> Naas Botha, South Africa v Ireland, Durban 1981
> Jean-Patrick Lescarboura, France v England, Twickenham, 1985
> Hugo Porta, Argentina v New Zealand, Buenos Aires, 1985
> Jean-Patrick Lescarboura, France v New Zealand, Christchurch, 1986
> Didier Camberabero, France v Australia, Sydney 1990
> Opeti Turuva, Fiji v Western Samoa, Nadi, 1994
> Neculai Nichitean, Romania v France, Bucharest, 1995

Albaladejo (left) and Keith Quinn, Dublin, 1999.

ROB ANDREW

England's Ace

Christopher Robert Andrew
Flyhalf
Born: Richmond, Yorkshire, February 18, 1963
Test debut: England v Romania, Twickenham, January 5, 1985
Test career: 1985-97 (76 matches - 71 for England, 5 for the British Isles)
Test points: 407 (2 tries, 87 penalties, 34 conversions, 23 drop goals)
* Played first class cricket for Cambridge University and Yorkshire
* Played a record 70 tests for England at flyhalf (the previous best was Dave Davies' 22)
* Scored 30 points against Canada at Twickenham in 1994
* His 23 drop goals place him second to Hugo Porta on the world test list
* His 396 points for England is the national test record

ROB ANDREW, one of the architects of a glorious England Five Nations era, will always be recalled for two crucial World Cup kicks. His drop goals sank Scotland in the semi-finals in 1991 and eliminated defending champions Australia in the quarter-finals in 1995. In a case of 'Cometh the hour, cometh the man', Andrew was very much the man.

Andrew often had to suffer snide remarks about being a 'kicking flyhalf' and was at times dropped in favour of the apparently more expansive Stuart Barnes. He was not a running flyhalf in the classic Welsh mould, yet when I saw him in action I was struck by his efficient, errorless play and the calming influence he had on the England team.

He adhered to a clearly-defined plan and helped England win three Grand Slams and beat every major rugby-playing nation. He was invariably one of those key players targeted by opposition, for he was a match-winner, not just because of his accurate place-kicking, but because he could dictate play so well.

Strangely, Andrew's sports career could have gone either way - he was a promising cricketer, good enough to captain Cambridge University and score a first class century. His boyhood sports ambition was to open the Yorkshire batting with Geoff Boycott. In his early years, Andrew swayed towards cricket, the main game on the family farm. He attended Barnard Castle School, where he was noted as a dashing all-rounder.

But rugby was *the* game at Barnard Castle and Andrew and another youngster of equally slight build, Rory Underwood, prospered, though neither made any rep sides until they left school. Andrew idolised Welsh flyhalf Phil Bennett and later paid close attention to Scottish flyhalf John Rutherford.

Andrew practised assiduously and his rugby leapt ahead. All the time, though, cricket was claiming a fair chunk of his time. He played for Cambridge University for two years, captaining the side in the 1985 Varsity match. He scored an unbeaten century for Cambridge against Notts in 1984 and was tipped for higher honours.

It was a close-run thing. He represented Cambridge at rugby from 1982-84, represented England under-23 in 1984, then made his test debut in the 22-15 win over Romania in 1985, contributing two drop goals and four penalties. It looked like England had unearthed a rarity, a flyhalf with a

cricketer's safe hands, 'two feet' and an unhurried ability to weigh up his options.

Instead, he was dropped soon after and his confidence plummeted. One England captain, John Scott, called him 'the worst to play for England'. Then, at the behest of Wallaby coach Alan Jones, he spent a season with the Gordon club in Sydney, having decided to take a rest from cricket. He'd had a reasonable year with the Yorkshire Second XI and had captained Combined Universities against Australia, so the decision must have involved some soul-searching.

His Australian sojourn benefited him greatly. Jones took him under his wing and Andrew was in the Wallaby dressing room at Eden Park the day in 1986 that the Australians whipped New Zealand to win the Bledisloe Cup. Back home, Andrew flourished under the new English management team of Geoff Cooke (manager) and Roger Uttley (coach). They decided they wanted

Grand Slam victories in the Five Nations Championship:

England	11 times
Wales	8 times
France	6 times
Scotland	3 times
Ireland	1 time

Triple Crown victories in the Five Nations Championship:

England	21 times
Wales	17 times
Scotland	10 times
Ireland	6 times

The grounds where England have hosted full rugby tests:

Birkenhead Park	Birkenhead
Rectory Field	Blackheath
Ashton Gate	Bristol
Crown Flatt	Dewsbury
Kingsholm	Gloucester
McAlpine Stadium	Huddersfield
Cardigan Fields	Leeds
Headingley	Leeds
Meanwood Road	Leeds
Welford Road	Leicester
Crystal Palace	London
Kennington Oval	London
Twickenham	London
Wembley	London
Fallowfield	Manchester
Old Trafford	Manchester
Whalley Range	Manchester
Otley RFC Ground	Otley
Athletic Ground	Richmond

Andrew as their flyhalf and the Yorkshireman responded to this vote of confidence. He'd been a bit-part extra at the 1987 World Cup, when Peter Williams was the top England flyhalf, but then asserted himself.

Andrew had a lucky break in 1989 when he was called up as a replacement for the Lions team in Australia and played the last two tests. In the second, he filled in nobly for an off-form Gavin Hastings as place-kicker, landing three vital goals in a 19-12 win.

At his best, Andrew was compared with two other famous flyhalves, New Zealander Grant Fox and Australian Michael Lynagh. Of the three, Fox was the best kicker and Lynagh the best runner. But Andrew was a good all-rounder, who had a deadly drop kick and an intimidating bomb. He was intelligent and undemonstrative and played to his team's strengths.

Though he was only 1.75m (5ft 9in) and 80kg (12st 8lb), he was a sturdy defender. He liked to stand deep to give himself a split-second's extra breathing space. He had a solid punt, could chip kick well and was a strong if not explosive runner. There was criticism that his outsides suffered because his plans seldom included them. Yet Rory Underwood set a try-scoring record on the wing during Andrew's reign, and Jeremy Guscott and Will Carling became recognised as world-class centres outside him.

Andrew is recalled now as a fine place-kicker, but for five years did not do that job for England. That duty fell mainly to Jonathon Webb, Simon Hodgkinson and Jonathan Callard. Even so, Andrew had some great days with the boot. In 1986 he scored 21 points against Wales. In 1994, in his first game back as England's kicker, he notched 18 points against France at Paris. Later that year he set two England test records during the first test in South Africa. His 27 points were a record and he became the first Englishman to achieve a test 'full house', with a try, two conversions, five penalties and a drop goal. Shortly after, he increased his England record with a 30-point haul against Canada.

It was assumed Andrew would bow out of international rugby after the 1995 World Cup, and he played well throughout the tournament. However, in 1997 he took the field as a replacement for the last 10 minutes of England's Five Nations match with Wales.

The thoughtful Andrew was seen as a possible England captain, especially as he'd shown leadership qualities as a cricketer. He led England against Romania in 1989 (the 58-3 win in his only test as captain makes him one of rugby's most successful skippers!) and led a British Isles XV to a 29-27 win over France in the French Revolution Bicentennial match that year. Andrew captained Wasps to the 1989-90 club title and London to the 1990 Divisional championship. Thereafter he led various provincial selections, but with Carling so successful as test captain, that road was blocked.

Andrew had a stint with the Toulouse club after the 1991 World Cup, but returned a year later.

A career that embraced three World Cups, three Grand Slams and spanned 13 seasons included many highpoints. But I doubt Andrew was ever more jubilant than after his two special World Cup moments. His drop goal in 1991 at Murrayfield broke a 6-6 deadlock with Scotland and put England into the final. And in 1995 at Cape Town he again revealed his temperament by dropping a booming 40-metre goal two minutes into injury time to earn England a 25-22 win over Australia.

On retiring, Andrew, previously a chartered surveyor, became a highly-paid director of rugby at the Newcastle club. **100**

MARK ANDREWS

High Flier

IT SAYS MUCH for Mark Andrews that though he has established himself as the best South African lock of the 1990s, his two most important games for the Springboks were at No 8. During the 1995 World Cup, coach Kitch Christie gambled on Andrews' adaptability and switched him from the second row for the semi-final against France and the final against New Zealand. Christie wanted Andrews to mark the tall Laurent Cabannes in the semi-final and the tactic worked so well that he used it in the final, where Andrews did a commendable job of combating All Black dangerman Zinzan Brooke.

Those two games aside, Andrews at lock has been a stable factor in a seemingly ever-changing Springbok scrum through the much of the 1990s. Before coach Nick Mallett settled on the pair of Andrews and Krynauw Otto, Andrews had had six other test locking partners. Six hookers came and went in three years. Mallett was Andrews' fifth Springbok coach in as many years.

Through it all, the lofty Natal player has provided South Africa with yeoman service, and in 1998 he became the first Springbok to reach the milestone of 50 tests.

He is a spectacular leaper near the front of the lineout, despite the special attention paid him. Often two of the opposition are despatched to mark him. While that creates opportunities for his team elsewhere, it can understandably be frustrating for the player himself. Similarly, Andrews is particularly adept at taking kick-offs, but the All Blacks, and some other opponents, now make a habit of never kicking to him.

Despite the burden he has shouldered, his class has shone through. Andrews has been to the Springboks what John Eales has been to the Wallabies and Ian Jones to the All Blacks. He has played in a World Cup-winning side and was a key member of the South African side which in 1998 equalled the world record with 17 consecutive test victories.

With such a CV, it's odd to reflect that Andrews' initial sports preference was water polo. He grew up in the Eastern Cape town of Elliot, where he plans to eventually return to farm. Andrews was attracted to water polo when attending boarding school in East London. He represented South Africa at junior level, but gave away the sport for pragmatic reasons. "Rugby was a nice way to get your frustrations out, but I preferred water polo. However, there is no money in water polo and not as many opportunities. If you applied to university and asked for a water polo scholarship, they would laugh at

Mark Gregory Andrews
Lock
Born: Elliot, February 21, 1972
Test debut: South Africa v England, Cape Town, June 11, 1994
Test career: 53 matches (1994-98)
Test points: 45 points (9 tries)
* In 1998 he became the first Springbok to play 50 tests
* Andrews' 9 tries was a world record for a lock (since equalled by Ian Jones of New Zealand)

you. Rugby has much more influence."

So Andrews, who began his rugby as a centre when he was five, began to concentrate on rugby. When his size - he is now 2m (6ft 7in) and 111kg (17st 7lb) - forced him into the forwards, he spent some time at prop, before finding his niche in the second row. His height, unusually large hands and the agility he developed through water polo stood him in good stead as he climbed through the rugby ranks.

He attended Stellenbosch University and, though he is now a fulltime rugby player, is close to completing a Bachelor of Arts in Social Science. In 1990, at the age of 18, he made the South African schools side.

His rugby benefited from a rugged few months he spent playing in Aurillac, France in 1991. Twenty-two games in 25 weeks turned him into a harder and more competitive player. In 1993 he toured Argentina with the Springboks, and a few months later he made his test debut, helping the Springboks to a storming 27-9 win over England at Cape Town. Andrews quickly established himself at the top level. He was outstanding for the Springboks in New Zealand in 1994, playing all three tests and surviving a torrid working-over from the experienced All Black pack. The Springboks, still suffering from the years of international isolation, weren't a match for New Zealand, but Andrews never took a backward step and was their most impressive forward.

In 1995, he played four matches in the World Cup and had a good end-of-year tour of Europe. Through 1996 and 1997 he was one of the constants in the South African team, but in 1998 Mallett developed the habit of using Andrews for 60 minutes then substituting him, which he didn't enjoy. There were suggestions Andrews, who struggled for a while with a shoulder injury, might be replaced at lock by flanker Andre Venter so that Bob Skinstad, the new wonderboy of South African rugby, might be accommodated as a loose forward.

From a New Zealand perspective, it all seemed rather bizarre. Andrews was only 26, but hugely experienced and totally committed. Not only was he a fabulous lineout leaper, but he had good ball-handling ability and had shown himself to be a surprisingly free mover in the loose.

Andrews has been a giant for Natal in the Currie Cup and Super 12 competitions. In 1994 he helped Natal beat England 21-6 and he helped Natal win back-to-back Currie Cup titles in 1995-96. But at provincial level he was even more of a target than he was in tests. Matters came to a head when the Sharks met New South Wales in a fiery Super 12 match in Sydney in 1998. He was twice ordered from the field for over-vigorous play, once to the sinbin and the second time for good.

The quietly-spoken Andrews was given the honour of leading South Africa onto Wembley against Wales for his 50th test in November, 1998 and played in every test on South Africa's end-of-year tour of Britain. He should have been entering his rugby prime; instead there was still speculation about his test place. Quite why is hard to work out. **100**

Mark Andrews became the first Springbok player to play 50 tests. Most of his tests were as a highly accomplished lock. His task was not made any easier by the problems the South African selectors had in finding him a consistent locking partner. A number of sporting publications listed him as having had 14 locking partners by the time he reached his 50th test appearance, in 1998. Below is the actual list of Andrews' locking partners in those 50 tests:

Steve Atherton, 1994-96	5
Drikus Hattingh, 1994	2
Phillip Schutte, 1994	2
Kobus Wiese, 1995-96	10
Johann Ackermann, 1996	4
Hannes Strydom, 1996-97	6
Krynauw Otto, 1997-98	18

Note: of Andrews' first 50 tests, one was as a replacement forward and two were as a No 8.

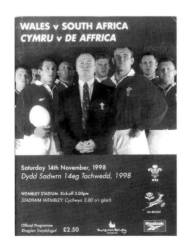

Andrews' 50th test, South Africa v Wales, 1998. He became the first Springbok to reach the 50-test milestone.

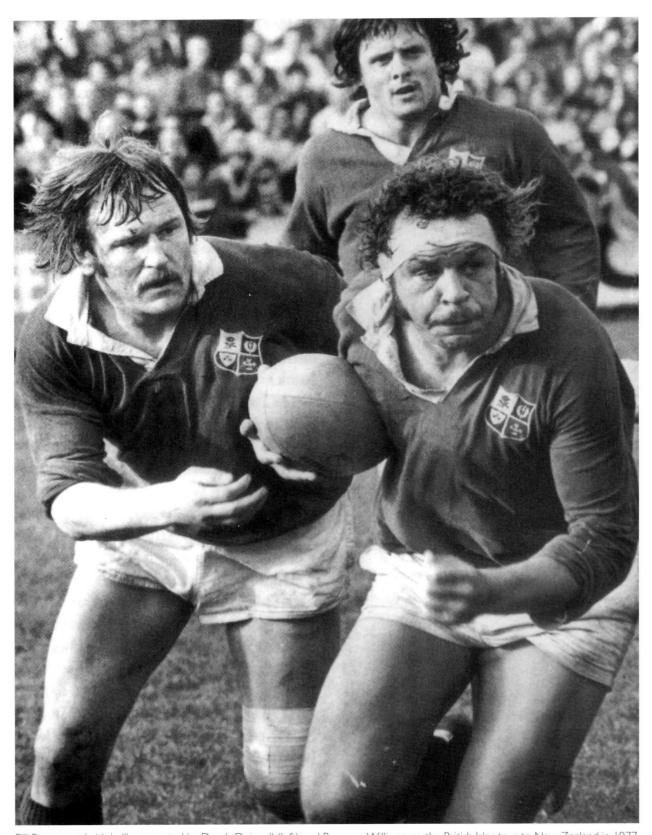

Bill Beaumont (with ball), supported by Derek Quinnell (left) and Brynmor Williams on the British Isles tour to New Zealand in 1977.

BILL BEAUMONT

England Expects

REPORTS FROM Britain in the mid-1970s suggested England had uncovered in Lancashire lock Bill Beaumont a player who might one day be his country's equivalent of Irishman Willie John McBride. Therefore it was staggering that when the 1977 Lions team to New Zealand was named, Beaumont was not chosen, even after Welshman Geoff Wheel withdrew. Beaumont eventually joined the Lions a third of the way through the tour, replacing the injured Nigel Horton, and what a revelation he was.

He was one of the old-school locks, with big backside, hips and thighs (he was known by team-mates as 'Bubble Bum'). He wasn't a great runner like Frik du Preez or Colin Meads, though he charged about the field energetically and hit rucks and mauls at full speed. But he was strong in the one-on-one situations and added significantly to the Lions scrum - prop Fran Cotton described him as a 'colossal scrummager'. In addition, during the 1977 tests he outplayed All Black Frank Oliver at No 3 in the lineouts.

Though he was the new boy in the Lions side, Beaumont quickly became a key figure. He played in 10 of the last 16 matches, including the last three tests. It was obvious he had qualities not only as a player but also a leader. The Lions pack was noticeably more spirited when Beaumont was involved.

That tour cemented his reputation. He'd made his test debut opposite McBride two years earlier when England had lost to Ireland 12-9, and had been a member of the England team since. They were depressing times for England. For instance, of Beaumont's first eight tests, seven were lost.

But after touring New Zealand in 1977, Beaumont never looked back, fashioning a record-breaking career as a player and captain and then becoming one of the personalities of British sport, a loveable bear of a man.

Beaumont was educated at Ellesmere College and at 16 started his rugby career as the Fylde sixth team fullback. A sharp increase in height and weight, to 1.90m (6ft 3in) and 95.5kg (15st) forced a move into the pack. By 1970, he was in the Fylde firsts.

Promotion came quickly. He first played for Lancashire in 1972 and the following year helped them win the county title with a 17-12 win over Gloucestershire at Bristol. There were appearances for England under-23, North Western Counties, then England. Beaumont was blessed with plenty of that North of England common-sense. He was a down-to-earth character who became an inspiring captain. Not only was he invariably one of his team's best players, but he had a fiercely competitive nature that his quiet

William Blackledge Beaumont
Lock
Born: Preston, March 9, 1952
Test debut: England v Ireland, Dublin, January 1, 1975
Test career: 1975-82 (41 matches - 34 for England, 7 for the British Isles)
Test points: 0
* In 1980, he led England to the Grand Slam and became the first Englishman to captain a Lions touring team in 50 years
* Captained England a record 21 times
* Was England's most capped lock (34)

Captains of British Isles touring teams (since 1910 when it is generally considered the first all-British and Irish teams were selected):

	Captain	Country
1910 to South Africa	Tom Smythe	Ireland
1924 to South Africa	Ronald Cove-Smith	England
1930 to New Zealand and Australia	Doug Prentice	England
1938 to South Africa	Sam Walker	Ireland
1950 to New Zealand and Australia	Karl Mullen	Ireland
1955 to South Africa	Robin Thompson	Ireland
1959 to New Zealand and Australia	Ronnie Dawson	Ireland
1962 to South Africa	Arthur Smith	Scotland
1966 to New Zealand and Australia	Mike Campbell-Lamerton	Scotland
1968 to South Africa	Tom Kiernan	Ireland
1971 to New Zealand and Australia	John Dawes	Wales
1974 to South Africa	Willie John McBride	Ireland
1977 to New Zealand and Fiji	Phil Bennett	Wales
1980 to South Africa	Bill Beaumont	England
1983 to New Zealand	Ciaran Fitzgerald	Ireland
1989 to Australia	Finlay Calder	Scotland
1993 to New Zealand	Gavin Hastings	Scotland
1997 to South Africa	Martin Johnson	England

style and unassuming manner sometimes covered. His players loved him and Gareth Edwards once observed, "His leadership was tinged with greatness."

He enjoyed his greatest moments during the 1979-80 season. After leading the Northern Division of England to victory over the Graham Mourie's All Blacks, he assured himself of national hero status by captaining England to their first Grand Slam in 23 years. When he led Lancashire to the county championship, he had completed a memorable treble. He was voted Player of the Year and Alan Gibson of *The Times* wrote: 'His appearance in the television age is familiar: the tubby walrus, one might say. This is not by any means a disparaging remark. Walruses, although undoubtedly well-moustached and tubby, are fast movers and capable of withstanding all sorts of weather. If you don't believe me, look up the natural history books and read Compton Mackenzie's novel *The Rival Monsters*. Old Bill is the hero in the end.'

Beaumont led the Lions to South Africa in 1980, the first Englishman to captain the Lions for 50 years. It was a difficult and controversial tour bedevilled with anti-apartheid protests, but he played as industriously as ever and behaved with dignity. The Lions lost the test series 3-1, a result they might have reversed given even normal luck with injuries.

Beaumont's career came to an abrupt end in 1982. During the English county final, Lancashire against North Midlands at Moseley, he had to leave the field, complaining of a injury which had affected him in several previous games. Diagnosis revealed a neck injury. He took medical advice and quit the game, right at the peak of his powers. Beaumont was just 29. He had captained his country a record 21 times and had played 33 consecutive tests.

His sudden retirement left a huge hole in English rugby, but he did not drift off the sports scene. As the managing director of a family textile mill in Chorley, Lancashire, he had plenty to do. But he remained involved in rugby by writing books (which eventually led to him being declared a professional and banned from taking part in rugby in any official capacity) and, with sponsorship assistance from Wimpey Homes, established the School of Rugby in 1985. He has become involved in rugby administration and is chairman of the RFU Playing Committee. He also became one of the 12 directors of the European Rugby Cup.

Through the 1980s, his battle-scarred, lived-in face became familiar not just with sports lovers but on a much wider stage. He became a rugby commentator for BBC television and for 13 years featured on the popular TV show *A Question of Sport*, along with opposition team leader Ian Botham and host David Coleman. Beaumont's modest, friendly personality and self-deprecating sense of humour shone through and it became clear why he'd been such a popular and successful captain. **100**

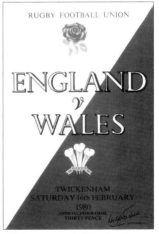

Bill Beaumont led England to a Grand Slam in 1980.

SERGE BLANCO

The Caracas Cracker

IN 1977, a few days before the All Blacks' tour of France began, I travelled with a television crew to Biarritz to interview former Wellington player Brian Hegarty, who was apparently getting paid to turn out for the local club. Back then, such a heinous crime merited a full investigation. We spent the day with Hegarty, who has been a friend since.

Hegarty introduced us to a quiet 19-year-old team-mate named Serge Blanco, who was said to be a promising fullback. There followed a stuttering conversation in our halting French and Serge's broken English and we quickly took a liking to him.

A few weeks later, Blanco played against the All Blacks for a French Selection at Agen. His team was well beaten 34-12, but Blanco looked a class player. I felt pleased to have been there at the dawn of his international career, so to speak, and over the next 15 years followed his fortunes with special interest.

He became one of the world's best players, adding a special French flair and sense of adventure to the fullback's normal accoutrements.

His was an unusual beginning for a test rugby star. His father was a Venezuelan policeman, his mother a Basque. As a young boy, he moved from Venezuela to France, but his exotic background left him with coffee-coloured skin that, when added to his brilliant play and charming manner, made him a sports hero in France. By the time he was seven, his ability and uninhibited attitude to rugby had captured the attention of local rugby followers.

Blanco was in the French Youth and B teams in 1978 and the following year graduated to the top team, initially for minor internationals against the likes of Tunisia, Yugoslavia and Italy. He made the French team that toured New Zealand in 1979, but couldn't dislodge Jean-Michel Aguirre as the test fullback. He played just four matches in New Zealand, but was given the unofficial international against Fiji in Suva.

His full test debut was against South Africa in 1980. France went down 37-15, but Blanco impressed with his decisive tackling and pace on attack. Thereafter he was rarely missing from the test side, though it took him a while to seal the fullback position. Serge Gabernet and Marc Sallefranque were initially preferred, leaving Blanco to make do with 12 appearances on the wing, a waste of his versatility and creativity. Once he was given an extended run at fullback, Blanco never looked back and came to be regarded

Serge Blanco
Fullback
Born: Caracas, Venezuela, January 31, 1958
Test debut: France v South Africa, Pretoria, November 8, 1980
Test career: 1980-91 (93 matches)
Test points: 233 (38 tries, 6 conversions, 21 penalties, 2 drop goals)
* Held the world record for test appearances when he retired
* Holds the try-scoring record by a fullback in tests
* Third on the all-time test try-scoring list

The top try-scoring fullbacks in tests:

32	Serge Blanco (France)	1980-91
25*	Christian Cullen (New Zealand)	1996-98
18	Gavin Hastings (Scotland)	1986-95
16*	Matthew Burke (Australia)	1993-98
13	John Gallagher (New Zealand)	1987-89
12	David Campese (Australia)	1982-96

* still playing

Totals include tries scored only when players appeared at fullback.

as the natural successor to Pierre Villepreux in the royal line of French fullbacks.

His 1983 Five Nations tally of 36 points broke the record Guy Camberabero had set in 1967. At nearly 1.84m (6ft 1in) tall and 85kg (13st 3lb), he was a perfectly balanced athlete who was always seeking the opportunity to attack. He could inspire his team with one spark of genius and was a huge crowd-puller.

Some of his tries are famous. New Zealanders saw his ability in 1984 when he scored a fine try in the first test at Christchurch, coming into the line to collect the ball, chipping ahead, then running on and scoring. On that same tour he scored an equally spectacular try against Wellington.

In 1987, though he was battling a thigh injury, Blanco hauled France into the World Cup final, and broke Australian hearts into the bargain, with a sensational last-minute try in the semi-final in Sydney. He'd already given his team a lifeline with a fantastic all-round performance in their first match, against Scotland at Christchurch, when he scored a try and kicked a conversion and two penalties in a 20-20 draw with Scotland. His try, in injury time, was so outrageous that no-one - spectators, cameras, Scots, or even the rest of the French - saw it. From 52 metres out and beside the touchline, Blanco spotted that the Scots were napping, so he tapped to himself, then sliced through the hastily regrouping Scottish defence to score under the posts. "It was a little bit contrary to logic, but you have to change now and then. It's the World Cup, so you have to do something new," he explained.

In the semi-final thriller, Blanco made a handling mistake in front of his posts and watched Michael Lynagh kick the ensuing penalty to give Australia an apparently match-winning 24-21 lead. Then it was a case of from the ridiculous to the sublime. Ian Borthwick described the moment like this: 'Blanco, having already participated in the movement, managed to find himself at the end of the chain, and sprinted 20 metres for the try of victory. Who could forget the moving and desperate plunge of Lawton attempting to stop him, or Blanco's expression of delight as he and Berbizier embraced?'

Blanco returned to Australia in 1990 and turned on the magic again in the second test at Brisbane. He elected to run from behind his own line and exhibited acceleration, speed and surprising strength to cover the length of the field, brushing off David Campese's despairing tackle. Not bad for 32-year-old legs.

At home, Blanco was a national celebrity. He was courted by various political parties, though he steered clear of politics. He was keenly sought by sponsors and advertisers and when he wasn't playing rugby was employed in a public relations capacity by some major French companies.

I always found him compelling to watch, as he played with singular panache. Occasionally there was a defensive lapse to remind you he was human, and his place-kicking ranged from outstanding to inconsistent. But he was always entertaining and seemed to genuinely love playing. The excitement he generated through his spectacular attacking and all-round skills was unmatchable. He was for some years regarded as the best fullback in the world and was in French sides that won or shared six Five Nations crowds, including two Grand Slams.

In 1990, Blanco was captain and assistant coach of the test side, and led

France in the 1991 World Cup, his farewell to top rugby. He played with tremendous passion, as evidenced by the goings-on in his final test, the quarter-final against England, which France lost 19-10. The French team's behaviour was shameful. They were obstructive and instigated several brawls. Blanco was not the prime culprit, but must take some responsibility. He became involved in one heated punch-up, revealing the volatile French side of his nature.

As a farewell to one of their favourite sports sons, the French later put on a testimonial dinner that had a special New Zealand connection. On an early tour of New Zealand, Blanco had befriended a youngster in Whangarei, north of Auckland. He offered the boy tickets to the forthcoming test and remained in contact with him. That lad, by then several years older, was flown to Biarritz for Blanco's testimonial dinner.

Blanco held the world record with 93 tests when he retired. (In addition, he played 14 unofficial tests, some against strong rugby nations like Scotland, Ireland and Italy.) His 38 test tries (including six on the wing) placed him third on the all-time test list behind Campese and Rory Underwood, a tribute to his attacking ability. The previous record for a fullback was Andy Irvine's 10 tries, which Blanco eclipsed relatively early in his career.

After his retirement, Blanco became president of his beloved Biarritz club. By 1999 he had risen to become President of the French Federation's League, with the responsibility of controlling club teams in the European Cup. **100**

Serge Blanco dives over in the corner for his match-winning try against Australia in the World Cup semi-final, Sydney, 1987.

NAAS BOTHA

Nasty Booter

Hendrik Egnatius Botha
Flyhalf
Born: Breyten, February 27, 1958
Test debut: South Africa v South America, Johannesburg, April 26, 1980
Test career: 1980-92 (28 matches)
Test points: 312 (2 tries, 50 conversions, 50 penalties, 18 drop goals)
* Twice equalled the world record with three drop goals in a test
* Captained South Africa on its return from international rugby isolation, in 1992
* Has scored most points for South Africa in tests
* Has kicked most penalties, conversions and drop goals for South Africa in tests
* South Africa's most capped flyhalf when he retired

NAAS BOTHA was known in rugby circles as 'Nasty Booter' and the tag, though a play on his name, was most appropriate. He *was* a nasty booter, whose ability to punt, drop goals and place kick won Northern Transvaal and the Springboks many vital matches.

As the Bennie Osler of his era, Botha seemed to attract criticism. His detractors claimed he was preoccupied with kicking, that he wouldn't tackle and seldom passed. But the criticism was not entirely fair.

I thought Botha was a fine flyhalf whose nonchalant and spontaneous kicking overshadowed his other talents. In 1980, in his debut season with the Springboks, he masterminded the 26-22 first test win over the Lions, yet kicked no penalties or drop goals. His vision and running ability helped the Springboks score five tries that day.

My first recollections of Botha are from the 1976 New Zealand tour of South Africa. The Northern Transvaal under-21s played several curtain-raisers to All Black matches and we became accustomed to the crowds arriving early to watch this flaxen-haired 18-year-old. The All Blacks were so impressed they requested he be chosen in the South African Barbarians team to play them late in the tour. The request was declined. All Black coach J J Stewart rated the young Botha above Gerald Bosch, the Springbok flyhalf that year.

Botha was already a potential sports star when he attended Hendrik Verwoerd School in Pretoria. He excelled at not only rugby, but also baseball and softball. Botha came from a sporting family - his brother Darius played a test for South Africa during the 1981 tour of New Zealand.

By the time Naas began attending Pretoria University, he was South African rugby's new wonderboy. He first represented Northern Transvaal at 19, but was unfortunate to arrive on the international scene as South Africa was being squeezed into rugby isolation because of the abhorrent apartheid policies of its Government. In 1979 he was South African Rugby Player of the Year.

Botha's test debut was in 1980, against South America at Johannesburg. He made a flying start, totalling 26 points in his first two tests. In his second test he equalled the world record with three drop goals. Back then, Botha was regarded as much more than a kicker. He was a quick and willing runner, read a game expertly and looked after the men outside him. That same year he was appointed captain of Northern Transvaal.

Botha places yet another kick to the Springboks' advantage in the Cavaliers series, 1986.

He had a fine tour of New Zealand in 1981. It was a torrid time for the Springboks as the tour was marred by constant protests. But Botha, fiercely competitive, kept to himself and piled up the records. He scored 31 points against Nelson Bays, reached his century after six matches, and finished with 129. Botha was the dominant figure among the tourists and their best chance of beating New Zealand. He guided them to victory in the second test with 20 points, the most a player had scored in a test against New Zealand.

Botha, 1.78 (5ft 10in) and 76.5kg (12st), was always well-balanced and his accurate kicking dominated reports. English writer Frank Keating later referred to the 'single-minded metronomic swing of his boot' and that's what it looked like to New Zealanders.

Keith Quinn (left) and Naas Botha, at Botha's home in Pretoria, 1999.

Ironically, he missed his most important kick of the tour, a moderately-difficult conversion in injury time during the deciding third test at Auckland. If he'd kicked it, the South Africans would have led 24-22. It was about the first time he had seemed fallible.

Thereafter criticism of Botha's style mounted. Already, after being a pivotal figure in the Springboks' 3-1 series win over the Lions in 1980, Botha had been criticised by famous Welsh coach Carwyn James, who wrote: 'He may be the new golden boy of South African rugby, but by world standards he is very ordinary.'

Players who have dropped the most goals in tests:

28	Hugo Porta (Argentina and South America)	1971-90
23	Rob Andrew (England and the British Isles)	1985-97
18	Naas Botha (South Africa)	1980-92
17	Stefano Bettarello (Italy)	1979-88
15	Jean-Patrick Lescarboura (France)	1982-90

For the Northern Transvaal Rugby union's celebration dinner to mark Danie Craven's 80th birthday, a leading South African artist completed a splendid oil painting of Craven's five favourite players - Naas Botha, Benoit Dauga, Gareth Edwards, Frik du Preez and Colin Meads - in action. At the dinner, the Northern Transvaal union backed Botha in bidding for the painting. Botha went as high as R20,000, but when the head of the Rembrandt Group, Anton Rupert, put in a bid for R25,000, Botha resigned himself to missing out.

The painting was duly sold to the hugely wealthy Rupert, who then stood up at the dinner and said, "No, I don't want the painting. I've only bid this high to give it to Naas."

The painting adorned Botha's study when I visited his house early in 1999 while researching for a Television New Zealand documentary on the All Blacks. It's one of the few rugby items in his huge house. I saw no photos or trophies, and he told me he'd given 125 jerseys to the Northern Transvaal union at the end of his career. The reason, he explained, was that he didn't want his children growing up with pressure on them to match his success.

It was the sort of stuff Botha would have to get used to. David Campese scoffed at a player who had shoulder pads built into his rugby jersey but never tackled. Scotland captain David Sole said his team called Botha the traffic policeman because of his eagerness to wave the opposition through.

Nevertheless throughout the 1980s, he was the greatest match-winner in South Africa and one of the country's sports superstars. On one famous occasion, he kicked all 24 points (four penalties, four drop goals) as Northern Transvaal beat Transvaal in the 1987 Currie Cup final. Botha played in 11 Currie Cup finals and nine times his team won. He really hurt the 1986 New Zealand Cavaliers, scoring 69 points in four tests.

Botha made news for other reasons, too. In 1983 he had a crack at the lucrative American Football scene, playing six games as kicker for the Dallas Cowboys, but was unable to land a permanent contract. (He was suspended from rugby briefly, until it was ruled that gridiron was not a competing code.) There followed a stint for Rovigo, in Italy.

He was still playing well when South Africa returned to the international fold in 1992. Approaching 35, he was slower, but his kicking boot was as accurate as ever. He captained the Springboks against New Zealand and Australia and then on a 13-match tour of Europe, where he impressed with his diplomacy. The South Africans were struggling to make the step back up to top rugby and their results were spotty, but Botha was still a beautiful technician. On a filthy day against England at Twickenham, he punted brilliantly and landed one great drop goal.

David Miller of the *London Times* wrote: 'Botha, marvellously proportioned physically and with that elusive secret of timing, makes his skills appear utterly natural to a degree that can unhinge the opposition in split seconds. He can swerve the ball off the outside of the foot and do things with it few can aspire to.'

But always there was criticism and controversy, much of it from South African journalists. One described him as 'toothless as an old hag'. He was chided because his shorts were too white, which apparently meant he didn't tackle enough. Botha tended to write it off as inter-provincial jealousy. When he retired after the European tour, he said: "Some people will be glad to see the back of me, but at least I retire with my head held high. I sacrificed everything for rugby and it was worth it."

He departed rugby with a plethora of records. What would those figures have been but for South Africa's exclusion? He was South Africa's most capped flyhalf, their highest points-scorer, and had kicked the most conversions, dropped goals and penalties. He'd had the longest test career of any Springbok. And he dominated even more at Currie Cup level.

Botha gained a reputation for being serious, even sullen. I did not find him that way. Some people do not understand that not all South Africans are as fluent in English as them. It is difficult to convey humour in your second or third language. I have worked with him as a television commentator and found him to be pleasant and knowledgeable.

His wife, Karen, was a champion long jumper who represented South Africa at the 1992 Barcelona Olympics. **100**

GERRY BRAND

Firebrand

PLAYERS DON'T qualify for greatness merely because of one extraordinary feat. However, often there is a defining moment in a player's career. With Ian Kirkpatrick, it was his try against the British Lions at Christchurch in 1971. Gareth Edwards capped off an amazing try for the Barbarians against the All Blacks at Cardiff in 1973. Pierre Villepreux kicked a never-to-be-forgotten 70-metre penalty at Athletic Park in 1968.

So it was with fullback Gerry Brand. He played for South Africa for 11 years and was keeper of the gate through one of the great Springbok eras. But despite his consistently classy performances, Brand is first recalled for his drop goal against England at Twickenham in 1932. Fielding a missed clearance at halfway, he let fly with a left-footed drop goal that drew gasps of admiration from the 70,000 spectators. His kick into a strong wind went on as if powered by battery, clearing the cross-bar and carrying well into the crowd. It was later measured at more than 85 yards (77 metres). After that he was known in Britain as 'Firebrand'.

In New Zealand, Brand is remembered for his great tour with the 1937 Springboks. He scored 109 points in Australia and another 100 in New Zealand. To hoist a double-century of points on tour was almost beyond belief back in those days when fields were poorly drained and the leather ball was often waterlogged and heavy.

But Brand was much more than just an accurate kicker. He was an astute positional player, a good defender and had an impressive turn of speed, not surprising as he was a winger when he broke into the test arena in 1928.

Brand hailed from a sports-minded family - his middle name of Hamilton represented the local rugby club, for which he later played. Brand's name certainly sounded different when his countrymen pronounced it. In New Zealand it tends to be reduced to the most basic 'Gerry Brand' but pronounced properly, with appropriate throaty guttural intonations, 'Herri Bront' has a rather exotic beauty.

Though a shy youth, his talent on the rugby field spoke for itself. But he had a difficult task breaking into the Western Province side of the mid-1920s. The selectors were able to fill their team with test players and leave still more on the sidelines. Despite his flair, accurate kicking - the result of many hours' practice - and devastating tackling, he was not chosen for any of the Western Province selections that faced Maurice Brownlie's 1928 All Blacks.

Gerhardt Hamilton Brand
Fullback
Born: Cape Town, October 8, 1906
Died: Fish Hoek, February 4, 1996
Test debut: South Africa v New Zealand, Johannesburg, July 21, 1928
Test career: 1928-38 (16 matches)
Test points: 55 (13 conversions, 7 penalties, 2 drop goals)

*   Brand's 293 points for his country (in 46 matches) remained the national record until beaten by Naas Botha in 1982
*   His 209 points on the 1937 tour of Australia and New Zealand is still the South African touring record

The town of Danville, in the west of Pretoria, has 48 streets named after Springboks. Some of them, like **Gerry Brand, Bennie Osler, Boy Louw** and **Frik du Preez**, are legends of South African rugby, though some greats such as Danie Craven. Hennie Muller and Gerhardt Morkel have not reached signpost status yet.

Test players from all over the world have been honoured by having parks, trophies, stadiums, tournaments and even racehorses named after them. Among the more notable are:

Danie Craven Stadium in Burgersdorp, Danie Craven Pavilion at Newlands, Danie Craven Rugby Stadium at Stellenbosch and Danie Craven Week, a festival for college teams.

Italians remember former rugby star, **Mario Battaglini** because the Rovigo Municipal Stadium is now named the Stade Communale Mario Battaglini. The Rovigo player represented Italy from 1940-53.

In New Zealand, Hamilton Boys High and Tauranga Boys High each year play for 'The Boot' - a trophy once worn by **Don Clarke** on the test fields of the world. New Zealanders have honoured former greats with the **George Nepia** Trophy, the Gallaher Shield (after 'Originals' captain **Dave Gallaher**) for the top Auckland club side, and the **Kelvin Tremain** Memorial Trophy for New Zealand rugby personality of the year. There is a Meads Street in Te Kuiti, the heart of **Colin Meads** country and racehorses have been named after stars like **Christian Cullen** and **Dave Loveridge**. **Jonah Lomu** had an item of food called the Jonah Burger named after him at McDonald's. At Waikeria Prison, in the central North Island, two of the buildings are named Meads House and Hillary House. The names, chosen by the inmates, salute two icons of New Zealand sport.

In Britain, there are the **Gwyn Nicholls** Memorial Gates at the Arms Park in Cardiff, not far from a magnificent statue of **Gareth Edwards.** The Stoop Memorial Ground, home of the Harlequins club is named after the great **Adrian Stoop**, while East Midlands and the Barbarians play an **Edgar Mobbs** Memorial Match.

The French renamed the Colombes Stadium State Yves du Manoir in memory of **Yves du Manoir**. The brilliant flyhalf played eight tests before dying at the age of 23 in a plane crash shortly before kick-off in the test against Scotland in 1928.

Australians have named the McLean Stand at Ballymore after the famous **McLean** rugby family and have honoured a recent great with the **David Campese** Field at Queanbeyan.

Gerry Brand was in superb form throughout the Springboks' 1937 tour of New Zealand.

When Brand was called into the second test team, the selection was criticised even in the *Cape Town Times,* which couldn't see why Brand, Western Province's No 2 fullback to the famous Jackie Tindall, should be chosen as a wing. He had a good debut, though, in a losing team, Charlie Lambe writing in the *Sunday Times,* 'Brand was most convincing, both on attack and defence, and a wonderful drop from the centre chalk-mark, which hit the uprights, deserved a better fate.' Brand played in the third test, but was omitted from the fourth test side.

By the time the Springboks toured Britain in 1931-32, Brand and Tindall were regarded as equals. When Tindall was badly injured early on, Brand moved into the test side and he held his spot as if by right through the 1930s.

New Zealanders first saw him in the 1937 Auckland-South Africa game when his form was indifferent. But in the next match, against King Country-Waikato-Thames Valley, he turned in a brilliant wet weather game. The *New Zealand Herald* reported: 'It was well for the Springboks that Brand was in such good form. He had plenty of work to do and accomplished it in very polished style. His handling under the conditions was excellent, while he showed cleverness in getting out of trouble. Against the loose rushes of the Combined team forwards he was quick to change direction. He kicked splendidly with his left foot and his right. It was easy to realise how he has made his great reputation as a fullback.'

The 1937 South Africans are often described as the best team to leave New Zealand and were the first tourists to win a test series in New Zealand. Besides a tremendous pack, they had two great backs in Danie Craven and

Brand. Graham Beamish of the *New Zealand Press Association*, summarising the tour, praised Brand glowingly, especially his ability to pick up a rolling, greasy ball, or a ball lying in a puddle, while going at top speed. All Black Charlie Oliver described Brand as the star of the Springboks and said: 'Without him the Springboks were like a ship without an anchor. I have yet to see a finer fullback. It was not only his play, but also the psychological effect he had on the rest of the team, for he was to them what Nepia was to the 1924 All Blacks.'

Though not physically imposing, Brand had undeniable presence. Sportswriter Maxwell Price wrote: 'Brand was always a silent, mystic figure, whose presence seemed to have an engulfing effect on the attackers. He would draw the player with the ball to his tackle like a human magnet.'

He was also perfectly groomed, his hair slicked back and everything clean from his jersey collar, to the left knee bandage he always wore, to his boots. After making a tackle, he would trot back to position, absent-mindedly dusting off his shorts.

Brand rounded out his international career with a virtuoso performance in the first test against the 1938 British Isles side, at Ellis Park, Johannesburg. There he landed several brilliant kicks, including a long drop-

kicked penalty which was taken from inside his own half. His test career ended suddenly, for shortly after the Ellis Park test, he was injured in a club game and missed the rest of the international season.

It was not quite the end of his career, for he played once more for Western Province, in 1945, at the age of 39. Like Bennie Osler and later Okey Geffin, he was declared a professional briefly because a make of boots bore his name. However he was reinstated on the condition that he received no money from the sale of the boots. 🏉

ZINZAN BROOKE

The Man who Scored a Goal at Wembley

ZINZAN BROOKE was the most competitive All Black I've seen. Whether it was golf or tennis, he loved competing. One day he watched a younger All Black spinning the rugby ball on his finger with some skill. Brooke went away and practised assiduously until he could do it better. He has been known to spend his Sundays playing Gaelic football or Australian Rules football. This competitiveness shone through in Brooke's rugby. He liked to be best at everything, which explains his penchant for drop kicking.

As a player with the physique of a forward and the skills of a back, Brooke was a unique rugby talent. He was skilful, versatile and durable. John Hart said when Brooke retired: "There will never be another player like him."

Brooke was superb at the back of the scrum, controlling the ball as he guided his pack towards the opposition line, then diving over for the try or picking up the ball and bullocking his way over. With the ball in hand he was nearly unstoppable. He was a merciless tackler and loved to play halfback and fire out reverse passes. He could drop kick and punt better than most backs and was a galloping runner in the loose.

When he departed international football in 1997, having played 100 games and scored 41 tries for the All Blacks, he left a gaping hole in the New Zealand team. This was the player who once induced esteemed Scottish commentator Bill McLaren to state that he was the best loose forward he'd seen.

Brooke was born in the north of New Zealand and grew up in a rugby family. One brother, Robin, became an outstanding All Black lock and another, Marty, went close to New Zealand honours. Zinzan attended Mahurangi College and by his early teens was showing unusual potential, playing at prop for the North Island under-16 team in 1981.

It was his efforts for the New Zealand sevens team that really caught the national selectors' attention. Three times in four years Brooke helped New Zealand win the Hong Kong sevens. After appearing for Auckland and New Zealand Maori in 1986, he was chosen in New Zealand's 1987 World Cup side.

He entered first class rugby as Murray Zinzan Brooke, but changed his name by deed poll to Zinzan Valentine Brooke to take his family history into account. In his early All Black days, he was Wayne Shelford's understudy at No 8, though he played as openside flanker against Argentina at Athletic Park in the 1987 World Cup. It was a big day for him. He led the haka and scored a try.

Over the next few years he struggled to hold a test place. Loose forwards

---

Zinzan Valentine Brooke
Loose forward
Born: Waiuku, February 14, 1965
Test debut: New Zealand v Argentina, Wellington, June 1, 1987
Test career: 1987-97 (58 matches)
Test points: 89 (17 tries, three drop goals)
* His 17 test tries is the world record for a forward

Most tries in tests by a forward

(from any country)

17 Zinzan Brooke (New Zealand)

16 Ian Kirkpatrick (New Zealand)

13* Michael Jones (New Zealand)

12 Sean Fitzpatrick (New Zealand)

11 Col Windon (Australia)

11 John Jeffrey (Scotland)

11 Michel Crauste (France)

11* Josh Kronfeld (New Zealand)

11* David Wilson (Australia)

11 Benoit Dauga (France)

* still playing

Shelford, Michael Jones, Mike Brewer and Alan Whetton were difficult to displace, and when Laurie Mains became All Black coach in 1992, Arran Pene and Jamie Joseph jumped ahead of him. In *Zinny*, his autobiography, Brooke revealed that Mains initially snubbed him on becoming All Black coach. The exhortations of Sean Fitzpatrick persuaded Mains to give Brooke another chance and by the end of 1993 he had stamped himself as a world class player.

Brooke faced public relations problems when selected to replace the charismatic Wayne Shelford after Shelford was sensationally dropped in 1990. But Brooke was always popular himself. The public liked his flair and the hint of mischief in his play. I felt at the time he was ready to replace the fading Shelford. Brooke brought skill, height, speed and passing skills to the position and had a tremendous instinct for the game. At 1.90m (6ft 3in) and 100kg (15st 10lb), his size and strength made him an asset as a lineout jumper. Shelford was a formidable operator when the going was tough, but Brooke, too, eventually proved himself against the best.

Three times Brooke dropped goals in test rugby. The first, against England in the 1995 World Cup semi-final, gained headlines because it was the first. But the most critical was the one against South Africa at Pretoria in 1996. That kick pushed the All Blacks into a virtually unbeatable lead and enabled them to win their first series in South Africa. I often wondered what induced halfback Justin Marshall to flick the ball back to Brooke when he had talented kickers like Andrew Mehrtens and Christian Cullen hovering. The video replay reveals that Brooke, standing behind Marshall, yelled out: 'Hey, hey, hey, hey, hey!' Marshall got the message, passed to Brooke and the rest was history. That was one of the most demanding tests I've seen. We realised how draining it had been when, 15 minutes after the game, Brooke walked into the interview room. He was asked to sign a ball, but couldn't. He just couldn't get his trembling hand near the ball.

Brooke's third test drop goal was against Wales at Wembley in 1997, a kick that enabled those of us in the commentary box to exclaim: 'Brooke's scored a goal at Wembley.' Few rugby players have that claim to fame.

The big Aucklander could easily have captained the All Blacks. He was Fitzpatrick's eyes and ears at the back of the All Black scrum and called many of the moves. He was an inspiring leader of the Auckland provincial and Super 12 teams, where his popularity within the team, plus his fierce desire to win, made him consistently successful. Brooke's test career closed in 1997 when he was beginning to lose his dynamism. Even just below his best he was a formidable competitor, but he was wise to retire rather than to linger.

He was always one of the most popular sports figures in New Zealand, taking over from David Kirk in the late 1980s as the heart-throb of All Black rugby. His trademark freckle under his left eye became a cartoonist's delight and the public warmed to the feats of the man they knew simply as 'Zinny'.

Many of his 161 first class tries (in 311 matches) were pushovers generated by the dominant Auckland pack. It made things somewhat repetitive from a commentary perspective, but as his career unfolded, Brooke showed he was far from a one-dimensional player. He was a central figure in Auckland's great era and rivalled wingers Terry Wright and John Kirwan as a try-scorer, surpassing Kel Tremain and Ian Kirkpatrick as the leading try-scorer among New Zealand forwards.

At least twice, Brooke was nearly lost to New Zealand rugby. He signed for Sydney league club Manly in 1990, then changed his mind. Later he was about to take up a professional contract in Japan when a business deal involving Sky Television was done to keep him in New Zealand. Eventually in 1998 he went to English club Harlequins as player-coach. **100**

MAURICE BROWNLIE

A Giant of his Time

For the last 30 years of the century, Colin Meads has been judged the player who epitomises an All Black - tough, proud, skilled and committed. He was regarded by New Zealanders, and many others, as the best forward of his generation. As the number who saw Meads play declines, I suppose another forward, perhaps Sean Fitzpatrick, will eventually replace Meads in the New Zealand psyche.

When I was growing up, Maurice Brownlie was still being cited as the greatest All Black forward. Many a rugby expert would look at a promising young forward and say, 'He'll never be another Maurice Brownlie.' He was the Meads of his time and the strongman of All Black teams in Britain, France, South Africa, Australia and at home during the 1920s.

Brownlie was one of three brothers - the others were Laurie and Cyril - who represented New Zealand, and helped launch the first great Hawkes Bay Ranfurly Shield era. Laurie, the youngest, represented the All Blacks first, against New South Wales, in 1921. Knee injuries cut short his career, but he did inspire Maurice and Cyril to get serious about their rugby. Maurice made his All Black debut in Australia in 1922, where his physical, robust game had critics in raptures.

Cyril became a quality forward, particularly adept in lineout play, but Maurice was the glamour player of his generation, a loose forward who had pace, ball-handling skills, ability to kick, courage and, most notably, strength. His work on the Puketitiri farm he and Cyril shared helped him develop tremendous body strength. There are stories of Maurice bounding up hills with a sheep under each arm, and of him pulling the family car out of the river. He was 1.83m (6ft) and just over 89kg (14st), but played well above that weight. Many of the stories of Brownlie on his farm are similar to those heard in the 1960s about Colin and Stan Meads and their feats of farming strength.

Brownlie was born in Wanganui and attended St Pat's College, Wellington, but it was in Hawke's Bay that he made his rugby reputation. By then he'd served with two brothers, Cyril and Tony (who was killed at Ankara), in the Palestine during the first World War.

His mentor was the great New Zealand rugby identity Norman McKenzie, who moulded the All Black-studded Hawkes Bay combination of the 1920s. McKenzie played Brownlie at lock in his rep debut, against Manawatu, but

Maurice John Brownlie
Loose forward
Born: Wanganui, August 10, 1897
Died: Gisborne, January 21, 1957
Test debut: New Zealand v Ireland, Dublin, November 1, 1924
Test career: 1924-28 (8 tests)
Test points: 6 (2 tries)
* One of three brothers who were All Blacks
* Held record for most appearances for New Zealand (61) for 28 years

never did so again. 'Maurice had too much ability to waste in the middle of scrums,' McKenzie explained. So Brownlie became a loose forward who could grind his way up the touchline, or could power clear in the loose, a 1920s version of Meads.

He was at his peak on the 1924-25 'Invincibles' tour of Britain. Even alongside brilliant forwards like Cliff Porter, Jim Parker, Jock Richardson and brother Cyril, Maurice was outstanding. He scored 11 tries in his 30 tour games and was described as the best forward in the world.

His greatest match was against England at Twickenham on January 3, 1925, the day Cyril became the first player to be ordered from the field in a test. Cyril received his marching orders from referee Albert Freethy for kicking a man on the ground, though no-one ever did find an English player who had been kicked. Maurice, seething with the injustice of it, played like two men and inspired the 14 remaining New Zealanders to such heights that they walloped 15 of England's finest 17-11. Maurice scored a barging, charging try in the second spell. He had Parker ranging up alongside him, but never considered passing. "Jim, I wouldn't have passed it out for 100 quid," he said later.

Brownlie was the captain and cornerstone of the Hawkes Bay side which defended the Ranfurly Shield 24 times from 1922-27 and in 1928 led the All Blacks on their first tour of South Africa.

Though the series was split 2-2, the best result a New Zealand side achieved in a series in South Africa for 68 years, it was not an entirely happy tour. There were questions about Brownlie's leadership qualities. Mark Nicholls, Brownlie's vice-captain, was omitted from the first three test teams, which caused the accompanying writers, including Nicholls' brother Syd, to mutter about poor selection and team leadership. Brownlie fell into the strong and silent mould, but commanded tremendous loyalty. Alan Robilliard, a team-mate on both his major tours, said that in South Africa Brownlie led by example and was a good talker and mixer. "He was a giant of a bloke," Robilliard recalled.

Jock Richardson, the 'Invincibles' vice-captain, agreed. "He was quite taciturn and didn't have a lot to say at team talks, but when he spoke he was sure of an attentive audience. Maurice was my idea of a captain. He'd talk up when he had to, but didn't shout his mouth off. He could be firm and inspired confidence."

The All Blacks in South Africa were handicapped by having to leave behind their Maori players, including the incomparable George Nepia, and by the unavailability of Bert Cooke. 'If we'd had Nepia and Cooke, we wouldn't have lost a match,' Brownlie said later. Still, Brownlie's form was good and in the fourth test, won 13-5, he was outstanding. Incidentally, as captain, Brownlie took the kick-offs for New Zealand and for Hawkes Bay.

The South African tour marked the end of his test career, though he played for Hawkes Bay against Great Britain in 1930. He was married and living in Gisborne by then, and his interest in rugby was waning.

For such a phlegmatic personality - he was seldom ruffled, even though he received plenty of physical attention - he had strong superstitions. Perhaps because of his war background, he would not talk to opponents before a game, treating the contest like a battle. And he became famously attached to a pair of faded blue dungaree shorts. Hawkes Bay's shorts were black, but Brownlie was the exception, and would invariably take the field in his trusty and battered blue shorts.

Because Maurice and Cyril were so close, it must have been a devastating

One of the extraordinary features of New Zealand rugby is how many world-class side-row flankers the country has produced. A few of these flankers are profiled in this book, but several more could easily have been included.

Before the first World War, Charlie Seeling - Bronco to his team-mates - played so well for the 'Original' All Blacks that British critics rated him the finest forward in the world. Next in the royal line was Maurice Brownlie, a giant of a player. After the second World War, Peter Jones, Bill Clark, Kel Tremain, Waka Nathan, Ian Kirkpatrick, Graham Mourie, Mark Shaw, Alan Whetton, Michael Jones and Josh Kronfeld have carried on the tradition. Some have been openside flankers, others blindside specialists. What they have had in common is that at some point each has been rated as good as any side-row forward in the world.

Maurice Brownlie leads the 1928 All Blacks out for the Cape Town test. New Zealand won 13-5, to draw the series 2-2.

blow when Cyril died in 1954. Less than three years later, Maurice was dead. Many felt the DDT he came into constant contact with during his farming years might have caused his ill-health.

Brownlie was an excellent all-round sportsman. He was a good young cricketer, a single handicap golfer (left and right-handed), an excellent shot and as a boxer in 1921 lost the New Zealand heavyweight final to fellow All Black Brian McCleary. But it was in rugby that he left an indelible mark. It is easy to picture him, jaw set, straight dark hair brushed back, sleeves rolled up his thick forearms, a solid athletic frame, ready to lead Hawkes Bay or the All Blacks into battle.

He was a supreme player, the Meads or Fitzpatrick of his era. 'He was the greatest side-row forward I ever saw,' Norman McKenzie once wrote, 'because he was great in every aspect, but particularly his ability to lead his forwards out of a corner, yard by yard up the touchline. For sheer tenacity, he was tops. He wasn't the lineout jumper Cyril was, and was only a passably quick runner, but he could kick well with either foot and had a formidably strong mind.' 🏉

In his time, Maurice Brownlie was regarded as a very big international forward. These days he would be about the size of some test scrumhalves and smaller than many wingers and fullbacks. Here are the sizes of some well-known All Black forwards in the first quarter of this century. All were variously described as 'big', 'huge' and 'giant' during their time:

		Height	Weight
Moke Belliss	1921	1.80m	89kg
Maurice Brownlie	1924	1.83m	89kg
Quentin Donald	1924	1.78m	80kg
Dave Gallaher	1905	1.83m	79kg
Bull Irvine	1924	1.71m	80kg
George Nicholson	1905	1.90m	84kg
Charlie Seeling	1905	1.83m	84kg
Alf West	1920	1.85m	82kg

In the 1924 'Invincibles' team, there were six forwards who weighed less than 83kg (13st). In the 1928 team Brownlie took to South Africa, there were five forwards less than 83kg.

Visiting forwards to New Zealand were just as small. In the 1921 Springbok side, there were two forwards over 109 kg (17st) and all the others were under 96.5kg (15st). In the 1921 New South Wales team, there were five forwards under 77kg (12st).

OLLIE CAMPBELL

Irish Charm

Seamus Oliver Campbell
Flyhalf
Born: Dublin, March 3, 1954
Test debut: Ireland v Australia, Dublin, January 17, 1976
Test career: 1976-84 (29 matches - 22 for Ireland, 7 for the British Isles)
Test points: 243 (1 try, 16 conversions, 61 penalties, 8 drop goals)
* His 217 points was the Irish test record

I DECLARED my hand on Ollie Campbell a long time ago. In a book I wrote after the 1983 Lions tour of New Zealand, I named Campbell as the team's best player and on a scale of 1 to 10, rated him 12. It seems like extravagant praise, but that was the impression he made on many New Zealanders that season.

It wasn't a great Lions team and lost the test series 4-0. The Irish flyhalf was the visitors' shining light. The All Blacks so feared Campbell's lethal place-kicking ability that they could not afford to concede penalties in their own half, and for two successive tests, Campbell did not get a penalty shot at goal.

What amazed New Zealanders was that Campbell did not seem to be universally appreciated back home. After one test, he was dropped and in 1981 was temporarily moved to centre. You don't get match-winners like Campbell often. To not fully use their talents seemed a waste.

Campbell came from a football family and says his father taught him to tackle. The lesson was well learned - there was never any open-door policy with Campbell as regards tackling. Unlike many flyhalves, he relished tackling and was uncompromisingly effective. At 1.80m (5ft 11in) and 77kg (12st 3lb), he wasn't especially robust, but he feared no-one.

Campbell was a schoolboy flyhalf at nine. He attended Belvedere College, where he lived for rugby, not study. "When we lost a first round Junior Cup match 6-3 against Newbridge I cried for three days," he told John Scally in *The Giants of Irish Rugby*. He recalls being so elated to be in the 1971 and 1972 Leinster Cup-winning sides that he cleaned some Lansdowne Road mud from his boots and kept it as a souvenir.

Surprisingly, Campbell did not kick at school, not even drop-outs or kick-offs. But when he was 17 and playing for Old Belvedere, his captain assumed that because he was a flyhalf he was a kicker. He enjoyed the challenge and applied himself with typical devotion. Soon he had honed the simple, economic kicking style that made him one of world rugby's greatest match-winners. He had absolute concentration when lining up a shot - Mike Gibson called his style 'a perfect isolated act'.

Campbell made his test debut against John Hipwell's Wallabies in 1976, but it was an unhappy occasion for him. He missed three straightforward penalty attempts, and played only moderately. Campbell was not seen at international level for another three years, but when he returned he extracted full retribution on the Australians.

He travelled as Tony Ward's understudy to Australia with the 1979 Irish touring party, but made the test side, his shock selection causing some debate within the team. Campbell responded in style. In the first test, at Brisbane, he piled on 19 points (including two place kicks from halfway and three from the sideline) in Ireland's upset 27-12 victory. He scored all his side's points - two drop goals and a penalty - in the second test at Sydney as Ireland sealed an unexpected series victory.

After that Campbell was ever-present in the test side until hamstring injuries ruled him out in 1984. In successive Five Nations campaigns, he registered record tallies of 46, 46 and 52 points, huge scoring for those days.

But even in his halcyon years, he was not a unanimous first-choice flyhalf. Ward, too, had many backers. The contrast was absolute: Campbell, pale, freckled, retiring by nature, a masterful kicker; Ward, with dark Mediterranean good looks, a popular television personality, a silky smooth player. Rugby critics argued their merits. There was talk of the Leinster-Munster divide, and the Irish class system.

The talk never affected Campbell. He (like Ward) was always personable, with never a bad word about anyone. In New Zealand we noticed that Campbell crossed himself before a kick-off. "Well, I am a Catholic, and I believe," he told me. He would ring a priest back in Ireland before each game.

He toured South Africa with the 1980 Lions, but, hampered by hamstring injuries, missed eight of the first nine matches. He still finished the tour with 60 points and played in three tests, but was not at best. He returned to South Africa with an Ireland team in 1981, but a broken wrist and concussion restricted him to 50 minutes' rugby.

In 1982, Campbell was the linchpin of Ireland's first Triple Crown since 1949, scoring 52 of his team's 72 points. Ireland sewed up the Triple Crown with a 21-12

There have always been controversies over selectors' choices and some of these public debates have severely affected the careers of the players involved. Ollie Campbell's rivalry with Tony Ward is one of the best examples. The Irish selectors had two great talents and understandably had difficulty deciding which player was more suited to their match plans. In the end, Campbell played 22 tests for Ireland and Ward 19.

Other great rivalries have included:

* Chris Laidlaw and Sid Going - the New Zealand halfbacks of the 1960s and 70s
* Allan Hewson and Robbie Deans - the New Zealand fullbacks in the 1980s
* Benoit Dauga and Walter Spanghero - French forwards in the 1960s and 70s
* Ciaran Fitzgerald and Colin Deans - the British Lions hookers on the 1983 tour of New Zealand
* Rex Willis and Roy Burnett - the Welsh halfbacks of the 1950s
* Mark Ella and Paul McLean - Australian flyhalves of the 1980s
* Rob Andrew and Stuart Barnes - England flyhalves in the 1980s and 90s
* Ron Dawson and Bryn Meredith - the British Lions hookers in New Zealand in 1959
* In 1959 Taranaki had two halfbacks, Roger Urbahn and Kevin 'Monkey' Briscoe, and two first five-eighths, Ross Brown and John McCullough, vying for places in the All Black test side

win over Scotland, Campbell kicking six penalties and a drop goal. The following year Ireland retained the Five Nations Championship, though they had to share it with France. Again Campbell recorded a 21-point haul, this time against England.

The 1983 Lions tour marked his peak, and he showed himself to be as good as Jackie Kyle, Barry John or any of the other great Lions flyhalves who had visited New Zealand. In 11 matches he scored 124 points. He described his tour as visiting the Holy Grail. He'd always loved New Zealand, recalling that as a nine-year-old he went to Lansdowne Road with his father and watched the All Blacks beat Ireland 6-5. "Kel Tremain and the great Don Clarke were their scorers. I was hooked by the All Black power and passion and from that day studied New Zealand rugby closely."

Of my many memories of Campbell in 1983, the most vivid concerns a game he didn't play. The Lions lost 22-20 to Canterbury and Hugo MacNeill missed a late conversion attempt that would have drawn the match. We finished our broadcast and the post-match interviews, and were packing up when out of the gloom, all alone, we saw the red-haired figure of Campbell walking onto Lancaster Park, ball in hand. He walked up to the spot where MacNeill had missed that vital last goal and lined up a shot. Straight through the posts the ball went. Campbell retrieved the ball and lined it up again. Three times he kicked for goal and three times the ball when through the top of the 'H'. Then, having proved a point to no-one but himself, he quietly departed.

So accurate a kicker was Campbell that Television New Zealand received complaints about not showing his misses in our edited highlights. It wasn't that - he just seldom missed.

His running in the last quarter of the first test at Christchurch completely spread the All Blacks in defence. He jinked and ran himself, or looped around to receive from the man he had just passed to. He would attack on the blindside or probe with flat kicks. It was a stunning individual effort that sadly for the Lions received insufficient support.

After my tour book was published, Campbell wrote me a charming letter, thanking me for my kind words. Since then, he has contacted me whenever I've visited Ireland. He must have some form of ESP. No matter how quietly I slip into Ireland, there'll be a phone call to my hotel and it will be Ollie, keeping in touch.

Campbell's devastating place-kicking overshadowed his other qualities. He was a brilliantly creative player, an expert passer and a twinkling runner. Invariably he was one of his team's best tacklers. He revealed all his attacking prowess in the test against Wales at Dublin in 1982 when his brilliant running destroyed the Welsh defence and produced two tries for Moss Finn and one for Trevor Ringland.

For such a great player, he did not play a lot of big rugby, but he scored 243 test points, including 217 for Ireland, the national record until Michael Kiernan beat it in 1988.

After departing test football, Campbell played three seasons for Old Belvedere, then turned to coaching. He never followed the well-worn path to the press box, saying he would feel uncomfortable having to criticise other players. He was never one to force his opinions, preferring to melt into the background. But he was always the consummate sportsman, displaying humility and warmth that is not always evident at top level.

Campbell, who attended Dublin College of Commerce, these days holds a senior position in the textile industry. **100**

DAVID CAMPESE

Goosestepping to Glory

DAVID CAMPESE jumped from an Australian under-21 representative to an international superstar remarkably quickly, and remained at that exalted level for 15 years. His first tour with the Wallabies was to New Zealand in 1982, when he was just 19. Playing on the wing, he encountered one of New Zealand's best, Stu Wilson, and consistently outplayed him, much to the amazement of All Black supporters.

By the end of the tour, critics were calling Campese a rugby genius and the best winger in the world, and over the years he more than lived up to that assessment. He was to score a record number of test tries and become the second player, after Philippe Sella, to reach a century of tests.

But there was always more to Campese than simply the matter of scoring tries. He was a unique character, whose streak of individualism thrilled and frustrated Wallaby coaches. Crowds flocked to watch him and journalists loved to interview him, for he was colourful and often irreverent. He is on the same pedestal as Gareth Edwards, Danie Craven and Colin Meads among the game's great personalities.

That 1982 Wallaby side was raw and under-rated. A mass withdrawal of experienced Queensland players meant coach Bob Dwyer had to lean heavily on youth. With Dwyer and his captain Mark Ella leading the way, there was a strong influence from the Randwick club. The Australians played exciting, innovative rugby and very nearly won the Bledisloe Cup.

I first saw Campese during a training session in New Plymouth before the tour opener against Taranaki. Even in training, the eye-catching ability of the teenager marked him out as something special. His team-mates called him 'Campo', and I figured I'd be hearing a lot more of that name.

Campese didn't play against Taranaki, but in the next match, against Manawatu, he scored a try and kicked two conversions and a penalty. He scored tries in his first five matches for Australia and finished the tour as leading try-scorer. In the test series, Campese continued his merry way, scoring two tries and giving Wilson all sorts of headaches with his pace, acceleration, sidestepping and swerving ability and his vision and flair.

It was the start of a magnificent career. Over the years he had huge highs. There was his sensational play during Australia's Grand Slam tour of Britain in 1984 and his memorable try against the Barbarians at Cardiff in 1988. He played in the first three World Cups and was the star of the second

David Ian Campese
Winger/fullback
Born: Queanbeyan, October 21, 1962
Test debut: New Zealand v Australia, August 14, 1982
Test career: 1992-96 (101 tests)
Test points: 315 (64 tries, 8 conversions, 7 penalties, 2 drop goals)
* Holds the world record for most test tries
* Was the second player to reach a century of tests
* Played in the first three World Cups

tournament, which Australia won. A shift in the mid-1980s to Sydney - and the 'Galloping Greens' of the Randwick club - from his home in rugby-weak Australian Capital Territory helped because it meant he was playing a sterner level of football at home.

He carried on, retiring more times than Dame Nellie Melba, as they like to say in Australia, but always returning to provide more thrills. Crowds loved him because he was spectacular, unpredictable and brilliant. With Campese, something was always about to happen, but no-one, even Campese, was quite sure what. "I don't think where I'm going. I just go where my legs go," he once said. He was a fearless improviser, quite willing to run the ball out even from behind his own posts. High-risk strategies held no fear for him. His skill and daring enabled him to unlock the tightest defences.

Even at school, he'd been different. The son of an Italian migrant winemaker, Campese attended Queanbeyan Primary School, where he played league and dabbled in junior rugby, without ever revealing his potential. In fact, he showed more promise at golf than rugby. On leaving high school, though, he went into first grade with the Queanbeyan Whites and that's where he began to blossom.

Playing mainly on the wing, but also turning out at fullback when required, he displayed genuine pace, a huge punt and a willingness to give anything a go and was promoted into the Australian under-21 side. Then came his big chance in New Zealand in 1982.

It was in New Zealand that international rugby followers first spotted Campese's trademark goosestep or stutter-step. This was not a sidestep, but a change of pace in which he brought one foot together with the other, then stepped off the same foot. It wrong-footed defenders all over the world, even when they had studied video clips of Campese and been warned about the goosestep. His high-stepping style of running made his goosestep all the more difficult to read.

Campese had a priceless attribute for a winger; he scored tries by the bucketful. Against the United States in 1983 he ran in four, to tie Greg Cornelsen's Australian test record. Twice more he was to score three tries in a test.

At Sydney during the 1987 World Cup, he scored his 25th test try, passing

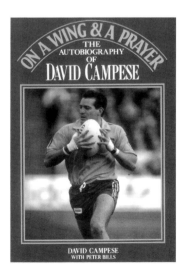

Campese's autobiography. The title says it all.

Most test tries			
64	David Campese (Australia)	101	1982-96
50	Rory Underwood (England/British Isles)	91	1984-96
38	Serge Blanco (France)	93	1980-91
35	John Kirwan (New Zealand)	63	1984-94
34	Ieuan Evans (Wales/British Isles)	79	1987-98
33	Philippe Saint-Andre (France)	69	1990-98
30	Philippe Sella (France)	111	1982-95
28*	Jeff Wilson (New Zealand)	42	1993-98
26*	Tim Horan (Australia)	67	1989-98
25*	Christian Cullen (New Zealand)	29	1996-98
25*	Joost van der Westhuizen (South Africa)	50	1993-98
25*	Vaea Anitoni (United States)	35	1992-98
25*	Marcello Cuttitta (Italy)	54	1987-99
25*	Jeremy Guscott (England/British Isles)	67	1989-99
* still playing			

Ian Smith's long-standing world record. It was one of five tries he scored during the tournament. Five years later at Cape Town, he brought up his 50th test try.

Like many great players, Campese occasionally found himself out of favour with selectors and he was dropped from the test side in 1990. But he bounced back and was at his greatest during the 1991 World Cup. In the preliminary matches, he scored two tries against Argentina and another against Wales. Then it was onto the quarter-finals, against Ireland at Lansdowne Road. Campese turned on a sublime exhibition, scoring two tries which were applauded even by the proud Irish supporters. It was Campese's desperate pass in those frenetic closing moments which enabled Michael Lynagh to crash over for the winning try.

In the semi-final he ran rings around New Zealand, scoring one fantastic try as he ran across the field and behind his arch-rival John Kirwan, and setting up another with an outrageous over-the-shoulder pass to Tim Horan. Australia beat their arch-rivals 16-6 to move into the final, against England. This was a tighter match and Campese had little room to manoeuvre, though his defence did save a sure Rory Underwood try on one occasion. He was the clear choice as Player of the Tournament.

The match programme for the 100th test played by David Campese, Italy v Australia, Padova 1996.

Besides these triumphs, there were some disasters, which, oddly enough, added to his appeal. His lowest moment came in the deciding third test against the British Lions at Sydney in 1989, when he fielded a miscued drop goal attempt from Rob Andrew behind his own line and threw a speculative pass to Greg Martin, rather than kick for touch. The pass went astray and Ieuan Evans pounced to score the vital try.

Everything about Campese was original. After his education in Australia, for example, he returned to his father's homeland in north-eastern Italy and began introducing rugby to soccer fanatics. He spoke good Italian and became a cult figure in Italian rugby, playing for Petrarca in Padova from 1984-88 and then the powerful Amatori Milano club from 1988-93. He helped each team win two national championships. In Italy he often moved to flyhalf when his team was on attack, calling the backline moves and scoring a string of tries himself.

Sometimes Campese looked so relaxed during a game that it seemed he didn't really care. But this casual on-pitch demeanour belied his dedication to fitness. You don't play international rugby for as long as he did relying on natural ability alone. He trained diligently to keep his 1.77m (5ft 10in), 89kg (14st 5lb) body in shape. No-one was more competitive. But he often made news for more than just his rugby. His outspoken views on opponents, coaches and even his own team-mates drew headlines. He was always particularly critical of England's style of play, calling them 'boring'. He had a major falling out with Wallaby coach Alan Jones, which he detailed in his autobiography, and even Bob Dwyer, coach of the 1991 world champions, had cause to say at one point that Campese 'has a loose wire between his brain and his mouth'.

On the other hand, Campese was often last off the field after signing autographs and did a lot of work helping young and promising players.

It seemed like his career would run out of steam before he could reach the magic century. He began to be overlooked by the Wallaby selectors and slowed noticeably, though he was still capable to great improvisation. Australian coach Greg Smith, however, chose him for his 100th test, appropriately against Italy at Padova. Campese broke a tradition by leading out the Wallabies ahead of captain John Eales. He got to the middle of the Plebiscido Stadium and looked around expecting to see his team-mates behind him, but found himself alone, as the 10,000-strong crowd saluted a rugby legend.

Besides his peerless record in test rugby, Campese was a brilliant sevens player. He enjoyed the space and the opportunity to have a go. For years he was one of the best sevens players in Australia. In 1988 he was named Player of the Tournament after helping Australia win the Hong Kong Sevens title, and in 1998 was still such a force in the abbreviated version of the game that he led Australia to a bronze medal at the Kuala Lumpur Commonwealth Games.

Campese was one of three great backs who ushered Australia through its finest era. Along with Michael Lynagh and Nick Farr-Jones, the iconoclastic Campese helped lift Australia to the top of world rugby. Along the way, he spurned several enticing rugby league offers, though this decision was made easier because of the lifestyle he was able to lead in Italy during the Southern Hemisphere off-seasons. He was calling himself a 'rugby millionaire' some years before the game went professional.

In Sydney, Campese has turned successfully to business, running *Campo's Sports Store*. In addition, he is in demand to assist in coaching in developing rugby countries. He has become manager of some well-known Australian sports personalities, including swimming champion Matt Dunn. **100**

WILL CARLING

Captain Fantastic

I WONDER IF Will Carling was treated fairly by the rugby media. By the early 1990s, the England captain was the world's most publicised rugby personality. Yet he had a love-hate relationship with the media, some of whom regarded him as aloof and self-serving.

My experiences with Carling indicated this assessment was well off beam. He toured New Zealand with the 1993 Lions side. It wasn't a happy tour for Carling, who was initially tipped to be captain, but saw the leadership go to Scotland's Gavin Hastings. Injuries and lack of form cost Carling his place in the test side. For such a successful player, the tour can't have been much fun.

Through my television commitments, I was required to interview Carling twice, once before the tour began and once after the Waikato fixture, when Carling led the Lions. Both times he could not have been more helpful.

The second interview was revealing. The Lions had been hammered 38-10 by Waikato and Carling had squandered a chance to reclaim a test spot. Immediately after the game I approached him as he trooped off the field somewhat disconsolately and asked if he would answer a few questions for television. At almost the same moment I was required to begin an interview with the Waikato captain John Mitchell, so was resigned to the fact that I would miss Carling. Throughout my chat with Mitchell, I was conscious of a figure just behind me. It was Carling, who remained behind when I'm sure he just wanted to slope off to the dressing room. He answered my questions fully and I know that in those moments of stress for a television journalist I greatly appreciated his actions. I thought they said a lot about the fellow. Funnily enough, I later interviewed both Carling and Mitchell in the same Twickenham studio in early 1999, while on a tour filming a documentary on the All Blacks.

With his English accent and his high profile, Carling was sometimes a figure of derision in New Zealand, but this said more about New Zealanders' innate suspicion of Poms than it did about Carling.

By a combination of skill, timing and good fortune he enjoyed a long and successful career during which he oversaw rugby's rush into the professional era. He bought himself out of the army (he was a 2nd Lieutenant) when told he would not be able to play rep rugby. The decision to focus on the business of rugby turned out to be a wise one. He was never far from the

William David Charles Carling
Centre
Born: Bradford-on-Avon, December 12, 1965
Test debut: England v France, Paris, January 16, 1988
Test career: 1988-97 (73 matches - 72 for England, 1 for the British Isles)
Test points: 54 (12 tries)
*   Led England in a record 59 tests
*   His 44 test wins as captain is the world record

When he became captain of England (against Australia, November 5, 1988), Will Carling was 22 years, 11 months of age - England's youngest captain since Peter Howard 57 years earlier. England won Carling's first match in charge 28-19.

He was to lead England in 59 tests, a world record ahead of Sean Fitzpatrick (New Zealand, 51) and Nick Farr-Jones (Australia, 36). Carling's 44 wins as a captain is the world record.

Carling's major captaincy successes were winning three Five Nations Grand Slams (1991, 92 and 95), four Five Nations Championships (including 1996), and reaching a World Cup final (1991) and semi-final (1995).

spotlight, whether through the work of his London-based promotion company *Insights,* or in 1995 for the liaison with Princess Diana, which ultimately destroyed his marriage.

Carling was the son of an army officer. He began playing rugby as a six-year-old with the Terra Nova School under-11s. At 15, he became the first fifth-former to play in the Sedburgh School First XV. He made seven appearances for England Schools, three as captain in 1984. When he moved to Durham University, where he read psychology on an army scholarship, he switched briefly to fullback before settling at centre. By 1987 he was in the England B team, and the following season he made his test debut in Paris in England's 10-9 loss to France.

By November that year, aged 22 and in only his seventh test, he had become England's youngest captain since 1931. England's solid defeat of Australia at Twickenham launched Carling's reign in fine style.

In 1991 Carling led England to its first Grand Slam since 1980 and to a runner-up finish in the World Cup - having beaten Scotland in the semis, England lost to Australia 12-6 in the final. In 1992 Carling became the first England captain to achieve back-to-back Grand Slams in 67 years. He was a huge sports figure in Britain and a major factor in the rise of rugby's profile.

As a player, Carling - 1.81m (5ft 11in) and 90kg (14st 3lb) - was sound rather than brilliant. He formed a record-breaking partnership in the centres with Jeremy Guscott and proved himself a good distributor with an ability to read the game well. He ran hard and tackled effectively, but lacked the spark of genius of a great midfield player. It is as a captain and a personality that he earns inclusion here. He was an organised and efficient leader who could appeal to the diverse temperaments in his teams. With his managerial abilities, he was the ideal person to lead England in the 1990s.

During the 1990s, he passed Nick Farr-Jones (36) and then Hugo Porta (43) to become the player who had captained his country the most times and the following year led England to an unprecedented third Grand Slam. It was a tumultuous year for Carling. At the very moment when his leadership seemed most secure and as he was focusing on the 1995 World Cup in South Africa, he was sacked as captain.

The decision was sparked by a television interview during which he made the throwaway comment that England's RFU committee was 'a

Keith Quinn interviews Will Carling at the Twickenham Rugby Museum, 1999.

bunch of 57 old farts'. England's rugby officials then proceeded to prove Carling correct by dumping him on the eve of the World Cup. It took two apologies before Carling was reinstated.

At the World Cup, England went well, upsetting Australia in the quarter-finals, before running into a fired-up All Black side. Carling scored two tries, but England were thrashed 45-29. The dominating figure in the match was Jonah Lomu, who scored four tries. "He's a freak, and the sooner he retires the better," Carling quipped afterwards.

Carling had one more year at the helm, leading England to another Five Nations championship and a Triple Crown, then stepped down from the captaincy. He held his test spot until his retirement in 1997. Near the end of his career he attempted to convert himself into a flyhalf and revealed previously unseen kicking and handling skills, showing himself a more accomplished player than many had suspected.

When he retired, he was England's second most capped player, after Rory Underwood. Besides his Five Nations triumphs, Carling led England to victories over New Zealand, Australia and South Africa. At home, Carling won two national club titles with the Harlequins club. His was a full rugby CV.

Carling never won anything like universal acclaim. Geoff Cooke, the England coach through most of the Carling era, said: "He is strong-willed and very intolerant of other people's weaknesses." Former test team-mate Jeff Probyn blamed Carling for the 1991 World Cup final defeat, saying: "His refusal to change tactics at halftime cost us the chance of the trophy." All Black skipper Wayne Shelford said: "Will was fairly good, but not that great."

Balancing that, England and Lions flanker Lawrence Dallaglio said: "Will has been a fantastic captain." Dennis Easby, who sacked Carling for his 'old farts' comment, said: "He is the most successful captain we'll ever have. He has been an absolute credit to English rugby and to his country in eight marvellous years." And Rob Andrew added: "No-one should underestimate what Carling has done as captain. It has been a period of unprecedented success … I don't believe anyone could have done more."

Carling was awarded the OBE in 1992, and made a fortune from rugby-related earnings, being much in demand as a speaker and from sponsors and advertisers. Late in 1998 he had a controversial autobiography published. With his profile and personality, it seems that even in retirement, he will never be far from the headlines. Early in the 1998-99 season, Carling made a return to rugby for the Harlequins and was contemplating a professional career in Japan. **⑩**

KEN CATCHPOLE

Captain So Young

IT WAS A tragedy that Ken Catchpole's glittering international career ended in such unhappy circumstances. The Australian scrumhalf was injured so badly in a test against the All Blacks at Sydney in 1968 that he never played top rugby again. Now when Catchpole's name crops up, that incident is invariably mentioned first - a pity, because he is worthy of recall as one of the world's greatest scrumhalves.

He was captaining the Wallabies when, near the end of first test of the 1968 series, he was pinned in a splits position under a ruck with one leg protruding. All Black lock Colin Meads grabbed that leg and pulled it hard in an effort to remove Catchpole from the ruck and clear the ball. There are diametrically opposing views of the incident. To Australians, it was a heinous act of barbarism. Ex-Wallaby Keith Cross sent Meads a newspaper clipping with a note attached saying: 'Colin, are you proud of this effort?' But to New Zealanders, while it was very sad, it was nothing more than a freak accident.

Either way, the effect was dramatic. "I could feel the muscles stretch like rubber bands reaching the end of their elasticity and snapping," said Catchpole. His hamstring muscle was torn from the pelvic bone, he had ripped and stretched groin muscles and a damaged sciatic nerve. Catchpole never blamed Meads, calling it a 'silly accident'. It marked the end of his eight-year, 27-test career, though he did later lead his Sydney club side Randwick with some success. He was picked to represent Sydney against the 1971 Springboks but a hand injury ruled him out, and he never did reappear at international level.

Despite the unsatisfactory end to his career, Catchpole did more than enough to stamp his name indelibly among rugby's greats. His speed of dispatch was the fastest I have seen from a scrumhalf. He would fire out wonderful spinning passes so quickly that they gave his flyhalf - usually Phil Hawthorne - plenty of time without the worry of having opposing loose forwards on top of him.

I have seen scrumhalves with longer passes, and others who could run and kick as well as or better than Catchpole. But he was supreme as a passer. He could pass equally well in either direction and scooped the ball straight from the ground, dispensing with backswing. He must have had immensely strong wrists and forearms, though at 1.65m (5ft 5in) and 63.5kg (10st), he didn't look particularly powerful. Catchpole had other assets too - particularly his tackling and intuitive flair for reading a game. He seldom looked rushed. What impressed critics was his ability to convert bad ball into good quality

Kenneth William Catchpole
Scrumhalf
Born: Sydney, June 21, 1939
Test debut: Australia v Fiji, June 10, 1961
Test career: 1961-68 (27 matches)
Test points: 9 (3 tries)
* Captained Australia on his test debut
* Was just 22 when appointed captain-coach of the 1961 Australian tour of South Africa
* Played 17 tests with Phil Hawthorne, the record at the time for a scrumhalf/flyhalf combination

Sad memories - Catchpole's last test, Sydney, 1968.

Australian Scrumhalves

Two Australian scrumhalves are profiled in this book. Ken Catchpole and Nick Farr-Jones earn their places comfortably among the all-time greats of the game. But to those two, at least another four Wallaby scrumhalves could have been added, for this has been a position in which Australia has been particularly well-served.

Between the wars, the outstanding scrumhalf was New South Welshman Syd Malcolm, who played 19 tests from 1928-34, captaining Australia three times and being one of the stars of the famous Waratahs 1927-28 tour of Britain. Next in the royal line came Des Connor, who played 12 tests for Australia in the late 1950s before crossing the Tasman and representing New Zealand with equal distinction.

After the Catchpole era, Australia was given superb service by John Hipwell, who played test rugby from 1968-82 and in his 36 tests proved that he was fit to be ranked alongside players like Sid Going, Chris Laidlaw, Gareth Edwards and Dawie de Villiers as the best in his era.

More recently, Australia has been fortunate to have in George Gregan a scrumhalf of flair and skill, a player who can launch an attack out of nothing and can defend brilliantly. Gregan has shone not just for Australia, but also for the Brumbies in the Super 12 competition.

ball, the litmus test for a scrumhalf. He was once described as 'a natural who did not waste his talent', and that sums him up perfectly.

Catchpole attended Coogee Prep School, and Scots College in Sydney. To overcome asthma as a child he did a lot of swimming, which developed his lungs and helped him when he began playing football, at the age of 11. He made the Sydney schools rep rugby side, and as a youngster also played a lot of tennis and dabbled with boxing.

Though he attended Sydney University, studying science, he played for Randwick. This is where his ideas on rugby were shaped, especially where he came into contact with two great thinkers, Cyril Towers and Wally Meagher.

He had a meteoric rise. From playing for Randwick under-21s in 1958, Catchpole was chosen to represent New South Wales against the British Lions in 1959 and handled his opposing scrumhalf, the highly-rated Dickie Jeeps, very well. He was reserve in both tests against the Lions that year.

When Catchpole was still just 21 he was not only picked to play for Australia in the three tests against Fiji in 1961, but was named as captain. In hindsight it put intolerable pressure on so inexperienced a player who was busy enough finding his own feet at test level. Catchpole was retained as captain-coach for the 1961 Wallabies' disastrous six-match tour of South Africa and for the match that followed, against France at Sydney.

Though struggling with the captaincy, Catchpole always looked the goods as a player. Like Nick Farr-Jones later, he seemed to control the match, chiding, encouraging and guiding the Wallaby pack around the field.

His play improved still further when the selectors took the captaincy off him. After trying Jim Lenehan and Peter Johnson, they settled on sturdy forward John Thornett. Catchpole thrived, calling the backline moves and concentrating more on his own game.

He became famous for his partnership with Hawthorne, a gifted player who looked twice as good when Catchpole was his scrumhalf. They eventually played a record number of tests together before Hawthorne turned to league in 1968. Their first great double act was in the third test of the 1964 series against the All Blacks when they electrified the Athletic Park crowd and engineered a memorable 20-5 victory.

'Catchy', as Australians knew him, was wooed repeatedly by league scouts and some of the offers were incredible, but he always resisted. He shone in South Africa in 1963 and the series victory over the Springboks at home in 1965. Then he took over the captaincy during the Wallabies' 1966-67 tour of Britain when Thornett was injured. It proved to be the peak of Catchpole's career. He was a pivotal figure in Australia's test wins over Wales and England. At the dinner after Australia had outplayed England 23-11, Duggie Harrison, the England Rugby Union president, described Catchpole as 'the greatest scrumhalf the world has known', not praise to be dismissed lightly.

How good was Catchpole? Using the logic that no-one recognises a good scrumhalf better than another one, I quote All Black halfback Chris Laidlaw from *Mud In Your Eye*: 'As the supreme exponent of all the skills, Catchpole stands beyond rivalry. He was years ahead of his time. His pass was never long - he considered that a waste of time. It was, however, phenomenally fast and his technique of delivery perfect. No elegant dive pass, no laboured swivel to avoid passing off the weak arm - just a flash of light to his flyhalf.'

After retiring from international rugby, Catchpole pursued his career as a chemical engineer, but he has remained involved with rugby. He is easily spotted with his bald head and distinctive beard as he assists with the ABC radio commentaries. His son Mark, more sturdily built, has also played rep rugby, as a scrumhalf, of course. **100**

MICHEL CELAYA

Très Formidable

MICHEL CELAYA has been one of the truest servants of French rugby. In a country where captains, coaches and players often seem to be dropped on little more than a whim, Celaya has shown himself to be a survivor.

He was a dynamic, versatile forward and, when occasionally omitted from the test side - no great surprise or shame in France - always fought back to reclaim his place. For a while he was captain, but even when he lost this job, he kept his test spot.

After drifting out of top rugby in 1961, he contributed greatly to French rugby in other areas. Besides coaching the test side in the late 1970s, Celaya for many years oversaw the progress of the country's promising youngsters as a development officer.

He also helped manage several French teams overseas, then in 1994 was Pierre Salviac's co-television commentator during the triumphant French tour of New Zealand. Celaya was nearly 64 by then, but had as much zest as ever for his beloved rugby. He was certainly pleased with France's 2-0 series victory over the All Blacks and his delight was obvious when Jean-Luc Sadourny capped off a wonderful length-of-the-field movement to win the second test in the dying moments.

Celaya, a product of Biarritz, reached national rugby prominence while studying at Bayonne Polytech. By the early 1950s, representing the Biarritz Olympique club, he was pushing for a test place. At 1.84m (just over 6ft) and 93kg (14st 8lb), he offered selectors the choice of playing him at lock or No 8. A committed, intelligent forward with excellent ball skills, he could play either position and sometimes also fitted in as a flanker.

L'Equipe's Denis Lalanne described Celaya as a split personality: 'Calm and retiring off the field, he was devilish on it.'

He made his test debut against England in 1953, playing at No 8 against John Kendall-Carpenter, who later became a noted administrator. France were captained that day by the famous Jean Prat, nearing the end of his career, but still an outstanding loose forward. It was not a great era for the French. Early in Celaya's career, they struggled to beat the established rugby nations.

In 1955 against England at Twickenham the selectors moved Celaya from No 8 to lock, which paid immediate dividends. He scored a try and had a storming game as France scored an upset 16-9 win. Just a year later, Celaya

Michel Celaya
Loose forward/lock
Born: Biarritz, July 27, 1930
Test debut: France v England, Twickenham, February 28, 1953
Test career: 1953-61 (50 matches)
Test points: 18 (6 tries)
* Captained France 12 times
* Was second to Jean Prat (51) in test appearances for France when he retired

was appointed captain, though his reign started inauspiciously with a 14-9 loss to England.

His best result as captain was France's 19-0 beating of Bob Davidson's Wallabies at the Colombes Stadium in March, 1958. This was followed by victories over Wales, Italy and Ireland. Celaya seemed ensconced as captain. On the field he didn't say much, but was so consistent and demanding of himself that he inspired team-mates to raise their level. He read a game well and had widespread support, which wasn't always the case with French captains of that era.

Unfortunately Celaya had a disastrous trip to South Africa in 1958. His team was packed with talent and the series was eagerly anticipated. In the first tour match, at Salisbury, Celaya so seriously hurt his knee he could play only three of the 10 tour games and neither test. The captaincy passed to Lucien Mias, a natural leader, and France won a famous series victory. Mias kept the job, even when Celaya returned the next season.

Nevertheless Celaya did what many good players could not - lose the captaincy, but hold a test spot. Over the next three years he played under four captains, Mias, Jean Barthe, Francois Moncla and Michel Crauste. His demotion did not seem a problem for him; indeed he said he preferred not to be captain, so he could concentrate on his own game. Certainly on the 1961 French tour of New Zealand, he seemed happy to leave the captaincy cares to others. No-one played more than his 11 matches in New Zealand and he had an fine tour, dividing his time between lock and loose forward.

With his chunky build, crop of dark hair and thick white headband (a decade before Mervyn Davies made it famous), Celaya was easily recognised. He, Crauste and Moncla had developed into a world-class loose forward combination.

Though Celaya made his name with Biarritz, he moved to the State Bordelais club during the last two years of his test career. His final test, in November 1961, resulted in a 5-5 draw with Romania at Bayonne. It wasn't a happy result for France, but was a memorable day for Celaya, who joined the select group of players to reach 50 tests.

Celaya didn't waste much time before making his presence felt in coaching and administration. He was assistant manager of the 1971 and 1975 French teams to South Africa and to Australia in 1972, and coached France in South Africa in 1980. In addition, he was for many years involved with the French youth and B teams. The number of players he helped prepare for test rugby must run into many hundreds. After his days with the French team were over, he continued to be actively involved in coaching, even being hired to work in Australia in 1989.

Celaya, an electricity draughtsmen and inspector, was awarded the French Rugby Federation's bronze medal in 1972. 🏉

France's most capped forwards:

63	Michel Crauste	(1957-66)
63	Benoit Dauga	(1964-72)
61	Jean Condom	(1982-90)
61	Olivier Roumat	(1989-96)
61	Abdelatif Benazzi	(1990-97)
59	Jean-Pierre Rives	(1978-84)
56*	Philippe Benetton	(1989-99)
56	Laurent Rodriguez	(1981-90)
55	Robert Paparemborde	(1975-83)
52	Amedee Domenech	(1954-63)
51	Walter Spanghero	(1964-73)
51	Jean-Luc Joinel	(1977-87)
51	Jean Prat	(1945-55)
50	Michel Celaya	(1953-61)
50	Philippe Dintrans	(1979-90)

* still playing

DON CLARKE

The Boot

ALL BLACK Don Clarke was world rugby's great figure 40 years ago. He was a giant of a fullback, a match-winning place-kicker who could land goals from so far out that he had an inhibiting effect on his opposition.

The first time I saw him play was in a match at Athletic Park in the 1950s. Clarke received the ball on about the halfway line and drop-kicked a goal with his right foot. A little later, again from near halfway, he dropped a goal with his left foot.

He was equally effective at test level. The 1959 Lions couldn't believe they'd lost the first test in Dunedin, despite scoring four tries. Clarke kicked six penalties and the All Blacks won 18-17. Clarke also won the second test at Wellington by scoring and converting a late try. I remember that occasion well, for I was a ballboy and fielded the ball after his last conversion. Later I walked proudly into the All Black dressing room to give it to him.

Clarke was a man for a crisis. There was his fulltime sideline conversion in the third test at Bloemfontein in 1960 that enabled the All Blacks to grab an 11-11 draw with South Africa. He kicked a penalty just before the final whistle to allow New Zealand to escape with a 9-9 draw with Australia at Athletic Park in 1962. Most amazing of all was his match-winning conversion of Kel Tremain's try against France at Athletic Park in 1961. There was an absolute gale blowing that day, and Clarke aimed his kick at the corner flag. The wind then swept the ball through the posts for an improbable conversion. Clarke was a juggernaut who attracted publicity wherever he went. He kicked an incredible 163 points while touring Australia in 1957. Once he landed an 84-yard goal at Te Kuiti.

So dominant was Clarke that there was a strong call (from overseas!) for rugby's rules to be altered to lessen the impact of the place-kicker. By the time he retired in 1965, Clarke had rewritten the New Zealand record book. Only the advent of round-the-corner kickers and much-improved modern kicking conditions have enabled his marks to be toppled.

Opponents tried everything … soaking the ball before a game, physically battering him, using balls which were out of shape or below the correct pressure, apparently even offering him bribes to miss kicks. But he took it all and maintained his form right to the end. Never was a nickname more appropriate than Clarke's. He really was 'The Boot'.

Clarke spent his early years in Taranaki, but his family moved to a farm in the Waikato when he was 10. He was always big for his age and actually

---

Donald Barry Clarke
Fullback
Born: Pihama, New Zealand, November 10, 1933
Test debut: New Zealand v South Africa, Christchurch, August 18, 1956
Tests career: 1956-64 (31 matches)
Test points: 207 (2 tries, 33 conversions, 5 drop goals, 2 goals from a mark, 38 penalties)

* Owned every major New Zealand points-scoring record, including most in first class rugby (1851), most for New Zealand (781) and most in tests (207)
* Was a first class cricketer, representing Northern Districts as a pace bowler

Star Sports, Saturday, July 18, 1959.

Clarke 18, Lions 17

Sad Fate For Unlucky Lions' Four Tries

RECORD CROWD

(By Our Correspondent with the Team.)

The saddest rugby test match that has ever been played in New Zealand took place at Carisbrook this afternoon. It was won by the All Blacks over the touring British Lions by one point—by 18 points to 17.

A crowd of 41,500 people watched today's test...

played netball for two seasons when no age rugby teams could accommodate him. But by his mid-teens, he was clearly a rugby player with a future.

He gained national attention as early as 1951 when, aged just 17, he lifted two penalties from a sea of mud at Rugby Park, Whangarei, to help Waikato wrest the Ranfurly Shield off North Auckland. It took him another five years to win his All Black place. The presence of Bob Scott, injuries and some poor trial form caused him to be overlooked.

When he did make it, against the 1956 Springboks, it was obvious he was there for good. Mick Williment, his deputy for five seasons, said: 'He was such a fantastic player. He had so much confidence and inspired a team. I had my good days, especially with my kicking, but I never felt anyone but Don Clarke should be the All Black fullback.'

Some suggested Clarke could be arrogant. He wasn't. Rather, as his team-mates will tell you, he was tremendously enthusiastic and would do anything for his team. This revealed itself during the 1963-64 tour of Britain under Wilson Whineray when he stated publicly that he wanted to duplicate George Nepia's feat of 40 years earlier and play every match. In the event, Clarke was injured early and his kicking form temporarily fell away.

Power was the key to Clarke's kicking. He didn't follow through like the classical kickers, but rather stabbed at the ball savagely, though his run-up and balance were perfect. Clarke was usually the heaviest man in the All Black team, weighing up to 111kg (17st 7lb). But appearances could be deceptive. He was a talented ball player, who handled well and moved with surprising speed.

He was also a first class cricketer from 1951-63 and went within a whisker of making John Reid's 1958 team to England as a pace bowler. At 1.88m (6ft 2in) he brought the ball down from a good height and had plenty of stamina. When Reid scored his famous 296 at the Basin Reserve in 1963, including the world record 15 sixes, Clarke was the only bowler not to be hit for six. I recall him bowling that day wearing purple shorts. He'd left his creams back at the hotel and soldiered on without them for the opening overs.

Yet there was a flip side to all this. He was the first superstar of the emerging New Zealand media. Before Clarke's time there was newspaper coverage, and some radio broadcasts, but Clarke's career coincided with the advent of television, so he became nationally recognised. New Zealand had some famous sportsmen at the time - John Reid, Bert Sutcliffe, Peter Snell, Murray Halberg, Colin Meads - but none were bigger than Clarke.

Four great All Black fullbacks: from left Billy Wallace, George Nepia, Bob Scott and Don Clarke.

In my estimation, he was an early victim of what has become known as the tall poppy syndrome. He received terrible barracking on occasions at Lancaster Park, because he didn't come from Christchurch. Stories spread about him, ridiculously petty stories. He cheated at golf, so it was said. Yet Clarke was a single handicap golfer, good enough to play as an amateur on the New Zealand circuit. He made a court appearance in the early 1970s on the most trivial of shop-lifting charges, amounting to something less than one dollar. He was not convicted, but the whispering grew.

Clarke and his wife Patsy moved to South Africa in 1977 and I am sure that the continual criticism he received at home contributed to his decision to emigrate. In South Africa, Clarke has been a huge success, setting up his own tree-felling and fishing businesses. But he's had his share of misfortune, too. On one occasion he was carjacked. On another, his son was shot even though he had obeyed some robbers' instructions and lain face-down on the road. In 1997 Clarke had a serious car accident, which put him out of action for some months. Even so, he says he's never regretted his move to South Africa.

But on the occasions I've met him, he has remained the most passionate of New Zealand supporters. "I'll always be a New Zealander as long as my backside points to the ground," he once told me in his typically colourful manner.

He appeared to make his own statement while helping with the studio presentation for the SABC's coverage during the 1995 World Cup. Every day Clarke wore a black pullover with a silver fern on it. He was commentating for a South African channel, but it was clear where his heart was. Clarke's coverage of the World Cup stood out like a beacon, for while he provided balanced and informed comment, his fellow commentators leaned outrageously towards South Africa.

Clarke turned up during the All Blacks' tour of France in 1995. I suppose it's a sign of the times that he when he went to the team hotel, very few players even knew who he was. That would never have happened in the 1960s when he bestrode the world rugby stage. **100**

Don Clarke came from a famous rugby-playing family. On one celebrated occasion, against Thames Valley in 1961, five brothers - Don, Ian, Doug, Brian and Graeme - played for Waikato. Doug, Brian and Graeme were solid provincial players. Ian, a durable forward, toured Britain twice and was an All Black captain. He later became president of the New Zealand Rugby Football Union. Ian Clarke died in 1997. A nicer person never walked onto a rugby field.

BERT COOKE

A Double Round of Applause

SPORTS WRITERS of the 1920s struggled for words to describe dual New Zealand international Bert Cooke. Freakish, mercurial, tricky, inimitable, sparkling and ghost-like were just some descriptions of the All Black centre. Cooke never merely 'scored a try', but always 'whizzed' or 'rocketed' over the line.

Having read reports of the big matches in which Cooke played, and spoken to some of his contemporaries, I have no doubt that Cooke was an extraordinary player whose gifts may not have been seen since. He was only a tiny fellow. He was 1.75m (5ft 9in) and his listed weight was 62.5kg (9st 12lb), though his real weight was probably closer to 54kg (8st 7lb). But had speed, timing and flair and tackled far better than someone his size should have. Crowds buzzed when he received the ball.

I caught an inkling of the affection spectators developed for Cooke when the 10 surviving 'Invincibles' held a 50-year reunion in 1974. They met at a hotel in Auckland and we had a terrific night with them. The following day, they attended a big match at Eden Park, where each player was introduced to the crowd. No-one got a bigger reception than Bert Cooke, who had begun his rep career for Auckland. He looked rather frail as he stood before the crowd dressed in a grey gabardine overcoat, but what memories his presence stirred. There was an interesting sequel to the story. The following day the Kiwis were playing a rugby league international across town at Carlaw Park and Cooke attended. Before the game the PA system announced called the crowd's attention to the presence of the great former New Zealand rugby league international Bert Cooke and again Cooke, still wearing his grey gabardine overcoat, received a standing ovation from a capacity crowd.

Like many players, Cooke established his reputation on the 1924-25 'Invincibles' tour of Britain where, despite his lack of size, he was a genuine superstar.

In a 10-season rugby career spanning four provinces, Cooke played in legendary teams in legendary games with legendary players, who regarded him as the greatest back of his time. He was rarely ordinary and often brilliant, scoring 119 tries in 131 first class matches. For the All Blacks between 1924 and 1930, he played 44 matches, including eight tests, and scored 38 tries.

He switched to rugby league in 1932 and despite being on the wrong side of 30, made an immediate impact, representing New Zealand with distinction

Albert Edward Cooke
Second five-eighth/centre
Born: Auckland, October 5, 1901
Died: Auckland, September 29, 1977
Test debut: New Zealand v Ireland, Dublin, November 1, 1924
Test career: 1924-30 (8 tests)
Test points: 12 (4 tries)
* Played 5 rugby league tests for New Zealand
* He scored 119 tries in 131 first class matches and was the first New Zealander to reach the milestone of 100 tries

The New Zealand provinces Bert Cooke played for:

Auckland	1923-24-25
Hawkes Bay	1926
Wairarapa	1927-28-29
Wellington	1930
Hawkes Bay	1931-32

against the 1932 British team and the 1935 Australians.

Cooke, who was educated in Hamilton, then Auckland, first played senior rugby in 1922, at the age of 20, and the following year marked his debut for Auckland against New Zealand Maoris with a try. He was reserve for the All Blacks against New South Wales that year.

His class was undeniable. After playing in the winning North team in the inter-island match in 1924, he was named as one of the 16 certainties for the tour of Europe. Throughout that tour he played sensationally, scoring 23 tries in 25 matches. Against France, he waltzed across for two tries. But Cooke's contribution was in more than try-scoring, where he led the field. He provided many opportunities for his wingers, two of whom scored more than 20 tries, and was an excellent defender. Cooke possessed fantastic acceleration and was not only a dazzling runner, but also had the uncanny knack of recovering his own kicks ahead.

A personal highlight was the match against Llanelli, the home of his father, where he played against doctor's orders. Llanelli presented him with a silver cigarette case, which was no doubt put to immediate use. Cooke was known to enjoy the odd vice. He smoked, was not adverse to a convivial drink or three and was often less than diligent in observing team curfews. George Nepia once told me that, except for himself, every member of the 'Invincibles' smoked.

Jock Richardson, the vice-captain of the 'Invincibles', was 92 years of age and living in a rest home in New South Wales when I interviewed him one day. His eyes sparkled when the name of Bert Cooke was mentioned. "Brilliant player, brilliant, the best ever," said Richardson emphatically. And what about as a tourist and team member? Richardson's eyes rolled. "He was a terror."

Cooke's effect on a team can be seen by his Ranfurly Shield record. He was in Hawkes Bay, Wairarapa and Wellington teams that held the Ranfurly Shield. He was an itinerant, unsettled type of person, but once he took the field, he was electrifying.

In 1928 Wairarapa tackled Canterbury for the Shield. Cooke was having a rather lacklustre game for Wairarapa and the Canterbury crowd were typically vocal about his apparent inactivity. Then, as Gordon Slatter recounts in *On The Ball*, 'The crowd were stunned to see him suddenly dodge through the defending team late in the game to score a try mathematically between the uprights and then, trusting no-one, to kick the conversion himself. Wairarapa 8, Canterbury 7, the scoreboard read at the conclusion of one of the greatest Shield games.'

Cooke played in all four tests against Great Britain in 1930, but was not required by the New Zealand selectors in 1931 after apparently arriving drunk for a North Island practice. His last rep rugby match was for Hawkes Bay against Wairarapa on June 3, 1932, when he scored two tries. Then he switched to league and developed a whole new army of supporters.

Perhaps the last word on the wandering genius should belong to George Nepia, himself a legend of that era, who had this to say after opposing Cooke in a match: "I couldn't compare. He was a ghost, a wraith. He had most wonderful acceleration and with it he spirited his way through an opening. He also had the surest of hands and his short punt over your head dropped exactly where he wanted it, your confusion being greater because he could make the kick without putting his eyes to the ball." 🏉

ALL BLACKS
SOUVENIR
1924~5

Major tours by the All Blacks were a big event, leading to many souvenir publications. This one marked the 'Invincibles' tour in 1924.

MICHEL CRAUSTE

The Marauding Mongol

RUGBY FOLLOWERS who hear the name of Michel Crauste recall the marauding, uncompromising French flanker of the late 1950s and 1960s. But whenever I hear his name, I think first of an Oamaru grandmother, Mrs P A Madsen, and an incident that occurred during France's 1961 tour of New Zealand.

The French were playing South Canterbury at Timaru and Crauste had taken over the captaincy for what was expected to be a straightforward midweek fixture. Instead South Canterbury played like men inspired and the French tumbled to a 17-14 defeat. It was a rough match and fortunately the referee was Pat Murphy, one of New Zealand's best.

The penalty count favoured South Canterbury 17-3 and afterwards even the French did not try to excuse their savage tactics. With 16 minutes left, Crauste was involved in a regrettable incident. After referee Murphy had turned his back, and several seconds after the whistle, Crauste punched Ted Smith on the jaw. Smith sagged to the ground and the players huddled around in concern. ("It was my fault," Smith said later. "I dropped my guard.") The incident, though missed by the referee, occurred in plain view of the spectators.

Suddenly out of the crowd marched quiet, retiring Mrs Madsen, who for 35 years had been an ardent rugby enthusiast. Bareheaded, fur-coated and utterly indignant, she marched up to Crauste, her right hand raised, and punched him on the back as hard as she could. Then, still clutching her umbrella, she turned and stomped back to her seat as thousands watching roared with laughter. "I didn't see a soul or think what I was doing," she explained. "I just went out there to retaliate for what was done to that poor boy."

Terry McLean, who reported the French tour, took a dim view of Crauste's 'species of devilry' and wrote that he could never regard Crauste as a player entitled to a great reputation because of some of the acts he saw him commit on that tour.

Such an opinion, from so experienced a critic, must carry weight, but on balance, I feel Crauste deserves inclusion in this collection of rugby greats. Some of his less wholesome actions would not be tolerated in today's video replay age, but in the 1960s there was more tolerance of punching and over-robust play.

Michel Crauste
Loose forward
Born: St Laurent de Gasse, July 6, 1934
Test debut: France v Romania, Bucharest, May 19, 1957
Test career: 1957-66 (63 matches)
Test points: 33 (11 tries)
* Held the French record for most tests
* Captained France in 22 tests

Progression of world record for most test caps since the year Michel Crauste made his debut:

47 Ken Jones (Wales/British Isles)
February 2, 1957

52 Jack Kyle (Ireland/British Isles)
March 1, 1958

63 Michel Crauste (France)
April 9, 1966

80 Willie John McBride (Ireland/
British Isles) March 15, 1975

81 Mike Gibson (Ireland/British Isles)
June 16, 1979

93 Serge Blanco (France)
October 19, 1991

111 Philippe Sella (France)
June 22, 1995

There can be no doubting Crauste's contribution to French rugby. He played a record 63 tests from 1957-66, scoring 11 tries, and was a central figure in a mighty era for the French. It included outright Five Nations Championship titles in 1959, 1961 and 1962 and a shared title in 1960.

Crauste was the son of a farmer. Among his childhood pals were Andre and Guy Boniface, who between them were to play 83 tests for France. Crauste was a student at the College d'Aire-sur-l'Adour and besides his rugby prowess was a good schoolboy athlete and boxer, prompting comparisons with Marcel Cedan, the world champion French boxer. After leaving school, he trained to work for the French Electricity Department. When he was 18, he moved to Paris, where he played for the prestigious Racing Club, which was runner-up in the national club championship in 1957 and won it in 1959.

He stood out as a courageous, ruthless loose forward and in August, 1957 was called into the French side for a test against Romania at Bucharest. France struggled to an 18-15 victory. In the return match at Bordeaux, France stormed to a 39-0 win and Crauste scored his first test try.

Urgent and remorseless, Crauste made such an impression that he was an automatic selection for the rest of his long career. His wife's illness forced him to miss the 1958 tour of South Africa, which he much regretted as France won the two-test series. But he was to enjoy many years of glory.

He became known as 'Mongol' and 'Attilla the Hun' because of the combination of his sallow, almost ghostly, complexion, a black moustache which curved like a wide U down his upper lip and his take-no-prisoners attitude. At 1.81m (nearly 6ft) and 85kg (13st 5lb), he was no heavyweight, but he was mobile and played with ceaseless ferocity. Generally he was a flanker, but he did turn out a few times at international level at No 8.

Crauste had such a competitive attitude that no task seemed beyond him. Once against Italy, when France's centres were unable to penetrate, he moved into the backline with startling results. In 1958, against England at Paris, he moved to lock, where he outjumped John Currie and David Marques, both of whom were considerably taller.

While Crauste possessed all the usual qualities of the outstanding loose forward - hands, feet and head - he had a unique ability to find his way through a crowded field with astonishing ease, more like a wing or a centre. He was a model support player, always on hand to keep a movement driving forward, and scored many tries because of his anticipation. He was a fearsome tackler and many an opposing inside back spent a sleepless night contemplating locking horns with Crauste on the morrow.

In 1960 he was voted France's top player and Jean Prat, the legendary French player of the immediate post-war years, said he had 'never seen a better, more complete forward'.

He first captained France at test level in 1961 and had immediate success, leading France to a 15-8 win at Sydney. But there remained doubts about his ability to lead and it wasn't until 1964 that he became the regular captain. By then he'd played under six test captains. Crauste built a reasonable record as a captain, the highpoint being the 8-6 win at Springs in the only test of the 1964 tour of South Africa.

Though he led by example, his critics said he lacked some of the subtleties of psychology of a top leader. He did not go out in triumph for France missed out on the Five Nations Championship in 1966 when Wales beat them 9-8 at Cardiff. Crauste had one more test, a 21-0 win over Italy at Naples, then retired.

The programme from the infamous France v South Canterbury match, 1961.

Many felt it was a premature decision. Certainly he was still as effective as ever and would have pushed hard for a place in any World XV through the 1960s.

Crauste's most notable individual performance was at the Colombes Stadium in 1962 when in a virtuoso performance he scored three tries in his team's 13-0 victory over England. He also turned on a memorable display against Wales in 1965, leading France to an upset 22-13 win over the reigning Five Nations champions. His 63 tests remained the French record until Benoit Dauga equalled it in 1972.

At domestic level, he achieved plenty of success, including achieving the rare feat of winning successive club championships with different teams. In 1959, after his success with Racing Club, he switched to the high-flying Lourdes side, winning national titles in 1960 and 1968. He captained Lourdes for much of the 1960s and was still a force at 36. Crauste's career was finally ended by a serious injury in a business-house match.

For many years Crauste worked for the French Electricity Department in Paris, Bigorre and Bearn, before entering local body politics in 1989. He was elected deputy mayor of Lons in Pau, representing the right-wing RPR party, and was given responsibility for finance, sport, the environment and information.

In 1964, Crauste received the French Rugby Federation gold medal. **100**

DANIE CRAVEN

Die Spiel is Router as die Mann

Daniel Hartman Craven
Scrumhalf
Born: Lindley, October 11, 1910.
Died: Stellenbosch, January 4, 1993.
Test debut: South Africa v Wales, Swansea, December 5, 1931
Test career: 1931-38 (16 matches)
Test points: 6 (2 tries)
* Played test rugby in four positions - scrumhalf, flyhalf, centre and No 8
* Captained South Africa in 4 tests
* Played for his country before representing his province
* Was one of the First XV inducted into the International Rugby Hall of Fame in 1997

DANIE CRAVEN was this century's most significant rugby figure - a brilliant and versatile player, a successful and innovative coach and a towering administrator. No-one has even approached Craven for overall impact. 'The Doc', as he was known, was out on his own.

His was a life devoted to rugby, particularly South African rugby. He lived and breathed the game, and never tired of talking about it. South Africans are adamant that Craven's ceaseless work advanced by years the unification of rugby in his country. He didn't live to see the Springboks win the World Cup at home in 1995, but did have the chance to savour the return of South Africa to the world rugby fold in 1992 after a decade of isolation.

Craven was born into a farming family in the small Orange Free State town of Lindley. Initially he was drawn to soccer, but at Lindley High School some Stellenbosch graduates introduced him to rugby. Craven's ability and reputation soon reached 'Oubaas' Markotter, the great man of South African rugby.

'Mr Mark' took one look at Craven when he arrived at Stellenbosch in 1928 and said, "This one I am keeping for South Africa." Markotter was to have a vast influence on Craven's life and the two shared many personality traits and principles.

In 1931 Craven, a theology student, went from the Stellenbosch First XV into Bennie Osler's Springbok team for the tour of Britain without having played for Western Province. He went away as understudy scrumhalf to the polished Pierre de Villiers and returned as an established test player.

His first match for South Africa was against Swansea, the day before his 21st birthday. It was a fiery match and when the South Africans won, they were pelted with stones by the miners in the crowd. Craven, a solidly-built 89kg (14st), impressed with his strength as well as his passing and kicking. Osler, the champion flyhalf, wanted him as his scrumhalf for the first test, against Wales, specifically to combat the burly home scrumhalf Wick Powell.

South Africa beat Wales 8-3 and Craven's play induced New Zealand rugby critic Syd Nicholls (brother of All Black Mark) to state: 'Craven played the best game I have seen played by a halfback in an international match. He carried South Africa on his shoulders.' Incidentally, throughout the tour, Craven addressed his captain as 'Mr Osler', a sign of respect for a man many years his senior.

The famous Craven dive pass, New Zealand v South Africa, Auckland, 1937.

The Springboks completed a Grand Slam of test victories. Craven was their special hero against Scotland when he spotted an inside gap near the posts, dummied, then scooted away to score the try which took his team to a winning 6-3 lead. He received rough treatment from the Scottish forwards and finished the game concussed, but never buckled.

The next year Craven played against the visiting Wallabies seven times, including in five tests. In the fourth test he showed his versatility by turning out at centre as the Springbok backline was adjusted to atone for the absence of fullback Gerry Brand.

With few tests in the 1930s, Craven's next tests were in Australia and New Zealand in 1937. Against Australia, he appeared at flyhalf and No 8. That meant he'd appeared in four different positions in successive tests. Furthermore, he played at fullback against Queensland.

He had a full array of skills allied to a superb rugby brain. His kicking and passing were outstanding, he was a lovely runner, light on his feet, and he had a tremendous workrate. He is sometimes cited as the inventor of the dive pass. This is not so. He learnt it from another Springbok, Dauncey Devine, and made it famous.

In New Zealand, his dive passing was a revelation. Though such a pass took him off his feet, it enabled Craven to get the ball away quickly and accurately under pressure. His flyhalf had a joy-ride and the outside backs thrived. The 1937 Springboks are still described as the finest team to leave New Zealand. They won the series 2-1 and proved too good as scrummagers. They were captained by lock Phil Nel, but Craven, the vice-captain, was regarded as the team strategist, constantly plotting and planning.

Nel retired after the tour and in 1938, Craven captained the Springboks against Sam Walker's Lions. As well as captaining Stellenbosch from 1933-

35, he had played for Western Province from 1932-35, Eastern Province in 1936-37, Northern Transvaal in 1938 and South African Universities, captaining all those teams.

The Springboks beat the Lions 2-1 and played a thrilling brand of running rugby. Craven was just 27, but it marked the end of his 16-match test career.

Craven goes into this collection of great rugby players without argument. Yet over the next 55 years he was to earn even more enduring fame in other spheres. Though New Zealanders viewed him with suspicion during the years when contact with South Africa was such a touchy subject, no-one doubted his commitment. When the scorn of world opinion rained down on his country's apartheid policies, Craven was seen by some as an apologist for the South African Government. Such charges were without real foundation. The cause Craven stood for was South African rugby, no more or less.

His desperate hope that international rugby might return to his country placed him in an invidious position over the 1986 rebel Cavaliers tour of South Africa. When tour details broke, Craven called the news 'too good to be true', which reflected his true feelings. Within days, wearing his International Rugby Board hat, he was calling for the cancellation of the tour. Ces Blazey, one of New Zealand's best administrators, felt Craven had betrayed him over the Cavaliers business. But Craven was trying his best for South Africa. He felt they desperately needed the tour and caps were awarded for the tests.

Politics cast a long, gloomy shadow over his final years as South Africa's 'Mr Rugby'. But it was through none of his endeavours that South African rugby was set adrift from the rugby world. Craven campaigned tirelessly to destroy rugby's racial barriers. If others imposed boycotts and protests against Springbok rugby, that did not deter him from hoping to see a multi-racial South African team accepted in world rugby.

Nothing could detract from his rugby feats. After the second World War, he quickly rose as a coach and administrator. He was a South African selector from 1949-56 and masterminded the Springboks' 4-0 whitewash of the 1949 All Blacks and the highly-successful 1951-52 Springbok tour of Britain. Asked about his rugby philosophy, he said: "We will concentrate on solid scrummaging - you must have that to obtain the ball. Then we must find gaps, make gaps, get the ball to the wings and make it come back to the inside backs and forwards." Craven was the driving force behind the powerful South African team which gave New Zealand 'The Battle for the Rugby Crown' in 1956. Craven's utterance - "It's all yours, New Zealand" - after the All Blacks had won the series is one of the cherished quotes in New Zealand rugby.

He became president of the South African Rugby Board in 1956, a position he still held in 1992. He continued as joint president of the new, non-racist body, the South African Rugby Football Union, until his death the following year. He served on the IRB from 1957-87 and was its chairman when it was South Africa's turn by rotation.

His was a life of achievement. In 1938, he was appointed director of Physical Education for the Defence Force. He became head of the Physical Training branch of the South African Military College, and was then promoted to Lieutenant-Colonel and Commanding Officer of the Physical Training Battalion. In 1947 he became the Head of the Department of Physical Education at Stellenbosch University, a position he held until his retirement in 1975. Subsequently he became Director of Sport and Recreation at Stellenbosch, then Director of Stellenbosch's Sport Institute.

When I visited Stellenbosch in 1995, his daughter, Joan Roux, was still living in the family home, just up the road from the rugby fields of Stellenbosch University.

He earned three doctorates - in anthropology, psychology (with emphasis on schizophrenia) and physical education. His thesis on *The Evolution of Major Games*, caused the examiner, Maxwell Howell, Professor of Physical Education at San Diego State University, to state: "There is simply no thesis in the Western World on sports and games that matches it in quality." He began this 700-page thesis in 1956 and finished it in 1978, at the age of 68. When he went overseas on rugby business, he would spend every spare minute in local libraries and bookshops sourcing relevant material.

Craven wrote many books and booklets, some biographical, some on coaching. My favourite is *Danie Craven on Rugby*, but all made good reading.

He was a difficult man to measure. I first heard him speak in 1963 when he and Winston McCarthy did a radio broadcast of a big college rugby match in Wellington, where he was attending an IRB meeting. He liked to project an image of reasoned affability, but underneath there was the iron will of a disciplinarian. He coached the top rugby team at Stellenbosch from 1947-91 and was like a father to his players. Former Springboks like Dawie Snyman and Jannie Engelbrecht speak with reverence about him. Engelbrecht once said to me: "Danie used to remind us, especially on a Monday, whatever the result had been the previous Saturday, 'die spiel is router as die mann' - the game is always bigger than the man."

Understandably, he is a huge figure at Stellenbosch and is immortalised at the university by a statue of him and his dog Bliksem in the courtyard outside the Craven Museum. In one hand he carries a rugby ball and with the other it looks as if he is making a point about coaching the game he loved.

In 1995, while filming at Stellenbosch University, we spent some time in the Craven Museum. The museum has a replica of Craven's study. Sitting on his table in the mock-up study was his bible and on numerous pages in pencil were his personal notations relating to life and to rugby. I would love to have had time to study that bible as I'm sure it would give a fascinating insight into a brilliant mind.

The statue of Danie Craven and his beloved Bliksem.

Craven was an innovative thinker. He sought to have twilight rugby introduced, wanted penalties awarded against teams whose supporters encroached on the field and favoured rugby being controlled by two referees. In 1995, when Stellenbosch played a game against a World XV to mark the opening of the Craven Stadium at the University, two referees controlled the match.

Craven Week, established in 1964, is a week of competition between the best of South Africa's provincial school teams and has been the nursery of many prominent test players. It is a fitting tribute to a giant of the game. 🏉

ERNIE CRAWFORD

The Right Sort of Alligadoo

William Ernest Crawford
Fullback
Born: Belfast, November 17, 1891
Died: Belfast, January 12, 1959
Test debut: Ireland v England,
Dublin, February 14, 1920
Test career: 1920-27 (30
matches)
Test points: 18 (6 conversions, 2
penalties)
*   Captained Ireland 15 times

NATURALLY, PLAYERS LOVE to be kindly reviewed by the media, but no praise ranks quite as high as that from their peers. That's one reason I rate Ernie Crawford, the Irish fullback of the 1920s, among the greats.

In his autobiography, George Nepia was generous in his praise of Crawford, both the player and the man. And as Nepia wrote his book when he was 58 years old, he was speaking with the wisdom of hindsight and able to put his comments into historical perspective.

'By our standards,' wrote Nepia, 'Crawford was an old man when we saw him, but until Bob Scott came along, Ernie was the greatest fullback I saw. Just watching him did me more good than dozens of lessons on the theory of fullback play.' Nepia described Crawford as an artist and a sure handler of the ball, but what most impressed him was his deadly tackling.

Crawford made a big impression on the 1924 All Blacks. He played against them twice, for Ireland and Ulster, and they rated his performances as good as anything they saw. On the morning of the New Zealanders' test against England at Twickenham, he visited them at their hotel and offered them advice and encouragement.

The Irishman was obviously a real character. He adopted the word 'alligadoo' to describe rugby officials and administrators. He incorporated the term, which was meant in a mildly disparaging way, in virtually every speech he made and it gained such wide usage that in Ireland it came to refer to any sports administrator.

On the field Crawford had a sharp tongue. Those who watched him swore that his ceaseless verbal abuse of Ireland's great forward, Jammie Clinch, and Clinch's replies, were worth the price of admission. "They used to abuse each other most dreadfully," said Nepia, "and inexperienced players felt they were about to witness the execution of one or the other by one or the other."

When Crawford wasn't rounding on Clinch, he was abusing the rest of the Irish team. He was several years older than his team-mates and because of his seniority and his rugby greatness, had their total respect. Apparently they never took exception to his comments, but were spurred to greater endeavours. His jibing never affected his popularity and he was described as a person with wit and wisdom.

Crawford lost some of his best rugby years to the first World War. He grew up in Belfast in the early years of the century, the only one of six brothers

The years this century when Ireland won the Five Nations Championship:

1906 (shared with Wales)
1912 (shared with England)
1926 (shared with Scotland)
1927 (shared with Scotland)
1932 (shared with England and Wales)
1935 (Ireland won on their own for the first time this century)
1939 (shared with England and Wales)
1948
1949
1951
1973 (quintuple tie - all five teams)
1974
1982
1983 (shared with France)
1985

interested in sport. He was educated at Methodist College, Belfast and at school shone equally at soccer and rugby. His rugby progressed well and he represented Ulster against a French team in Paris in 1910 and against the South African tourists in 1912. He continued to play soccer, too, even when he was a rugby international. He'd turn out for Cliftonville, the top soccer team in the area, at the end of the rugby season and reached minor rep level.

During the war Crawford joined the Sixth Inniskillin Dragoons and served later in the London Irish Rifles. He was an accountant before the war, but afterwards became a lawyer.

When Ireland were scrambling to field a team in the 1920 Five Nations Championship, he was chosen for his test debut against England, at the rather advanced age of 28. To general surprise, Ireland pushed a strong England team to the wire and it was obvious the Irish fullback was there to stay.

Crawford remained ensconced at fullback for eight seasons, except for an incredible selectorial decision in 1924 when he was dropped for one match. He'd been prevailed upon by the selectors to play against England at Belfast, though suffering from bad back pains. He played poorly and the selectors thanked him by dropping him for the next match, against Scotland. He'd have called them 'right alligadoos'.

Many of his contemporaries spoke of the 'mystical' quality of Crawford's play, particularly his defence. He was said to be like a magnet who could draw attackers to him, even in one-on-one situations. Wavell Wakefield, the England captain of the 1920s, wrote: 'Though Crawford is the most cheery of companions off the field, he has always seemed sinister to me during a game, a kind of brooding intelligence, directing play, crouching and waiting like a spider for the unfortunate man who had to try to pass him.'

Crawford was said to be like an octopus, for he was almost impossible to pass and his anticipation was so good he always seemed in position to receive a kick. He had a longish punt but his defence, plus his streak of individualism, were his major attributes. Many years after the 'Invincibles' tour, All Black Jim Parker was still talking about the way Crawford had chased him and smother-tackled him when a try seemed certain. Parker was a champion sprinter, so was not used to being caught from behind.

Crawford also developed the habit of imitating opposing players' voices, which could wreak havoc in an opposing attack. He was known, when confronted by two attackers, to call out 'Pass, pass', then take the intercept.

He rounded out his international career by leading Ireland to a share of the Five Nations Championship in 1926 and 1927. His last test, when he was 35, was against Wales, and resulted in a 19-9 triumph for Ireland. The *Rugby Football Annual* wrote: 'Few men have rendered their country such service on the playing field as Crawford - he certainly must rank among the great fullbacks. It will be no easy manner to find his successor.' This proved prophetic and it wasn't until the arrival of Tom Kiernan more than three decades later that Ireland unearthed a fullback who could stand alongside Crawford.

Crawford later became a member of the Irish Rugby Union, serving as its president in 1957-58. He became one of the great characters of rugby as an official (an alligadoo), a media commentator and a general rugby sage. **100**

MARCELLO CUTTITTA

The Italian Connection

WHEN RUGBY followers discuss the great modern wingers, players like David Campese, Jonah Lomu, Jeff Wilson, Ieuan Evans and Chester Williams are compared. It's unlikely that Marcello Cuttitta's name would often enter the reckoning, yet the Italian is a winger to compare with any of them. He happens to play for an emerging, rather than an established, rugby nation, so does not enjoy the same worldwide profile. Yet throughout the 1990s, Cuttitta and Paolo Vaccari were as potent a pair of wingers as any country could boast.

I first saw Cuttitta during the 1987 World Cup, when he scored tries against Argentina and Fiji and was not disgraced even when Italy were over-run by New Zealand in the tournament opener. It was his debut season in international rugby and it was obvious he was set for a long career.

Cuttitta and his twin brother Massimo have become stalwart members of their national test side, helping Italy earn the right to compete in the new Six Nations Championship, after almost a century of Five Nations play.

Though the Cuttittas were born in Latina, they grew up in Durban, South Africa, moving there when they were just three. Their father was involved in the construction industry. The Cuttittas not only learned excellent English, but also developed their rugby, representing Natal Schools. They were inspired as seven-year-olds by watching Willie John McBride's famous 1974 Lions team. By the time the twins returned to Italy, at the age of 19, they were pushing for places in the Natal representative side, though there was never any danger of them jostling for the same position in a team - Marcello was a winger with a gift for try-scoring and the sturdier Massimo a hard-working prop.

In Italian rugby, Marcello enjoys cult status. He represented the small L'Aquila club until 1988 and from 1989 has turned out for the mighty Amatori Milano team (now known as Amatori Calvisano). The Cuttittas' rugby improved markedly in Milan, where they encountered tough Argentinian coach Manuel Ferrari and discovered what hard training was all about.

Marcello has been part of four national championship-winning sides for Amatori Milano, as well as representing the club in the European club tournament from 1996-98. His try-scoring in the national first division club championship has been astounding. In 1989-90, he scored 31 in just 24 games. The following season he improved on even this impressive ratio with 32 in 23 games. After 251 matches, spread over 12 seasons, he had scored 222 tries and had five times been the season's leading try-scorer.

Cuttitta's potential was quickly recognised. Within a year of playing his first big club game, he had sped through the ranks of the Italian youth team

Marcello Cuttitta
Winger
Born: Latina, September 2, 1966
Test debut: Italy v Portugal, Lisbon, January 18, 1987
Test career: 1987-99 (54 matches)
Test points: 110 (25 tries)
* The only player to have scored tries in each of the first three World Cups
* Italy's leading try-scorer in tests
* His twin brother Massimo holds the Italian record for most test appearances
* The Cuttittas have played in more than 30 tests together

Marcello Cuttitta scored a good try in the 1991 Italy v England World Cup match at Twickenham.

Marcello Cuttitta shows his powerful fend for Italy v Argentina, World Cup, 1987.

and Italy B and was in the national team to play Portugal at Lisbon. He scored a try on debut and has kept on scoring them ever since.

He has played in three World Cups, scoring a total of seven tries from as many matches in those tournaments and has totalled 25 in all tests, easily the Italian national record.

Cuttitta, Italy's most capped winger, is solidly-built - 1.80m (5ft 11in) and 87kg (13st 11lb) - and while nippy, scores tries more through inventiveness than pure pace. His trademark is his ability to beat a man on the outside with a swerve at full speed. I especially like his aggression and combativeness. He never seems overawed, regardless of an opponent's reputation.

It seemed as though his test career might have closed in 1995 when he had an unhappy time of it at the World Cup. He played only one game, against the feisty Western Samoa side. After scoring a try just before halftime, Cuttitta had a nightmare second spell as the Samoans ran rampant, winning 42-18. The Italian defence crumbled and coach Georges Coste pinpointed Cuttitta as a chief culprit, dropping him for the rest of the tournament.

There was talk of Cuttitta returning to play in Natal, but Coste recalled him in 1996 and the winger has continued to play in Italy. Massimo has become something of an international celebrity, captaining Italy and signing for the prestigious Harlequins club in England. But at home, it is Marcello who is the rugby star. His try-scoring magic is a magnet and he is the sort of player who can draw huge crowds.

Cuttitta has also had some memorable outings in various Barbarians and exhibition games, as well as playing three matches for World XV teams. He travelled to Sydney in 1996 for the David Campese Testimonial match (when he and Campese both declined to wear the No 11 jersey as a mark of respect for Jonah Lomu, who was also playing), and proved a popular guest. In 1998 he turned on a three-try effort in helping the British Barbarians rout Leicester 73-19. **100**

BENOIT DAUGA

Le Tour Eiffel

IT WAS TYPICAL OF FRENCH RUGBY to produce two superlative forwards in the same era, each able to play brilliantly at lock or No 8. It was also equally French that the two, Walter Spanghero and Benoit Dauga, should have so major a falling out that they eventually could not be included in the same team. The drama concluded in a typically French manner. When Dauga had such a bad accident in a club match that he was paralysed, one of the first people to hurry to his hospital bedside was his bitter rival Spanghero.

Dauga was an immensely strong man who justified his lofty reputation when he toured New Zealand with the 1968 French team. He was a lineout specialist, an expert leaper and despatcher of the ball to his halfback. At 1.95m (6ft 5in) and 110kg (17st 5lb), he was a formidable sight. I remember him in New Zealand with his rugby jersey stretched to its absolute limit and socks that could not pass over his calf muscles.

He was sometimes called the 'control tower' of French lineout play, or the 'Eiffel Tower'. He was an imposing presence on the field and made a lasting impression.

Dauga was the son of a farmer in the south-west of France. By the time he gained a diploma at the Saint-Sever School of Agriculture, it was apparent he was going to be an outstanding sportsman, though his initial preference was for basketball. He really only applied himself to rugby when he was 18, playing briefly for the Saint-Sever club before joining the Army for his national service.

His time in the Army toughened him considerably. He shone for the French Forces against their British counterparts and was mentioned as a test contender. On leaving the Army, he joined the Mont-de-Marsan club which boasted the talented Andre Boniface.

Dauga made his test debut against Scotland in 1964, a sorry occasion, for France went down 10-0. It wasn't until his fifth test, against Italy, that he was in a winning team.

For the next few years, Dauga was one of the rocks of the strong French pack. He and Spanghero, who also arrived on the international scene in 1964, locked the scrum in 15 tests for France and were a tough, uncompromising pair who helped France sweep to a Grand Slam in 1968.

Yet though both were popular, friction developed between them. It was exacerbated when Spanghero was critical of Dauga in his book. He wrote: 'It does no service to Dauga to make him No 8. He is better as a lock.' It was a

Benoit Dauga
Lock/loose forward
Born: Montgaillard, May 8, 1945
Test debut: France v Scotland, Edinburgh, January 4, 1964
Test career: 1964-72 (63 matches)
Test points: 34 (11 tries)
* Dauga's 63 tests equalled the national record
* Captained France in nine tests

Benoit Dauga feeds from a lineout, France v England in the Five Nations Championship.

complicated situation. Both were excellent locks, but each preferred playing at No 8, where their pace and ball skills were of more use. Obviously it would have suited Spanghero to have Dauga at lock. The selectors tried every sort of combination, even using each man as a flanker.

The situation deteriorated until the selectors had to opt for one or the other. (There was one exception: against Romania at Bucharest in 1970, when Spanghero, trying to re-establish himself in the test side, played at lock under Dauga's captaincy.) During this period, Christian Carrere, Jean Trillo and Pierre Villepreux were chosen as captain, to enable both great forwards to be played without loss of face. Then Dauga was appointed captain, and led France nine times (for four wins, two draws and three losses).

Came February, 1972 and the team to play England was named. Dauga's name was missing, and Spanghero was the new captain. The Dauga era was over. He was still in his rugby prime, but had become the victim of an impasse. Jean Prat described him as the best forward produced by France, and others agreed. Mervyn Davies rated him the best No 8 he played against. Colin Meads couldn't decide if Dauga was better at No 8 or lock, but acknowledged his ability in both positions.

Dauga had three successful tours to the southern hemisphere - to South Africa in 1967 and 1971 (when he was captain) and to New Zealand and Australia in 1968. In South Africa, Dauga impressed with his menacing but constructive brand of rugby. Frik du Preez said he was the finest forward he had encountered. Danie Craven went further and said he was the greatest player to visit South Africa.

In New Zealand, Dauga and Spanghero were pick of French forwards in a brutal series. They gave no ground to perhaps the best All Black pack ever fielded. In the Wellington test, won 9-3 by New Zealand, referee John Pring had to work overtime to maintain a semblance of control. Several times he asked captains Brian Lochore and Marcel Puget to calm down their teams. Lochore said it was the dirtiest game he was involved in.

Colin Meads, asked afterwards about what had gone on, pointed the finger at Dauga and flanker Bernard Dutin. I recall taking offence on their behalf when my sensibilities (honed by barely passable School Certificate French) were offended by Meads pronouncing their names in his best nasal New Zealand accent, with no effort to make them sound French!

The All Blacks felt the French were the best visiting team since the 1956 Springboks. At home, it was a triumphant time for the French, who won the Five Nations Championship in 1967 and completed a Grand Slam in 1968. Dauga, mean and menacing, was an integral part of the side.

When Dauga was forced out of the French side, he had played 63 tests, equalling the national record that Michel Crauste had set in 1966, and scored 11 test tries.

He continued to play good club rugby until in January, 1975 when he broke his neck in a national championship game. His arms and legs were paralysed and he was hospitalised for many months. Eventually his iron determination and resilience enabled him to make such a full recovery that he was added to the French selection panel.

Through most of his rugby career, Dauga played basketball to a high level, feeling his it helped him develop his athleticism and his ball-handling ability.

Dauga tried a variety of jobs. He was a fertiliser rep, then worked in public relations for a liquor company, and ran a cafe in Mont-de-Marsan. His contribution to rugby was noted when he was awarded the national Order of Merit. **100**

France's Five Nations Championship victories:
1954 (shared)
1955 (shared)
1959
1960 (shared)
1961
1962
1967
1968
1970 (shared)
1972 (quintuple tie)
1977
1981
1983 (shared)
1986 (shared)
1987
1988 (shared)
1989
1993
1997
1998

France's Grand Slam triumphs:
1968
1977
1981
1987
1997
1998

DAVE DAVIES

One Half of "Dave and K"

William John Abbott Davies
Flyhalf
Born: Pembroke, June 21, 1890
Died: April 26, 1967
Test debut: England v South Africa, Twickenham, January 4, 1913
Test career: 1913-23 (22 matches)
Test points: 24 (4 tries, 3 drop goals)
* Captained England 11 times without defeat.
* Remained England's most capped flyhalf until 1989

THROUGH THE FIRST half of this century, England did not produce a finer back than William John Abbott Davies, known to all in rugby circles as Dave. He was the flyhalf and captain of the champion England teams of the early 1920s and formed a lethal partnership with scrumhalf Cyril Kershaw - 'Dave and K', they were called.

Davies had all the gifts of the accomplished flyhalf, including pace, vision and timing. A contemporary critic described him as 'an elegant flyhalf, who wheedled his way through with a length of stride incredible but factual'. Yet it was not Davies' running, or his sure tackling, or his flair for the unexpected, which drew most praise. He had a wonderful feel for a game so that even in times of crisis he seemed utterly calm and unconcerned. Like all class sportsmen, he had time to spare.

But what set him apart was his superb kicking. Until Davies' arrival, flyhalves tended to pass the ball on nearly every occasion, but the Englishman expanded the horizons of the flyhalf game with his long touch-finders, his deft chip kicks and his expert left-footed drop-kicking. Few players have such an impact on rugby that they take the game to another level, but Davies was one such man.

He made his test debut against Billy Millar's South Africans at Twickenham in 1913. (Initially there was some discussion about whether Davies, through his family connections, should be representing Wales, but he was clear that England had the major claim on him.) It was not a happy beginning for Davies, taking over the flyhalf position left vacant by the vastly-respected Adrian Stoop, for England were well beaten.

However, he held his test spot and for the rest of his 11-year international career was never again on a losing test side. He played 22 tests in all, for 20 wins, a draw and that solitary loss to South Africa. Davies remained England's most capped international flyhalf for 66 years until Rob Andrew bettered his mark.

Because of the first World War, Davies really had two rugby careers. Before the war he played eight tests and formed a fine partnership with scrumhalf Francis Oakeley. Tragically, Oakeley was killed in a submarine - he was one of the first England internationals to die in the war. After hostilities ceased, Davies resumed his career and captained England until his retirement in 1923.

Davies had a life associated with the sea, which happily gave his rugby the chance to prosper as well. In 1905, aged 15, he became an apprentice in the Pembroke Dockyard. His rugby developed as he attended the Royal Naval Engineering College, Keyham, then, in 1910, Greenwich Naval College. He captained the United Services at Portsmouth, showing the calming leadership qualities that would stand England in such good stead a decade later.

During the war Davies served with the Grand Fleet on *HMS Iron Duke* and *HMS Queen Elizabeth*. He was a Lieutenant-Commander of the Naval Constructor Corps and served on the staff of the commander-in-chief of the fleet at Jutland. In 1919 he was awarded an OBE.

Afterwards, he remained stationed at Portsmouth, where in 1939 he rose to the rank of Chief Constructor. During the second World War he was Assistant Director of Warship Production and later, stationed at Clyde, became Superintendent of Warship Production. By 1950, he was Director of Merchant Shipping and Repairs.

Following the first World War, Davies captained the powerful Royal Navy team for five years, led Hampshire and then, for 11 tests, England. His partnership with Kershaw began in a match for the Grand Fleet against the Rest of the Navy in 1919. Thereafter 'Dave and K' were rugby inseparables, and were often to be seen practising at Portsmouth's famous Services ground.

By the time he was done, Davies had become the scourge of other Home Nations teams. With Davies at flyhalf, England won all six of their matches against Scotland, all four against Ireland and all three against Wales. During Davies' 22 tests, England scored 72 tries and conceded just 22.

Davies, a teetotaller, was a model of fitness - while at Greenwich, he won the Champions Cup as the Athlete of the Year - and was always immaculately turned out.

His last big game was in 1923 when he captained a combined England-Wales team to victory in a celebration match at Rugby School to mark the centenary of the birth of rugby union.

When Davies retired, England lost something special. Wavell Wakefield, his great contemporary in the England team, described him as 'an artist and philosopher of that rugby period'. E H D Sewell wrote in *Rugger: The Man's Game*: 'I can see him now, gliding, or slithering, rather than running along, pouching passes when going full bat, or dropping a much-needed goal with telling accuracy. His short punts into touch, never overdone, were proverbial, and helped the chances of his side beyond all compute.'

Davies became an England selector for four years in the 1920s and was president of the Civil Service Football Club from 1937-66. 🏉

GERALD DAVIES

Welsh Dazzler

Thomas Gerald Reames Davies

Winger/centre

Born: Llansaint, February 7, 1945

Test debut: Wales v Australia, Cardiff, December 3, 1966

Test career: 1966-78 (51 matches - 46 for Wales, 5 for the British Isles)

Test points: 81 (23 tries)

*   When he retired, he was equal Welsh record-holder for tries in tests
*   His 46 tests for Wales was a national record for a three-quarter

GERALD DAVIES embodied in a rugby sense the Beatles era. He had a Sergeant Pepper's moustache, and played an exciting, innovative brand of rugby. He was a brilliant winger, blazingly fast, tricky and the owner of a devastating sidestep.

It was New Zealand's good fortune to see him at the peak of his career, with the 1971 British Isles team. That Lions side had some wonderful backs, but none shone brighter than the sinewy right-winger Davies. His potency and verve electrified spectators. Davies missed the first few games while he completed his exams back home. But once he arrived he was a revelation. He played 10 tour games, including all four tests, and contributed 10 tries.

He scored three test tries, including a vital one in the third test, but the game most New Zealanders recall was when the Lions played Hawkes Bay at Napier. He ran in four tries that day in a virtuoso display. His first try came after he kicked ahead, then picked up the ball at full speed. Two minutes later he collected a cross-kick and scored. Before halftime he'd completed his treble by taking a long pass from halfback Gareth Edwards, slipping through the Hawkes Bay backline and running 25 metres. His fourth try was the most memorable. He spotted that Hawkes Bay centre Mick Duncan was up too close, went around him, then cut across the entire Hawkes Bay backline on a darting, jinking run. The Lions have sent some superb wingers to New Zealand, but none have been better than the lightning Welshman.

Davies (known to team-mates by his middle name of Reames) was obviously always something special in rugby, representing Welsh secondary schools in 1963 before attending Loughborough College. At this time he was a centre, slightly wayward on occasion, but with undeniable brilliance. He made his test debut in 1966 against the Wallabies, in the same match as did Barry John, and became a fixture in the Welsh side for the next 13 years.

In 1968 he was selected for the Lions' journey to South Africa, but torn ligaments, then a dislocated elbow, spoilt his tour and he was fit for only one test. Even so, he scored one of his never-to-be-forgotten tries, against Boland, when he received the ball from a lineout in his own half, dog-legged through the opposition, twice side-stepped past the cover defence and finally dotted down after running 70 yards.

Davies toured New Zealand with Wales in 1969. It was an unhappy tour for the Welsh but a significant one for Davies, who was persuaded to move from centre to wing. There was never a question about his courage, but at just 73.5kg (11st 7lb), he was too slightly built for the crash-ball type of

The great Welsh rugby writer J B G (Bryn) Thomas wrote 30 books about the game during a professional career of more than 40 years. He went on nine consecutive British Lions tours and covered nearly 300 internationals. Bryn Thomas died in 1998. Here is his published *Welsh XV from players after World War II.*

Fullback: JPR Williams - 'A fierce competitor, and a powerful, skilful and slightly arrogant individual.'

Wingers: Ken Jones and Gerald Davies - 'Jones was the best winger of his era. He had a smiling modesty and enthusiasm and revelled in the open spaces which were fewer then. Davies produced many moments of wonder for watchers and despair for opponents. Always showed exciting, elusive brilliance.'

Centres: Bleddyn Williams and Jack Matthews - 'Matthews the powerful striker with magnificent defence; Williams the brilliant attacker. They went together like eggs and bacon.'

Flyhalf: Cliff Morgan - 'He gave pleasure to so many with his abundant skills, tolerance and bubbling good humour.'

Scrumhalf: Gareth Edwards - 'The complete rugby player. Often one was at a loss for fresh adjectives to shower on him. Truly a great one!'

Number 8: Mervyn Davies - 'He read the game quickly and accurately, while his leadership was inspirational.'

Flankers: Haydn Morgan and Clem Thomas - 'Morgan had strength pace and superb athleticism to go with safe hands and an all-embracing tackle. Thomas spared no-one with his close marking ... and made life very uncomfortable for all opponents.'

Locks: Roy John and Rhys Williams - 'John was the greatest jumper of all. So good was he the IRB amended the lineout laws. Williams was strong, reliable and indestructible.'

Props: Courtenay Meredith and Graham Price - 'Meredith was as hard as teak in the scrums, supportive in the lineout and lively in the loose. Price's strength and consistency were invaluable for Wales in 41 matches. He was developed in the furnace of the Pontypool front row.'

Hooker: Bryn Meredith - 'The complete forward who did everything well. A controller on the field, a humourist off it.'

centre game then in favour. Davies, who had played his first 12 tests as a centre, was reluctant to move out wider. He feared he would not see enough ball and later this was true. However, when he had a distributor as good as John Dawes inside him, this was not a problem and he was free to give full rein to his brilliance.

Of all his attributes, the one that most amazed me was his ability to sidestep at full speed. In a one-on-one situation he was unstoppable. Rarely did a defender lay even a finger on him as he jetted by. David Duckham, who opposed him many times, once said: "You know he is going to sidestep. You also know there isn't a thing you can do about it."

Davies played a lot of his rugby in England, for Cambridge University, whom he captained in 1970, and London Welsh. He was extremely well suited to sevens rugby and had some glorious days at the Middlesex sevens. However he was fiercely loyal to Wales and was a key figure in his country's golden reign of the 1970s. He was unavailable for Lions tours in 1974 and 1977, but toured Australia with Wales in 1978, rounding out his test career by scoring a try in each of his last two tests. He finished with 23 test tries, including 20 for Wales, which put him equal top with Edwards on the Welsh lists.

Through the 1970s, Davies became an increasingly visible figure in Welsh rugby. In 1975 he beat Edwards in the race for captaincy of the Cardiff side and proved to be an innovative and inspiring leader who helped his club develop the 15-man game for which they were to become well-known through the early 1980s. He read the game well, having studied rugby in a manner befitting the schoolmaster he was.

Davies had excellent understanding of positional play and seldom died with the ball. Even into his 30s, he remained a potent weapon, full of pace and verve. In a Schweppes Cup match at Pontypool in 1977, he scored four tries for Cardiff, each with sustained sprints from near halfway. The Cardiff forwards were comprehensively outplayed and Davies received the ball only five times, yet his team won the game.

Davies was a real crowd-pleaser, one of those players who pulled spectators through the turnstiles. There was an obvious stir of excitement when he got the ball and with his speed and acceleration, he seldom disappointed.

I saw him in a moment of poignant reflection in 1995, when he wandered through the rooms and foyer of the Southern Cross Hotel in Dunedin. It was a very popular stop, apparently, and Davies thoroughly enjoyed reflecting on the happy memories from the 1971 tour.

In sport, a person's style of play often reflects his personality. But for all his dazzling play, Davies was a quiet, thoughtful person off the field. I've always found him a thorough gentleman and as a rugby critic, either for television or for *The Times* of London, always worth taking note of. **100**

MERVYN DAVIES

Merv the Swerve

MERVYN DAVIES entered big rugby suddenly, and left it even more dramatically. At 22 years of age, he was picked for Wales in 1969, only three months after making his first appearance for the London Welsh club side. He quickly impressed as a tall, angular loose forward with exceptional ball-winning ability at the back of the lineout.

For the next eight seasons he made the No 8 spot his own, in both the Welsh and Lions teams. The stringy Davies became the most influential British forward of his era.

Then his career was sensationally snuffed out. Playing for Swansea against Pontypool in a Schweppes Cup semi-final in 1976, he collapsed near the end of the match. It transpired he'd suffered a brain haemorrhage and for some time his life hung in the balance. After a lengthy battle he survived, but his rugby career was over.

By 1976 he was the captain of Wales, and a successful one at that with only one defeat in nine matches, and had been earmarked to lead the 1977 British Lions to New Zealand. Instead, still in his late 20s, his rugby days had ended. Whether it was the haemorrhage, or the fate which had befallen him, it was said his personality changed. He lost much of his humour and became a more sombre individual. But he remained around rugby, writing for English newspapers and coaching, and in recent years seems more like his old self.

The long-limbed Davies did more than enough on the international scene to stamp himself as a great and left memories of an uncompromising and disciplined No 8 who became a benchmark player to those who followed. Halfback Gareth Edwards, who played in all Davies' tests, once wrote of his team-mate: 'I conjure up an image of a sort of rugby-playing octopus: a participant who gathered in all around him - ball and players - and gave the game shape and coherence.'

Davies was easily identified because he wore a thick white headband, had the moustache of a western outlaw and ran with a characteristic hunched action. He had wide shoulders and a tapering body and was invariably taller than his opposite No 8. In the 1970s, there were few No 8s who were nearly 1.95m (6ft 5in) and 95kg (14st 12lb).

I regard him as a pioneer of the No 8 position, not only for his unique body shape, but because of the way he dominated lineouts, for his athleticism, strength and ability to read a game. He wasn't the fastest loose forward off

Thomas Mervyn Davies
No 8
Born: Swansea, December 9, 1946
Test debut: Wales v Scotland, February 1, 1969
Test career: 1969-76 (46 matches - 38 for Wales, 8 for the British Isles)
Test points: 7 (2 tries)
* Played his 46 tests consecutively
* Captained Wales for two seasons and they won the Five Nations Championship both times
* Was the world's most capped No 8 when he retired

Most tests as a No 8:

54	Dean Richards (England and British Isles)
52	Zinzan Brooke (New Zealand)
46	Mervyn Davies (Wales and British Isles)
43	Willie Duggan (Ireland and British Isles)
43	Tim Gavin (Australia)
39*	Gary Teichmann (South Africa)
34	Murray Mexted (New Zealand)
33	Guy Basquet (France)
31	John Scott (England)
29	Derek White (Scotland)
*	still playing

Note: this table includes only appearances at No 8

the mark, but anticipated superbly and was inevitably one of the first to a breakdown, or was there to make the vital tackle.

Davies certainly made his mark in New Zealand with the 1971 Lions. In fact, All Black captain Colin Meads nominated Davies and centre Mike Gibson as the two players who contributed most to the All Black defeat in that series. 'It was not just that Davies achieved domination for the Lions at the back of the lineout,' wrote Meads after the tour. 'He moved with quite startling speed and intelligence - an instinctive reaction almost - to trouble-spots, killing ball till the Lions could regroup.'

For a long time it did not seem as if Davies would amount to very much as a rugby player. He was born into a rugby family - his father had been a Welsh Victory international. Davies learned his rugby at Penlan Comprehensive, and later graduated to the Swansea College of Education, where he played minor rep rugby and basketball. He had a few games for Swansea then trod the well-worth path from Wales to London, where he became a teacher and played for London Welsh.

Then he was pulled into the Welsh test side for the test against Scotland at Murrayfield. Fullback JPR Williams made his debut the same day and they helped Wales to a convincing 17-3 victory.

Later that year he toured New Zealand with an outclassed Welsh side that was hammered in both tests. From the seeds of those defeats grew the determination to gain revenge two years later with the Lions.

Davies was part of what is known as the second golden era of Welsh rugby. Wales had some brilliant backs, including Edwards, John, Bennett, Dawes, Williams and Gerald Davies in the backs. The forwards were solid, but it was the Pontypool front row and the multi-talented Mervyn Davies at No 8 who lifted the pack to real class.

Known as 'Merv the Swerve' (Swerve to his good mates), Davies was at his best on his two major tours, to New Zealand in 1971 and to South Africa in 1974. But he had great times at home, too. He clinched a draw for the Barbarians against the All Blacks at Twickenham in 1974 with a fine one-handed try in the closing minutes and was in five Welsh teams that won the Five Nations Championship.

He spent half his career based in London, but in 1972 returned to live in Swansea and in 1975 became a popular captain of Wales. Though he was more the strong silent type than a fire-and-brimstone leader, he enjoyed total respect from his players. Under Davies, Wales won the Five Nations Championship in 1975 and 76 and the Grand Slam in the latter year. **⑩**

GREG DAVIS

Transplanted Kiwi

GREG DAVIS was New Zealand's gift to Australian rugby. After struggling to break into top rugby in New Zealand, Davis shifted across the Tasman in 1963, joining Sydney's Drummoyne club. He was an instant success and was soon being acclaimed as one of the world's best loose forwards, a committed, competitive player whose fierce tackling destroyed the morale of opposing backs.

The prematurely balding Davis became one of Australia's most significant players ever. He captained the Wallabies for four seasons and closed his career by leading them to New Zealand in 1972. It was a poor side, tagged the 'Awful Aussies', and lost all three tests heavily. Live television broadcasts were introduced into New Zealand that season, so the Australians' inadequacies were graphically exposed. But Davis, although 33, was still outstanding. His play never faltered and he led the team with quiet dignity, showing New Zealanders what they had missed out on.

Davis was educated at Auckland's Sacred Heart College. He began his rep career as a midfield back with Thames Valley in 1958, scoring a try on his debut against Combined Services.

In 1960 he made two moves - to Auckland, and to the position of flanker. Though he scored a try in an All Black trial in 1961, his career stagnated, especially when he returned to Bay of Plenty. Before the 1962 season, Davis made a short tour of Australia with a Tauranga Sub-union team and was encouraged by the opportunities there for his work as a wool classer and in rugby.

So the following season he lined up for Drummoyne in Sydney. The Australian selectors took one look at the 1.80m (5ft 11in) 83kg (13st) loose forward and named him in their test side. He made his debut against England, marking the occasion with a try, one of two he scored in test rugby.

Then followed the historic 1963 Wallaby tour of South Africa, when the Australians upset predictions by drawing the series 2-2. After losing the first test 14-3, the Australians, led by John Thornett, scored a stunning 9-5 win at Cape Town in what was perhaps Davis' finest game. South African writer Norman Canale remarked: 'The crash tackle by the fair-haired Wallaby flank forward Greg Davis of Springbok Keith Oxlee in the opening minutes not only shook Oxlee down to the tip of his size seven boots, but reverberated

Gregory Victor Davis
Loose forward
Born: Matamata, July 27, 1939
Died: Rotorua, July 24, 1979
Test debut: Australia v England, Sydney, June 4, 1963
Test career: 1963-72 (39 matches)
Test points: 6 (2 tries)
* Played for Thames Valley, Bay of Plenty and Auckland, and in an All Black trial, before moving to Australia
* Captained Australia in 16 consecutive tests

through rugby-playing South Africa.'

Davis, in tandem with equally destructive Queensland flanker Jules Guerassimoff, so destroyed the Springbok backline that Oxlee was dropped. Australia went on to take the third test 11-9 and another critic, Fred Labuschagne, wrote: 'His anticipation is uncanny. Local flyhalves have been ruing the day Davis left New Zealand.'

The *Australian Rugby Almanac* named Davis one of its five Players of the Year and Wallaby manager Bill McLaughlin said: "I wish I had a whole packful of Davises." Later, when he was the Australian Rugby Union president, he said: "Greg was the greatest leather-hunter I have seen. He'd be tackling a man and he'd leave him in mid-air if he saw the ball was loose. He and Guerassimoff made a devastating pair."

Despite the media attention, Davis remained a quiet, modest man who deflected glory onto his team-mates. He toured New Zealand in 1964, starring in the Wallabies' shock 20-5 victory in the third test at Athletic Park, the All Blacks' biggest defeat in 36 years. Davis and Guerassimoff were described as 'the scourge of the open'.

By now Davis was a senior member of the Wallaby side and in the following years travelled to Britain and France, made a short tour of Scotland and Ireland, and led Australian teams to South Africa, France and New Zealand. He was unfortunate with his timing, for when he became the test captain, against Wales at Sydney in 1969, many of the fine players of the early 1960s had either retired or switched to league.

Australian lost that test to Wales 19-16 and were whitewashed 4-0 in the series in South Africa shortly after. His feat of playing 21 of the 26 matches in South Africa earned him the tag 'Iron Man'. A tour correspondent wrote: 'His team-mates held him in awe for the manner in which he kept going.'

Davis was certainly hard. In Ireland in 1968 his nose was badly broken. Told he needed an operation, he grabbed a soft drink bottle and knocked it back into shape.

It says much for Davis' ability that he showed his class even in teams that were generally struggling. Of his 39 tests, Australia won just 10.

The example of Davis leads me to wonder about other players who have failed to make the All Blacks. In the 1960s, New Zealand was served by such fine flankers as Waka Nathan, John Graham, Kel Tremain and Ian Kirkpatrick and it's not certain that Davis would have represented the country of his birth. Yet he showed when he wore Australia's green and gold that he was among the best players this century.

After his rugby days, Davis returned to live in Rotorua, where he was diagnosed as having a brain tumour. He died three days before his 40th birthday. When his former Drummoyne team-mates heard of Davis' illness they formed a committee to raise money to pay his medical bills. The club played a Barbarians side that included French star Jean-Pierre Rives as part of the Davis Benefit. Small clubs from all over Australia contributed to the fund, which raised more than $60,000. The trustees paid for Davis' house, invested the balance for his wife, two sons and daughter and paid their school and medical fees.

The Davis rugby line continued in 1998 when his nephew Scott Robertson broke into the All Blacks, as a flanker, of course. ⬤

MORNE DU PLESSIS

Like Father, Like Son

THE NAME du Plessis means double nightmares for New Zealanders. Lock Felix du Plessis captained South Africa in three tests in 1949, the year the Springboks whitewashed the All Blacks 4-0. In 1976 New Zealand received more of the du Plessis treatment when Felix's son Morne led the Springboks to a 3-1 series victory.

Felix and Morne du Plessis are the only father and son to both lead their country in tests. But whereas Felix's international career lasted one season, Morne became a major figure in South African rugby, a superb No 8 and leader, and a capable administrator.

There was no lack of sport in Morne's background. Besides his father's rugby prowess, his mother Pat was a South African hockey captain and his uncle Horace Smethurst was a South African soccer captain. Another uncle played soccer for South Africa and 1920s Springbok Nic du Plessis was Felix's uncle.

Soon Morne revealed all the family's sports and leadership qualities. He attended Klerksdorp Primary School and Grey College in Bloemfontein. Naturally he played rugby, at flyhalf, centre, fullback and eventually lock. He was tall and appeared somewhat gawky, but had natural timing and co-ordination. He also excelled in tennis and swimming, was the college athletics Victor Ludorum and represented South African Schools in 1967 and later Western Province at cricket.

On the rugby field, the rangy du Plessis had tenacity to match his exceptional talent. Danie Craven took a look at him when du Plessis turned up at Stellenbosch University, switched him from lock to No 8, and became a vehement supporter. While at Stellenbosch, where he eventually graduated with an honours degree in industrial psychology, du Plessis captained the Western Province under-20 rugby team.

He made the Western Province senior side in 1970 and the following year, aged 21, was one of a batch of brilliant loose forwards in Hannes Marais' team to Australia. It says much for du Plessis' potential that even with Jan Ellis, Piet Greyling, Tommy Bedford and Thys Lourens on hand, he played all three tests. His big individual moment came in the New South Wales match when he charged the last 15 metres to the tryline to finish off a sweeping move that had begun in the South African 22.

Strangely, du Plessis' career then faltered. He was dropped during the

---

Morne du Plessis
Loose forward
Born: Krugersdorp, October 21, 1949
Test debut: South Africa v Australia, Sydney, July 17, 1971
Test career: 1971-80 (22 matches)
Test points: 12 (3 tries)

* Felix and Morne du Plessis are the only father and son to have both captained their country in a rugby test
* Captained South Africa in 15 tests
* Managed the 1995 World Cup champion Springbok side
* Also represented Western Province at cricket

Felix and Morne du Plessis are the only father and son who have both led their country in rugby tests. However, here are three interesting variations on the theme:

1. Ray Dalton was vice-captain of the 1949 All Blacks and captained the side in a number of tour matches. His son Andy captained New Zealand in 17 tests.
2. Clive Rowlands captained Wales 14 times and his son-in-law, Robert Jones, has also captained Wales.
3. Frank Oliver captained New Zealand in three tests in 1978. His son Anton has captained New Zealand Colts.

Springboks' unhappy series loss to the 1974 Lions, though he was hardly alone - the South Africans used 33 test players that year. He came in for an inordinate amount of criticism outside Western Province, being labelled 'too soft' and 'too rough' at the same time! In the north he was called 'Maureen' and 'Moffie' because he was soft, then 'Meanie' after punching a player. The critics couldn't agree on what they didn't like; they just knew they didn't like him.

Du Plessis made the Springbok team that won both tests in France in 1974, and within a year was captaining the test side against France at home, South Africa's 36th test skipper. He answered criticism in the only effective manner - with repeated quality performances. He had ample grit and self-discipline and when he became Western Province captain, it was obvious he was a born leader.

He always appealed as a person capable of bringing together the different factions of South African rugby. In 1975, he captained a racially mixed Invitation side, including four coloured and black players, against the French at Newlands. His team won 18-3 and one of the four, John Noble, scored a brilliant try. The match was an important early step in the march towards apartheid-free rugby.

Du Plessis was 25 when he led the Springboks to two victories against France in 1975. By then he was playing for Villagers, the first player from the club to captain South Africa since Bennie Osler in 1931.

He was the favourite to captain South Africa against the 1976 All Blacks and cemented the position when he led Western Province to a 12-11 win over the visitors. Du Plessis had broken his jaw three weeks earlier and had to pass a fitness test to play. I was most impressed with his cool leadership, especially when Western Province trailed 11-0.

Du Plessis was a dominant figure in the test series. Flyhalf Gerald Bosch broke All Black hearts with his deadly place-kicking, but du Plessis was equally crucial. He was an outstanding No 8, who played in a similar fashion to All Black Murray Mexted. He was a great leaper, using his 1.94m (6ft 5in) frame to maximum advantage, very athletic, always seemed at peak fitness and was a dogged competitor. Unlike a couple of his 1976 team-mates, he did not bother himself with rough or dirty play.

In 1977, du Plessis led the Springboks to victory over a World XV skippered by Willie John McBride and including Gareth Edwards, Andy Haden, Jean-Pierre Rives, Ian Kirkpatrick and J P R Williams. By now he had established himself as the Springbok captain in a way few men have. He took his team to South America in 1980, where they won two tests - in Uruguay and Chile - against the Jaguars, the Argentinian side in mufti.

Then came a career highlight, the hard-fought 3-1 series win over the 1980 Lions, when his captaincy drew widespread praise. As a leader he was both thoughtful and inventive. He read a game well, but knew when it was time to try something different - a short lineout, a mini-scrum, a flip pass, or a long gridiron pass.

South Africa was girding itself for the major tour to New Zealand in 1981 when du Plessis dropped a bombshell by retiring. It was a torrid, protest-marred tour and the Springboks were pipped in a tight series. Many South Africans felt that with du Plessis at the helm the balance might have tipped the other way.

From 1975-80, he led the Springboks 15 times and lost only twice. He led his country to wins over the All Blacks, a World XV, the Jaguars, the Lions

Two great test captains - Morne du Plessis and Jean-Pierre Rives - feature on this programme for the South Africa v France test, Pretoria 1980.

Morne du Plessis (right) leading from the
front for Western Province

and France. Du Plessis also played 112 games for Western Province, captaining the side 103 times.

Craven said: "His example, his leadership, stamped him as one of the immortals."

In retirement, the boyish-faced du Plessis remained a powerful figure in South African rugby. He was one of the few leading rugby figures to retain the trust and friendship of the non-white population, especially the large number of non-white players on the Cape, to whom he was a hero. He was an active supporter of President Nelson Mandela and worked hard to make rugby in his country integrated.

In 1995, with South Africa emerging from its harrowing period of international isolation, du Plessis was pitchforked into Springbok team manager's job after Jannie Engelbrecht had been appointed then dropped. Du Plessis worked well with coach Kitch Christie and helped create the environment for the Springboks to win the World Cup, beating the All Blacks 15-12 in extra time in the final.

Unbelievably, du Plessis, like captain Francois Pienaar and Christie, was soon gone, a victim of the vagaries of South Africa's often inexplicable internal rugby politics.

Outside rugby, the popular du Plessis is much in demand as a public speaker and is a director of a successful sports goods company. 🔟🔟

FRIK DU PREEZ

Lineout Leaper

IN THE BOARDROOM at Pretoria's Loftus Versfeld ground is an incredible photo of Frik du Preez jumping in a lineout. I swear the great Springbok lock of the 1960s is all of 75cm (30 inches) off the ground. In du Preez's time, lifting in the lineout was not permitted and there isn't a supporting hand in sight. He has climbed a fair way to the sky on his own, yet at 1.88m (6ft 2in) he was not tall for a lock.

Du Preez's jumping was for me the most spectacular skill he brought to rugby, but because he did so many things well, he was one of the players of his generation. Du Preez, Irishman Willie John McBride and New Zealander Colin Meads were the world's three pre-eminent locks for a decade and they staged some titanic battles. It was wonderful to see them at the big International Hall of Fame dinner in London in 1997. After all those years locked in combat, the spirit of camaraderie was obvious.

How good was du Preez? Well, Carwyn James said in his superb book *The World of Rugby* (written in conjunction with John Reason): 'Du Preez was an astonishing player, possibly the only lock of modern times who had every one of the skills necessary to the completely equipped forward. He could jump a truly remarkable height in the lineout, he could scrummage, he could kick, he could maul, he could tackle, he was hard, he could handle, he could pass and as if all that was not enough, he was as quick as almost any back in the world and could sustain his extraordinary pace for more than half the length of the field.' From a rugby thinker like James, that is praise indeed.

From what I saw, du Preez merited every word, with one proviso: while he was certainly the rock of the Springbok forward pack, there was a suspicion that he was not always in top gear. Perhaps the game was too easy for him. He always seemed poised, but sometimes there wasn't quite the urgency you'd expect of such a fine athlete. As his arch-rival Meads wrote: 'Frik would have been greater still had he unfailingly applied himself. He was inclined to take rest periods, but as an all-round lock, he had just about everything and that included the capacity to be a punishing runner with the ball.'

Having said that, it is still incredible when flicking through South Africa's test history to see just how many times du Preez was dropped and how many tests he missed - a case of selectors not appreciating talent when it was directly in front of them. South Africa's opponents always rated du Preez on the top

Frederik Christoffel Hendrik du Preez
Lock
Born: Rustenberg, November 28, 1935
Test debut: South Africa v England, Twickenham, January 7, 1961
Test career: 1961-71 (38 matches)
Test points: 11 (1 try, 1 conversion, 2 penalites)
* Equalled the South African record for test appearances
* One of the First XV inducted into the International Rugby Hall of Fame in 1997

Most tests for the Springboks:

53*	Mark Andrews	1994-98
50*	Joost van der Westhuizen	1993-98
47*	James Small	1992-97
39*	Gary Teichmann	1995-98
38	Frik du Preez	1961-71
38	Jan Ellis	1965-76
35	Hannes Marais	1963-74
34*	Andre Joubert	1989-97
34*	James Dalton	1994-98
33	Jannie Engelbrecht	1960-69
33	John Gainsford	1960-67
33*	Henry Honiball	1993-98
32*	Ruben Kruger	1993-97

* still playing

rung of the rugby ladder, but his own selectors sometimes could not see it.

There was no question of Du Preez's durability and toughness - you don't play international rugby for a decade in the middle of the scrum without those attributes - but he always appealed as a person with a good sense of humour and the utmost modesty. This was illustrated by his retirement after the Australia-South Africa test in Sydney in 1971, when he was given the honour of leading the Springboks onto the paddock. Afterwards at a team function, there were moving tributes from Flappie Lochner, Johan Claassen and Hannes Marais, but the great lock could find no words with which to reply, and leant against a wall, slowly turning a can of beer in his fingers. As Kim Shippey wrote: 'In silence they showed their respect for him, and in silence he acknowledged their adulation. It was the most eloquent non-speech I've never heard …'

Du Preez played his initial rugby at Standerton High School, as a flyhalf. Later he joined the South African Air Force at Pretoria and represented Northern Transvaal. By then he was a forward - he was 98kg (15st 6lb) when he first played test rugby - and was equally effective as flanker or lock. With his love of running with the ball in hand and his speed, he thrived more on his hard home grounds than the softer fields of New Zealand and Britain.

His first peep of the international stage was for South African Combined Services against the All Blacks in 1960. He earned a spot on the Springbok tour of Britain and France at the end of that year, playing the England and Scotland tests. His kicking was almost as useful as general play. He kicked 49 points on tour (as well as scoring three tries) and became known as a prodigious if inconsistent goal-kicker. His most famous kick was a 77m monster drop-kick in the thin air at the Loftus Versfeld Stadium.

Du Preez was a central figure in a great Springbok era and helped win series against Australia (three times), the Lions (twice), France (twice), and New Zealand. It wasn't until his 11th test, against France in 1964, that he suffered defeat.

He gave opponents all manner of reasons for remembering him. Future All Black wing Bill Birtwistle recalls an 85m sprint for a try against the Springboks in 1965 when the only man to chase him was du Preez. Birtwistle, a real flier, made the tryline, but was unable to gain even a metre on the big lock. Another All Black, Ian Kirkpatrick, talks about getting penalised for lifting du Preez in a lineout during a centenary match in England in 1971. "I was actually further away from him than the referee," says Kirkpatrick, "but Frik got so high the ref thought he could only have got there by being lifted, which he most certainly wasn't."

The 1968 Lions remember a try du Preez scored at Loftus Versfeld when he won a lineout just inside the Lions half, and began a charging run around the front of the lineout. He over-ran winger Keith Savage and halfback Gareth Edwards, then swerved past fullback Tom Kiernan to score a sensational try.

Du Preez played 38 tests - 31 as a lock, seven as a flanker - and won friends all over the world. At his 80th birthday party, Danie Craven was asked to choose five great players from the world of rugby. He chose Gareth Edwards, Colin Meads, Benoit Dauga, Naas Botha and du Preez.

While in South Africa during the 1995 World Cup, I was given the responsibility of contacting him to see if he had anything he might be able to donate to the Hall of Fame. I phoned him in Namibia, where he lives, and received a typically friendly message back, in a strong South African accent, offering all sorts of souvenirs. He was as good as his word and sent all manner of valuable memorabilia. **100**

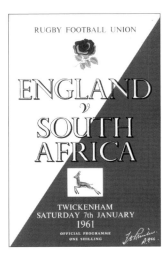

Frik du Preez's test debut; South Africa v England, Twickenham, 1961.

JOHN EALES

The Complete Footballer

BEANSTALK WALLABY lock John Eales fits most people's idea of the perfect forward. Not only has he proved over the past decade to be the world's best lineout jumper, but he is a superb ball player, able to catch, pass and run like as back. Eales is also one of the best goal-kickers around. If he ever decided to focus on his kicking, he might well rate alongside the likes of Michael Lynagh and Grant Fox. These days, too, Eales is the Wallaby captain, bringing his own brand of flair and verve to the job.

New Zealanders describe Zinzan Brooke as the complete footballer, but Brooke was never a place-kicker to match Eales, or a test captain.

Since he burst into test rugby in 1991, the softly-spoken Eales has impressed me hugely. The All Blacks' lineout specialist through most of the 1990s has been the Ian Jones, but even loyal New Zealanders would not dispute that Eales has consistently outplayed Jones in this crucial department.

Eales was a brilliant schoolboy athlete at St William's and Marist Brothers College in Brisbane. He shone at cricket, but displayed talent at any ball game he turned his mind to.

He began to attract wider rugby attention in 1990 when he won the Best and Fairest competition in Brisbane club rugby and made his Queensland debut against Canterbury in Christchurch. Early in 1991, he was a member of the Emerging Wallabies side to Europe. Under coach Bob Hitchcock, the team played eight matches in a month and Eales, Jason Little and Willie Ofahengaue marked themselves as future internationals.

In Eales' case, there was little time to wait. Though he was a No 8 during his school days, he has made his reputation for Australia at lock. He showed he was made of stern stuff when he ignored constant barging and shoving tactics to outplay Wade Dooley in the lineouts and help Queensland beat England 20-17 in 1991. In his test debut a few days later the Wallabies thumped Wales 63-6. Eales' play - not just his spectacular lineout leaping, but his coverage around the field - was a revelation. The Queenslander arrived when Australia had good locks in Steve Cutler, Bill Campbell and Rod McCall. But Eales was special and played in all 10 tests for Australia in 1991. In his second test outing he outjumped Martin Bayfield, England's lineout specialist and the tallest man to play rugby for his country.

Eales was a junior member of the Wallaby team that won the 1991 World Cup by beating England 12-6 at Twickenham in the final. Though he played

---

John Anthony Eales
Lock
Born: Brisbane, June 27, 1970
Test debut: Australia v Wales, Brisbane, July 21, 1991
Test career: 1991-98 (64 matches)
Test points: 165 (2 tries, 30 conversions, 32 penalties)
* Has scored the most points in test rugby by a forward
* Has captained Australia in 33 tests, second only to Nick Farr-Jones (36)

every match of Australia's World Cup campaign, he reserved his best for the final, jumping superbly, especially in the exciting closing stages, and making one brilliant tackle from behind that halted a likely England scoring movement.

At 2.01m (6ft 7in) and 114kg (17st 12lb), he is a major physical presence. But even up against taller players like Bayfield, his timing and agility enable him to dominate lineouts. For such a tall man, he is very nimble - he would have made a superb basketballer. He showed his athleticism during the 1998 Super 12 competition when he stood between the posts awaiting an opposition penalty, then leapt high and batted the ball back as it sailed over the crossbar, sparking discussion about whether he had knocked the ball on. For me, the inspiration and athleticism of his action spoke volumes for Eales' ability.

Since 1991 Eales, nicknamed 'Slippery' for obvious reasons, has been a must selection for Australia when available. He missed the entire 1993 year because of a shoulder injury, but bounced back as good as ever in 1994. Besides his contribution as a forward, Eales has emerged as a classy goal-kicker.

Sometimes his teams use him as their No 1 place-kicker, and he invariably comes through for them. He kicked all four conversion attempts against Romania at the 1995 World Cup and has generally been Queensland's kicker in the Super 12 competition. In 1998, Eales emphasised what a handy kicker he was during the test against the All Blacks at Sydney. With first-choice kicker Matthew Burke struggling, Eales took over in the second half and landed goals from everywhere to guide his team to victory. At the end of 1998, the Wallabies were pushed to their limit by a fired-up England team at Twickenham. With Burke absent injured, Eales kicked four penalties to guide his side to a heart-stopping 12-11 win.

Eales' kicking would be laudable for a fullback, but is even more amazing lock. He gets his legs pummelled, pushes himself in rucks, scrums and mauls, then brushes himself down, takes a deep breath and kicks with rare technique and balance. By the end of 1998 he had scored the most test points by a forward and had topped 500 for Queensland. Sadly, early in 1999, he again suffered a serious shoulder injury and missed the Super 12 competition.

The main danger for Eales, as the end of the century approaches, is that Australia rely on him so much. Nick Farr-Jones has predicted he will be a great Wallaby captain. Certainly his dynamic play and sincere, humble manner draw the best from the teams he captains. He took over the reins in 1996, before the first Tri-Nations series, and hasn't looked back. Perhaps the psychology degree he completed at the University of Queensland helps.

More worryingly for Australia, Eales is such a lineout force that the Wallabies tend to rely too much on him. The temptation is to continually throw the ball

A selection of the nicknames of the century's famous players, variously reflecting a player's physical build, a special rugby skill or a diminutive of his name.

John **'Parramatta'** Eales (Australia): named after the Sydney-based rugby league team the Parramatta Eels. He is also sometimes called **'Slippery'**, a reference to his surname.

Ian **'Mighty Mouse'** McLauchlan (Scotland): because he was short in stature - for a prop, that is!

Billy **'Carbine'** Wallace (New Zealand): named after a champion New Zealand racehorse.

Don **'The Boot'** Clarke (New Zealand): he could kick 'em from anywhere.

Jeff **'Goldie'** Wilson (New Zealand): everything he touches turns to gold.

Michael **'Noddy'** Lynagh (Australia): derived from his habit of nodding in agreement with his coach at team talks.

Matthys **'Boy'** Louw (South Africa): a common South African nickname (note Boy de Villiers and Boy Morkel). Perhaps it was bestowed as a reference to Louw's heavyweight build, or because he was one of a family of nine boys.

Colin **'Pinetree'** Meads (New Zealand): tall, sturdily-built, but immensely powerful.

Wayne **'Buck'** Shelford (New Zealand): familiar New Zealand tag, referring to a young deer's strength and speed.

Wavell **'Wakers'** Wakefield (England): the familiar shortening of a surname.

Mervyn **'Merv the Swerve'** Davies (Wales): taken from an admiring rhyme matching his name with his rugby talent.

John **'J P R'** Williams (Wales): there were two John Williams in Welsh rugby in the 1970s. When both made the test team they were distinguished by their initials. One became 'J J' and the other became 'J P R'.

Pierre **'Monsieur le Drop'** Albaladejo (France): the great 1960s drop goal specialist.

William **'Willie John'** McBride (Ireland): he was named William James McBride, but everywhere in the rugby world, including all references in this book, he is known as Willie John. This was attached to him during his touring days with the Irish and British Lions teams.

David **'Campo'** Campese (Australia): seldom referred to as David during his long career.

Tim **'Helmet'** Horan (Australia): of indistinct origins, perhaps referring to a haircut he favoured at one time.

Daniel **'Doc'** Craven (South Africa): after all, he had no less than three University doctorates.

Naas **'Nasty Booter'** Botha (South Africa): nicknamed by New Zealanders, who feared his goal-kicking prowess.

Hennie **'Greyhound'** Muller (South Africa): Named for the way his distinctive play hounded opponents.

Andre **'Jouba'** Joubert (South Africa): an abbreviated version of his surname.

to Eales, knowing he will produce the goods - not the best long-term strategy.

Under Eales, Australia have played entertaining, expansive rugby. Against the All Blacks in Christchurch in 1998, they scored a try after 18 phases, which sums up Eales' commitment to a non-stop, exciting style. In 1998, the Wallabies enjoyed their best season against New Zealand, winning three successive tests for a Bledisloe Cup whitewash. Eales' wide smile, as he held aloft the massive Bledisloe Cup in Christchurch, was a sight to behold.

Eales is so crucial to the Wallaby efforts that he has been the target of some foul and unsavoury play by various opponents. He seldom resorts in kind, preferring to prove his point with skill. The once exception I have seen was in the Melbourne Bledisloe Cup test in 1997 when Sean Fitzpatrick, an expert niggler, got under his skin and provoked a few snarls and grizzles from Eales in response. But normally Eales is totally composed, seems to be genuinely enjoying the battle, and thrives on the contest of skill.

I've especially admired Eales for two reasons - though for some years he has been praised as a great lock, he has continued to improve, and all the while he has remained a genuinely good bloke, someone of the highest calibre. The leading Wallabies, like Eales, Farr-Jones, Lynagh and David Campese, remember the days before their 1991 World Cup glory, when rugby was only the third or fourth winter code back home and they struggled for scraps of publicity. They've not let the game's more elevated recent position change them and remain untouched by fame. Leading players from other countries could take a leaf from their book. **100**

Edwards (left) and his great All Black rival, Sid Going.

GARETH EDWARDS

The One and Only

RANKING THE WORLD'S BEST rugby players is impossible, given the difficulties of comparing different positions and eras. But that doesn't stop people from trying. In 1996, the British magazine *Rugby World* compiled a top 100 and placed Welsh halfback Gareth Edwards No 1. There was no outcry, even from the leading southern hemisphere countries.

Edwards comes out near the top in virtually every poll. He was the British rugby personality of the 1970s, and was such a legendary figure in Wales that he became known simply as Gareth. The surname was superfluous.

I have certainly never seen a better scrumhalf. He was a star even in great teams; the teams he played for won major titles and series; he had every facet of his position mastered; he made the players around him better; he could dominate a match; he had longevity and durability.

Edwards was educated at Pontardawe Technical School, Millfield and Cardiff Training College (where he studied physical education), and joined the Cardiff club, where he remained until his retirement. As a youngster, he dreamed of playing rugby for Wales, though he was a good soccer player (he was offered a pro contract by Swansea Town) and won the All-England Schools 200-yard hurdles title, beating by 15 yards Alan Pascoe, later an Olympic hurdles silver medallist.

Edwards was 19 when won his first cap against France in 1967. Soon after, he linked with flyhalf Barry John at Cardiff, for Wales and, in South Africa, for the 1968 Lions. The young Edwards was no great passer, but was put at ease by the nonchalant John, and a famous partnership was born. They played 23 tests for Wales, and five for the Lions. When John retired, Edwards formed another enduring combination, with Phil Bennett.

New Zealanders first glimpsed Edwards in 1967. He was in the Welsh side that was beaten 13-6 by Brian Lochore's All Blacks, captained East Wales to a 3-3 draw with the tourists and played for the Barbarians in the last game of the tour.

Two years later Wales, the Five Nations champions, toured New Zealand. Like the other much-touted Welsh backs, Edwards played only moderately. Sid Going outplayed him on that tour, as Chris Laidlaw had in Britain in 1967.

It all changed in 1971 when the Welshmen, now wearing Lions jerseys, returned to New Zealand. Edwards had early problems with injury, but once

Gareth Owen Edwards
Scrumhalf
Born: Gwaun-cae-Gurwen, Wales, July 12, 1947.
Test debut: Wales v France, Paris, April 1, 1967
Test career: 1967-78 (63 matches - 53 for Wales, 10 for the British Isles
Test points: 85 (20 tries, 2 conversions, 3 drop goals)
* Held world record for most tests by a scrumhalf
* Held Welsh test records for most appearances and most tries when he retired
* Was world's youngest test captain at 20 years, seven months
* Was inducted into the First XV of the International Rugby Hall of Fame in 1997

Through the 1970s Welsh rugby very much revolved around Gareth Edwards, as is illustrated by this well-worn joke:

Wales and England were playing a test at Twickenham. A young Welsh fan couldn't get a ticket, so stood outside the ground in the pouring rain. He would repeatedly call up to the England supporters inside the ground, "What's happening? What's happening?" Finally the English supporters, tiring of the youngster, told him all the Welsh team except Edwards had been carried off injured.

A few moments later there was a roar from the crowd. The Welsh fan called out: "What's happening? What's happening? Did Gareth score?"

An example from the 1970s of how one advertiser viewed the strength of the Welsh team - Gareth Edwards in every position.

into his stride was a big factor in the Lions' series win. That tour lifted him into world class.

In South Africa in 1974 he teamed with Bennett and wrought more destruction. And his work with No 8 Mervyn Davies really upset the Springboks. The South African loose forwards were confounded by the control of Davies and Edwards at the back of the scrum and were reduced to impotence as they struggled not to stray offside.

Through the 1970s, Edwards remained the central figure in the second golden era of Welsh rugby. After his last test, in 1978, he could look back on a harvest of three Grand Slams, five Triple Crowns and seven Five Nations Championships.

He had memorable battles against the likes of Springbok Dawie de Villiers, and All Blacks Laidlaw and Going. After a while, no-one bettered him. Even Going, so strong and such a match-winner, lacked the consistency to match Edwards.

Along the way there were some amazing personal highlights, including these three tries:

* Against France at Paris in 1969 he turned, spun and dodged through a succession of tacklers from 30 metres out.

* Against Scotland at Cardiff Arms Park in 1972, Edwards broke from the scrum in his own 22, fended off and jinked past the opposition and sprinted downfield. As the cover-defence converged, he chip-kicked over the fullback's head, ran round him, kicked on again and dived on the ball, forcing down just inside the in-goal area. Spike Milligan wrote: 'Edwards was a poet that day, not a rugby player. He was a ballet dancer, a pugilist, a mathematician. He was a miracle.'

* For the Barbarians against the All Blacks in 1973, television's most replayed try. Early in that sweeping end-to-end movement, Edwards sprinted through, then sent out a perfect pass as he sprawled to the ground. Yet there he was 30 seconds later, up with the action, to take the final pass and score. When you next see that try on TV - and you will, because it's played so often - note the quality of the picture as Edwards takes the final pass and dives over for the try. The capacity crowd of 60,000 at Cardiff roared so loudly they distorted forever the television recording.

The match programme for the Barbarians v New Zealand in 1973. Within two minutes of the game starting, Edwards had scored one of rugby's classic tries.

Edwards was more than a superb technician. He was a humble, but humorous person and an exciting player. Once when asked by the Welsh selectors to prove his fitness after a hamstring injury, he cleared a space in the foyer of the Angel Hotel, then did a back somersault. Television New Zealand has footage of him dropping a goal, then doing a forward roll, virtually in the same motion.

Before the test against Scotland in 1977, he shot off to America to compete in a TV *Superstars* contest. Anyone else would have faced questions about commitment, professionalism and prizemoney, but Gareth got away with it. His waistline thickened, but his form never slipped, and he was still dominant in his last Five Nations campaign. In the crucial fixture that season, against France, he turned a 7-0 deficit into a 13-7 halftime lead, dropping a goal and absolutely taking charge.

He was the ringmaster of the great Welsh and Lions teams and would guide his pack about the field rather as Australian Nick Farr-Jones did a decade later.

Edwards' kicking was a lethal weapon. His precise tactical kicking was heartbreaking for opponents, and he mastered the kick down the line and the grubber kick. But Edwards also had a robust defence, absolute concentration, and, because of his strength and low centre of gravity, could bullock his way over for improbable tries.

Curiously for such a popular, talented player, he was not a convincing captain. Gerald Davies was preferred at Cardiff and John Dawes and Mervyn Davies led Wales for extended periods. Edwards did captain Wales 13 times and set a record as test rugby's youngest captain. He was just 20 years, seven months when he led Wales against Scotland at Cardiff in 1968 in his fifth test. Perhaps he was a shade too humble to be an effective captain, though he could be imposing and imperious as a scrumhalf. John described him as 'an explosion just waiting to happen'.

There was no doubting Edwards' tremendous natural gifts, to which he added a singular competitiveness. He was strongly built - 1.72m (5ft 8in) and nearly 83kg (13st) - and had such natural timing that he could even turn his hand to place-kicking. But the work he put into his game should not be overlooked. Initially he did not have a big pass, so he studied Laidlaw's spin pass and worked on his own until passing became a strength.

It says much for his physical resilience that he played his 53 tests for Wales consecutively over a 12-season span, never being dropped or missing a match through injury.

Like all great players, he left shoes too big to fill. Welsh rugby spent years trying to find 'another Gareth' and I felt sorry for Terry Holmes and others who were saddled with such a daunting tag.

After retiring, Edwards worked with Bill McLaren in the BBC TV commentary box. I thought he never quite sounded at home behind the microphone, perhaps because he did not relish criticising players. He has also been involved with the print media, through newspapers and in the publication of half a dozen books. His autobiography *Gareth* is said to be the highest-selling rugby book ever, which says something about the popularity of the subject. Edwards has also broadcast and written about his other sports passion, fishing.

The Welsh have done Edwards proud. In the centre of Cardiff is a fine statue of Edwards passing in that familiar style, to remind future generations of this once-in-a-lifetime player.

This poem by Max Boyce pays tribute to Edwards' quality and longevity:

A man came home one afternoon and found his child in woe
And asked him: "What's the matter bach, pray tell what ails you so? Your little eyes are swollen red, your hands are white and shaking."
"Oh, Dad," he said, "I've got bad news. My little heart is breaking. Gareth Edwards has been dropped, 'twas on the news just now. The Welsh selectors must be mad; there's bound to be a row."
His father said: "Now dry your eyes and don't get in a state. Let's be fair, mun, after all - the man is seventy-eight!"

They don't give caps away in Wales for any old reason. Gareth Edwards once told me that the Welsh Rugby Union gave him a cap to mark his test debut. When, in 1977, Edwards became the first player to reach the milestone of 50 tests for Wales, he was given a second cap.

That cap has an unusual history. In 1998, Dr Dafydd Rhys Williams, a Canadian resident, became the first Welsh-born astronaut. He wanted to take a piece of Welsh memorabilia into space on the *Columbia* shuttle. So the Welsh union asked Edwards for his 50th test cap. That cap duly travelled 6.3 million miles around the world in 263 orbits over a 16-day period. Dr Williams returned the cap to Edwards and it now sits proudly in his study.

MARK ELLA

Ella! Ella! Ella!

Mark Gordon Ella
Flyhalf
Born: Sydney, June 5, 1959
Test debut: Australia v New Zealand, Sydney, June 21, 1980
Test career: 1980-84 (25 matches)
Test points: 75 (6 tries, 3 conversions, 8 penalties, 7 drop goals)
* Was one of the First XV inducted into the International Rugby Hall of Fame in 1997
* Scored tries in each test on the Wallabies' 1984 Grand Slam tour of Britain

LIKE RON JARDEN and Barry John, Wallaby flyhalf Mark Ella retired early from test rugby and has therefore stayed perpetually young in the memory. Ella, the first Aborigine to captain Australia at sport, was 25 and at his peak when he departed top rugby in 1984. During his five-season career, he reached a level that has seldom been matched.

Ella's casual exterior masked his passion for rugby. He was an intuitive player, an artist, but his thinking was ahead of its time. His insistence on calling moves from flyhalf, even when not the captain, his habit of standing close to his scrumhalf and much closer to the advantage line than was the norm, and his use of short, quick fingertip passes became fashionable after his retirement. He was extravagantly talented and used his gifts well.

Amazingly, Ella at 13 was playing the same brand of rugby that was to stun the world a decade later. Ella, his younger (by half an hour) twin brother Glen and their younger (by 13 months) brother Gary performed miracles of innovation and sleight of hand for the Matraville High School First XV. Wallaby coach Bob Dwyer recalls watching the immaculately-attired, much-touted St Joseph's College First XV play a scruffy-looking Matraville team: "It was worth travelling far to see. The Matraville boys were not merely having the better of the contest; they were running rings around their opponents. The St Joseph's XV looked entirely bewildered. They could not stop tries being scored."

Dwyer was so impressed with the play of the Ellas that he visited their home and persuaded them to play for his Randwick club, where they came under the influence of Cyril Towers, the grand old man of Wallaby rugby. They were playing first grade at 17 and in their first outing at that level, Randwick whipped Northern Suburbs 63-0. Mark Ella later said: "Many of the backline moves the Australian team used in the early 1980s, such as the bafflers, the waggas, the cut-outs and the loops were moves we had used in the Matraville under-15s. We took them with us as we moved up the ladder - to Australian schoolboys, Randwick and finally the Australian side." The Ellas helped the famous 'Galloping Greens' of Randwick win five successive club premierships.

The Ellas grew up in La Perouse, a down-trodden area of Sydney. There were five girls and seven boys in the family and conditions were rudimentary. The family slept on shared mattresses, there was no privacy and no sewerage.

The bath was a communal trough in the yard. Perhaps Mark's competitive rugby drive came from his upbringing - the 12 children had to battle for whatever came their way.

Initially the Ellas dabbled in rugby league, but at Matraville High they switched to rugby union with startling results. Mark, the pick of the trio, toured New Zealand with a Combined High Schools side in 1975 and Mark, Glen and Gary toured the world for nine weeks with a brilliant Australian schoolboys team in 1977-78. The olio of talented players went through 16 matches unbeaten. British critics forecast that the Ellas would soon be playing international rugby - they were stars even before they left college.

Mark, 1.78m (5ft 10in) and 74kg (11st 7lb), toured Argentina with the Wallabies in 1979, but couldn't prise the test spot from Tony Melrose. His test debut came against New Zealand at Sydney in 1980 and he then jostled with Queenslander Paul McLean for the Wallaby flyhalf spot. They were so good that selectors often picked both, moving McLean further along the backline. On the 1981-82 Wallaby tour of Britain, Ella got two of the four tests.

In 1982 Dwyer became Wallaby coach and promoted the Ellas, dropping Queenslanders McLean and Roger Gould to clear the path. There followed a mass withdrawal of Queenslanders before the team to tour New Zealand shortly after was chosen. So Dwyer named Mark Ella, only 23, as captain and included his two brothers. Though the Australians lost the series 2-1, they played exciting rugby. The Ellas' consummate passing and mutual understanding reminded New Zealanders of the fabulous Going brothers of the 1970s. Their uncanny reading of each other's play brought suggestions of telepathic Aboriginal powers and when viewing some of their moves it was

Australia v New Zealand, Wellington, 1982 - Mark Ella's first test victory as Wallaby captain

Celebrating the 1984 Wallaby Grand Slam of test victories: from left, Mark Ella, David Campese and Andrew Slack.

hard to argue otherwise. Strangely, though Gary played six tests, Glen four and Mark 25, they never all appeared in the same test.

Alan Jones was the Wallaby coach when the team next toured Britain, in 1984. This was a superb combination, and included emerging stars Michael Lynagh, Nick Farr-Jones and David Campese. Lynagh played outside Ella. The Wallabies completed a Grand Slam of test victories and Ella scored tries in all of them. His play against Ireland, when he dropped goals with either foot and scored a critical try, was acclaimed as the finest of his career.

It says much for Ella that he played so well, despite having lost the test captaincy to Andrew Slack and having in Jones a coach he had little time for. As captain, Ella had led inexperienced teams without great scrumhalves and his record was not outstanding. He prospered when able to concentrate on his own game. On the return plane journey from Britain, Ella shocked Australian journalists by retiring. He'd already won the Order of Australia medal and been voted Young Australian of the Year, but it seemed a waste - there was much more good rugby in him. He was a player with marvellously soft hands, anticipation, speed off the mark and an almost supernatural ability to spot an opening. He was superb at putting his team-mates into a gap and seemed to turn up in unlikely places at the most opportune times. After passing the ball he invariably looped around the outside to support the attack. For me, Ella's passing was his trademark. He believed in short passes to create room out wide and would pass over and around opponents. He had reverse passes, cut-out passes and dummies.

Cyril Towers summed him up: "Ella runs from the shoulders down, with the fingers, hands and arms completely relaxed; he takes the ball on one side and passes before the foot comes down again; his concept of the flyhalf position is that it is semi-restricted - the attack must be further out. He is difficult to think against - if you think ahead of him he will slip inside, and it's no good thinking four or five moves ahead, because he hasn't invented them yet."

Ella resisted some big league offers. He made a brief return to club rugby in 1989 and has remained involved in other areas, coaching in Milan, doing TV commentaries, writing a newspaper column and working for the Australian Rugby Football Union. In 1998 he coached the Australian sevens team at the Commonwealth Games and he has ambitions to becoming Wallaby coach, although in December 1998, he resigned as national sevens coach.

He is a polished public speaker. I recall sitting alongside him at the New Zealand rugby awards dinner one year. He was nervous about having to speak in front of so many big names, but he soon won over the audience with his quietly-spoken, nonchalant manner and was extremely well-received. I have worked alongside Ella in the commentary box during the Hong Kong sevens and found him knowledgeable and an enjoyable companion. Tennis critics used to claim that Evonne Goolagong, the Aborigine star, played on natural ability and without great insight as to technique and tactics. There was an element of that in Ella, but he also showed that he had a sound grasp of rugby.

Ella has become an unofficial human rights activist for Aborigines and took an Aborigine cricket team to England.

He has a rare place in Australian sport. He enjoyed cult status as a player and when he was dropped there would be public outrage. Not only was he a dashing, dazzling player, but he was immensely entertaining. He was one of those rare individuals who could draw crowds. Terry Smith was right when he wrote that Ella was 'as indigenous to Australia as kangaroos, koala bears, Edna Everidge, Paul Hogan and a Foster's tinny'. 🏉

Australia's most capped flyhalves:		
64	Michael Lynagh	1984-95
25	Mark Ella	1980-84
21	Phil Hawthorne	1962-67
17	Paul McLean	1974-82
13*	Stephen Larkham	1998
11	Tommy Lawton Snr	1920-32
10	Neville Emery	1947-49
10	Arthur Summons	1958-59
* still playing		

JAN ELLIS

The Red Devil

IT WAS JAN ELLIS' red hair that first grabbed my attention when I watched the 1965 Springboks in New Zealand. Perhaps because I'd not seen many red-haired test rugby players, the 'Red Devil', as he was known, became a source of fascination for me. However, I soon forgot about the colour of his hair as the power and pace of his play became evident.

He was just 23 on that tour, and new to international rugby, but after a few slightly hesitant performances, improved dramatically and shone in a beaten Springbok team. He played all four tests and in his 16 tour matches, he scored nine tries. In his book on the tour, All Black fullback Don Clarke remarked on the young South African's dedication. Ellis was one of the hardest trainers in the Springbok side and left nothing to chance. 'His training methods were reflected in his play,' wrote Clarke, 'for he was a tireless worker and even in the last minutes of a match, he could still corner flag efficiently.'

I see that the *New Zealand Rugby Almanack* described Ellis as 1.85m (6ft 1in) and 98kg (15st 5lb), but he seemed bigger - perhaps he was still growing. Certainly over the next decade, he became one of the giants of the world rugby scene. Even now, I cannot recall having seen a faster flanker and he had a demoralising effect on opposition inside backs. In 1970, he and his equally brilliant partner, Piet Greyling, were rampant against the All Blacks and outplayed even great All Black flanker Ian Kirkpatrick.

Opponents of Ellis and Greyling (it is hard to separate them because like great fast bowlers in cricket, good flankers tend to hunt in pairs) used to stress that not only were they big and fast, but they were also constructive, more so perhaps than Hennie Muller, the famous South African loose forward of the late 1940s and early 50s. Eventually Ellis and Greyling played a record 24 tests together. For a dozen of those tests, they had another outstanding loose forward, Tommy Bedford, at No 8, a formidable trio if ever there was one. Like all good flankers, Ellis had a nose for a try. He scored 32 in his 74 appearances for his country.

Ellis grew up in far-flung South-West Africa (now Namibia), where the nearest rugby club was 60 miles away. This isolation proved little handicap and by his late teens he was clearly an international in the making, combining his size and co-ordination with the promise he'd shown as a junior athlete.

He was the only player from South-West Africa chosen for the 1965 tour of New Zealand, where his loping style of running, ball engulfed in one hand, captured the imagination.

Jacobus Hendrik Ellis
Flanker
Born: Brakpan, January 5, 1943
Test debut: South Africa v New Zealand, Wellington, July 31, 1965
Test career: 1965-76 (38 matches)
Test points: 21 (7 tries)
* Jointly (with Frik du Preez) held South African record for test appearances
* South Africa's most capped flanker

Jan Ellis' first test - South Africa v New Zealand, Wellington, 1965.

For several major series, Ellis was a benchmark player for Springbok sides. He didn't say much off the field, often preferring his own company, and was accused of being aloof. But there was an intensity about him that made it obvious he was focusing entirely on producing his best rugby. He made it a matter of pride to be first to a breakdown and had good ball-handling skills. In addition, he contributed far more in the scrums than did many flankers.

Ellis needed all his dedication for he played much of his rugby in a politically-charged atmosphere, never more so than on the Springboks' tour of Britain in 1969-70. It proved a frustrating time for Ellis, because in the second match he injured his shoulder and he missed half of the tour games. Even when he played, he sometimes struggled.

However, he stormed back to his best near the end of the tour, helping the Springboks draw 6-6 with Wales and then playing a blinder against the Barbarians at Twickenham. He scored two tries that day, the second of which ranks as one of the all-time great tries. From just inside the Barbarians' half, he grabbed the ball, zipped between Gareth Edwards and Barry John, dummied past J P R Williams and outpaced Mike Gibson to score what proved to be the winning try.

Then it was onto the 1970 series against the All Blacks, who hadn't been beaten for five years. As Colin Meads said, 'Ellis and Greyling exploded the myth in 1970 that All Black loose forwards were still the fastest in the world.' Fergie McCormick added: 'Ellis was all vitality and energy. He had so much get up and go, this bloke. He was a bloody nuisance, hounding away at Chris Laidlaw and Earle Kirton. Ellis and Greyling made us look like clodhoppers in getting to the loose ball.' There were many reasons South Africa won that series, but the two explosive Springbok flankers were certainly an important factor.

Ellis continued to represent South Africa with distinction even after Greyling's retirement. Finally, aged 33, he was dropped from the Springbok side after the first test against the 1976 All Blacks. By then he had slowed down noticeably and was clearly past his best. It was a sad end for such a great player, but by then his niche in South African rugby history was secure. More than two decades after his retirement, his is still a revered name in South Africa. 🏉

Flankers who have played the most tests:		
65	Fergus Slattery (Ireland/British Isles)	1970-84
65	Peter Winterbottom (England/British Isles)	1982-93
60*	David Wilson (Australia)	1992-98
59	Jean-Pierre Rives (France)	1975-84
59	Simon Poidevin (Australia)	1980-91
54*	Michael Jones (New Zealand)	1986-98
51*	Massimo Giavanelli (Italy)	1989-99
49	Noel Murphy (Ireland/British Isles)	1958-69
49	Laurent Cabannes (France)	1990-97
46	Jean-Claude Skrela (France)	1971-78
44*	Philippe Benetton (France)	1989-99
44	Tony Neary (England/British Isles)	1971-80
40	John Jeffrey (Scotland)	1984-91
38	Jan Ellis (South Africa)	1965-76
* still playing		

IEUAN EVANS

Try, Try and Try Again

HOW IEUAN EVANS would have prospered playing for the mighty Welsh sides of the 1970s. Instead, fate decreed he would fill the right wing position for Wales from 1987-97, the most dismal period in his country's rugby history.

As it was, Evans compiled a marvellous record. As he approached his 34th birthday, he was forced into international retirement because of injury, but by then he held virtually every Welsh test and club record worth having and had led Wales to a Five Nations Victory in 1994 - a rare bright spot in a gloomy decade.

When I recall Evans' fine play for the Lions, I wonder what his impact would have been if he'd played in a national side that was dominating world rugby, instead of providing canon fodder for leading teams. As another great winger, Gerald Davies, said on Evans' retirement: 'Ieuan would have shone in any generation of Welsh rugby.'

Evans' father, John, played for Aberavon and it wasn't long before Ieuan was showing unusual promise. At 1.78m (5ft 10in) and 85kg (13st 5lb), Evans grew into a solidly-built young man, but had a sprinter's speed and an insatiable appetite for try-scoring. He attended Salford University, gaining a BA in geography (and later an honorary MA), and at the same time established his position in Welsh rugby.

His test debut was not propitious - a 16-9 defeat by France - but he'd already made his name with a six-try effort against Spain for Wales B at Bridgend in 1985.

At the inaugural World Cup, Evans captured headlines by scoring a Welsh record-equalling four tries in the 40-9 win over Canada at Invercargill (the world's southernmost city). It was to be a rare moment of sunshine for Evans in Welsh colours.

There followed:
* A 49-6 hammering by New Zealand in the 1987 World Cup semis.
* The 1988 team's whitewash tour of New Zealand, where the tests were lost   52-3 and 54-9.
* Hugh defeats by New South Wales (71-8) and Australia (63-6) in 1991.
* A sad 16-13 defeat by Western Samoa at the 1991 World Cup.
* A 34-9 thumping by New Zealand at the 1995 World Cup.

Off-setting these disasters were a Triple Crown in 1988, the Five Nations title in 1994 and precious little else.

Ieuan Cenydd Evans
Winger
Born: Pontardulais, March 21, 1964
Test debut: Wales v France, Paris, February 7, 1987
Test career: 1987-98 (79 matches - 72 for Wales, 7 for British Isles)
Test points: 157 (34 tries)
* Led Wales a record 28 times in tests
* Has played most tests for Wales
* Holds the Welsh test try-scoring record

A mark of how soul-destroying life could be with Wales is that his two tries accounted for two-thirds of the entire Welsh try tally for the 1992-93 Five Nations season. One of them was critical, though - his try against England at Cardiff turned likely defeat into a 10-9 victory and made him a national hero for life. Despite Wales' fluctuating results, Evans soldiered on, showing pride and commitment despite a run of shocking injuries. He had to cope with a recurring dislocated shoulder that required two operations, a serious ankle injury and, in 1994, a broken left leg.

Some of his best days were with the Lions. He pounced on an error by David Campese to score the winning try in the third test decider against Australia at Sydney in 1989. He played with distinction throughout the 1993 tour of New Zealand and, before returning home with a groin injury, was a senior member of the 1997 side that beat the Springboks.

While the northern English league clubs decimated Welsh rugby, contracting players like Jonathan Davies, Scott Quinnell and many others, Evans stayed loyal, despite the results of the national team. He was a stalwart member of the Llanelli club for 13 seasons. He scored the winning try as Llanelli beat Australia 13-9 in 1992 and helped the Scarlets complete the League/Cup double in 1992-93. Evans played a record 230 games for Llanelli and scored 193 tries, making seven Cup final appearances for the club. He was the first player to score 50 tries in Welsh league matches.

In 1991, he became captain of Wales. Few of his predecessors had as difficult an assignment, yet Evans was an inspiring figure and captained the side effectively, even from way out on the wing. Along the way to his try-scoring record, Evans passed some famous figures. During the qualifying games for the 1995 World Cup, he indulged in a try splurge against Romania, Portugal and Spain and zipped past first Arthur 'Monkey' Gould, then joint record-holders Gerald Davies and Gareth Edwards. By the time he retired, in early 1998, he had added 13 tries to the Welsh record of 20 that Davies and Edwards had held since the 1970s. With his one try for the British Lions, his total test tally of 34 placed him fifth on the world list when he retired.

Evans belongs alongside these celebrated names. With his pace and acceleration, plus a nifty sidestep, he was difficult to stop and had an eye for the slightest chance of a try. He encountered some of the most famous wingers in rugby history, including John Kirwan, David Campese and Rory Underwood, and was seldom bettered. He was a sturdy defender who set an example his team-mates sometimes neglected to follow.

Though usually on the losing side, Evans, ever modest and pleasant, played consistently well in New Zealand. I recall, especially, his try for the 1993 Lions against the New Zealand Maoris at Athletic Park. For the third test in 1993, at Eden Park, I was working on the sideline and got a close-up look at Evans' speed and determination as he thundered past me. It was a telling reminder of the force needed to play at the top level.

Ian McGeechan summed him up accurately by saying: "He was one of the outstanding wingers of the last decade. He was always a great threat to the world's best defences and, on top of that, was an outstanding ambassador. It is the respect he had outside Wales when Welsh rugby wasn't at its strongest that made him stand apart."

Near the end of his career, Evans signed a two-year contract worth £75,000 with English club Bath and helped them win the 1998 European Cup. He continued to work as a finance company business development executive, ensuring he had a career to move into when his rugby days were over.

The top 10 Welsh test caps	
72	Ieuan Evans (1987-98)
64*	Neil Jenkins (1991-99)
62*	Gareth Llewellyn (1989-98)
55	John (JPR) Williams (1969-81)
54	Robert Jones (1986-95)
53	Gareth Edwards (1967-78)
46	Gerald Davies (1966-78)
46	Phil Davies (1985-95)
44	Ken Jones (1947-57)
42	Mike Hall (1988-95)

* still playing
Excludes test matches for the British Isles.

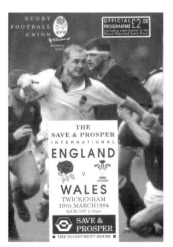

Ieuan Evans captained Wales to the Five Nations Championship in 1994.

NICK FARR-JONES

He Brought the Cup Home

NICK FARR-JONES, great scrumhalf though he was, never forgot rugby was to be enjoyed. Along with coach Bob Dwyer, he was responsible for the worldwide popularity of the Wallabies in the early 1990s.

During the 1991 World Cup, the open and friendly Australians built such a following that their semi-final against New Zealand in Dublin was like a home game for them. In the final, Australia ventured to Twickenham and beat England. Their attractive tactics and approachability won much praise even from English supporters.

If the theory that every dog looks like its master can be applied to rugby, then Farr-Jones deserves credit for this. The All Blacks under coach Alex Wyllie and captains Wayne Shelford and Gary Whetton were tough-talking and tough-drinking. Under Laurie Mains and Sean Fitzpatrick they were introverted and suspicious. Under John Hart and Fitzpatrick and then Taine Randell, they became noticeably more open and friendly.

Through the 1991 World Cup, Dwyer and Farr-Jones were incredibly receptive to the media. Farr-Jones' laid-back attitude at times irritated former Wallaby coach Alan Jones, but did his team a power of good. Not that Farr-Jones was a pushover. I'd heard that as a youngster he had a hot temper, and on a couple of occasions saw examples of this as he either rounded in on a journalist or simply walked away during an interview if he felt the questions were not worthy of serious consideration.

Farr-Jones was always his own man. As captain he discussed the thorny issues of professionalism and South Africa's re-emergence with maturity and insight, and he introduced a new regime in the Wallaby camp. Early in his captaincy, he turned up in the dressing room after a test against the All Blacks with his wife and baby, which raised a few eyebrows but signalled a new era.

Above everything, though, Farr-Jones had wonderful skills as a scrumhalf and was a worthy successor to great Wallaby scrumhalves Des Connor, Ken Catchpole and John Hipwell. By the late 1980s, he was acknowledged as the best in the world.

At 1.78m (5ft 10in) and 84kg (13st 2lb), Farr-Jones was on the big side for a scrumhalf, built more like a loose forward, and operated like an extra flanker. He was a good all-rounder - competitive, aggressive, a strong runner, a long passer and an inveterate talker. He seemed to steer his team around the field, urging his forwards to greater endeavours, marshalling his backs,

---

Nicholas Campbell Farr-Jones
Scrumhalf
Born: Sydney, April 18, 1962
Test debut: Australia v England, Twickenham, November 3, 1984
Test career: 1984-93 (63 matches)
Test points: 37 (9 tries)
* Captained Australia a record 36 times
* His 62 tests as a scrumhalf is a world record for one country
* Farr-Jones and Michael Lynagh played 47 tests together, the world record for any positional combination in test rugby

Players who captained their sides in the most tests:

59	Will Carling (England)
51	Sean Fitzpatrick (New Zealand)
43	Hugo Porta (Argentina and South America)
36	Nick Farr-Jones (Australia)
34	Jean-Pierre Rives (France)
34	Philippe Saint Andre (France)
33*	Gary Teichmann (South Africa)
33*	John Eales (Australia)

* still playing

Nick Farr-Jones' greatest moment. The match programme for the Rugby World Cup final, Australia v England, 1991.

calling the plays and always looking to use the blindside.

His particular flair was in reading the game and switching tactics midstream when necessary. He played in contact lenses and was short-sighted, but there was nothing myopic about his play. His vision and flair were inspirational.

I have fond memories of Farr-Jones, not just as a player. He was a tour group leader in South Africa during the 1995 World Cup, when he was also a television commentator. As a tour leader he was immensely popular. He socialised extensively with his group and was most generous.

As a commentator, he was astute and frank. He was at Cape Town to call the quarter-final between Australia and England and had to work hard to remain unobjective as Australia were pipped 25-22. Then, while the many Australian supporters trooped out of the stadium to drown their sorrows or analyse the disaster, Farr-Jones stayed behind to co-commentate the following match, New Zealand v Scotland at Pretoria, off a monitor. After the excitement of the preceding hours, there were only the two commentators left inside the vast Newlands stadium. It must have been an eerie experience.

As a youngster in Sydney, Farr-Jones shone at a variety of sports from swimming and athletics to cricket and surfing, but didn't appeal as a potential rugby star. He could not make the Newington College First XV, being deemed too small.

His rugby stocks rose when he became a boarder and law student at Sydney University's St Andrews College and worked with former Wallaby coach Dave Brockhoff, whom he regards as one of the great influences on his career. By 1984 he had caught the eye of the eloquent and unconventional Alan Jones, who selected him for a short tour of Fiji and then for the end-of-year tour of Britain.

In Britain, Farr-Jones and Jones developed a curious relationship. The player received more than one dressing down for keeping late hours and having less than his entire focus on rugby. However, his skills were undeniable and he was elevated above the smaller Phillip Cox as Australia's first-choice scrumhalf, playing all four tests and forging a strong partnership with flyhalf Mark Ella.

The Australians achieved the Grand Slam of test victories and Farr-Jones admitted later he was surprised how easy it was. Having the brilliant Ella there must have helped. Once, asked how he wanted the ball, Ella replied: "Just chuck it out. Good ball, bad ball, I'll be there."

Thereafter, Farr-Jones' career was really one long success story. The next highpoint, after the Grand Slam tour, was the 1986 2-1 away series win over the All Blacks. He struggled with injury through the 1987 World Cup, but the following year was chosen by Bob Dwyer as the Wallaby captain, ahead of the more experienced Simon Poidevin.

With their eyes on the 1991 World Cup, Farr-Jones and Dwyer built Australia's stocks. They were assisted by the presence of Michael Lynagh, who stepped comfortably into the flyhalf role when Ella retired prematurely. Lynagh was an excellent goal-kicker and he and Farr-Jones went on to set the world record for the most tests together as a scrumhalf/flyhalf combination.

Farr-Jones was hindered by injury during the 1991 World Cup. He suffered agonies when, having left the field during Australia's quarter-final against Ireland, he watched his team pull back from the brink with a last-minute try by Lynagh. But Farr-Jones was back to lead the Australians past New Zealand

and England and became only the second captain to hold aloft the Webb Ellis Trophy.

In 1992 Australia confirmed their status by beating New Zealand 2-1, then set their sights on the Springboks. There had been sniggers from South Africa that Australia could not really call themselves the best as they had not beaten the Springboks. In 1992, New Zealand edged out South Africa 27-24 at Johannesburg. Then a fortnight later the Wallabies smashed the Springboks 26-3, their heaviest defeat in a century, conclusively ending any debate about their right to be called world champions.

Farr-Jones retired, but returned to the test fray in 1993 when his successor Peter Slattery injured his hand and helped the Wallabies beat South Africa at home. Then he was prevailed upon to play against New Zealand at Dunedin. It was not such a happy match. His form was only reasonable and Australia were well beaten.

His 62 tests at scrumhalf (there was also one as a replacement winger) was a world record for a scrumhalf for one country and his 36 tests as Australian captain was also a record.

Though he had a remarkably full career, Farr-Jones found time to qualify and practise as a lawyer. He became heavily in demand as a guest speaker and, especially after the 1991 World Cup, was a huge celebrity at home.

Typically for a man who was ever the individual, he based himself in Paris for much of the 1990s. He was keen to live his life as Nick Farr-Jones, rather than Farr-Jones the Wallaby, and was beginning to find the rugby-associated fame in Australia cloying. **100**

SEAN FITZPATRICK

Twelve Seasons at the Top

Sean Brian Thomas Fitzpatrick

Hooker

Born: Auckland, June 4, 1963

Test debut: New Zealand v France, June 28, 1986

Test career: 1986-97 (92 matches)

Test points: 55 (12 tries)

* His 92 tests is the most by a New Zealander and the world record for a forward
* Played a world record 63 consecutive tests
* Played 128 matches for New Zealand, second to Colin Meads' 133
* Played 347 first-class matches, second in the New Zealand lists to Meads' 361
* Captained New Zealand in 51 tests. Only Wilson Whineray (30) had previously led his country in more than 19

AFTER I'D DONE some promotional work with Sean Fitzpatrick in 1998, he drove me to his home in an exclusive Auckland suburb. As we approached his impressive-looking house in his large sports car, he looked at the carpenters working on his neighbour's property and said with feeling, "That could have been me." Fitzpatrick's simple statement summed up what rugby has done for him.

He was an All Black for 12 seasons, developing markedly as a player and a person. He did so well from rugby that he was able to change his career in midstream. A carpenter by trade, these days he is a marketing executive with Coca-Cola and is associated with several other companies. As befits his status in New Zealand, he is in demand for television ads, commercial endorsements and public speaking engagements.

Fitzpatrick is the classic example of someone who has taken his chances. He was born into a rugby family - his father, Brian, was an All Black second five-eighth in the early 1950s. Through his teenage years, Fitzpatrick enjoyed consistent sports success. He was in the Sacred Heart College cricket First XI for four years and a prop/hooker in the First XV, representing New Zealand secondary schools at rugby in 1981.

I first saw him in 1981 when former All Black Grahame Thorne pointed to a chunky-looking teenager and said he was 'B B J's boy', B B J being Brian Fitzpatrick. In later years, Brian came to be described as Sean's father.

His Auckland debut came in 1984, but it was a harsh introduction. On Auckland's world tour that year, Fitzpatrick ran foul of lineout specialist Andy Haden. At training once, he threw the ball into the lineout, but not where Haden wanted, and was invited to do better. Again Fitzpatrick threw inaccurately. "You're no good," said Haden. "Abo [hooker Iain Abercrombie], you're in."

Auckland coach John Hart took Fitzpatrick aside soon after and spelt out two home truths: he would not become a regular for Auckland unless he improved his lineout throwing and stopped conceding penalties.

Fitzpatrick heeded the advice. He was to spend countless hours practising his throwing. "I equated myself to Grant Fox. He practised kicking as well as general play, and I practised throwing." Eventually Fitzpatrick became a brilliant thrower into lineouts.

The penalties problem was also solved. In his early years Fitzpatrick was

aggressive, niggling, physical and sometimes headstrong. He remained a constantly rasping thorn in his opposition's side, but became more canny. He learned to rile opponents without incurring the referee's wrath. He was always a talker on the field. Wallaby hooker Phil Kearns, described Fitzpatrick as 'the world's best referee'.

In 1986 Fitzpatrick was still Abercrombie's deputy for Auckland. Then the Cavaliers went to South Africa, defying their national union, and were suspended for two tests. All Black coach Brian Lochore selected Bruce Hemara as his test hooker against France. When Hemara popped his rib cartilage, Fitzpatrick was called up, leap-frogging Abercrombie. It was the first of several strokes of good fortune for the Aucklander.

When the Cavaliers became eligible again, Fitzpatrick was dropped for

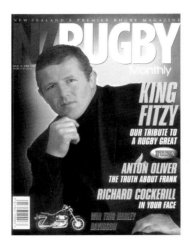

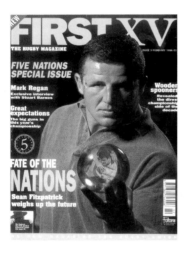

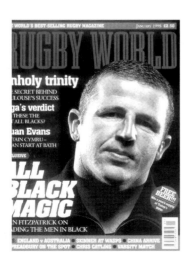

Sean Fitzpatrick: a superstar around the world.

Hika Reid. But he continued to impress with his strength, bullocking play, all-round ball skills, composure and attitude. He was named as Andy Dalton's deputy for the 1987 World Cup. Then, a second slice of luck. Dalton pulled his hamstring before the tournament opener and Fitzpatrick was promoted. Dalton never recovered and Fitzpatrick retained his place … for the next decade. He played above himself during that World Cup, then shortly after when the All Blacks won a tough Bledisloe Cup match in Sydney, scored two tries.

Fitzpatrick wasn't the first hooker to become a pseudo-loose forward. But he developed a special ability to turn up on the blindside wing and storm across for tries. Opposing wingers didn't fancy having the 1.83m (6ft) 106kg (16st 9lb) Fitzpatrick charging at them.

He had a third lucky break in 1992. By then he was the world's best hooker. He'd been part of the champion 1987 World Cup team and was a big name in the brilliant Auckland side, but had suffered the disappointment of a flawed 1991 World Cup campaign. He contemplated retirement, but lingered to see if he might regain his enthusiasm under new coach Laurie Mains. In the final trial at Napier, Mike Brewer, Mains' choice as All Black captain, injured his leg. Faced with having to find a new captain within an hour, Mains opted for Fitzpatrick.

At that stage, Fitzpatrick was no national celebrity. TVNZ had a studio set up at the ground for the live crossover to interview the new captain. When Fitzpatrick's name was announced, one of the TV crew was dispatched to fetch him and came back holding the arm of a puzzled Steve McDowell.

The captaincy changed Fitzpatrick's life. During the six years he led the All Blacks, he matured and became a more endearing personality. Earlier he was one of the Aucklanders who had formed a strong clique in the All Blacks. He was prickly towards me because I'd praised his early rival, Hika Reid, as having played the three outstanding games as hooker for the All Blacks during the 1980s.

He improved every year as a captain, his greatest achievement being to lead the All Blacks to a series win in South Africa in 1996. By the end, he was an accomplished leader. He was uncompromising on the field and became a humorous and diplomatic interview subject. His well-worn phrase 'full credit to the opposition' became famous nationally, as did his analysis that it had been 'a game of two halves'.

Despite his belligerence on the field, he suffered from slight insecurity. He has told me about his early uncertainties as an All Black and when he was appointed captain. He began his test captaincy with a loss to a World XV and it flicked through his mind that he hoped something would happen to take the leadership off him.

He was described by no less a judge than Terry McLean as 'a dirty player'. Early in his career, I said during a radio debate that Fitzpatrick would have 'stomped on his granny' to get the ball. One prominent Auckland referee says that if he ever saw Fitzpatrick bleeding 'you could feel no sympathy for him, as he would have dished it out tenfold along the way'.

But he could take punishment, too. In 1992, Irish hooker Steve Smith broke two of his teeth at Athletic Park and in 1994, Springbok Johan Le Roux chewed his ear on the same ground. The All Blacks undoubtedly suffered food poisoning before the 1995 World Cup final, but Fitzpatrick seemed uneasy afterwards about statements by coach Laurie Mains that the poisoning had been deliberate. The strongest reply I've ever heard him give to such a suggestion was, "You'll have to ask Laurie about that."

He was a great trainer and incredibly durable, virtually never leaving the field during a test. Until his dicky knee affected his farewell tour at the end of 1997, injury never prevented him from being available for the All Blacks. In his last test, in November, 1997, when he virtually limped onto Wembley to replace Norm Hewitt, he was 34 years, 178 days old.

Fitzpatrick was never challenged for his All Black spot. His one sub-standard match was the second test against the Lions in Wellington in 1993, and it was interesting to see his response to criticism of his performance. I was a TV producer that season, and for the third test positioned my cameraman, Roger Duncan, near the 22-metre line to shoot close-up action. I stood alongside Roger, the closest I have been to a test. You could hear the bones crack! The All Blacks played superbly. At one point, they came rushing towards our camera and tumbled across the touchline in front of us. It was the end of another furious passing sequence that had involved Fitzpatrick. As he marched back onto the field of play, he passed right by me. He paused, then snapped at me through gritted teeth: "Is this good enough for you?"

The Aucklander set a formidable array of All Black records. His 92 tests (for 74 wins) is the New Zealand record, but for me the statistic which sums up his value is his sequence of 63 consecutive tests, a series broken only when he stood down for the 1995 World Cup pool match against Japan.

Fitzpatrick made other contributions to New Zealand rugby, including his leading role in the pro rugby contract negotiations in 1995, when he successfully argued that the All Black captain should have another $50,000 tacked onto his salary. And though few would have credited it at the start of his career, he became a unifying influence in rugby, illustrated by the way he was equally close to bitter rivals Mains and John Hart during their tenures as All Black coach. By the time he retired, he was a national icon.

It was a back-handed compliment to Fitzpatrick that he was a figure of scorn and derision in South Africa, where he said he feared for his life, and Australia. Ian McIntosh, the Springbok coach, shared a speaking engagement with Fitzpatrick and showed a nice touch of black humour. McIntosh was the first speaker to address the hundreds gathered and said, "You South Africans are priceless. When Fitzy was playing, all of South Africa was telling him to shut up. Now you are here paying money to hear him talk!"

Spectators in those countries fully understood the influence he exerted on a game. But he was always well-received in France. One day in Toulouse, the All Black team arrived at the Stade Municipal venue before kick-off and wandered onto the field to savour the atmosphere. The local crowd welcomed them with a shout, then roared their approval when the French side arrived. After the teams left the field, Fitzpatrick stayed to have a final check of the breeze. I watched as he finally walked to the tunnel. A huge burst of applause rose from the crowd, and swelled ever stronger. Fitzpatrick looked around, expecting to see a local dignitary arriving. At the last moment, just before ducking into the tunnel, he realised the ovation was for him, gave a faint wave of recognition and was gone.

His career spanned many changes in rugby, from the amateur days to the era of great wealth for leading players. He began in the pre-World Cup period, but played in three World Cups. During his career, the laws of the game changed significantly and his game evolved accordingly. He made his All Black debut with Joe Stanley and made his final All Black tour with Stanley's son, Jeremy, as a team-mate. **100**

When I interviewed Sean Fitzpatrick on television after the All Blacks' test win over the Wallabies in Melbourne in 1997, I called him the 'winningest' test rugby player of all time. Quite rightly he winced at the choice of such an Americanised intrusion into rugby commentary. Nevertheless his record stands. His career win/loss record over the various test opponents is:

Opponent	Played	Won	Lost	Drew
Argentina	7	7	0	0
Australia	24	16	7	1
British Isles	3	2	1	0
Canada	2	2	0	0
England	3	2	1	0
France	12	8	4	0
Fiji	2	2	0	0
Ireland	4	4	0	0
Italy	3	3	0	0
Scotland	8	8	0	0
South Africa	12	9	2	1
Wales	6	6	0	0
Western Samoa	2	2	0	0
World XV	3	2	1	0
USA	1	1	0	0
	92	**74**	**16**	**2**

GRANT FOX

Points-scoring Genius

Grant James Fox
First five-eighth
Born: New Plymouth, June 16, 1962
Test debut: New Zealand v Argentina, Buenos Aires, October 26, 1985
Test career: 1985-93 (46 matches)
Test points: 645 (1 try, 118 conversions, 128 penalties, 7 drop goals)
* His test points tally is the New Zealand record
* His 1067 points for New Zealand is the record
* Scored 20 or more points in a test nine times
* Is New Zealand's most capped first five-eighth
* His 4112 points in 303 matches is the New Zealand first-class record

GRANT FOX WAS PERHAPS the greatest match-winner in All Black history. Strange, then, that his play often earned only grudging praise. No-one quibbled with his goal-kicking accuracy, but his general play at first five-eighth was not as universally acclaimed.

I didn't go along with that thinking. Obviously his fabulous kicking boot was a factor in his test selection, but he was a very sound player. Early in his career, it became a national discussion point as to whether the All Black selectors should be choosing the safety-first Fox or the brilliant Frano Botica. Similar arguments have raged elsewhere: Australians debated the merits of Mark Ella and Paul McLean, Englishmen were divided over Rob Andrew and Stuart Barnes.

Fox's critics overlooked his many attributes. Though he had lovely balance, he wasn't a runner to compare with Ella or Botica, so developed other skills. His passing - especially the skip pass - was outstanding, and his tactical kicking, touch-finding and drop-outs from set play were amazingly accurate, while his snow-capped up-and-unders put even the bravest opposing fullbacks under intense scrutiny.

But Fox really scored in his vision and ability to read a game. He knew when a move was 'on' out wide and how to take advantage. If the opposition defence was disorganised, Fox took advantage. He was much more than just a kicking first-five. For instance, Fox's timing and reading of a game made John Gallagher a force as a running fullback in the late 1980s. Wingers like John Kirwan and Terry Wright enjoyed a feast of good possession outside the man Wayne Shelford dubbed 'The Little General'.

Fox was a great talker on the field, organising and calling moves. At 1.75m and 75kg, he was on the small side and was not a frequent tackler, though he did the job when required.

Though Fox was born in New Plymouth, he is an Aucklander through and through. He made a big impression at Auckland Grammar, where he was in the First XV for three years and shone at cricket. In 1980 Fox captained the New Zealand Secondary Schools rugby team in Australia. By 1982 he was playing impressively for Auckland and the New Zealand Colts.

He was obviously a future All Black. His poise and tactical understanding were there for all to see. And always there was that magical kicking boot. In 1984 he became the first player to exceed 300 points in a New Zealand season.

Fox first played for New Zealand in Fiji in 1984, against a President's XV. However his first home game for the All Blacks didn't come until the 1987 World Cup. He made his test debut in 1985 in the first test against Argentina at Buenos Aires, though fullback Kieran Crowley did the goal-kicking duties. Fox did manage a drop goal, which became statistically important later as Fox was to score in all 46 of his tests.

After touring South Africa with the rebel Cavaliers in 1986, Fox was unable to displace Botica in the test side in France later in the year. Their rivalry continued until Botica switched to rugby league in 1990, though Fox had forged ahead in their personal rivalry by then.

Fox had a magnificent 1987 World

Grant Fox's first class career:

	Matches	Tries	Con	Pen	DG	Total
Auckland	189	25	613	441	31	2746
NZ (tests)	46	1	118	128	7	645
NZ (other)	32	1	107	64	4	422
Others	36	2	63	50	5	299
	303	29	901	683	47	4112

Grant Fox's highest points tallies in tests:

26	v Fiji, 1987	(10 conversions, 2 penalties)
25	v Western Samoa, 1993	(2 conversions, 7 penalties)
22	v Italy, 1987	(8 conversions, 2 penalties)
22	v Argentina, 1987	(2 conversions, 6 penalties)
22	v Scotland, 1987	(2 conversions, 6 penalties)
22	v Wales, 1988	(8 conversions, 2 penalties)
22	v France, 1990	(2 conversions, 6 penalties)

The match programme from Grant Fox's most successful day as a kicker, New Zealand v Wales, Auckland, 1988. He landed 10 from 10.

Cup. His tournament tally of 126 points was easily the highest, and he set test records for most conversions (10 against Fiji) and most penalties (six against Australia and Scotland). He contributed 17 points in New Zealand's 29-9 victory over France in the final.

All Black coach John Hart dabbled with Botica while in Japan in 1987 and Laurie Mains replaced Fox with Walter Little for four tests in 1992, but both selectors soon reverted to Fox. The All Blacks felt a lot more secure having him in their side. In 1989, he collided with Matthew Ridge during an All Black practice in Wales and missed three successive matches. Botica filled in superbly but, when he was fit, Fox was restored to the top lineup.

Fox played in an era when the All Blacks were rampant, but if they did get into trouble, he generally rescued them. In the second test against Scotland in 1990, New Zealand conceded more tries than they scored for the first time in Fox's career, but Fox, with five penalties and a conversion from six attempts, saw them home. In 1992, the All Blacks were heading for defeat in the third test against Australia, and a series whitewash, until Fox dropped a goal six minutes from time.

His kicking accuracy was no fluke. He spent countless hours practising and eventually added many metres to his place-kicking. New Zealanders soon became familiar with his kicking routine. After the methodical, slow walk to the top of his run-up, he'd wiggle his fingers - to shake out the last remnants of nerves - then run in and let fly, placing his faith in the hours of practice. Often it took him a full minute to complete his kick. On nearly a dozen occasions, he went through a test without missing a kick.

Fox played against some great flyhalves. On his test debut, he was matched against the incomparable Hugo Porta and later he lined up against Michael Lynagh and Rob Andrew. Though he wasn't as good an all-rounder as Lynagh or Porta, the average New Zealand bloke would have taken Fox over anyone. We came to admire his reliability and were always happy to have him in the No 10 jersey.

He played through the 1991 World Cup with an injury, electing not to publicise it. While his form was still good, he was not at his peak and it was felt his career might be winding down. But he fought back after Mains dropped him the following year, giving another season of top service to the All Blacks.

When he departed, there wasn't a major New Zealand points-scoring record Fox didn't own. Aided by the artificial leather ball and kicking off a tee, Fox set records in Ranfurly Shield play, for Auckland, New Zealand and in tests.

Fox, who heads an Auckland sports marketing firm, now works in the Television New Zealand commentary box where I've come to appreciate why he was such a great kicker. At Melbourne during the 1997 Bledisloe Cup match, he said: "It's good to play at night because you can see something behind the goal posts in the stand. A kicker will look for a light high in the grandstand and will focus on that light, not the posts." He talks about how to judge the wind, angles of approach and so on, and has given viewers an insight into the science of place-kicking.

As a player, Fox regarded the media with suspicion. He was outspoken and had strong opinions, but was rather intense and took criticism to heart. As a commentator, he remains serious about his rugby. He does not criticise lightly, but if he prefaces his remarks with, "I've gotta say ...", viewers know Fox is about to offer some less than complimentary comments about the players or the referee. **100**

DANIE GERBER

Midfield Strength

DANIE GERBER scored tries, buckets of them. The powerful Springbok centre, whose career spanned the years of South Africa's international rugby isolation, made an impression on virtually every team he encountered. When his test career ended in 1992, he held the South African test try-scoring record and was regarded as one of the finest players of his generation.

Gerber wasn't as big as the famous Springbok centre of the 1960s, John Gainsford, but at 1.83m (6ft) and nearly 89kg (14st), took a lot of stopping. He had all the attributes of a class centre but his capacity for scoring tries made him special. With his thick, piston-like thighs, he was quick off the mark, could hold his speed and he had a nose for a try. Gerber, always the most urgent of players, proved a real menace from broken play.

It says much for Gerber that though he played when the Springboks generally had to make do with series against South American combinations and rebel teams like the Cavaliers and the South Seas Barbarians, he was still acknowledged as one of the world's best.

But then Gerber was always destined to be a champion. While at school in Despatch, near Port Elizabeth, he was so impressive that he became one of the rare few to represent South African schools three years in succession, captaining them in 1977.

He played well for Eastern Province from the moment he made his debut in 1978, but had to wait until late in 1980, when he was 22, to get a sniff of test rugby. South Africa had two fine centres, Willie du Plessis and David Smith, who initially kept Gerber off the international scene. However, in two matches against Bill Beaumont's 1980 Lions, for Orange Free State and the Junior Springboks, he showed he was a player of the future.

Gerber toured South America with the 1980 Springboks, scoring six tries in five matches. He played both tests against the Jaguars, at Montevideo and Santiago, scoring tries in each. After that, he was a front-line player for the next decade.

Wherever he went, he scored tries. In 1981 he notched up two against Ireland at Newlands, one of them sensational. From near halfway, he cut back inside the Irish defence, stepping past Fergus Slattery and Willie Duggan, then jinked and side-stepped his way to score under the posts. Gerber rates this as his best moment in rugby.

New Zealanders saw Gerber during the stormy 1981 Springbok tour. He

---

Daniel Mattheus Gerber
Centre
Born: Port Elizabeth, April 14, 1958
Test debut: South Africa v South America, Montivideo, October 18, 1980
Test career: 1980-92 (24 matches)
Test points: 82 (19 tries, 1 conversion)
* Held South African test try-scoring record
* Scored three tries against England at Johannesburg in 1984

Players who have held the South African test try-scoring record:

Tries		Period	Year record was set
2	Theo Samuels	1896	1896
3	Bob Loubser	1903-10	1906
5	Jan Stegmann	1912-13	1912
6	Boetie McHardy	1912-13	1913
7	Ferdie Bergh	1931-38	1937
8	John Gainsford	1960-67	1965
8	Jannie Engelbrecht	1960-69	1969
12	Gerrie Germishuys	1974-81	1980
19	Danie Gerber	1980-92	1984
20	James Small	1992-97	1997
25	Joost van der Westhuizen	1993-98	1998

played all three tests and, with Naas Botha, was one of the stars of the side. It was a tight series and there wasn't the opportunity for Gerber to do much more than tackle hard and feed his wingers. It was a compliment to him that the All Blacks marked him closely at all times.

Elsewhere he continued to score sublime tries, three against the Jaguars at Bloemfontein in 1982 and then, even more remarkably, a hat-trick within 18 minutes to help South Africa beat John Scott's England side 35-9 at Ellis Park in 1984.

When the New Zealand Cavaliers toured in 1986, Gerber played in all four tests. In the decisive third test, he broke an 18-18 deadlock 10 minutes from time with a magnificent try. He touched the ball twice in a sweeping 80m movement and outpaced and out-thought the Cavaliers' defence in his final 25m run.

Gerber shone on other rugby stages, too. In 1983 he had two matches in Britain for the Barbarians, scoring two tries against Scotland and really turning on the magic with a four-try virtuoso display against Cardiff. The following year, playing for a President's XV as part of the 75th anniversary celebrations of the Twickenham ground, he scored the mandatory try. In South Africa he was named 1984 Player of the Year. In the first test against Argentina that year, he doubled as the place-kicker, landing one conversion.

He was one of five South African players invited in 1986 to celebrate the centenary of the International Rugby Board. At Twickenham Gerber scored two tries to help the Overseas Unions beat the Five Nations 32-13 and was acclaimed by some English critics as the world's best centre. This tied in with the assessment of the *Rothmans Rugby Union Yearbook* which in 1984 had named Gerber as one of the two South Africans, along with Morne du Plessis, in its team of the decade.

But as the international boycott of South Africa bit, players like Gerber ran out of international opportunities. By 1992, when South Africa was readmitted to the test arena, Gerber was 34, but was selected for the Springboks against Australia and New Zealand. He reminded the All Blacks of his class by contributing two tries, even though he was in a side that was outplayed.

The Springboks toured France and England at the end of 1992 and Gerber, on his farewell tour, scored tries in both tests of the split series with France. He closed out his test career against England when South Africa went down 33-16.

His 19 tries (in only 24 tests) was the South African record, which until his arrival had belonged to Gerrie Germishuys with 12. He held the mark until James Small surpassed it in 1997. But Gerber was more than a brilliant individualist and formed potent midfield combinations with both du Plessis brothers, Willie and Michael, with whom he played a total of 14 tests.

Gerber was a big figure on the domestic scene as well. He played mainly for Eastern Province, for whom he made well over a century of appearances, though he had a short stint for Orange Free State in 1980 while doing army training at Tempe. In 1990 he represented Western Province, appearing at

Danie Gerber scored yet another try for South Africa against the Cavaliers, Pretoria, 1986.

wing, flyhalf, centre and fullback, but then resumed playing for Eastern Province, even when living in Cape Town.

Eastern Province is the only major province which has never won the Currie Cup, but Gerber remained their most staunch supporter. Similarly, he was a loyal member of the Despatch team which won national club titles twice in the 1980s. Gerber was sorely tempted by a lucrative league offer from Wigan in 1985, and his love of home was one of the factors which influenced his decision to stick with rugby union.

He did, however, play for Italian team L'Aquila in 1994, helping the previously unrated club to a shock Italian championship victory.

When I think of Gerber I recall a superbly-fit, confident, competitive player. As a sports administrator he apparently could fit in two hours' solid training a day and obviously used his time wisely - it was said he would kick off his sessions with a quick 300 sit-ups.

In 1997 while in South Africa for the All Black-Springbok series, Grant Fox (my co-commentator) and I were walking towards Ellis Park when we happened across Gerber, who was on the footpath promoting his biography. The friendship between these two great players, rivals for years, was so warming that I broke one of my rules and joined them for a pre-test drink.

These days Gerber works as a sports organiser and coach among disadvantaged people in Port Elizabeth. 🏉

MIKE GIBSON

The Pride of Belfast

FOR 16 YEARS Irishman Mike Gibson was rated among the world's best players and it is difficult to name a skill he didn't possess. Fergus Slattery, a fine forward, replied when asked about Irish players he most admired: "The giant of Irish rugby is C M H Gibson. The rest are also-rans." All Black great Colin Meads said: "Gibson was as near to the perfect player as I have seen."

I recall Gibson for more than just the quality of his play. He was a pleasure to deal with - quiet, modest and charming. He was a tee-totaller and an independent person who liked to have time to himself. But he was always enjoyable company.

In 1976 a New Zealand television crew travelled with the touring Irish team. Gibson and co proved such delightful companions that the TV soundman, Kieran Horgan (a true-blue New Zealander, despite his name) abandoned New Zealand and moved to Dublin. Using his Irish-sounding name and a newly-acquired Irish accent, he has gone on to forge a successful career and has been involved in major films such as *The Field* and *The Boxer*.

New Zealanders received an early taste of the Gibson magic when he turned out as flyhalf for Cambridge University against Wilson Whineray's All Blacks in 1963. In a soundly beaten team, Gibson was a revelation, scoring a try and lighting up the backline. Terry McLean wrote that Gibson 'looked miraculously good'.

But Gibson's play was no shock to those who had followed his career. The Belfast lad played scrumhalf at his prep school before moving to Campbell College and the position of flyhalf. He was in the First XV for two years and already attracting outside attention when he ventured to Queen's College, Cambridge in 1963 to study law. Two matches, against the All Blacks and the Varsity match that year, cemented his reputation. He scored a try, guided the Light Blues to an 19-11 victory over Oxford and was quickly pulled into the Irish test side.

From there, his career was one long success story. On his test debut against England at Twickenham, he was part of a magnificent 18-5 Irish victory. He received three rugby Blues, captaining Cambridge in 1965. By 1966 he was good enough to be selected for the first of a record-equalling five Lions tours.

His law exams forced him to miss the early stages of that tour, in Australia, but he made up for lost time in New Zealand, where he slipped happily into centre outside established flyhalf David Watkins. He played the most games (19) and topped the try-scoring list with nine. I recall particularly his display against the New Zealand Juniors at Athletic Park. It was an appalling day and

Cameron Michael Henderson Gibson
Centre/flyhalf
Born: Belfast, December 3, 1942
Test debut: Ireland v England, Twickenham, February 8, 1964
Test career: 1964-79 (81 matches - 69 for Ireland, 12 for the British Isles)
Test points: 115 (9 tries, 7 conversions, 17 penalties, 6 drop goals)
* Equalled the record with five British Lions tours
* His 81 test appearances was the world record
* Was one of the First XV inducted into the International Rugby Hall of Fame in 1997
* Still holds the Irish record for most test appearances

Breakdown of positions Mike Gibson played during his British Isles and Irish test career:

69 tests for Ireland - 40 as a centre, 25 as a flyhalf and 4 as a wing.

12 tests for British Isles - 8 as centre, 3 as a flyhalf and 1 as a replacement flyhalf.

The match programme for Mike Gibson's last test, Ireland v Australia in 1979. Ireland won the match to gain a surprise series victory.

conditions underfoot were treacherous, but Gibson at flyhalf never put a foot wrong. He made a searing 40m break to set up winger Dewi Bebb for a try, landed a vital penalty out of the slush and handled impeccably.

Gibson toured again with Lions teams to New Zealand in 1971 and 1977, and to South Africa in 1968 and in 1974. His greatest tour was in 1971, when even in a backline of superstars he was something special. Colin Meads, the All Black captain, nominated Gibson and forward Mervyn Davies as the two figures most responsible for the Lions historic test series victory.

With players the calibre of Gareth Edwards and Barry John inside him, Gibson was given the time and space to show all his talents and he dazzled New Zealand rugby fans. There seemed nothing he couldn't do. Many famous players had one remarkable attribute, but it is difficult to single out one aspect of Gibson's game.

He had unnerving speed, a wicked sidestep and an eye for a gap; trained diligently so that he was always in peak condition; had wonderful timing on the pass; was a total team player and, though not especially sturdily built - 1.80m (5ft 11in) and 81.5kg (12st 10lb) - was a superb and courageous tackler. While he prided himself on doing the basics well, he had a flair for the unorthodox and must have been a nightmare to mark. He was an efficient place-kicker but was not often required in this department.

Gibson was an excellent rugby thinker. In fact, he resembled Grant Fox in this regard. Both had rare understanding of the tactical side of the game. For me, Gibson's stamp of class was the way he always had time to spare, because of his balance. Like great tennis players and batsmen, he was seldom flustered, even in the middle of a torrid international.

Though he played beautifully in all 15 of his games on that 1971 tour, it was his display against Wellington, when he scored two tries in a 47-9 thrashing of one of New Zealand's proudest provincial sides, which really fired the imagination. The way the Lions, with Gibson their inspiration, played that day was sensational. Wellington completely altered their style after that and became one of the most exciting teams in the country, which had a filter-through effect on New Zealand rugby.

In 1969 Gibson switched from flyhalf to the centres, where he felt he had the freedom to express himself and more licence to run. If anything, the move made him even more dominant and he is recalled today as the prince of centres.

The only time I saw him look out of sorts was in New Zealand in 1977. He did not see eye to eye with coach John Dawes, suffered a run of injuries and was unable to break into the test side. Yet he was the only touring player not to play in a losing team. His continued omission was inexplicable and New Zealanders, who greatly admired the Ulsterman, were sad for him. He further endeared himself to New Zealanders when he played for Auckland club Ponsonby in a couple of charity games.

Near the end of his career, Gibson turned out for Ireland on the right wing and he enjoyed a happy finale to test rugby by helping Ireland score two upset test wins in Australia in 1979. By then he was in his 37th year, extraordinary for a back, especially a wing. Eventually, Gibson eclipsed Willie John McBride as the world record-holder for test caps.

Often in sport, a person's personality is reflected by the way they play their sport. With Gibson this was not so. Off the field he was reserved and modest. On the field he was, through the dynamism of his play, invariably the centre of attention.

Since his retirement, Gibson, a Belfast solicitor, has kept rather a low profile, though I have seen him occasionally at rugby functions where he is as warm as ever. ⬤⓪⓪

SID GOING

The Maromaku Special

THERE HAS ALWAYS been debate about Sid Going's place among halfbacks. Even 20 years after his retirement, the discussion continues - he has not been included in the New Zealand Sports Hall of Fame, though 22 rugby players are.

Arguments over Going are waged along these lines: his backers say he was an incomparable match-winner and a rare rugby talent; his critics say he was selfish and inhibited his backline. I am in the pro-Going camp. He could turn a match given a sniff of a chance and I'm sure he was the player his opponents were keenest to negate.

It's true he often thought of his forwards before his first-five, but from 1967-77, the All Blacks were mighty grateful to have him. He was their big star and their major weapon in his 29 tests. I'm sure he would be just as effective today.

This 1.7m (5ft 7in) tall, 80.7kg (12st 10lb) man of steel was a match-winner for his Mid-Northern club, North Auckland and the New Zealand Maoris, where his genius was enhanced by his understanding with brothers Brian, at first-five and Ken, at fullback. He was targeted by opponents and took many fearful knocks, but always retained his combativeness and personified the courage of great All Blacks.

His effect on All Black rugby was so profound that BBC commentator Cliff Morgan remarked: "That is why people say New Zealand without Going is only half a team," after he scored against Ireland in 1973.

The chunky Going had fantastic upper body strength, fine footwork and acceleration, and a low centre of gravity. He was a nightmare to stop near the line, especially as he had an uncanny instinct for sniffing out a try. There was a question mark over his passing but his tactical kicking, especially into the box, was superb and he was a ruthless defender. In South Africa in 1976 he was sometimes the All Black test goal-kicker, which was cruel considering he was performing miracles of strength at halfback, but was an indication of his versatility.

Sidney Milton Going (Milt to team-mates), a product of Maromaku, made his North Auckland debut in 1962. He was then lost to rugby for two years as he took up a Mormon mission in Canada.

In 1967 he was picked to replace the injured Chris Laidlaw for the Jubilee test against Australia at Athletic Park. This began four years of debate over

---

Sidney Milton Going
Halfback
Born: Kawakawa, August 19, 1943
Test debut: New Zealand v Australia, Wellington, August 19, 1967
Test career: 1967-77 (29 matches)
Test points: 44 (10 tries, 1 conversion, 2 penalties)
* One of two brothers to represent the All Blacks and three who represented North Auckland
* Played 86 matches for New Zealand, scoring 33 tries

While not wanting to bring racial questions into any summary of the century's great players, it is appropriate to recognise the great Maori players who have graced the world rugby scene and gained a wide following with their exuberant style of play. Four Maori players feature among the 20 All Blacks profiled in this book.

Keith Quinn's list of the century's top Maori players and personalities:

1 George Nepia
2 Sid Going
3 Wayne Shelford
4 Zinzan Brooke
5 Johnny Smith
6 Tori Reid
7 Waka Nathan
8 Albert Pryor
9 Hika Reid
10 Tane Norton

the abilities of the two outstanding halfbacks. Going's passing was often compared to Laidlaw's and I would place him second only in that category. But his darting runs around the lineouts and the base of the scrum were unequalled. Laidlaw was generally, but not always, preferred, though coach Fred Allen has since said Going was the better footballer.

Going was preferred against France at Paris in 1967 and scored the first of his 10 test tries. In the third test against the touring French in 1968, he scored two solo tries and in South Africa in 1970 blindside breaks set up tries in the first and fourth tests for Bryan Williams.

Every season from 1967-72, Going won the Tom French Cup for outstanding Maori player. He was a crowd-puller everywhere and adored in Northland, where he was placed on the same pedestal as rugby idols Johnny Smith and Peter Jones. Going led North Auckland through an exciting, if short, Ranfurly Shield reign in the early 1970s.

I thought Going suffered in the public relations department. He was a private, rather distant individual and did not drink alcohol. Back when the All Blacks drank much more, this was construed by some as being anti-social. He was bracketed with some trouble-makers on the 1972-73 tour of Britain and France, though this had more to do with the company he kept than his own actions. In fact, he was shy and had a flat, expressionless visage. Having said that, when he smiled, he lit up a room.

On the field, he had wonderful battles with the great Welsh halfback Gareth Edwards - supporters of their respective countries will claim their man came out on top. He suffered in Britain and South Africa from being penalised for feeding the ball under his hooker's feet. This seemed pin-pricking officiating - Going was no worse an offender than other halfbacks.

In the early 1970s, we took a television crew to the far north to do a story on the Goings. On their back lawn they re-enacted their magic moves, including a triple scissors called 'The Special'. Such moves are common today, but back then were unheard of and the Goings, with their sleight of hand, were a big attraction. Sid was a delight to interview during that story - relaxed and open. It was the closest I got to him, for though I toured often with him, he was generally introspective though never unfriendly.

Some of his play was incredible. In 1972-73, Going, the All Black vice-captain, initiated a try for Keith Murdoch against Wales and scored tries against Scotland and Ireland. His try at Murrayfield broke Scottish hearts. The All Blacks were grimly defending a 10-9 lead when Going intercepted a pass by Alastair McHarg and scuttled 50 metres into the fog to score the try that sealed the match.

Through the 1970s, Going had a love-hate relationship with the selectors. He was dropped for the Australian tour in 1974, but coach J J Stewart was then so keen to have Going back that he was offered assistance in the management of his dairy farm while he toured Ireland and Wales with the All Blacks at the end of the year. His older brother Ken made his one All Black tour with that team.

In 1976, Going toiled manfully in South Africa. He contributed eight points with goal kicks during the second test victory and added a special piece of magic when he flick-passed the ball between his legs to first-five Doug Bruce, who dropped the goal.

Against the Lions in 1977, Going scored a typically brilliant solo try in the first test, but was dropped after the second. His replacement, Lyn Davis, a solid halfback and a consistent passer, wasn't a shadow of the player Going

Sid Going in action. A rare photograph of him kicking on the All Blacks' 1976 tour of South Africa.

was, which emphasises that the All Black selectors felt Going's individual style was hindering his backline.

Despite public debate about his style and erratic support from selectors, those who played with Going were emphatic about his quality. Peter Whiting said he was 'pound for pound, the greatest footballer New Zealand has seen'. Bryan Williams added: "Sid Going was criticised for his passing, but I so often saw him pass well and the balance of his game was outstanding."

The public were in no doubt about Super Sid. He was a national folk hero and his autobiography remains one of the biggest selling sports books in New Zealand.

Going and his wife Colleen had five children, but their eldest daughter was tragically killed in a motor accident. One of their sons, Milton, reached provincial and Super 12 level. Sid became the North Auckland provincial coach, but had only moderate success. His individual instincts and shy nature were perhaps not suited to the job. 🏉

KEN GRAY

The Snarl that Frightened Opponents

Kenneth Francis Gray
Prop
Born: Porirua, June 24, 1938
Died: Plimmerton, November 18, 1992
Test debut: New Zealand v Ireland, Dublin, December 7, 1963
Test career: 1963-69 (24 matches)
Test points: 12 (4 tries)
*   Lost only 2 of his 24 tests

AN ENDURING MEMORY I have of Ken Gray is of him standing near the front of the lineout at Wellington's Athletic Park, squinting into the low-setting winter sun. That squint took the form of a fearsome-looking snarl and as Gray played outstandingly for Petone, Wellington and New Zealand at Athletic Park for a decade, it was seen often and must have struck trepidation into many an opposing prop.

During the 1960s, Gray was the world's best prop, according to those who knew best - his peers. At 1.88m (6ft 2in), he was tall for a prop, and had a farming-hardened 108kg (17st) physique that made him exceptionally strong. Gray expanded the horizons of his position. Not only was he an outstanding scrummager, but he was, for his era, uncommonly mobile, had good ball skills and was an exceptionally good jumper at No 2 in the lineout.

Nearly three decades later, Chris Laidlaw's summation of him in *Mud in Your Eye* does not seem excessive: 'Perhaps the finest forward in his position the game would ever see. He was, with Meads, indisputably the most talented forward I saw, and any prop he played for or against could hardly hesitate before naming him the greatest.'

Gray, a gentleman off the field, brought incredible intensity to his play, seeking to dominate all opponents. I felt one flaw in his game was that he was inclined to lose his temper. I saw him punch opposing players even at club level, often with little cause. If he took such action in the modern era, he would be out of the game. Even in the 1960s, with a different attitude towards what constituted a masculine rugby player, it was horrible to see. He had all the rugby skills necessary, and when you got to know the man and realised how intelligent he was, the reckless punching just didn't make sense.

Gray attended Plimmerton Primary School and Wellington College, playing his rugby mainly in the backs. As a sixth former at Wellington College in 1963, I listened proudly as two of our old boys, Ralph Caulton and Gray, addressed us before departing for Britain with the All Blacks. Wearing their new All Black blazers they made quite an impression. I remember them mentioning that neither of them had made the First XV, which offered hope to many.

After leaving college, Gray was too shy to visit his local Paremata club until prompted by his brother. Over the next few years he earned various Wellington minor rep honours at No 8 and lock while playing second division club football. I first saw him when a group of us schoolboys went along to

Illustration courtesy of Murray Webb.

watch the Wellington B team practise. We had never heard of Ken Gray of Paremata and wondered who he was, but we left that practice in no doubt that he was going to be a great player.

He moved to the famous Petone club in 1959 and began his long association with the Wellington provincial team, playing at lock against the British Lions. It wasn't until 1961 that Gray began propping for Wellington, after the retirement of Ivan Vodanovich, whom he credited with teaching him about front row play.

In 1963, after appearing in his fifth All Black trial, he was selected in Wilson Whineray's team for the big tour of Britain, France and Canada. From then until his sudden retirement in 1969, Gray was a must All Black selection.

He could play at either loosehead or tighthead, and even turned out for the All Blacks at lock. Gray played with All Black legends like Colin and Stan Meads, Kel Tremain, Whineray, Brian Lochore and Waka Nathan, and helped lay the platform for a grand era of New Zealand rugby.

Gray's lineout jumping was a huge bonus. In 1965, he was so dominant in the first test against South Africa that lock Tiny Naude was delegated to jump against him, which, of course, gave the other All Black jumpers that much more freedom. In 1967, a severe knee injury forced him out of the Jubilee test against Australia and it appeared he would miss the end-of-year tour of Britain, but coach Fred Allen was desperately keen to include him. Folklore in Wellington has it that Gray was required to turn up at the menswear shop run by former All Blacks Vodanovich and Tom Morrison, was asked to do 20 press-ups and was pronounced fit to tour.

He then broke his hand in the tour opener in Vancouver and did not play again until the seventh match, though his hand had still not healed properly. New Zealand-born pressman Wallace Reyburn wrote: 'As the tour progressed, I understood why the New Zealand selectors had kept a place open for the injured Gray. And I knew why, when he was injured on tour, he was put back to work before the injury was thoroughly healed. The All Blacks needed him. They were not nearly as good a side without the Gray.'

The Wellingtonian was in rampaging form in the two home tests against Wales in 1969, scoring the fourth of his test tries, then retired. He was 31 and still at his peak. It transpired he had quietly quit rugby, rather than be selected to tour South Africa in 1970. He explained that though he missed the challenge of not playing in South Africa, he made the decision not to tour 'from my own readings and my own feeling'.

Just before naming their team for South Africa, the selectors asked Gray to reconsider, though he had not been playing, but he turned them down. Gray remained a staunch opponent of South African politics. Having played against them in 1965, he marched against them in 1981, when the Springboks toured New Zealand, which did not endear him to dyed-in-the-wool rugby types.

Gray's record for Wellington was superb. He was captain in more than half of his 133 appearances from 1959-69, leading them to a 23-6 victory over the 1965 Springboks and a 20-6 victory over the 1966 Lions.

Gray later became involved in equestrianism, following the successes of his children, and threw himself into politics, at local body level, then nationally. He unsuccessfully sought the Labour Party nominations in the 1987 and 1990 general elections, but had secured the nomination for Western Hutt for the 1993 election when he died of a heart attack in late 1992, aged 54. In was a tragedy, for many agreed with his former team-mate Earle Kirton's assertion that Gray would have made a fine Prime Minister. At the time of his death, he was the chairman of the Health Sponsorship Council. **100**

PIET GREYLING

Unbending Commitment

'OF ALL SOUTH AFRICANS, the one who most epitomises my vision of the Springbok would be the loose forward Piet Greyling, for his total, unbending commitment to their cause.' So wrote All Black captain Brian Lochore, who tangled with the mercurial flanker in 1970.

Greyling, though he played 25 tests over a six-season span, encountered the All Blacks in only one series, but what an impression he made. Here is what some of the other stars of that 1970 New Zealand team later wrote of him:

Colin Meads: 'When Piet Greyling and Jan Ellis got to the loose ball, they were constructive, Greyling especially.' Fergie McCormick: 'Greyling was a mean loose forward, a real ripper of the ball. When he tackled you, you stayed tackled. He hunted the ball relentlessly.'

Sid Going: 'Greyling was very quick off the back of the lineout and did a lot of damage to the opposition.' Ian Kirkpatrick: 'Ellis and Greyling were a terrific pair, big fast men, and Greyling, especially, was a deadly tackler.'

It's natural to mention Greyling and Ellis together. They were South Africa's flankers in 24 tests and wrought havoc with opposing backlines. But though they were both wonderful players, they must be treated as separate entities. Ellis often caught the eye, but Greyling was a relentless player who had fire in his belly and demanded total respect. They were brilliant players and it was South Africa's good fortune that they arrived on the international scene virtually together and that for some time they worked in harness with another fine loose forward, No 8 Tommy Bedford.

Though Greyling was born in Rhodesia, he was educated at the Central High School at Bloemfontein. He moved about a lot, beginning his rep rugby in Rhodesia, then playing for Orange Free State, Northern Transvaal and Transvaal. He captained Transvaal when they won the Currie Cup in 1971 and 1972.

Greyling made a stunning test debut against France at Durban in 1967. He scored two tries and spearheaded a 26-3 Springbok victory. Raw-boned and utterly committed, Greyling was immediately compared with the world's great flankers.

What impressed critics and daunted his opposition was that he was both a creator and a destroyer. At 1.88m (6ft 2in) and 89kg (14st), he was a potent lineout force, yet got about the field like a bloodhound. He was a crushing

Pieter Johannes Frederik Greyling
Flanker
Born: Zastron, May 16, 1942
Test debut: South Africa v France, Durban, June 15, 1967
Test career: 1967-72 (25 matches)
Test points: 15 (5 tries)
* Was partnered with fellow-flanker Jan Ellis in 24 tests

There is no doubt that a pair of world-class flankers can have a decisive bearing on a match. They can stifle opposition attacks and initiate those of their own side. Some of the great flanker combinations have been:

Piet Greyling and Jan Ellis (South Africa)	1967-72
Jean-Pierre Rives and Jean-Claude Skrela (France)	1975-78
Jean-Pierre Rives and Jean-Luc Joinel (France)	1978-84
Greg Davis and Jules Guerassimoff (Australia)	1963-67
Michel Crauste and Francois Moncla (France)	1959-61
James McKay and James McCarthy (Ireland)	1948-52
Fergus Slattery and Roger Uttley (British Isles)	1974
Michael Jones and Alan Whetton (New Zealand)	1987-91
Kel Tremain and Waka Nathan (New Zealand)	1962-67
Graham Mourie and Leicester Rutledge (New Zealand)	1978-79
Graham Mourie and Mark Shaw (New Zealand)	1980-82
Jim Calder and David Leslie (Scotland)	1981-85
Finlay Calder and John Jeffrey (Scotland)	1985-91

Note: the years refer only to the years when the flankers operated together in pairs

assaulter of halfbacks and had a nasty habit (for the opposition) of being on hand to grab and feed the ball after his partner in crime, Ellis, had made the initial tackles. Greyling was always superbly fit, so was still playing as strongly as ever at the end of 80 minutes when others were slowing. It made him even more effective as a match wore on. With his fitness and rugby intelligence he was amazingly consistent. It's not easy to recall him turning in a sub-par performance.

Greyling came into international rugby just as South Africa was starting to bear the brunt of anti-apartheid protests, never better illustrated than on the 1969-70 'demo' tour of Britain. Nearly every day of that unhappy tour was marred with a demonstration. The Springboks had a terribly difficult task to keep their minds on rugby and never won a test. But Greyling was consistently superb. He scored tries against England and Ireland (when he carried four tacklers across the line with him) and helped his side salvage at least the dignity of test draws with Ireland and Wales.

He peaked against the All Blacks in 1970. Through the 1960s, New Zealand had prided itself on the quality of its loose forwards - Kel Tremain, John Graham, Brian Lochore, Waka Nathan and Ian Kirkpatrick were just some of the famous All Black loose forwards of that era. But Ellis and Greyling proved a revelation. They were big, fast, menacing and remorseless. Greyling sustained a hairline fracture of a rib during the first test, but during the second, playing with his ribs strapped, he was the best forward on the park.

After helping the Springboks repel New Zealand 3-1, Greyling was deservedly selected in a World XV to help celebrate the Rugby Football Union's centenary in 1971. It was a memorable year for Greyling, who helped South Africa win series at home against France and then whitewash Australia 3-0 in Australia.

In 1972, Greyling captained the Springboks when John Pullin's England side upset the South Africans 18-9 in a one-off test. Greyling did little wrong, though he kicked himself for not picking up a pass at his feet when he was only two metres from the line. "If I had held it I would have been over and we might have won," he said.

By 1972 he was a towering figure in South African rugby. Not only was his play of the highest order, but he had a sharp rugby intellect. He concerned himself with the style of his teams and analysed play shrewdly. He seemed set to lead the Springboks to New Zealand in 1973 when New Zealand Prime Minister Norman Kirk cancelled the tour.

Greyling led his team on an internal tour instead, then retired to devote himself to his business commitments. Of his 25 tests, in which he scored five tries, South Africa had won 16 and drawn four others. He later became a Transvaal selector. **100**

JEREMY GUSCOTT

Model Centre

DESPITE JEREMY GUSCOTT'S outstanding test record, it has always seemed to me that his talent has been under-utilised. If he'd played for a nation other than England, who have a predilection to kick from their insides, his skills would have been more widely exposed.

Guscott, a tall, elegant centre, has been one of the great modern rugby players. He is a sharp and elusive runner, always threatening with ball in hand, and was part of the early 1990s England backline that oozed class. Rob Andrew, Guscott, Will Carling and Rory Underwood were fine players, but the safety-first kicking tactics that England adopted did not allow them to use the full range of their abilities.

Besides the quality of his play, Guscott has been a significant figure in other areas. He was one of the first black players to cement a permanent spot in the England team, and must surely have been a role model to a whole generation of youngsters. Off the field, he was a much-publicised personality - a part-time model, a BBC television presenter, and in demand from advertisers and sponsors. He epitomised the modern, professional age of rugby, even before the game officially went pro. He always seems determined to enjoy life. Almost as a sidelight, it seems, he is a public relations officer for British Gas.

With his glamorous lifestyle, which includes mandatory trappings such as mobile phone, flash car and good clothes, Guscott has always stood out. Yet I've never found him aloof. Touring New Zealand with a World XV in 1992 and the Lions the following year, he was much in demand but was never less than approachable and helpful. He is a sardonic, low-key character and good company.

Guscott is Bath born and bred. He was educated at Bath's Ralph Allen School and first ventured onto a football field when playing mini-rugby as a seven-year-old.

As a senior player, he had a meteoric rise in the late 1980s. He made his debut for Bath in 1985, a cocky youngster who had a touch of brilliance but perhaps not the application. But in 1989 he had two outings for England B, scored three tries in his test debut for England against Romania, and helped the Lions win two tests in Australia. The previously unknown Guscott was a sensation in Australia. He replaced the injured Carling in the second test at Brisbane and scored a breathtaking try to set up a 19-12 victory, then had

Jeremy Clayton Guscott
Centre
Born: Bath, July 7, 1965
Test debut: England v Romania, Bucharest, May 13, 1989
Test career: 1989-98 (67 matches - 59 for England and 8 for the British Isles)
Test points: 120 (25 tries, 3 drop goals)
* Scored three tries on his test debut
* Formed a centres combination with Will Carling in 46 tests

another big game in the deciding third test, which the Lions also won.

After that, Guscott, 6ft 1in (1.85m) and 13st 10lb (87kg), was a must selection for several years. He once said: "I'd always heard the England team was a bunch of Oxbridge tossers." But his opinion changed once he became involved. During Geoff Cooke's time as England coach, Guscott and Carling did sterling work in the midfield, though they could often have qualified for the unemployment benefit, so little ball did they see. Amazingly, after 16 tests, Guscott had reached double figures in tries, which said more about his brilliance than about England's tactics. For most of his career, Guscott, who declined to wear the No 13 jersey, played alongside the less-superstitious Carling and they finally set a record for the most test outings by a centres combination.

I've been impressed with the way Guscott has fought back from injury. He missed the entire 1993-94 season with a groin injury and also had to miss a chunk of the 1997 season. But always he has come back stronger than ever.

He is a stylish, upright runner in the traditional English mould. Whereas Carling alongside him provided the brawn, Guscott did it more by stealth, using his devastating acceleration to glide through opposing defences. He has a full range of skills - being a lovely passer and a good kicker, and is decisive on the tackle. Mike Cleary once wrote that he was 'no gilded butterfly, a precious species craving gentle handling'.

He thrived on the cut and thrust of international rugby. One match I recall well was for the Lions against Canterbury in 1993. It hadn't been all plain sailing for the visitors and they needed a win against Canterbury. In a ferocious match, Guscott tackled superbly and provided the spark that helped the Lions win 28-10.

Guscott's career has been one of great highs. He has helped Bath become the dominant England club side, with a hatful of league and Pilkington Cup titles. For England, there was a runner-up finish in the 1991 World Cup and an unprecedented run of three Grand Slams in five years. The Lions provided Guscott with many great days. There was the series win in Australia in 1989. Then at Wellington in 1993 he helped the Lions score a record 20-7 win over New Zealand. And in South Africa in 1997, Guscott snapped a drop a goal in the closing minutes of the Durban test to earn the Lions an 18-15 win and give them an unassailable 2-0 lead in the series.

Despite the impressive results, Guscott told Ian Stratford of *Rugby World* in April 1998 that he felt a sense of frustration when recalling those record-breaking years with the England team. "It was time wasted, not just for me but for our whole backline. We had so much talent in the backs but the coaching game plan concentrated on ten players. I often wish I'd said something, but then results are everything in this game. If you win, you can have anything you like, and we were winning."

Even in his 30s, Guscott has remained a force in big-time rugby. Jack Rowell provoked a storm by dropping him in 1996, but Guscott fought his way back, sometimes appearing on the wing, which seemed not the best use of his skills. When he turned out against Wales in 1998, Guscott joined the select few who have appeared 50 times for England.

While his coaches have not always used his talents fully, his opposition invariably targeted him as a danger player. Chris Rea spoke for many when he said: "In rugby terms Jeremy Guscott is a national treasure. If he was a building he would be listed." 🏉

A selection of prominent players from the Bath Rugby Football Club in England:

Adedayo Adebayo
Stuart Barnes
Jonathan Callard
Mike Catt
Gareth Chilcott
Ben Clarke
Phil de Glanville
Jeremy Guscott
John Hall
Richard Hill
John Kendall-Carpenter
Nigel Redman
John Sleightholme
Victor Ubogu
Jon Webb

England centres who have played for the British Isles in tests:

8	Jeremy Guscott	1989-97
6	Mike Weston	1962-66
5	Carl Aarvold	1930
4	Jeff Butterfield	1955
4	Colin McFadyean	1966
3	Phil Davies	1955
3	Maurice Neale	1910
3	Anthony Novis	1930
2	Paul Dodge	1980
2	Clive Woodward	1980
1	Will Carling	1993
1	Basil Nicholson	1938
1	Bill Patterson	1959

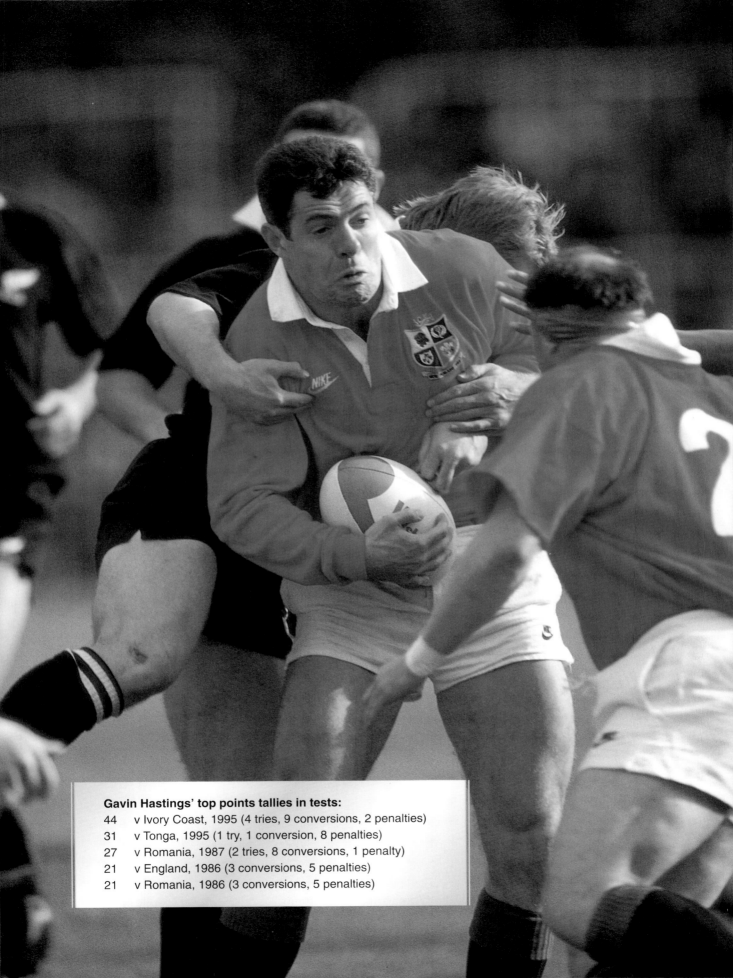

Gavin Hastings' top points tallies in tests:

44   v Ivory Coast, 1995 (4 tries, 9 conversions, 2 penalties)
31   v Tonga, 1995 (1 try, 1 conversion, 8 penalties)
27   v Romania, 1987 (2 tries, 8 conversions, 1 penalty)
21   v England, 1986 (3 conversions, 5 penalties)
21   v Romania, 1986 (3 conversions, 5 penalties)

GAVIN HASTINGS

Scotland's Braveheart

NEW ZEALANDERS came to regard Gavin Hastings as an adopted son. The amiable Scottish fullback seemed to be in New Zealand virtually every second season throughout his long career and his skills and solid temperament were always much admired.

The All Blacks first encountered him when he played for Edinburgh against them in 1983. Four years later he visited New Zealand for the World Cup, then remained in Auckland and played out the season for University. Hastings was back with the Scottish team in 1990 and two years later returned as part of a World XV for the New Zealand Rugby Union centenary celebrations. In 1993 he captained a Lions that went within a whisker of winning the series in New Zealand.

With that history, it was appropriate that Hastings' last test should be the 1995 World Cup quarter-final against none other than New Zealand.

The Scotsman was a courageous, hard-running fullback with a thundering punt and an ability to kick long-range goals. Both Hastings and his younger brother Scott - also a quality test player - were marvellous company. I recall one especially enjoyable night on the tiles at the Hilton Hotel in London in 1989 when the Hastings brothers, David Sole and one or two others proved most congenial company. In interview situations, Hastings was unfailingly polite, answering with honesty and humility in his quiet Scottish burr.

Hastings told me he was very glad he played in the amateur era and never wanted to play for money. "How could anyone replace the thrill of playing for one's country? Money couldn't buy that," he said.

Hastings was born into an Edinburgh rugby family. His father, Clifford, played No 8 for Edinburgh and Watsonians, and four Hastings sons - Gavin, Scott, Graeme and Ewan - played rugby to at least a good club level.

Gavin attended George Watson's College and then Cambridge University. He represented Scottish schoolboys and Scotland under-21, earned five caps for Scotland B and won Blues for Cambridge University in 1984-85, captaining Cambridge to victory over Oxford the second year. In 1985 he toured North America with Scotland.

His first test, against France in 1986, was memorable for several reasons. Scott made his debut that day too, the first time this century bothers had made their international debuts for Scotland in the same match. Gavin muffed his first touch of the ball, putting the kick-off into touch, from which France scored. But he made amends, kicking six penalties in Scotland's 18-17 win, to set a national record for points on debut. His 52 points in the Five Nations

Andrew Gavin Hastings
Fullback
Born: Edinburgh, January 3, 1962
Test debut: Scotland v France, January 17, 1986
Test career: 1986-95 (67 matches - 61 for Scotland, 6 for British Isles)
Test points: 733 (18 tries, 87 conversions, 160 penalties)

* Gavin and his brother Scott made their test debuts in the same match
* Scored 18 points on his test debut
* Set a short-lived IRB test record by scoring 27 points against Romania in the 1987 World Cup
* Set another short-lived IRB test record by scoring 44 points against Ivory Coast in 1995
* Is third on the all-time test points-scoring record

Gavin Hastings once told me a classic story about how rugged the world of international rugby can be.

After Hastings played in the World Cup in 1987, he stayed on in Auckland and played seven or eight games for University, helping the team win the Gallaher Shield. He became very good mates with players such as John Drake, Grant Fox and, especially, Sean Fitzpatrick.

A few months later he was invited to play for the President's XV in the last match of the All Blacks' tour of Japan. Early in what might have been considered a semi-social conclusion to the tour, Fox put up an enormous high kick. Hastings recalls he was hit by 'a bloody tank' (Fitzpatrick) and knocked 'all over the place'. As he recovered, he looked up and there was Fitzpatrick's face right next to his. "Sorry, mate," said the grinning All Black hooker.

The top points-scorers in tests for Scotland:

667	Gavin Hastings	1986-95
273	Andy Irvine	1972-82
210	Peter Dods	1983-91
166*	Craig Chalmers	1989-98
106*	Tony Stanger	1989-98
104*	Rowen Shepherd	1995-98
95*	Kenny Logan	1992-99
80	Michael Dods	1994-96
72	Ian Smith	1924-33
71	Ken Scotland	1957-65
71	Doug Morgan	1973-78

* still playing

Excludes points scored while representing British Isles

Championship was another Scottish record.

Hastings, who played for the London Scottish and Watsonians clubs, was his country's natural successor to Andy Irvine. He was always immaculate on the field, in dress and demeanour, and at 1.88m (6ft 2in) and 94kg (14st 10lb), was big for a fullback. He didn't have the blistering speed of Irvine, but would use his strength and size, plus a good fend, to burst through, and was an imposing presence. It must have been reassuring for the Scottish forwards to know that the indomitable and capable Hastings was guarding the rear. During the 1987 World Cup he scored 62 points in four games.

Hastings was a key member of the 1989 Lions team to Australia, scoring a vital try in the second test and kicking 15 points in the decider to guide the Lions to a 2-1 series win.

There was more glory in 1990 when he was part of his country's Grand Slam team. Then he toured New Zealand and though the All Blacks won both tests, Hastings played outstandingly, especially in the second when it required a late penalty by Grant Fox to kick the All Blacks to a 21-18 win.

Scotland reached the semis of the 1991 World Cup and Hastings contributed a total of 63 points during the six-match campaign. England beat Scotland 9-6 in the semi-finals and Hastings kicked himself later for having missed a penalty that was well within range.

He took over the test captaincy in 1993, leading Scotland to a 15-3 win over Ireland in his first match in charge. He was to lead Scotland in 20 tests and while not a fire and brimstone leader, inspired by personal example. He was softly-spoken and understated, but commanded total respect.

Hastings was much-praised for his leadership of the Lions in New Zealand in 1993. In the first test of the tour, at Christchurch, the Lions led 18-17 with just three minutes remaining. At that point Hastings had kicked six penalties and the All Blacks had scored one try, an eerie turnaround from the first test of the 1959 Lions tour when Don Clarke kicked New Zealand to an 18-17 win in Dunedin. The 1993 result also eventually worked out in New Zealand's favour because Grant Fox landed a penalty in the dying moments.

One of Hastings' career highlights was the Lions' emphatic 20-7 win in the second test at Wellington. Though the All Blacks clinched the series in the third test at Auckland, I was left with memories of Hastings' courage and skill. The All Blacks decided to pepper Hastings with bombs, and had in Fox a man to execute the plan brilliantly. Hastings stood up to the barrage fearlessly. He dropped one, which the All Blacks turned into a try. But he caught everything else, even with the rampant All Black forwards bearing down on him. He was indeed Scotland's rugby Braveheart.

Hastings was last seen in the test arena during the 1995 World Cup in South Africa. He again set a world record during a World Cup, and again saw it bettered quickly. He scored 44 points against Ivory Coast, but eight days later Simon Culhane bettered this total for New Zealand against Japan.

With Jonah Lomu a dominant figure, the All Blacks beat Scotland 48-30 in the quarter-finals. Hastings took the loss with typical class and made a dignified exit from test rugby. All Black captain Sean Fitzpatrick, summed up the feelings of many by saying: "Gavin has simply been a great rugby figure, a player respected wherever the game is played."

Hastings' 61 tests was a Scottish record, subsequently beaten by his brother Scott. His 733 points in test rugby, including 66 for the Lions, was second (behind Michael Lynagh) on the all-time list. His points haul could have been higher as for a while Craig Chalmers did the place-kicking for Scotland.

These days he is a sports marketing executive in Edinburgh and is still often seen on the rugby circuit as a commentator. **100**

TIM HORAN

Midfield Magic

TIM HORAN COMBINES three qualities most required in a top inside centre - speed, vision and uncompromising defence. He had those attributes when Bob Dwyer plucked him from the Queensland B team and put him on the park against the All Blacks at Auckland in 1989, and still had them a decade later, despite a morale-sapping series of injuries.

It is impossible to talk of Horan without quickly mentioning Jason Little, his partner in the Wallaby centres in 32 tests. They go together like pie and schooner, as they say in Australia. Not only are they a classy rugby pairing but they are good mates, which makes their combination all the stronger. Horan has represented Australia in most backline positions, but I've always felt he was more dangerous when in the centres, particularly when partnering Little. The two schoolboy chums have a special understanding that has helped Australia win the World Cup title in 1991 and score an unprecedented number of victories over the old rival - New Zealand - in the 1990s.

Though Horan was born in New South Wales, he was educated in Queensland. His father played league in Sydney before becoming a farmer, then a Member of Parliament, in Queensland. Initially Tim played rugby league for the All Whites and Toowoomba State School. When he moved on to Downlands College, he was drawn to rugby union, appearing first at flyhalf.

Horan was a natural. He made the Australian under-17 and schoolboys teams and established his partnership with Little, though the two had been football team-mates and opponents back to the age of 11. They helped Australia beat New Zealand 16-3 in an under-17 international and combined impressively when the Australia met Ireland in a schoolboy international.

When Horan left school he joined the Southern Districts club in Brisbane, and captained Queensland under-19 in 1988. A year later he was reserve for Australia against the Lions. Then Dwyer took the plunge and selected him against New Zealand. He did not finally represent Queensland until 1990.

From the moment he stepped into test football that day at Eden Park, Horan looked the part. Though he was just 19, and the New Zealand centres were the experienced John Schuster and Joe Stanley, Horan obviously belonged at that level. Even in a losing Wallaby effort, he looked composed and efficient.

Timothy James Horan
Centre
Born: Darlinghurst, May 18, 1970
Test debut: Australia v New Zealand, Auckland, August 5, 1989
Test career: 1989-98 (67 matches)
Test points: 120 (26 tries)
* Horan and Jason Little have been Australia's centres combination in 32 tests
* Is second to David Campese on the list of Australian test try-scorers
* Represented Australia before representing his state

Tim Horan scores the try which killed off the All Blacks' hopes in the 1991 World Cup semi-final.

He had another string to his bow in those early days, for he was also one of the world's best sevens players, turning on some brilliant displays in the Hong Kong tournament.

Horan is slightly chunkier than Little (who joined the test side later in 1989) and not quite as quick, but is the ideal inside centre. Sharp is the word that comes to mind - he's a sharp thinker, a sharp passer and a sharp mover. He has outstanding vision and quick reactions. With his solid build - 1.83m (6ft) and 87kg (13st 10lb) - and combative attitude, he is a formidable opponent, able to burst through even solid tackles. And not only is he a deadly tackler himself, but he has perfected the art of following up a bomb, making a big a tackle on the opposing fullback to shake the ball free, then pouncing on it to score.

His eye for a try is shown by the fact that in 1998, in his 60th test, he joined the elite group of players to have scored 25 test tries.

Horan hasn't had an easy time through the 1990s, when he has been plagued by injuries. He hurt his knee in 1990, but bounced back to be a decisive influence through the 1991 World Cup. In 1992-93, free from injury, he was in his pomp, causing headaches for opposing backlines around the world. However in 1994 he suffered an horrific injury while playing for Queensland in the Super 10 final against Natal. He badly damaged the cruciate ligaments in his knee and was out of rugby for the season. Coincidentally, 10 minutes later, Little too had to leave the field with a bad knee injury.

There have been several more injuries since, but whenever he has been able to take the field, Horan has played up to his own high standards. His case has not been helped by the tendency of the Australian selectors to use him as a jack-of-all-trades, playing him at flyhalf, centre, wing and fullback. He can play anywhere but New Zealanders have always most feared him at inside centre.

Horan was outstanding during the 1991 World Cup, scoring four tries in six matches, including a crucial one in the semi-final against New Zealand. He accepted a miracle overhead pass from David Campese, burst past winger John Timu and dashed towards the posts for the try that was the final nail in the All Black coffin. In the final, Horan and Little marked the more experienced Will Carling and Jeremy Guscott and never put a foot wrong, their ruthless defence stifling any England attacks.

I got to know Horan in 1995 when I was part of a Channel 7 Australian test commentary team, with Chris Handy. Horan, recovering from injury, was temporarily out of the Wallaby side and was contracted to add his expert comments. He was well-prepared, professional and a pleasure to work with. Like many Wallabies, he was fairly quiet - shy even - off the field, very well-presented and thoroughly likeable. In fact, I was struck by the contrast in the two Horans: off the field he says little and is under-stated; on the field he is dynamic and fiercely competitive.

The All Blacks have been unstinting in their praise of Horan. For instance, in their biographies, Ian Jones and Grant Fox nominated him as the best test second five-eighth they encountered. Fox summed him up: 'Young, strong, great attacker and defender, the best by a country mile.' Jones wrote: 'Horan has acceleration and a keen eye for a gap. He's a bootlace tackler.'

Horan now makes his living mainly as a rugby player, having been a promotions officer for a brewery. Earlier in his career, he rejected some massive offers to turn to rugby league, which his style of football would have suited. **100**

The leading Australian test points-scorers:

911	Michael Lynagh	(1984-95)
354*	Matthew Burke	(1993-98)
315	David Campese	(1982-96)
260	Paul McLean	(1974-82)
165*	John Eales	(1991-98)
120*	Tim Horan	(1989-98)
117	David Knox	(1985-97)
114	Marty Roebuck	(1991-93)
92*	Jason Little	(1989-98)
82	Roger Gould	(1980-87)
80*	Ben Tune	(1996-98)

* still playing

The birth of a partnership - Tim Horan and Jason Little joined forces in the Wallaby midfield for the first time during the series against France in 1989.

ANDY IRVINE

Rugby's Free Spirit

Andrew Robert Irvine
Fullback/winger
Born: Edinburgh, September 16, 1951
Test debut: Scotland v New Zealand, December 16, 1972
Test career: 1972-82 (60 matches - 51 for Scotland, 9 for the British Isles)
Test points: 301 (12 tries, 26 conversions, 67 penalties)
* When he retired he held the world record for most points in tests
* He was Scotland's most capped fullback

ANDY IRVINE GOT ME into a bit of trouble when he toured New Zealand with the 1977 British Lions. The Scottish fullback was the team's undoubted star, turning on some sublime displays and heading the try-scoring charts with 11. His play was an eye-opener for New Zealanders as he showed the impact a talented running fullback could have.

Television New Zealand covered the entire tour, and each night the highlights would invariably feature Irvine. All winter, it seemed, I was on TV praising Irvine for another piece of rugby wizardry. Eventually someone wrote a letter to *Rugby News* asking whether Keith Quinn was "in love with Andy Irvine, or are they just good friends?"

Well, I don't know about being in love with Irvine, but he was a pleasure to deal with and I rank him among the greats of his era. His fullback rival was Welshman JPR Williams, but they were different players. Williams was more physical. He was a big tackler and a rocklike defensive player. Irvine, who had a light frame - 1.78m (5ft 10in) and 80kg (12st 8lb), was a rugby cavalier. He had blistering speed, was always looking to counter-attack and could turn a game in seconds. For him the kick into touch was a last option. He was a good goal-kicker who could rock his opposition by landing a penalty from long-range.

In many ways, Irvine was ahead of his time, though he told me in 1999 that he was very glad his career did not coincide with the professional era. Fullbacks tended to be defence-minded, safety-first players until the Scotsman's arrival. But he turned conventional thinking upside down and certainly made a huge impression in New Zealand. It's interesting that since then the All Blacks have fielded in Allan Hewson, John Gallagher and Christian Cullen three fullbacks who could win games through their running skills.

Irvine was always going to be a top fullback. At George Heriot's School in Edinburgh, he had the weight of destiny on his side, for seven previous Scotland fullbacks - Dan Drysdale, Jimmy Kerr, Tommy Kerr, Ian Thomson, Ken Scotland, Colin Blaikie and Ian Smith - had also attended the school.

Irvine had speed, timing and imagination even in his school days. He was the school sprint champion and used his pace magnificently on the rugby field. He was so obviously gifted that even when the fullback position was filled, coaches incorporated his ability by playing him on the wing. You wouldn't dare leave a match-winner like Irvine on the sideline. So he played

on the wing when he joined Heriot's FP and found Blaikie was wearing the No 15 jersey. For Edinburgh District, Arthur Brown initially had the fullback position, so Irvine again played on the wing. But it always seemed to me he was at his best at fullback, where he had the time and space to do justice to his skills.

Injuries to other leading fullbacks cleared the way for Irvine, a 21-year-old Edinburgh University student, to make his test debut one murky day in December, 1972, against Ian Kirkpatrick's All Blacks. Scotland lost a tight match 14-9, but Irvine kicked two long penalties and signalled the arrival of a special player.

He was selected for the Lions tour of South Africa in 1974 and responded so well to the challenge of being JPR Williams' fullback understudy that he

Typical Andy Irvine, ball in hand, pressuring defenders. This photo was taken during a festival match in New Zealand in 1978.

141

Keith Quinn's ranking of the century's 10 greatest Scottish players and personalities:
1 Andy Irvine
2 Gavin Hastings
3 Ian Smith
4 Ian McLauchlan
5 Arthur Smith
6 David Sole
7 John Bannerman
8 Bill McLaren
9 Sandy Carmichael
10 David ("Darkie") Bedell-Sivright

Though he misses inclusion in this book on purely playing ability, David Bedell-Sivright, known to all as "Darkie", was a major figure in Scottish rugby before the first World War.

He attended Cambridge University at the turn of the century, then specialised in medicine at Edinburgh University.

Bedell-Sivright, a fiery forward who sometimes strayed too far into the realms of foul play, made 22 appearances for Scotland from 1900-08 and captained the 1904 Great Britain side to Australia and New Zealand in 1904 (when he was captain). New Zealanders found his attitude could be patronising, but he was admired for his play, especially his fearsome tackling and skilled dribbling.

Bedell-Sivright had an interesting life outside rugby. He was a Scottish heavyweight boxing champion and at one time reared stock in Australia. He served as a surgeon in the Royal Navy and died of food poisoning at Gallipoli in 1915.

played the last two tests on the wing. He 156 points not only topped the Lions lists, but was a record for such a tour. South Africans took the boyishly enthusiastic, personable and dazzlingly talented Irvine to their hearts as they had Tony O'Reilly 19 years earlier.

It was Irvine's misfortune to hit international football at about the time the Scottish forwards were going through a lean patch. He had to make do with bare scraps of possession and his team was generally going backwards. However, he still enjoyed some glorious moments and throughout his 11-season career, was indisputably Scotland rugby's No 1 pin-up boy. No-one could light up Murrayfield like Irvine.

His first big moment for his country was in 1974 when he scored a try and kicked a last-minute penalty to earn Scotland a 16-14 win over England. In 1979, he scored tries against Wales, Ireland and France in the Five Nations Championship. That same season he led Heriot's to their first Scottish League championship.

One of his famous days was at Murrayfield, against France in February 1980. Irvine had been in poor kicking form, duffing six kickable penalties and a conversion. The crowd had even begun to boo him. With 12 minutes remaining, France led 14-4, but then Irvine caught fire. He scored a great try in the corner, after handling twice in the movement, converted it, then scored another try and kicked two penalties. His 16 points stunned the helpless French, who went down 22-14. *L'Equipe* headlined his performance 'Le Triomphe de Baroque' and rechristened Murrayfield 'Irvinefield'.

Oddly, while Irvine was acknowledged as a world great, there were always caveats. The Scottish selectors sometimes preferred Bruce Hay at fullback, and the word in rugby circles was that Irvine was fragile - he was not a strong tackler, tended to lose concentration or was shaky under the high ball.

When Irvine toured New Zealand with the 1977 Lions, news of his apparent susceptibility raced through the country and he was peppered with skiers. He may have dropped one or two but he was as good as most at taking the ball and lethal at using the possession to launch counter-attacks even from inside his own half. On one golden day at Taumarunui he scored a record five tries against a combined Wanganui-King Country side. There was another incredible solo effort from his own 10-metre line against a combined South Canterbury-Mid-Canterbury-North Otago side when he beat all 15 of the opposition. Irvine was not only very fast but had electric acceleration and could swerve off either foot.

As well as his lethal running, Irvine was a useful goal-kicker. Even when he wasn't his team's regular kicker (such as when Phil Bennett was in the 1977 Lions team), he would still be called up on occasion. I recall one successful penalty from near touch inside his own half in terrible conditions at Athletic Park in the first test of the 1977 tour. It was the first minute of the match and really took the wind out of the All Blacks.

When he retired in 1982 because of recurring injuries, Irvine held the world record for most test points with 301, including 11 tries. He captained Scotland 15 times.

Irvine was a chartered surveyor even when playing test rugby and is now senior partner in Scotland of Jones, Lang, Wootton. Though busy at work and a family man with four children, Irvine has stayed close to rugby, through his BBC television and radio commentaries, through coaching and more recently as a member of the Scotland Rugby Union's executive board. He is now chairman of Scotland's International Game Board In 1999, he made headlines again when he resigned from the Scotland Rugby Union in a major dispute over the future direction of the game. **100**

PETER JACKSON

The Speedy Ghost

FUNNY THINGS, FIRST IMPRESSIONS. I first saw Peter Jackson when he was touring New Zealand in 1959 with the British Lions and was immediately struck by the paleness of his complexion. "The All Blacks will have no trouble with this bloke," I thought, showing the deep powers of analysis that could be expected of a 13-year-old.

In fact, the All Blacks were to have a great deal of trouble with the brilliant England winger. Jackson's pallid face and body colour (the legacy of a childhood kidney complaint) made him seem less than imposing, but in his case looks counted for nothing. 'Nikolai', as he was nicknamed, had a marvellous tour, scoring 16 tries in 14 matches. The other famous Lions winger that year, Irishman Tony O'Reilly, scored 17 tries, and between them they set New Zealand abuzz.

Though he played with flair and originality, Jackson always wore a serious, dignified expression on the field. To my youthful eyes, he looked very upper class, perhaps like a king.

For a decade, Jackson left opposing defences floundering with his bag of tricks, which often seemed to have a hypnotic effect on his opposition. He was quick-footed and beautifully balanced, but there was more to it than that. He had all manner of ploys to throw an opponent off guard, including an array of dummy passes, sometimes to no-one in particular. Another Jackson favourite was to shape to chip kick over his opponent's head. Often his opponent had turned and begun his chase for the ball before he realised it was still in Jackson's hands. Like all good wingers, Jackson seldom died with the ball. He would run back infield towards his supports, so tended to set up tries for his backline, as well as scoring more than his share.

The Englishman scored several memorable tries during the 1959 Lions tour, including two in the three tests he played in New Zealand. The best was in the fourth test when he received the ball from fullback Ken Scotland about 35 metres from the line with three defenders fanning out in front of him. He embarked on a jinking, zig-zagging run, threw in a couple of dummies and left several All Blacks sprawled behind him as he dived over in the corner in Ralph Caulton's tackle.

He began that tour with two tries against Hawkes Bay and scored tries in his first six matches, including four against West Coast-Buller (when he played on the left wing) and against a combined Marlborough-Nelson Bays side. According to O'Reilly, Jackson became such a crowd-pleaser on tour that it

Peter Barrie Jackson
Winger
Born: Birmingham, September 22, 1930
Test debut: England v Wales Twickenham, January 21, 1956
Test career: 1956-63 (25 matches - 20 for England, 5 for the British Isles)
Test points: 21 (7 tries)

was suggested to the Lions the Englishman be equipped with a one-wheeled bicycle and three juggling balls to keep the crowd entertained when play was not on his side of the field.

New Zealanders shouldn't have been surprised at his try-scoring exploits. After all, the year before against the Australians at Twickenham he scored one of the most famous tries in rugby history. It was 6-6 deep into injury time, England were a man short and the Wallabies were pressing for victory when the ball reached Jackson's wing. Though he looked to be well bottled up by the defence, Jackson began an amazing side-stepping run. He brushed off his opposing wing, Rod Phelps, feinted inside, then ran around fullback Terry Curley. Again he beat Phelps, who had recovered and gone after him, and then he twisted past the cover defence before he crashing over in the corner for a try that one writer said 'gave him life membership in the Twickenham Hall of Fame'.

Jackson attended King Edward's School in Birmingham, shining not only as a flyhalf in rugby, but also in athletics. He set school records for the 100 yards, 220 yards and 880 yards. After leaving school, he played for the Old Edwardians club for six years before joining Coventry in 1954. He first played in an England trial in 1950, but had to wait six seasons for his test debut.

Typically self-effacing, Jackson claims he was too selfish to be a flyhalf and that his coaches moved him onto the wing where he could do less damage to his team's attack. In fact, he was a natural winger, with his speed, elusiveness and powers of invention.

He made his international debut against Wales in 1956 and played his last test in 1963. Strangely for such an outstanding player, he missed a lot of matches through non-selection. He had only three full seasons for England - 1957, 1959 and 1963 - and after his triumphant 1959 Lions tour played only five more times for England. In all he played 20 tests for England and another five for the Lions.

His last big season was 1963 when he helped England win the Five Nations Championship. He captained Warwickshire from 1960-64, leading them to a hat-trick of county titles. He also represented the Army and North Midlands.

Jackson thought deeply about his rugby. For instance, he often said it was a waste to have wingers throwing in the ball at lineouts as they should be freed to play more positive roles in general play. He was right - these days hookers do the throwing into lineouts. Jackson also once outlined the unusual theory that he became a better winger as he got older and slower. He explained that in his younger days his feet used to move too fast for his brain, but that as his feet slowed down, he became more co-ordinated, in effect catching up with himself. He became a successful businessman, rising through the ranks at the Cadbury firm, then in 1960 becoming managing director of Exports Packers Midlands Ltd.

I met Jackson in 1997 in London during the inauguration ceremony for the first 15 members of the International Rugby Hall of Fame. He looked somewhat pale and grey, but still very dignified, just as I remembered him nearly 40 years earlier. 💯

Jackson's six tries for England (in 20 tests), places him well down the list of England test try-scorers, though most of those above him represented England many more times. The try-scoring leaders are:

49	Rory Underwood	1984-96
24*	Jeremy Guscott	1989-99
18	Cyril Lowe	1913-23
13	Tony Underwood	1992-97
12	Will Carling	1988-97
10	Jack Birkett	1906-12
10	David Duckham	1969-76
9	Arthur Hudson	1906-10
8	Gordon Robinson	1897-1901
8	Chris Oti	1988-91

* still playing

RON JARDEN

The Idol of Athletic Park

RON JARDEN WAS THE Wellington rugby idol of the 1950s, a left winger who could turn the most unlikely situations into tries and who could also kick goals. He was a real hero and as schoolboys, we tried to copy his mannerisms as well as his play.

He was a distinctive looking person with a high forehead, a Roman nose, and a sprinter's backside. Jarden had incredibly fast leg speed. In fact, when he was at full tilt, his legs seemed a blur.

But there was much more to his game than mere speed. He could sidestep or chip and charge, and had a characteristic swerve which would leave defenders flat-footed. He also had a super centring kick, often to his club and rep team-mate Bill Clark. On countless occasions Clark, a quicksilver flanker, would charge down the field in his distinctive white headgear, grab Jarden's kick and dive over for a try. Rugby league players use the centring kick effectively and I don't know why more use is not made of this valuable weapon in modern rugby.

Besides being a prolific try-scorer - 145 in 134 matches - Jarden was a valuable left-footed goal-kicker. When Wellington played the Springboks in 1956, Wellington received a penalty in front of the posts. Jarden took no run-up at all, but merely stabbed the ball between the posts. That impressed we schoolboys.

Later, as I grew to understand more about rugby, I realised what a talented individual Jarden was. He always did things his way. He scored a record number of tries, helped the All Blacks beat the Springboks in 1956, then retired, aged just 26. He turned himself into a high-flying businessman, lending his name to a successful stockbroking firm. In his 40s, he represented New Zealand at yachting, a crew member of *Barnacle Bill* in the 1975 Admiral's Cup at Cowes. Jarden might well have been a champion athlete (he was a schoolboy sprint sensation and a national junior 440 yards champion) or a golfer (in his limited spare time, he sliced his handicap to six). Sports ability must have run in his family. His mother, Jean, was one of the world's best croquet players.

But it was to rugby that he devoted himself. At Hutt Valley High School he starred in a crack First XV that included champion sprinters Don Jowett and Lionel Smith and a clutch of future rugby stars.

By 1949, he was in the Wellington rep team. Though play back then tended

---

Ronald Alexander Jarden
Winger
Born: Lower Hutt, December 14, 1929
Died: Wellington, February 18, 1977
Test debut: New Zealand v Australia, Sydney, June 23, 1951
Test career: 1951-56 (16 tests)
Test points: 42 (7 tries, 6 conversions, 3 penalties)
* Against the Australian team Central West in 1951, he scored 38 points (6 tries, 10 conversions) for a world record that lasted 23 years
* In 1951 he became the first rugby player to win the New Zealand Sportsman of the Year award
* Scored 213 points for New Zealand (35 tries, 36 conversions, 12 penalties)
* Represented New Zealand in the Admiral's Cup yachting competition

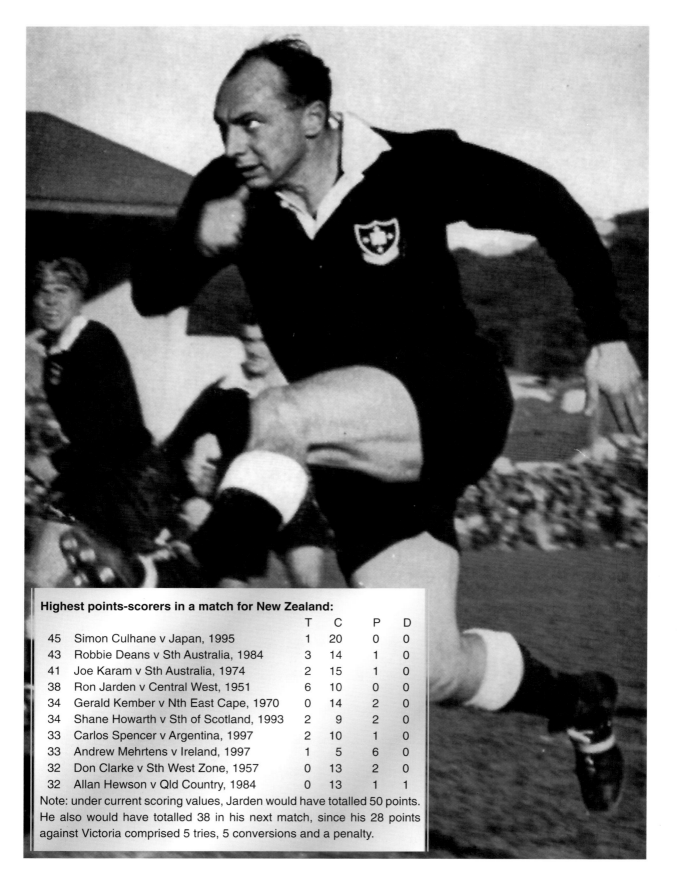

Highest points-scorers in a match for New Zealand:

		T	C	P	D
45	Simon Culhane v Japan, 1995	1	20	0	0
43	Robbie Deans v Sth Australia, 1984	3	14	1	0
41	Joe Karam v Sth Australia, 1974	2	15	1	0
38	Ron Jarden v Central West, 1951	6	10	0	0
34	Gerald Kember v Nth East Cape, 1970	0	14	2	0
34	Shane Howarth v Sth of Scotland, 1993	2	9	2	0
33	Carlos Spencer v Argentina, 1997	2	10	1	0
33	Andrew Mehrtens v Ireland, 1997	1	5	6	0
32	Don Clarke v Sth West Zone, 1957	0	13	2	0
32	Allan Hewson v Qld Country, 1984	0	13	1	1

Note: under current scoring values, Jarden would have totalled 50 points. He also would have totalled 38 in his next match, since his 28 points against Victoria comprised 5 tries, 5 conversions and a penalty.

to be unimaginative, Jarden 1.73m (5ft 8in) and a rather chunky 82.6kg (13st), proved himself a try-scoring freak. When he scored three tries on Eden Park for a Barbarians team against Auckland in 1950, it was obvious he was an All Black in the making.

Within a year, he was a national celebrity. He toured Australia with the New Zealand Universities side and was asked to remain in Australia to link up with the All Blacks. Anything but overawed, he produced a series of record performances. Against Central West, he scored a world record 38 points. In his next match he added a further 28 and after six All Black appearances had scored 88 points, an unprecedented rate in those days.

Jarden looked the most natural footballer in the world. But away from the crowds he spent hours training. Not just running, but repetition sprints, lineout throwing and place-kicking. In an amateur era Jarden prepared like the modern professionals. When wretched weather deterred his mates, his single-mindedness wouldn't allow him to miss a session. Physical fitness was all-important. He didn't smoke and seldom drank. For years his team-mates called him 'the Lemonade King'.

By his standards, he didn't have a super tour of Britain in 1953-54, though he topped the points list and scored 15 tries in his 22 matches. He suffered from homesickness and seemed bored. "I didn't enjoy the tour," he said later. "We played negatively, without enterprise. The whole thing became a chore."

Back home the points piled up. In 1954 he scored 155, including 20 tries, and the following year he topped 200 and scored 30 tries in only 16 matches, incredible figures for those times.

His last season of big rugby was 1956, when he was one of the special heroes in the series against South Africa. In the first test he intercepted and sprinted 40 metres for a crucial try. In the hard-fought third test he leapt high and pulled down a Ross Brown kick to score another try. He was so dangerous that the Springboks tended, as did other teams, to spend so much time watching him that gaps opened up inside.

His most famous effort that year was his 'non-try' for New Zealand Universities against the Springboks. Jarden beat nearly the entire visiting side before he dotted down. Only then was everyone's attention drawn to a linesman's flag way back up the field. Jarden had stepped into touch at the beginning of his amazing run, so the try didn't stand, though the memory of that run certainly remains.

He was still in his rugby prime when he retired. He'd scored 945 points at rep level and Winston McCarthy ranked him as the best winger he ever saw.

But Jarden preferred to move on. "I'd reached my potential. My general manager at Shell Oil had given me an opportunity to put my business career on course." So Jarden changed direction, but not pace. He raced through business life, using the same gifts of intelligence, application and determination he had applied to his rugby.

Jarden's father Benjamin had suffered heart problems and close friends of Ron suggest he may have known he, too, had a problem with his heart. He preferred to continue his frantic pace of work and in the end it cost him his life.

He died in 1977, aged just 47, so young for one of his dynamism and energy. At the time he was chairman of the Broadcasting Corporation (and effectively my boss!). His death shocked rugby followers, but in hindsight Jarden had lived life at the pace he wanted - the individual to the end. ⓿

The match programme for Ron Jarden's last test: New Zealand v South Africa, Auckland, 1956.

NEIL JENKINS

Making a Point

Neil Roger Jenkins
Flyhalf
Born: Pontypridd, August 18, 1967
Test debut: Wales v England, Cardiff, January 19, 1991
Test career: 1991-99 (67 matches - 64 for Wales and 3 for British Isles)
Test points: 767 (8 tries, 94 conversions, 177 penalties, 3 drop goals)
* Kicked a world record eight penalties against Canada in 1993
* Kicked a then world record 11 conversions in the World Cup qualifying match against Portugal in 1994
* He shares with Michael Lynagh the world test record for the most penalties.
* Second on all-time test points-scoring list

IT BAFFLES ME WHY Neil Jenkins has received such grudging praise in his native Wales. The versatile and diligent Jenkins has already amassed more than twice as many points in tests as any other Welshman.

Considering the Pontypridd flyhalf has often been one of the few class acts in a struggling Welsh side, he has not exactly received rave reviews from the critics. However, I've always thought he was a fine player. Sure, he's not a gifted runner in the Jonathan Davies mould and doesn't have the effortless grace of a Barry John. But he has strengths which are not always acknowledged.

He is, of course, a relentlessly accurate place-kicker, a mirror image of All Black Grant Fox, right down to the shaking of the finger tips at the top of the run. Jenkins studied videos of Fox when he was attempting to perfect his style and the results have been telling. ("It's four steps back, two to the left and concentrate, concentrate, concentrate," he says.) Jenkins is often described in semi-disparaging terms as a great kicker, the inference being he has few other skills.

Yet this same player has scored a vast number of tries for his Pontypridd club side and has shown the sort of rugby nous that has enabled him to be selected at centre and fullback for Wales - in his first 50 test caps, he played eight times at centre and seven at fullback. He has a steely nerve and is a strong tackler, which can't be said of all history's great flyhalves. While he may be under-rated in Wales, his value is certainly recognised overseas and he is always a player targeted by opposition.

Jenkins was educated at Bryn Celynog Comprehensive School. After joining Pontypridd when he was 14, he stuck loyally with the club in the face of mouth-watering offers from other British rugby and rugby league clubs. For many years his income was boosted by his position as a PR consultant for Just Rentals Limited, though when he first dipped his toe in international rugby, he was a scrap metal dealer.

Jenkins was always going to be a test player. That was obvious to anyone who watched the determined teenager practising his kicking and other skills at Cad Fardre, his local field just outside Pontypridd. He climbed through various age rep sides, and by the time he reached the East Wales under-21 and Welsh youth sides in 1989-90, was pushing hard for a test spot. He turned in some good performances in under-21 tests for Wales during the 1990-91 season, scoring 14 points against New Zealand and 15 against Scotland.

At the start of 1991 he became an international, making his debut at Cardiff in a 25-6 loss to England. He kicked a penalty in that match and contributed a try and a dropped goal in his next outing, against Italy. But then his career faltered. During Wales' World Cup build-up tour of Australia that year, Jenkins lost his test place to Adrian Davies.

He subsequently missed selection for the World Cup squad, the other flyhalf chosen being the popular 30-test veteran Mark Ring. As ace goal-kicker and captain Paul Thorburn had quit test rugby after 'Welsh rugby died of shame' on their tour of Australia (a 63-6 loss in the only test), Wales went into the World Cup under-manned. In hindsight, the omission of Jenkins was a blunder. Wales lost to Western Samoa and Australia in that tournament and failed to make the quarter-finals.

Jenkins, 1.78m (5ft 10in) and 84kg (13st 3lb), established himself during the next Five Nations Championship. Since then, the ginger-haired Jenkins, with his trademark jug ears, has been a familiar sight on rugby fields throughout the world.

Various Welsh coaches, seeking that elusive commodity called flair, but not wanting to sacrifice Jenkins' match-winning place-kicking, have shunted him to centre and fullback. Generally Jenkins has grinned and done his best. He has endeavoured to increase his speed and has focused on improving his running and passing.

But things came into a head in 1998 when coach Kevin Bowring put him at fullback with the nifty Arwel Thomas at flyhalf. Wales were pummelled 60-26 at Twickenham, and Jenkins, who looked uncomfortable in the No 15 jersey, decided enough was enough. "I never want to play fullback again," he said. "I'm not a fullback. I don't like playing there. I'm a flyhalf by nature and number ten is my proper position."

Having declared his hand, Jenkins then returned to his favoured flyhalf position. Bowring's replacement as Welsh coach, New Zealander Graham Henry, who had coached Grant Fox and knew the value of a solid, dependable flyhalf, elected to keep Jenkins in that position. During the 1998-99 home season, Jenkins responded to that vote of confidence with some of the best rugby of his career.

There weren't many high points for Wales in the 1990s, but Jenkins played a major role in any. He scored 48 points in four matches when Wales won the Five Nations Championship in 1994 and had a record 30 points against Italy in 1999. He was Welsh Player of the Year in 1994 and 1995.

Jenkins was also a key player in the Lions' 1997 trip to South Africa. He finished the trip with 110 points and scored 41 in the three tests, helping the Lions to a notable 2-1 series victory.

Jenkins, the sixth player to top 50 test caps for Wales, became the Welsh record-holder when he passed Thorburn's 304 points. By the end of the 1999 Five Nations Championship, he was the second-highest points scorer in test rugby. 💯

The top Welsh points-scorers in tests:		
726*	Neil Jenkins	1991-99
304	Paul Thorburn	1985-91
173*	Arwel Thomas	1996-98
166	Phil Bennett	1969-78
157	Ieuan Evans	1987-98
152	Steve Fenwick	1975-81
90	Barry John	1965-72
88	John Bancroft	1909-14
88	Gareth Edwards	1967-78
81	Mark Wyatt	1983-87
81	Jonathan Davies	1985-97

* still playing

Note: excludes points scored when playing for British Isles

BARRY JOHN

The King

Barry John
Flyhalf
Born: Cefeneithin, January 6, 1945
Test debut: Wales v Australia, Cardiff, December 3, 1966
Test career: 1966-72 (30 matches - 25 for Wales, 5 for the British Isles)
Test points: 120 (6 tries, 9 conversions, 18 penalties, 10 drop goals)
* Was one of the First XV inducted into the International Rugby Hall of Fame in 1997
* His 90 points for Wales was a national test record when he retired

HIS BRITISH TEAM-MATES anointed Barry John 'the King' after his wonderful play on the 1971 tour of New Zealand. Handsome and richly gifted, the Welsh flyhalf became rugby's first television superstar when extensive coverage of that tour was beamed back to Britain.

Not only was John the model flyhalf, but he was amazingly accurate as a place-kicker, racking up 180 points in New Zealand - more than double the previous Lions record. He was a pivotal player in what some call the greatest backline ever: Gareth Edwards, John, Mike Gibson, John Dawes, David Duckham, Gerald Davies, JPR Williams.

There were many heroes in that Lions team, but to New Zealand rugby followers John shone. Nearly three decades later, his reputation in New Zealand is secure.

But for those who have run into John in recent times, his change in physical appearance has been sad. He retired from rugby in 1972, having just turned 27 and still at his peak. There followed years in which he wrote or put his name to several books. He became involved with the media and still covers rugby for BBC radio.

At the launch of the International Rugby Hall of Fame in 1997, he was accompanied by his son, who acted as his driver. I couldn't help notice his hand shaking as he autographed balls and other items that evening. What made the sight all the more poignant was the memory of the fit, athletic, easy-going player of the early 1970s.

John attended Gwendraeth Grammar School - a great nursery of Welsh rugby. He had the good fortune to grow up across the local park from famed Welsh coach and former test flyhalf Carwyn James, who became his mentor and, of course, coached the 1971 Lions.

At school, John shone in several sports and was notably talented at soccer, which may have contributed to his remarkable kicking skills in rugby. He made his rep rugby debut for Llanelli and spent three seasons with the club. During his final year at Trinity College, Carmarthen, he was chosen for Wales in their 1966 test against Australia. He held his place for the following test, against Scotland, and was then dropped for David Watkins.

Things really happened in the next off-season. Watkins turned to league and John switched to the Cardiff club, linking with Wales' new halfback, Gareth Edwards. It was the start of a wonderful six-year partnership. There

seemed to be a special chemistry between the pair who went on to play 28 tests together for Wales and the Lions.

Edwards confessed that initially he was concerned about being able to deliver enough good quality ball, but was immediately put at ease by the laid-back John, who said casually: "Look Gareth, you throw them - I'll catch them."

John and Edwards toured South Africa with the 1968 Lions and were just hitting their straps when John broke his collarbone in the first test and was forced out of the tour. The following year they toured Australia and New Zealand and did little of note in a Welsh side that was twice outplayed by the All Blacks.

But by 1971 they were really humming. Wales sewed up their third consecutive Five Nations Championship, and the Grand Slam, with a brilliant 9-5 victory over France in Paris. Critics rated it John's finest game for Wales. He broke his nose making a try-saving tackle, but stayed on the field to score a brilliant individual try and kick a penalty.

Then it was on to New Zealand. Amazingly, John wasn't even Wales' No 1 kicker at the start of 1971 and Englishman Bob Hiller was expected to be the Lions' top points-scorer. Hiller did indeed contribute 102 points, but lagged far behind the unerringly accurate John. With his round-the-corner kicking style, John inadvertently launched a revolution in New Zealand as throughout the country youngsters (and some not so young) emulated his technique.

The stylish John had a major impact on the test series. In the first test, he clinically tormented experienced All Black fullback Fergie McCormick with a string of diagonal cross-kicks that seemed to be forever just out of reach as they bounced into touch. McCormick, all at sea, was dropped from the test side, never to play for New Zealand again. John scored a try in the crucial third test and contributed 30 points in the series.

But he wasn't just a place-kicker. He had mastery of all manner of kicks, including a lethal drop goal, and was a swift, elusive runner who made liberal use of a good sidestep and was able to glide through opposing defences. Like all class players, John seemed to have all the time in the world to weigh up a situation. He exuded confidence and was hard to rattle. At 1.75m (5ft 9in) and 75kg (11st 11lb), he wasn't a huge tackler, but I cannot recall opponents being able to exploit this possible chink.

While it's true that John was fortunate to play outside such a fine player as Edwards, he used possession well. We saw a touch of his genius in the game against New Zealand Universities at Wellington. It was just a midweek encounter and the Lions won it going away, 27-6. But one moment from John lit up the match. Late in the first half he received the ball, feinted to drop a goal, then embarked on a scuttling run which took him through the opposition defence and eventually to the tryline.

John - 'B J' was another name his team-mates called him - was a popular tourist. He took all the praise heaped on him with good grace and was most accommodating. After the fourth test I asked him rather diffidently if he could come outside for an interview. No, he replied, it would be better if I went into the dressing room. Then, with celebrations taking place all around him, he asked me how he could help.

Back home, he played only three more tests for Wales, then retired, in mid-career really. He had played 30 tests, including five for the Lions, and scored 120 points. I suppose he could argue that he'd done it all and there was no reason to carry on. But I suspect he retired because he found all the attention too cloying. He was offered all manner of endorsements by businesses keen to capitalise on his amazing popularity.

Phil Bennett, who followed John as the next great player to emerge from the Welsh flyhalf factory, called the peerless John 'a one-off genius' and it's hard to argue with that assessment.

When weighing up John's place in the rugby pantheon, his early retirement must be taken into account. There have been great flyhalves like Hugo Porta and Michael Lynagh who have endured for years and years. John was more like a shooting star, flashing across the skyline. But he certainly burned brightly while he was there. ◖100◗

CLIFF JONES

Flyhalf Flair

CLIFF JONES DIDN'T HAVE a long international career, but in one match he did enough to ensure New Zealanders recalled his name forever. Jones was one of a clutch of brilliant backs who plotted Wales' 13-12 defeat of the 1935 All Blacks, the second of three occasions that Wales has beaten New Zealand.

Wales had a fabulous backline, with a schoolboy halfback in Haydn Tanner and other stars like Vivian Jenkins, Wilfred Wooller, Claude Davey and Idwal Rees. But the man who formulated the pre-match tactics and marshalled the backline was flyhalf Cliff Jones. It was Jones who kicked through so Davey could score under the posts, and it was Jones who repeatedly broke downfield or made space for Wooller at inside centre.

The *Sunday Referee* said: 'Jones was always a source of trouble to the New Zealanders and the credit for the fine display of the Welsh backs must go to him and Wooller.' Dai Gent in the *Sunday Times* pointed to Jones as the spearhead of the Welsh attack. The *United Press Association* said Jones was simply too good for his opposite, Jack Griffiths. Teddy Morgan, the famous winger of the first golden era of Welsh rugby, said: "I have said that Cliff Jones is a greater flyhalf than Percy Bush. He proved me right."

Jones had flypaper hands, a mastery of the teasing short punt, an electrifying sidestep and great self-confidence. Most importantly, though, he was a real rugby thinker. It showed in his book *Rugby Football,* first published in 1937, that ran to six editions and it showed in his relentless push for better coaching systems in Wales.

Yet it could so easily have been soccer. At Porth County School, Jones played soccer with a passion and hero-worshipped Cardiff FC. But when he moved to Llandovery College in 1928, he came under the influence of school coach T P Williams, a disciple of running rugby. Williams, known as 'The Pope', was inspired by the great Oxford (and Scottish) three-quarter line of the 1920s and moulded his teams accordingly.

Jones, 1.72m (5ft 8in) and 70kg (11st), had flair and the kicking skills he'd picked up at soccer, and adapted quickly to rugby. His speed set him apart. He was not only phenomenally fast, but he ran in a jinking style that made him a nightmare to try to stop. Often he'd leave two or three defenders sprawling before being halted. One of the most memorable of his many fine tries was a 40-metre effort against Scotland when he weaved and side-stepped his way through a succession of defenders.

William Clifford Jones
Flyhalf
Born: Rhondda, March 12, 1914
Died: Bonvilston, November 27, 1990
Test debut: Wales v England, Cardiff, January 20, 1934
Test career: 1934-38 (13 matches)
Test points: 6 (2 tries)
* During the 1935-36 season, he was in an unbeaten Welsh side which won the Five Nations Championship and beat New Zealand

Most common names in Welsh test rugby history:

Jones	60
Davies	56
Williams	46
Evans	45
Thomas	36
Morgan	22

At least 72 players named Jones have appeared in test rugby. Not surprisingly, Wales leads the way with 60, followed by New Zealand 4, Australia 3, South Africa and England 2 and Scotland 1.

The best-known players named Jones have been:

Cliff Jones (Wales)	1934-38
Ian Jones (New Zealand)	1990-98*
Ken Jones (Wales/British Isles)	1947-57
Lewis Jones (Wales/British Isles)	1950-52
Michael Jones (Western Samoa/New Zealand)	1986-98*
Peter Jones (New Zealand)	1954-60
Robert Jones (Wales/British Isles)	1985-95

* still playing

Of course, this takes no account of derivatives of Jones, such as Nick Farr-Jones, and does not include the likes of noted 1980s Wallaby coach Alan Jones.

He was already a fine rugby player when he went up to Cambridge University in 1933, aged 19. He and Wooller played in that year's University match while still freshmen. Cambridge lost 5-3, but Jones and the no-nonsense Wooller were blameless. Five weeks later they were playing for an outclassed Wales against England at Cardiff. As Jones recalled: "I rarely had a pass all afternoon, with [England flanker] Harry Fry breathing down my neck and a scrumhalf with a damaged hand. It was some baptism."

Gradually Wales built their superb backline. In 1935 two schoolboys, Tanner and Willie Davies, played with remarkable maturity to mastermind Swansea's defeat of the All Blacks. They were cousins and there was pressure for them to be chosen for the All Black test. The selectors stuck with Jones and were richly rewarded. Davies was some player, though, and there was much debate about whether he or Jones was the better flyhalf. Other countries would have grabbed either.

Jones captained Wales in 1938, then retired prematurely. He was never a very sturdy player. He suffered several broken bones in his teens, broke his collarbone in 1936, and in 1939 a serious elbow injury confirmed his decision to hang up his boots. Though just 25, he'd done enough to confirm his place in rugby's hall of fame. The *Rugby Football Annual* said: 'There was the spark of genius in his running and kicking ahead. Every now and then his play was sheer pyrotechnics.'

When I spoke to older Welshmen about Cliff Jones, I'd naturally mention Barry John. Was Jones as good as Barry John? Not Barry John, they'd say. Imagine Gerald Davies playing at flyhalf. That was Cliff Jones.

Wooller, a straight-talking individual who played with Jones for Cambridge University, Cardiff and Wales, was past his 80th birthday when asked who he rated best Welsh flyhalf. Wooller talked of Cliff Morgan and especially Barry John, then said: "Cliff Jones was the best I ever played with and the best I ever saw."

Though he played just 13 tests, Jones knew some great days in rugby. The Cambridge side in 1934 scored six tries in winning the University match 29-4, a stupendous margin then. For Wales he enjoyed the immortal triumph against the 1935 All Blacks and a Five Nations Championship that season. Later he captained his country.

After his playing days, Jones, a lawyer, developed an interest in antiques and became nationally known as an antiques dealer.

He was never far from rugby, though. He became a Welsh selector in 1957 and served on the Big Five for 21 years. The secret of selecting, he said, was to build a team without losing individual brilliance, which sums up the way he played.

Always he stressed the importance of coaching. In the late 1950s, he made himself unpopular in Wales with his attempts to coach the test side on an informal basis. The British seemed to regard coaching as little more than a sly form of cheating. Later Jones became a coaching co-ordinator and was a prime mover in Wales setting up its effective squad system for training the national team. "I always knew the value of good coaching, but the way people felt back then, you had to sell them the concept like some sort of spiritual experience - a religious revival," he once said.

The dapper Jones, with his ever-present youthful smile, was already a respected elder statesman of Welsh rugby when in the Centenary year of 1980 he became Wales Rugby Union president. It fell to Jones to host the Queen at Cardiff Arms Park when the All Blacks played Wales. He described this as one of the great honours of his life. **100**

KEN JONES

The Olympic Speedster

IT'S DOUBTFUL IF TODAY we'd ever see a sportsman like Ken Jones, the flying Welsh right winger of the immediate post-war years. Not only was Jones arguably the best winger in the world at his peak, but he was also a champion athlete.

As professional rugby's seasons expand, there is less chance for players to apply themselves to a major second sport. For instance, Jeff Wilson, the crack All Black winger, has had to give away cricket, at which he represented New Zealand at one-day level. But previously Jones and others such as his countryman Wilf Wooller (who led Glamorgan at county cricket level for many years), could successfully combine major sports.

Jones did more than merely run internationally; he shone. He won a sprint relay silver medal for Great Britain in the 1948 London Olympics (for three days it was a gold, until the USA was deemed to have been wrongly disqualified) and was a semi-finalist in the 100m. He won a bronze medal in the 220 yards and was sixth in the 100 yards at the 1954 Vancouver Empire Games. For years he represented his country at meets all over the Continent and in 1955 he captained Britain at the European champs at Berne. In 1958 Jones managed Welsh team at the Cardiff Empire Games.

Not only was Jones fast, but his running career endured. He won the Welsh 100 yards championship seven times in eight years, missing out only in 1950 when touring New Zealand with the Lions, and won eight national 220-yard crowns.

Despite this heavy involvement with athletics, Jones is primarily recalled for his rugby exploits. He was a real crowd-pleaser, for he scored record numbers of tries through a combination of thrilling pace and flair.

Nowhere is Jones' lethal try-scoring ability acknowledged more than in New Zealand, against whom he scored two memorable tries. The first was for the 1950 British Lions. In the fourth test at Eden Park, he raced 60 metres, chased all the way by New Zealand sprint champion Peter Henderson. But no player outpaced Jones, not even the quicksilver Henderson.

Even more significant was Jones' try for Wales against Bob Stuart's 1953-54 All Blacks - the first live rugby telecast in Wales. The All Blacks appeared to have a spirited Welsh side under control until Clem Thomas unexpectedly cross-kicked and Jones capitalised on a kind bounce to grab the ball and elude his marker, Ron Jarden, to score under the posts. Wales thus turned likely defeat into a famous victory.

Kenneth Jeffrey Jones
Winger
Born: Blaenavon, December 30, 1921
Test debut: Wales v England, Cardiff, January 18, 1947
Test career: 1947-57 (47 matches - 44 for Wales, 3 for British Isles)
Test points: 57 (19 tries)
* A champion athlete who won an Olympic silver medal in 1948
* Played 43 successive tests for Wales
* Held the world record for most tests played

Ken Jones' breathtaking run to score for the British Isles v New Zealand, Auckland, 1950.

Keith Quinn's ranking of the century's 10 greatest Welsh players and personalities:

1 Gareth Edwards
2 Barry John
3 Haydn Tanner
4 Gwyn Nicholls
5 John "JPR" Williams
6 Cliff Morgan
7 Ken Jones
8 Gerald Davies
9 Bleddyn Williams
10 Cliff Jones

At 1.80m (5ft 11in) and just over 76kg (12st), Jones was strongly built, with very long legs. He was more of a swerver (like Jarden) than a side-stepper. Besides his speed, he had good hands and was a fearless tackler. They loved him in New Zealand in 1950. Not only did he average a try in each of his 16 matches (including scoring two in his three tests), but he was likeable and self-effacing. Jones, dubbed 'the Flying Welshman', was one of several backs - including Bleddyn Williams, Jackie Kyle and Jack Matthews - who helped make the side so attractive to watch.

Jones was from a sports-minded family. By nine, he was playing rugby at Blaenavon Boys School and in the late 1930s, when attending West Monmouthshire Grammar School, he was fortunate to come under the eye of former Pontypool forward Gilbert Granett. Jones' rugby progressed well and in the 1939-40 season he captained the school first season and made the Welsh secondary schools side.

On to St Paul's Training College, Cheltenham, where it became clear he had all the attributes of a class winger. He was wiry and robust and in 1941-42 captained the college team. However, rugby was far from the primary focus in those troubled days and when he turned 21 he entered the Royal Air Force. He found time while on duty in South Africa and India to play wartime rugby and to win any sprint races going.

Immediately after the war he was chosen for the Newport side, which he was to represent with honour for over a decade. Jones attended Loughborough College, qualifying as a PE teacher, then returned to Wales, to teach at Newport High School. Wales couldn't pick him quickly enough, and his debut, against England in 1947, came in Wales' first post-war test.

When he retired in 1957, Jones' 47 tests represented the world record. The span of his test career was amazing for a winger whose debut was delayed some years by war. And let's not forget, he was sprinting for all he was worth each summer. Jones was part of Welsh teams that won two Grand Slams and six Five Nations titles.

His try-scoring ratio was impressive, especially as the rules of the time did not encourage expansive backline play. For years rugby critics bemoaned the fact that the lethal winger was not provided with more ball by either Newport or Wales.

It is unusual to have a winger captain a rugby team, but Jones successfully led Newport in the 1950s. His ability to analyse rugby could be seen after his retirement by his work as the *Sunday Express* rugby correspondent. ⑩⓪

MICHAEL JONES

Fire and Ice

FLEET STREET WRITER John Reason's trenchant criticisms never endeared him to dyed-in-the-wool New Zealand rugby fans. However, he silenced his critics when he nominated All Black loose forward Michael Jones as the greatest rugby player he'd seen.

'Jones really was poetry in motion,' wrote Reason, 'a combination of grand prix-winning car and a Shakespeare sonnet. He won gold medals across the board, whether jumping, handling, running, tackling, positioning, improvising or thinking. He even stood at the top of the dais when it came to behaviour and sportsmanship. Michael Jones was indeed a man apart.'

Was Reason's praise too fulsome? Could any player - any person - have all those qualities? In this instance, Reason was absolutely accurate. After Jones had sensationally launched his All Black career during the 1987 World Cup, John Hart observed: "This boy could play at centre in a World Cup final and not look out of place." Graham Mourie, himself a great flanker, once observed: "At times I feel Michael has played as well as any international loose forward could hope to play."

This was heady stuff, but if ever a person was unlikely to be affected, it was the unassuming Jones. Fine player though he was, I admired him even more as a person, for he epitomised the ideals of fair play. Off the field he was a gentle, generous soul, with time for everyone. He was quietly-spoken with an endearing, almost child-like giggle.

Over a quarter of a century, on countless tours with rugby teams, I have only once had an All Black offer to help me with my luggage. In Sydney in 1988 I was startled to find Jones lugging my bags into a taxi for the airport. It's a sad indictment that by this one simple action Jones should stand out, but there it is.

Jones' strong Christian beliefs precluded him from playing rugby on Sundays. I'm sure that when he entered the test arena in 1986 he had no idea how far-reaching the decision would be. I interviewed him in South Africa before his 50th test and asked him to nominate his greatest moment in the All Blacks. He considered for some time, then replied: "Every time I play for the All Blacks I praise the Lord."

Because of his stand on Sunday play, he missed dozens of tests. Sceptics were soon won over by his obvious sincerity. Lesser players would have struggled to hold their places under those circumstances, but Jones was not

Michael Niko Jones
Loose forward
Born: Auckland, April 8, 1965
Test debut: Western Samoa v Wales, Apia, June 14, 1986
Test career: 1986-98 (56 - matches, 55 for New Zealand, 1 for Western Samoa).
Test points: 56 (13 tries)
* His 53 tests as a flanker is the New Zealand record
* Was the first player to score a try in the first two World Cups

a lesser player. Successive All Black coaches Brian Lochore, Alex Wyllie, Laurie Mains and Hart all rated him tops.

Though a dynamic player and ferocious tackler, Jones never resorted to foul tactics. He justified his crunching tackling by saying with a grin, "The Lord says it is better to give than to receive." His team-mates called him 'The Iceman', and he certainly had ice in his veins. It was amazing he could play with so much fire while being so cool and clinical.

Jones grew up in west Auckland and was a sports star at Henderson High, the best batsman in the First XI, the First XV captain for three years, a brilliant athlete and basketballer. He credits basketball for giving him the skills that served him so well in rugby. Jones represented Auckland at rugby at various age levels and progressed to the North Island under-18 side.

Auckland coach Hart quickly spotted him as an exceptional talent and Jones repaid his faith when drafted into the Auckland side in 1985. Chronically shy off the field, he was the equal of anyone on it and scored three tries on his provincial debut, against South Canterbury.

Jones was born in Auckland, but his brother and sisters were born in Samoa and it was for Western Samoa that he played his first test, against Wales at Apia in 1986. It was a violent match and the rookie Jones would have required all his ethical skills to steer clear of the trouble. I have no doubt he managed, though, for I never saw him throw a punch, despite sometimes being sorely provoked.

During a visit to Britain with a Barbarians side in March, 1987, Jones was so brilliant he became a must selection for the World Cup shortly after. Yet just a couple of months before when the All Blacks selectors had named 70 World Cup possibles, he was one of the last chosen. His meteoric rise reminded me of the emergence of another Auckland loose forward, Waka Nathan, 25 years earlier.

Jones was sublime at the World Cup, scoring the first individual try of the tournament, against Italy, and forming, with Wayne Shelford and Alan Whetton, one of the best All Black loose forward trios. I recall him charging up the field against Fiji in Christchurch, his loose-limbed, relaxed style reminding me of great Cuban 400m-800m runner Alberto Juantorena. His other try in the tournament was the first of the final, against France.

By the time Jones played his 13th test, against Argentina at Athletic Park in 1989, he was the world's best loose forward. But in that test he suffered an horrendous injury, tearing and shredding both cruciate ligaments, plus his medial ligaments. All Black doctor John Mayhew said it was the worst knee injury he'd seen in rugby. It was feared his career was over. But placing his faith in the Lord, Jones quietly and calmly worked his way back to fitness. When he returned a year later, in the Ranfurly Shield match against Southland in 1990, he received an emotional welcome from the crowd and celebrated with a try.

The increase in Sunday play meant he missed much of the early season in New Zealand, including the South Pacific Championship and that competition's various spin-offs. At the 1991 World Cup, he was again the tournament's first try-scorer, against England at Twickenham, but had to sit in the stands and watch the All Blacks being hammered by Australia in the semi-finals. Perhaps that experience persuaded coach Mains to exclude Jones from the 1995 All Black World Cup team, a decision I agreed with.

There were other problems. A broken jaw in 1993 cost him a tour of Britain, and in 1997 he injured his knee in the first test of the season and was

New Zealand v England, Twickenham 1991. Michael Jones, for the second time, scored the first individual try at the World Cup.

Michael Jones scores the first try by an individual in the Rugby World Cup, New Zealand v Italy, Auckland, 1987.

sidelined for the year. But always he came back: rugby's bionic man.

Though he was never the physical phenomenon of his pre-injury days, he was very nearly as good afterwards. He could be an effective No 8 and from 1996-98, John Hart used him as blindside flanker, his anticipation and deadly tackling more than atoning for a lessening in his speed.

In assessing Jones the player, it is easy to overdo the superlatives. He was solidly built at 1.85m (6ft 1in) and 98kg (15st 6lb), but played above his height and weight. At the back of the lineouts his leaping ability made him a big asset. He had searing pace for a forward, read the game well and had ball-handling skills that most backs would have envied. And always there was that magnificent tackling. He ended up playing 74 games for New Zealand and scoring 16 tries .

I recall Jones' play for the gentle touches. In 1994 the crowd roared when he took the field as a replacement in the third test against South Africa at Auckland (wearing the No 23 jersey, as he'd left his own at the hotel). As he positioned himself in the lineout, he leaned across and shook the hand of his opposite, Francois Pienaar.

Jones' career was eventually stalled by his mounting injuries. He returned repeatedly, often playing in considerable pain, and Hart kept him in the All Blacks until well into 1998. I was concerned Jones' wonderful play of earlier years might be overlooked if he hung on too long and eventually he was dropped, a difficult decision for Hart.

Though immensely popular with team-mates, and the best man or groomsman at more than a dozen of their weddings, Jones was not an inspiring Auckland Blues captain in the Super 12 competition. While he became more eloquent over the years, he didn't have the forceful, driving personality to be a successful captain.

Jones was an unusual mix for a national rugby hero. New Zealanders traditionally admired hard men like Colin Meads, with their absolute commitment to rugby. While Jones loved rugby and cherished the honour of being an All Black, it was always only one facet of his life. His religion, family and career - he earned a masters in geography and a Bachelor of Town Planning - all played important roles. He was a well-balanced individual, able to keep all aspects of his life in perspective. Not every rugby player could say that. 🏉

ANDRE JOUBERT

Rugby's Rolls Royce

IN SOUTH AFRICA, Andre Joubert is, with good reason, known as the Rolls Royce of fullbacks. The quiet Natal star's play reflects the changing role of the fullback since 1970. Previously fullbacks were the last line of defence, but a change in the kick-into-touch rules opened up the game. Players who had previously been required to religiously find touch at every opportunity were now able to launch counter-attacks and bring more individuality to their game. The game has opened still further with more rule changes in the 1990s.

Though at 1.90m (6ft 3in) and 87kg (13st 6lb), Joubert is big even for an international fullback, he epitomises the modern game with his excellent running, explosive counter-attacking, safe defending and tidy left-footed place-kicking. He is South Africa's answer to Jean-Luc Sadourny of France and New Zealand's Christian Cullen. On the field Joubert is dynamic and exciting; off it, he is one of the nicest of people, courteous and friendly.

After attending Ladysmith High School, Joubert began to make a name for himself in the late 1980s, eventually playing 93 times for Orange Free State before switching to Natal in 1992. His flair and pace captured the attention of the national selectors and in 1989 he made his test debut, taking the field as a replacement against a World XV at Newlands.

South Africa's international rugby isolation bit into his career, even though he was long recognised as a class fullback - he was a South African Player of the Year finalist as early as 1991. That was also the year when British rugby fans got their first inkling of his brilliance. Playing for the Barbarians against Scotland at Murrayfield, he set up a glorious match-winning try in the final minute with a break from under his own posts that didn't end until he was deep in Scottish territory. When South Africa re-emerged as a test-playing nation in 1992, Theo van Rensburg was the test fullback. When he suffered a groin injury during the Springboks' 1993 tour of Australia, Joubert, aged 29, was called in as a replacement. It was a chance he grabbed.

The Natal player - a bank official by occupation - quickly made up for lost time. He scored two tries and added two conversions in the 65-5 defeat of Queensland Country and kicked two conversions and four penalties in the 31-20 victory over Sydney. These performances enabled him to leapfrog the original No 2 fullback, Hugh Reece-Edwards, and gain selection for the decisive third test at Sydney.

Even then it wasn't all plain sailing, for he had to hold off the challenges of Chris Dirks and Gavin Johnson before cementing his place as the

Andre Johan Joubert
Fullback
Born: Ladysmith, April 15, 1964
Test debut: South Africa v World XV, Cape Town, August 26, 1989
Test career: 1989-97 (34 matches)
Test points: 117 (10 tries, 8 conversions, 17 penalties)
* Has played the most tests for South Africa by a fullback
* His total of 38 points for South Africa against Swansea in 1994 is a national record

Springbok test fullback. His cause was helped by a good tour of Argentina late in 1993, when he scored a try in the second test victory.

Joubert's career continued to soar in 1994. Whether playing for his Harlequins club, Natal or South Africa, he was in consistently superb form.

His polished all-round display and deadly place-kicking were pivotal in Natal's 21-6 upset of England. In the first test a fortnight later, he kicked five penalties, and in the second he scored a try, a conversion and two penalties, giving him the handy total of 28 points in the two tests.

Then it was onto New Zealand where, though operating in a well-beaten side, he was generally one of the South Africans' best performers. Joubert played in all three tests, the second only as a replacement for van Rensburg. In his eight tour games he totalled 56 points, second to van Rensburg. New Zealanders were impressed with his running from deep defensive positions and his ability as a support player.

On South Africa's end-of-year tour of Scotland and Wales, Joubert was brilliant, totalling 75 points in eight matches. He played well in both tests, but his most talked-about effort was his virtuoso display against Swansea: four tries and nine conversions for a national record of 38 points in the 78-7 rout. Joubert was voted International Player of the Year by overseas critics, but inexplicably missed being named South African Player of the Year for 1994.

By 1995 he had established himself as South Africa's No 1 fullback and played five matches in the World Cup. He had to play the semi-final against France and the final against New Zealand with a bandaged broken hand, the result of an injury in the quarter-final against Western Samoa. Coach Kitch Christie was desperately keen to keep him in the side and reckoned even an injured Joubert was a better bet than any other fullback available to him. Joubert did not let him down, and in the final his cool head and experience helped South Africa escape from some tricky situations.

After the World Cup, Joubert, though into his 30s, became one of the glamour players in the Springbok side. He played 11 tests in 1996 and proved himself a prolific try-scorer. His appearances became more spotty in 1997 as he was plagued by injuries and the talented Percy Montgomery began push him for his test spot. But Joubert ended the year having played 34 tests, the most by any South African fullback.

Joubert distinguished himself in other spheres as well. He represented South Africa at sevens from 1992-94 and at various times played for South African, French and British Barbarians sides.

He has been a consistent scorer in Super 10 and Super 12 matches. In the 1994 Super 10 match against Western Samoa at Auckland, he scored 33 points. Joubert helped Natal reach the competition final against Queensland that year. In 1996, playing for the Natal Sharks (as the team was then known), his 12 tries in the Super 12 competition placed him second overall, behind teammate James Small. Joubert had a magnificent semi-final, scoring two tries and kicking two conversions as Natal convincingly beat Queensland 43-25. He scored another try in the final, against the Auckland Blues, but couldn't prevent a 45-21 defeat.

At Currie Cup level, Joubert was in the Natal side that lost the 1993 final to Transvaal 21-15, but gained some revenge by helping Natal beat Western Province 25-17 in 1995 and Transvaal 33-15 in 1996.

In early 1999 Joubert suffered an allergic reaction to a bee sting while playing golf and had to be resuscitated in a hospital trauma unit. Typical of his strength, he was soon back playing brilliantly for the Sharks in the Super 12 competition. **100**

PHIL KEARNS

Australia's Rock

WALLABY COACH Bob Dwyer gambled bravely and successfully by throwing rookie hooker Phil Kearns into the Australian team in 1989. Kearns, just turned 22, was playing for Dwyer's old club, Randwick, in the Sydney reserve grade competition when picked for his test debut against New Zealand at Eden Park.

It wasn't easy for him. He didn't know some team-mates, was replacing a top hooker in Tommy Lawton, was moving from minor club to test rugby, and was pitted against the redoubtable Sean Fitzpatrick. When the first scrum packed down, the resounding crunch could be heard in the stands. As the two front rows were pulled apart, Fitzpatrick stared grimly at Kearns and said: "Welcome to the big time." An enduring rivalry had begun.

Initially Fitzpatrick, who had rated Lawton very highly, was disparaging of Kearns. He taunted, niggled and did all he could to make the new Wallaby's life miserable. But Kearns enjoyed a delicious moment of revenge at Athletic Park in 1990 in the third test of the Bledisloe Cup series. New Zealand turned round leading 9-6, but then Kearns swooped on a loose ball near the All Black line and dived over for a try. He did not let the moment pass without making some pointed remarks to Fitzpatrick nearby, and finished by offering the classic Churchillian gesture. Asked later what he'd said, he replied: "I invited Sean to a barbecue … no, two barbecues."

Through the 1990s, the durable Kearns became part of a Wallaby era that brought him World Cup and Bledisloe Cup triumphs, the test captaincy and the record for the most tests by an Australian hooker. He is popular throughout the rugby world and has remained a modest, approachable person who typifies the down-to-earth Australian attitude towards sport and sports fame.

Like his future test captain Nick Farr-Jones, Kearns attended Newington where, also like Farr-Jones, he couldn't make the First XV. Either boys developed late at Newington or there were some poor rugby judges at the school.

Shortly after, Kearns was captaining the Australian under-21 team with distinction and making good progress at Randwick, the breeding ground for so many Wallabies. Dwyer, seeking to build a team that would peak for the 1991 World Cup, plucked players like Kearns and Tim Horan from nowhere in 1989 and had his youth policy justified.

Kearns rates the 1991 World Cup a career highlight. He played every

Philip Nicholas Kearns
Hooker
Born: Sydney, June 27, 1967
Test debut: Australia v New Zealand August 5, 1989
Test career: 1989-98 (61 matches)
Test points: 34 (8 tries)
* Has played the most tests by an Australian hooker
* Captained Australia between 1992 and 1995

Phil Kearns on one of his aggressive runs, Australia v South Africa, 1993.

match and was many critics' choice as the hooker in the tournament, proving mobile, a powerful scrummager, and being very aware tactically. His front row partnership with props Ewen McKenzie and Tony Daly, which began in 1990, was critical. The trio went on to set a world record for tests played together.

New Zealanders were scornful of Kearns in his early days, nicknaming him 'Lightning' because, they said, his lineout throws never struck the same place twice. But soon the Sydneysider with the distinctive flat-topped haircut was acknowledged around the world as a great.

There were many similarities between Kearns and Fitzpatrick as players, leaders and personalities. They are built along the same lines - Kearns is 1.83m (6ft) and 108kg (16st 12lb) - and played the modern-style hooking game. Both were nimble and possessed good ball skills. As Kearns' career progressed, he even developed Fitzpatrick's habit of turning up on the wing and scoring tries. The two fed off each other, pushing each other to greater heights. Ian Jones summed up the situation in his autobiography *Unlocked*: 'I've appreciated Kearns' no-nonsense approach. I used to listen in on his verbal battles with Fitzy and he gave as good as he got. He never allowed himself to be intimidated and never backed down.'

Kearns captained Australia several times when Michael Lynagh was absent injured, the first occasion being during the tour of Ireland and Wales in 1992, then took over permanently when Lynagh retired in 1995.

Unfortunately, a severe Achilles tendon injury removed him from test

An unlikely front row but a victorious Wallaby trio following Australia's win over New Zealand, Wellington, 1990. From left: David Campese, Phil Kearns and Tim Horan.

rugby for nearly three years. He did exceedingly well to return to the international arena in 1998 after many had written him off and played an integral role in helping Australia whitewash the All Blacks 3-0 in the Bledisloe Cup series. By then the captaincy had passed on to John Eales, but Kearns was the senior pro and an influential, inspiring figure in the test side.

Kearns had shown ability before to fight back from adversity. In 1991 during the World Cup, he scored a try against Argentina at Llanelli, then injured his Achilles tendon and was forced to leave the field. There was talk that his career might be over and I recall his parents crying at the news. Yet within five days the resilient Kearns was back in the Wallaby side and contributing as well as ever.

My most poignant memory of Kearns was his after-match speech at the Sydney Football Stadium in 1995, following the test against the All Blacks. New Zealand won 34-25 in their best performance of the Laurie Mains era. Kearns, addressing the large crowd, said: "To all the Australian supporters here today, we thank you. It's been terrific having your support and whatever happens in the future we hope you and the union support us. We thank you."

As Wallaby captain, Kearns had led the negotiations with the two rival groups bidding for the players' signatures as rugby rushed into the professional era. When he made that speech he believed the Wallabies would be signing for the World Rugby Corporation and thus would be turning their backs on their national union. As it transpired, the Wallabies, with Kearns still chief negotiator, elected not go to WRC.

Kearns attended the University of New South Wales, then became involved in marketing and promotions. He has used that experience to produce and sell rugby memorabilia under the *Great Moments* banner. More recently, he has become a general news reporter for Channel Nine in Sydney. The channel has, not surprisingly, assigned him to preview rugby tests, which creates the unusual situation of Kearns interviewing team-mates and opposition on prospects for a forthcoming test in which he will be involved. **100**

Australia's most capped hookers:
61* Phil Kearns (1989-98)
42 Peter Johnson (1959-71)
41 Tommy Lawton Jnr (1983-89)
21 Edward Bonis (1929-38)
19 Peter Horton (1974-79)
* still playing

JOHN KIRWAN

Rugby Globe-trotter

John James Kirwan
Winger
Born: Auckland, December 16, 1964
Test debut: New Zealand v France, Christchurch, June 16, 1984
Test career: 1984-94 (63 matches)
Test points: 143 (35 tries)
*   Was the third-youngest All Black test player ever when he made his debut
*   His 63 tests was the New Zealand record at the time
*   Holds the New Zealand test try-scoring record with 35
*   He holds the New Zealand record with 199 tries in first class rugby
*   In 1993, he scored eight tries in a Ranfurly Shield match against North Otago

JOHN KIRWAN'S IS THE classic story of what rugby can do for a young man in New Zealand. The first public image of Kirwan, in the early 1980s, was of a teenaged Auckland butcher's apprentice. He ended his career as a worldly, Italian-speaking international sports star.

Kirwan was more than a great winger. He was a pioneering rugby globe-trotter who spent the northern winters playing for the Italian club Treviso. With his eye-catching rugby and his bubbly manner, he became one of the most famous people in New Zealand.

He retired from rugby in 1994 and was later signed by the Auckland Warriors league club. Television New Zealand led its national news that evening with a nine-minute item about Kirwan's switch of codes.

In his prime, from 1987-90, Kirwan was as good as any winger in the world. He drew large crowds and became a sports hero, first in Auckland, where he was tagged Saint John, then nationally. He was often to be seen on the field long after his team-mates had disappeared, signing autographs for endless lines of children.

Kirwan was educated at Auckland's De La Salle College, In 1980, he was the First XV halfback, but on leaving school, he grew nearly a foot in a year and played on the wing for the Marist club.

In 1983 John Hart plucked him from the third grade and put him in the Auckland side in a stroke of selectorial inspiration. My first memory of Kirwan stems from that year when, playing for his province against the Lions, he galloped back at impressive speed to the in-goal area to touch down on defence. He was only 18, but being big - 1.90m (6ft 3in) and 92kg (14st 7lb) - and fast, oozed promise. That year he represented Auckland, New Zealand Colts and the North Island and prompted comparisons with an earlier wing of electric ability, Bryan Williams.

Early in 1984 Kirwan made the first of three appearances for the national sevens team in Hong Kong, and was just 19 years, 182 days old when he played his first test, against France at Lancaster Park.

Through the rest of the 1980s, Kirwan was a headline performer in the Auckland side that set a record for Ranfurly Shield defences and dominated the national championship.

Kirwan was one of only two All Blacks (along with David Kirk) to decline invitations to tour South Africa with the rebel Cavaliers in 1986. The next

John Kirwan at his elusive best, New Zealand v British Isles, 1993.

year he lit up the inaugural World Cup with an incredible try against Italy at Eden Park in the tournament opener.

In a breath-taking zig-zagging 70m run, he left the Italians floundering. It was a memorable day for the All Blacks, who passed 50 in a test for the first time since 1913 and unveiled the brand of rugby that was to earn them World Cup honours. But Kirwan was clearly the individual star. After his try, he jogged back to halfway with the setting winter sun directly behind his head. It looked like Kirwan was wearing a halo, and that would have been entirely apt in the eyes of the adoring Eden Park masses.

Kirwan caused the Welsh nightmares in the semi-final, scoring two tries, and added another in the final against France, giving him six for the tournament.

Throughout 1987, Kirwan was virtually unstoppable, totalling 35 tries for the All Blacks, Auckland, North Zone and a New Zealand trial team. David Kirk summed him up: "He's got natural physical ability in size, strength and speed, but has developed his skill through hard training. His try-scoring and rugby-playing ability is without peer."

For all Kirwan's boyish enthusiasm, he was a good rugby thinker with an instinctive ability to do the right thing. Though he was quick, his chief attribute was his size. He was very difficult to stop and could swerve outside his opposite number, sidestep off either foot or bust through. He was always happy to bring his strong fend into play. Kirwan was also adept at standing

The leading New Zealand try-scoring wingers in tests:

35	John Kirwan	1984-94
28*	Jeff Wilson	1993-98
19	Terry Wright	1986-91
17	Stu Wilson	1977-83
16*	Jonah Lomu	1994-98
11	Craig Green	1983-87
10	Bryan Williams	1970-78
8	Ralph Caulton	1959-64
7	George Hart	1930-36
7	Ron Jarden	1951-56

* still playing

Includes tries scored only when playing on the wing

in a tackle and off-loading. Very seldom did he die with the ball. His chief weakness was his lack of kicking skills, while his defence was adequate but not intimidating.

There was a period when he became needlessly aggressive but generally he acquitted himself well, especially considering he was so often in the spotlight and was an opposition target.

Kirwan showed character by returning from major injuries in 1984 (shoulder) and 1989 (achilles tendon). Never afraid to speak out, he called for Hart to replace Alex Wyllie as All Black coach in 1991, saying he might not play if Laurie Mains was appointed. Mains duly got the job and Kirwan was dropped shortly afterwards. He regained his test spot, but in 1993 Mains omitted him from the team to tour Britain. Kirwan battled back again, reclaiming his test jersey in 1994. When he was dropped again after the series against the Springboks, he called it a day, saying Mains had 'lost the plot'.

A big farewell match for him at Auckland's Mt Smart Stadium was televised live and tributes flowed in from around New Zealand and overseas.

Then came Kirwan's switch to league. During his two years with the Warriors, he trained hard and improved his defensive skills so that he was an asset to his team, though he was not the devastating finisher he had been in rugby.

When he left the Warriors at the end of 1996, he headed for Japan, replacing Joe Stanley in the NEC club side in Tokyo. He eventually became the team's back coach.

Kirwan scored so many tries it's no easy task nominating a few as outstanding. Besides his never-to-be-forgotten effort against Italy, one that stands out came in 1988 when he ran off Michael Jones in the third test against Australia at the Concord Oval. The memory of 'J K', as he was known, steaming up alongside Jones, taking the ball, then charging towards the goal line is vivid. After he dotted down, dozens of jubilant New Zealanders carrying flags swarmed onto the field to slap him on the back and congratulate him.

There were other sensational days, including his four tries against Wales at Christchurch in 1988 and, at domestic level, his 40 points (eight tries) for Auckland against North Otago in a 1993 Ranfurly Shield match.

Kirwan stayed in the news. He became involved in helping to produce television sports programmes and videos, then in 1992, his biography *Running on Instinct* was published. In it he delivered the sensational news that he suffered from bouts of clinical depression. By discussing these black periods, Kirwan increased awareness for this mental illness and helped others understand and come to terms with it. In my dealings with Kirwan, I never saw any signs of depression. He was always good to interview, friendly and up-beat. The fact that he was such an effervescent character made his revelation all the more startling.

The big Aucklander was criticised for spending his off-seasons playing in Italy and there were years when he did seem stale and sluggish on returning to New Zealand. But his Italian experiences were critical to Kirwan. Indeed, his wife, Fiorella, is Italian.

Kirwan's record entitles him to comparison with the best. He played 96 matches for New Zealand and scored a record 67 tries. His 35 test tries almost doubled Stu Wilson's record mark of 19. He once scored tries in eight successive tests. In all first-class rugby, he scored 199 tries in 267 games, well ahead of his nearest challenger, Terry Wright, on 177. ⬤

John Kirwan designed the cover of his biography himself.

JACKIE KYLE

He Carried the Rugby Message

John Wilson Kyle
Flyhalf
Born: Belfast, January 10, 1926
Test debut: Ireland v France, Dublin, January 25, 1947
Test career: 1947-58 (52 matches - 46 for Ireland, 6 for the British Isles)
Test points: 30 (9 tries, 1 drop goal)
*   He held the world record for tests by a flyhalf when he retired
*   Captained Ireland 6 times

IRISH FLYHALF Jackie Kyle must have been something special. When he toured New Zealand with the 1950 British Isles team, he was compared with Bert Cooke, the brilliant centre of the 'Invincible' All Blacks. New Zealanders had always revered Cooke, whose rugby genius, they'd say, was unequalled.

Until Kyle turned up. This is what the *New Zealand Rugby Almanack* said of the Irishman after that tour: 'The very fact that he was so often measured up as in the class of A E Cooke indicates the impression he left behind - the complete footballer.'

The *Almanack* summed him up: 'Quietly confident in his approach, Kyle

was primarily an excellent team man, faultless in his handling, able to send out lengthy and accurate passes and adept at making play for his supports. The possessor of a good side-step, his instantaneous reacting, quick thinking and neat footwork enabled him to flash through the occasional opening in an elusive break that usually spelt danger. A feature of his play was his sturdy defence and solid tackling, while his kicking, either into a gap or defensively to touch was snappy and accurate." The *Almanack* has been published each year since 1935, and generally shies away from superlatives. I cannot find a more glowing description of a player in any edition.

Kyle certainly impressed Bob Scott, the New Zealand fullback who played against Kyle from 1945-54. "He was brilliant, a classic type of player, polished, always balanced and in position," says Scott. "He was the best player in the 1950 Lions team and in all the years since, I have never seen a better first five-eighth [flyhalf]."

Who was this Irishman who had New Zealanders so in awe of his skill?

Kyle attended Belfast Royal Academy, captaining the school rugby (from fullback) and cricket teams. He became a medical student at Queen's University in Belfast in 1943 and at 18 was playing rugby for Ulster.

New Zealanders got an early look at him when he played against Charlie Saxton's Kiwis Army team. While still a teenager, he was selected for Ireland in five Victory Internationals after the second World War.

At 20 he was the complete player and only Cliff Morgan of his future opposition was considered his equal. Kyle made his test debut in 1947, against France, and for the next 12 seasons was the best player in the Irish side. In the late 1940s Ireland had some good forwards, Karl Mullen among them, but it was the slightly-built - 1.75m (5ft 9in) and 79kg (12st 6lb) - Kyle who added the spark of brilliance to the team. He guided Ireland to the only Grand Slam it has ever won, in 1948, and to three Five Nations Championships in four years.

In New Zealand in 1950, Kyle played in 16 of the 23 matches and scored six tries. The best was in the first test when he gathered the ball and flashed past the New Zealand backline. Racing diagonally towards the goal-line between the All Black fullback and wing, the Irishman scored a magnificent try. Kyle had earlier revealed his ball-handling skills in scoring three tries against the West Coast in the slush at Greymouth when no-one else seemed able to hold the ball.

Kyle bowed out of top rugby after the 1958 season, ending on an appropriate note when Ireland beat Scotland 12-6. The Scots must have hated him. He played them 10 times and never lost.

What made his play all the more remarkable was that in his time, flankers had much more latitude in hunting down opposing backs and Kyle was naturally singled out as the danger man. Even so, with his distinctive pitter-patter style of running, he proved too elusive for most of them.

Ironically, for someone so sharp on the football field, he was inclined to be forgetful. One time he famously turned up for a test practice with only one boot. He was inevitably last onto the train or bus, though never seeming to be in a hurry. But he had such a genial nature, no-one could ever be annoyed with him.

He was often the butt of good-natured banter. One day the Irish centre Noel Henderson (Kyle's brother-in-law) caused a shock at a team meeting. Henderson was normally very reserved, but for once piped up when captain Karl Mullen asked if there were any questions. "What I would like to know is," said Henderson, "is there any way of knowing whether the out-half be taking his man for a change?"

Winston McCarthy described Kyle as 'the most unforgettable character I have met'. As a strict tee-totaller, a choral singer, a Sunday School bible reader and a diligent autograph-signer, he was a model sportsman. McCarthy spoke of Kyle's bush of black, curly hair, his twinkling feet, shy eyes and friendly smile.

Kyle meant everything to Ireland. He masterminded them through their greatest rugby years, still known as 'the Jackie Kyle era', and provided Irish supporters with excitement and pride that only Mike Gibson had subsequently matched.

For all his class, Kyle received precious little coaching, explaining it once like this: "Just like a girl who is born beautiful can only enhance her looks a little bit, you can only achieve a limited amount in rugby by coaching. It's really a question of natural ability."

During his long career, Kyle was showered with tributes, though he shrugged them off with absolute modesty. In John Scally's *The Giants of Irish Rugby*, he nominates the accolade which meant the most: "The famous poet Louis MacNiece was doing a radio broadcast in Belfast one evening. He was asked if he could make one wish, what it would be. His answer was that he would love to play rugby like Jack Kyle. That's the compliment that meant the most to me."

After retiring from rugby, Kyle lived in Malaysia from 1962-64 and then moved to Chingola, Zambia where he spent more than 30 years as a medical missionary. 🏉

Flyhalves who have appeared in the most test matches:

75	Rob Andrew (England/British Isles)	1985-97
66	Hugo Porta (Argentina/South America)	1971-90
64	Michael Lynagh (Australia)	1984-95
56*	Craig Chalmers (Scotland/British Isles)	1989-98
55	Stefano Bettarello (Italy)	1979-88
52	Jackie Kyle (Ireland/British Isles)	1947-58
48*	Gareth Rees (Canada)	1986-98
46*	Neil Jenkins (Wales/British Isles)	1991-99
46	Grant Fox (New Zealand)	1985-93
44*	Diego Dominguez (Italy)	1991-99
41	John Rutherford (Scotland)	1979-87
* still playing		

Keith Quinn's ranking of the century's 10 greatest Irish players and personalities:

1. Willie John McBride
2. Mike Gibson
3. Jackie Kyle
4. Fergus Slattery
5. Ernie Crawford
6. Ollie Campbell
7. Tony O'Reilly
8. Karl Mullen
9. Tom Kiernan
10. Des O'Brien

TOMMY LAWTON Snr

Grandfather Leads the Way

Thomas Lawton
Flyhalf
Born: Waterford, January 16, 1899
Died: Brisbane, July 1, 1978
Test debut: Australia (New South Wales) v New Zealand, Sydney, July 24, 1920
Test career: 1920-32 (15 matches)
Test points: 64 (1 try, 17 conversions, 9 penalties)
* Won a Rhodes Scholarship and earned three rugby blues and an athletics blue for Oxford University
* In 1993, his test career was extended posthumously by a further nine matches when New South Wales' internationals of the 1920s were upgraded
* His 51 points was an Australian test record

THERE HAVE BEEN TWO great Tom Lawtons in Australian rugby. One was the 110kg (17st 4lb) hooker who played 41 tests for the Wallabies through the 1980s. Imposing and aggressive, Lawton deserves to be rated alongside Phil Kearns as among the greatest of Wallaby hookers.

But much as the tough hooker was admired, it was Lawton's grandfather who really captured the hearts of the Australian rugby public. Tommy Lawton senior had a varied and exciting career in which he:

* represented Queensland while still a schoolboy.
* was a key member of the magic Waratahs team that toured Britain and France in 1927-28.
* led Australia to an historic series victory over the All Blacks.

Lawton was the idol of Brisbane Grammar, one of Brisbane's most prestigious schools. He was in the cricket First XI for four years, captain for two. His colossal scoring earned him newspaper headlines. He rowed well, was a promising tennis player, a champion high jumper and hurdler, and excelled as a swimmer.

But it was in rugby union that he shone brightest. He was in the First XV for three years and the school magazine remarked on 'his ingenuity in originating passing rushes, his clever raking in of wild passes and his sure foot'. He was rated the school's outstanding back in 1916 and 1917, not merely for his attacking skills but for his strong defence.

While still at school he was selected for interstate rugby, but any advance in his favourite sport was delayed while he zipped off to serve in France as a gunner with the 12th Field Artillery Brigade during the first World War.

Incredibly, on his return from Europe he was forced to turn to rugby league, as the University of Queensland, which he was attending, had no union team. Shortly after, he transferred to Sydney, ostensibly to pursue a medical course at St Andrew's College, though the lure of rugby union was another powerful incentive for his move south.

Sydney rugby followers quickly came to appreciate Lawton's skills. Though he was built more like a loose forward than a back, he passed well, was seldom flustered and, as a bonus, was an exceptionally accurate goal-kicker for the times. In 1920 he represented New South Wales twice against Jim Tilyard's touring All Blacks.

The following year, having earned a Rhodes Scholarship, he began his studies at Oxford University, residing at New College. Three times he played in the annual Oxford-Cambridge game and in 1923 he found himself embroiled in a furore over the captaincy. The captain was chosen by the players, not the selectors, and the Australian was a unanimous choice. He was an outstanding player in the side and immensely popular. However Lawton and fellow Rhodes Scholars Victor Grenning and Banjo Paterson were suspended because it was discovered they had played rugby league. The drama ended with the sacking of the selector who had so thoughtfully released news of Lawton's league appearances to prevent a colonial becoming captain, and the three Australians were reinstated.

Besides his rugby, Lawton represented Oxford University at the shot put and in swimming and water polo. He was named as a reserve for England against the All Blacks in January, 1925.

Lawton returned to Australia in time to travel with New South Wales on an 11-match tour of New Zealand in 1925, leading the team in the only test. New Zealand rugby was particularly strong at the time - the unbeaten 'Invincibles' had just returned from their long tour of Britain and France - but the New South Welshmen won nine of their 11 games and the sturdy stand-off led the scoring with 49 points.

The highlight of Lawton's long career was the 1927-28 Waratahs tour of Britain and France. This was a special team, containing legendary players like the captain, Johnny Wallace, Cyril Towers, Alex Ross and Syd Malcolm. The Waratahs beat Ireland, Wales and France and lost narrowly to England and Scotland. They played a fluent, flowing game that was years ahead of its time, and are still recalled fondly in Britain.

For Lawton, the tour was one long triumph. He played 33 of the 35 matches and scored 124 points, 70 more than anyone else, to break by two points the record tally Phil Carmichael had set while in Britain with the 1907-08 Wallabies. Lawton scored just one try, but those outside him scored 40, a mark of his greatness. Wallace said: "Tommy smoothed the way for us."

The *Daily Express*, which covered the tour comprehensively, described him as an unselfish, deceptive stand-off. 'With his long legs and his long stride, he seems slow to the casual spectator ... but watch Lawton closely and you will see how he draws an unwary opponent, and so times his pass that the attack is likely to prosper. He scores few tries himself, but helps his comrades to many. He is always in the right place, his defence is excellent, his kicking well-judged.'

Lawton returned to Queensland in 1929, but his rugby continued to prosper. He captained Australia to an historic three-test clean sweep over the All Blacks and was described by New Zealand captain Cliff Porter as 'the loping ghost'. His tactical acumen was again acknowledged in 1930 when he led Australia to victory over the British Lions.

In 1932, at the age of 33, he led Australia in the first two tests against the All Blacks, for a win and a loss (the second of only two test defeats as captain), and was then sensationally dropped.

He was a charismatic personality, a popular leader and a complete flyhalf whose powerful hips and thighs and long stride left many a would-be defender stranded. **100**

Keith Quinn's ranking of the century's 10 greatest Australian players and personalities:

1   David Campese
2   Mark Ella
3   Nick Farr-Jones
4   John Eales
5   Michael Lynagh
6   Ken Catchpole
7   Mark Loane
8   Cyril Towers
9   Tom Lawton Snr
10 Phil Kearns

MARK LOANE

For Queensland and Country

Mark Edward Loane
Loose forward
Born: Ipswich, July 11, 1954
Test debut: Australia v Tonga,
Sydney, June 23, 1973
Test career: 1973-82 (28
matches)
Test points: 8 (2 tries)
* Was 18 when he made his
  test debut, the second-
  youngest Wallaby
* Captained Australia in seven
  tests

MARK LOANE WAS one of the giants of Australian rugby literally and figuratively, and his influence was seen in many ways.

* He lead Queensland's rugby resurgence. During his decade in the maroon jersey, he became a folk hero and built a huge following among his loyal fans at Brisbane's Ballymore ground.

* He helped Australian rugby regain respectability. Loane was among a core of players who put some pride back in the Wallabies after poor test results in the early 1970s.

* He spent time in South Africa and was so impressive that he was on the brink of the Springbok side when he returned to Australia.

New Zealand didn't see the best of Loane. He was injured on the 1978 tour and returned home, and he retired before the increase in trans-Tasman tests in the 1980s. However, he made a significant impact in one match, captaining the Wallabies to a 12-6 victory over the All Blacks at Sydney in 1979 to earn Australia the Bledisloe Cup for the first time since 1949. I recall the unfamiliar (to a New Zealander) sight of the Wallabies doing a victory lap of the Sydney Cricket Ground. Loane was rampant at No 8, marshalling an impressive forward effort that overwhelmed the All Blacks.

Only rarely did Loane not make an impact. He had self-discipline and defiance and I admired his appreciation of the ethics of rugby. He was an inspiring leader whose team-mates raised their game to try to match their super-charged skipper.

There was a strong sports influence in the Loane family - his father was a good rugby league player, his mother was a Queensland athletics rep and his two older brothers were talented athletes. Initially Mark played hockey and rugby league, but once he attended Christian Brothers College, first at Gympie, then Brisbane, rugby union drew him. He first played rugby at 14, as a lock, but was so good an athlete and reader of the game that he was more suited to No 8.

Loane's was a swift rise. He joined Brisbane University club in 1972 and had a season in the lower grades, making the state under-19 team. The next year, though eligible for age group rugby, he played in his club's senior side. Within months he was a Queensland rep, helping the state to a surprise 27-19 win over New South Wales.

Wallaby coach Bob Templeton chose him to play against Tonga when he

Mark Loane, always an aggressive runner with the ball, in action for Queensland v Scotland, 1982.

was three weeks short of his 19th birthday. He became the second youngest Wallaby and one of the youngest forwards to appear in international rugby. Loane turned in a dynamic, storming display in a 30-12 win, but made defensive errors in the second test and was dropped. The *Sydney Morning Herald* declared that Loane should hang onto his Australian jersey as it would be his last. The newspaper overlooked the teenager's determination. As Loane said: "I had a mono-maniacal desire to win."

He quickly re-established himself with his commanding play for Queensland. In his home state, Loane, Paul McLean and Tony Shaw were called 'the Holy Trinity', with Loane nominated as 'the Father'. When Loane came into rep rugby, he was disgusted with the way Queensland would capitulate to New South Wales - "The effort of the Queensland team was pathetic. It lasted about the same time as the psyche-up talk." By the time he departed top rugby, Queensland was one of the world's great rugby regions. The flow-on effect to Wallaby rugby was telling. Bret Harris in *The Marauding Maroons* wrote: 'Loane was the saviour of Queensland rugby and the avenger of past defeats'.

One of Loane's proudest moments was in 1976 when Queensland

Former Wallaby captain Andrew Slack composed this limerick about Mark Loane, capturing Loane's individualism and unique view of life:
Our leader's name was Loane;
Rather than smile he'd groan.
His idea of debauchery
was to visit a mauchery
or Iguazu Falls on his own.

thrashed New South Wales 42-4. At one point Queensland went 20 matches without defeat. They became the best team in Australia and regularly beat top New Zealand provinces, plus Japan and Fiji.

Though hindered by injury, Loane had a good tour of Britain in 1975-76, and his clash with Mervyn Davies in the Barbarians match was a classic. Loane studied medicine for four years until the end of 1977, and several times resisted lucrative league offers.

Loane was a fine blend of team player and individualist. Bob Templeton, the Wallaby coach, called him 'the dogmatic doctor'. He was always happy with his own company and, like many great captains, stood slightly apart. He had strength of character, which came through in his rugby. Though he always seemed to look scruffy and dishevelled on the football paddock, he was well organised and did everything to the best of his ability.

He worked hard in sprint training even though he was a giant of a man - 1.91m (6ft 3in) and 104kg (16st 6lb) - always tackled ferociously and had an unyielding commitment that was legendary around the rugby world. Loane was a marauding, immensely strong player able to make thundering bursts from the base of the scrum. Often he crashed over his opponents' line with several opponents clinging to him. As one critic said: 'He was like a train without a station'.

After leading Australia against the All Blacks in 1979, Loane captained the Wallabies on a two-test tour of Argentina, then headed for South Africa, partly to further his medical career. He spent 15 months in trauma and obstetrics training before returning home.

In South Africa he led Natal, forming the back row with other Wallabies Gary Pearse and Dick Cocks. He was honoured with the captaincy of the South African Barbarians against the Lions. When he was selected for the Junior Springboks and was short-listed for Springbok team it became apparent how highly he was regarded.

In Australia in 1981, Loane regained his Wallaby jersey but not the captaincy, which Tony Shaw retained. Loane was Australian Player of the Year in 1981 and toured Britain with the 1981-82 Wallabies, taking on the captaincy when Shaw was dropped. In 1982, he led Australia in two home tests against Scotland, the second producing an exciting 33-9 win at Sydney.

It was Loane's test farewell, for he joined nine other high-profile players, nearly all Queenslanders, in withdrawing from the Wallaby side to tour New Zealand under new coach Bob Dwyer of New South Wales. Loane denied there was interstate rivalry in his decision, saying he could no longer afford the financial sacrifices of playing international rugby and had just had enough.

While working with former Wallaby skipper Andrew Slack during the 1998 Commonwealth Games sevens tournament at Kuala Lumpur, I mentioned that I was compiling a list of the century's 100 greatest rugby players and we discussed outstanding Australian players. Slack was adamant Loane deserved inclusion, stressing that for nearly a decade he was a towering presence in the Wallabies and that his contribution was still being felt.

Loane played 28 tests, a total restricted by injury, his stint in South Africa and the fact that he retired when 27.

His decision to specialise in ophthalmology led to him studying in Adelaide and San Diego. He completed two fellowships, one in corneal transplantation and one in glaucoma and in 1990 returned to Australia to set up his own practice. **100**

JONAH LOMU

The Phenomenon

SEAN FITZPATRICK TELLS A story that sums up the Jonah Lomu phenomenon. In South Africa in 1996 the All Blacks, after doing an in-store promotion, went into the manager's office for a quiet talk. Then Fitzpatrick, the All Black captain, left to return to the team hotel. A large elderly white woman with a pen and new white rugby ball approached him for his autograph. "I was halfway through signing," Fitzpatrick explains, "when Jonah walked out of the manager's door. The woman screamed 'Jonah', grabbed the ball and pen and rushed towards Jonah. Somewhere in South Africa an elderly woman has a white rugby ball which has two signatures - Jonah Lomu and Sean F."

It is hard to comprehend the extent of Lomu's fame, even beyond the traditional rugby-playing countries. I feel that at the 1995 World Cup, his impact was the most sensational of any player at any time in rugby history. The irony is that until he scored a couple of tries in the final trial at Whangarei, he was not a World Cup certainty.

At 1.95m (6ft 5in) and 118kg (18st 9lb), Lomu in South Africa was entirely different from any previous winger. Once he had a head of steam on, he was almost impossible to tackle. But he wasn't just big. He was agile, pacey and quick off the mark. He cut a swathe through the best that Ireland, Wales, Scotland and England could offer as New Zealand romped into the final. There were two storming Lomu tries against Ireland, but it was England who really felt his full power. He scored four magnificent tries in the All Blacks' 45-29 semi-final victory. One, when he burst out of one tackle and ran over England fullback Mike Catt while stumbling for balance, defied belief and made commentators stumble for words.

His play was so sensational, and it was on such a world stage, that he became the hottest name in rugby. The Springboks marked him closely and held him off while winning the final in extra time, but he remained a potent threat. Colin Meads, asked if he had ever seen a player like Lomu, replied: "Yes, I've seen plenty of them. But they were all locks and I found them in the middle of a lineout." Lomu was able to harness the bulk of a forward with the athleticism of a back.

The name of Lomu shot around the rugby world. Later in 1995, the All Blacks toured France and visited Nancy, in east France. This is the home of Michel Platini and is a soccer stronghold. The All Blacks stayed in an old

---

Jonah Tali Lomu
Winger
Born: Auckland, May 12, 1975
Test debut: New Zealand v France, Christchurch, June 26, 1994
Test career: 27 matches (1994-98)
Test points: 80 (16 tries)
* Lomu's test debut at 19 years, 45 days old makes him the youngest test match All Black
* Scored four tries in the 1995 World Cup semi-final against England
* Scored 12 test tries in 1995, a record for a calendar year by any player (since equalled by New Zealand's Christian Cullen in 1997)

hotel near the town square. A dozen children waited outside and hardly batted an eyelid as stars like Fitzpatrick, Jeff Wilson and Zinzan Brooke came out. When Jonah emerged, he jogged past them into the square. They turned and followed. Jonah went into a barber's and they queued up outside. Ten minutes later he emerged and threw the children into crisis. Eventually six jogged back across the square behind their hero to get his autograph while the other six went into the barber's to scoop up equally prized souvenirs of hair.

Yet for some years in Lomu's life, jail, rather than sports fame, beckoned. He grew up in a tough area of Auckland and, following the example of his peers, was getting into increasingly serious trouble by his early teens. His best friend, Danny, was killed in a fight as a teenager and his uncle was decapitated in a local shopping centre brawl. "I was in trouble, police trouble, but they couldn't put me in jail because I was too young," he recalls.

His despairing parents sent him to board at Wesley College in Pukekohe and Lomu's life turned around. He discovered rugby and the discipline and camaraderie that the sport involved. Lomu, playing as a loose forward, towered over his mates and was in the First XV for five years. By 1991 he was a lock in the New Zealand under-17 side and in 1994 made the New Zealand Colts. His first class debut came in May 1994, on the wing for Counties, but even before then he had the country buzzing with his breathtaking play for the New Zealand sevens team at the annual Hong Kong tournament.

Lomu's second first-class game was an All Black trial, where John Kirwan was at full stretch marking him. He was included in the test side for the 1994 series against France. I felt at the time it was unfair - he'd played just four first-class games and at 19 years, 45 days old, was the youngest ever test All Black. Lomu, lacking rugby savvy, looked out of his depth, though his potential was glaringly obvious. Over the next few months, there were questions about his rugby acumen, his tactical appreciation, his slow reactions and his lackadaisical attitude to training.

Despite these caveats, and the fact that Lomu failed to make the All Black test side against Canada on the eve of the World Cup, he loomed as a huge weapon for the All Blacks in South Africa. Just before the tournament, I spoke to Steve Smith, Clive Norling and Alastair Hignell, who were covering the World Cup for ITV. None had so much as heard of Lomu. I suggested they get used to saying his name. This indicates just how quickly Lomu rose to rugby superstardom, for these were three knowledgeable and well-prepared rugby commentators.

After the World Cup, Lomu played to the same sensational level in two hard-fought tests against Australia. He scored a try in each and really was the difference in the sides. Who would have believed that within a year he would be dropped from the test side? Yet in 1996, following some niggling injuries, Lomu was demoted to the reserves' bench in South Africa. He has not yet recaptured his brilliance of 1995, though during the latter part of 1998 he was near his best and showing more understanding of defensive and positional aspects of rugby. He's been unlucky, for a major kidney disorder cost him almost all of 1997 and may have been affecting his play before that.

Regardless of his form, Lomu has continued to be the biggest person - literally and metaphorically - in world rugby. He passes the first name test … with him, it needs no more than 'Jonah' for the rugby world to know precisely who is being referred to.

I've watched Italian schoolchildren at Bologna wait for hours after an All Black game just for a sight of him. I've seen how thrilled staff and patients at

Keith Quinn's rankings of this century's great wingers, using the "PITS" criteria: Pace, Impact, Talent, Skill:

1. Jonah Lomu
2. David Campese
3. Ken Jones
4. Gerald Davies
5. Ron Jarden
6. Ian Smith (Scotland)
7. Tony O'Reilly
8. Jeff Wilson
9. Cyril Lowe
10. Ieaun Evans
11. Chester Williams
12. Bryan Williams

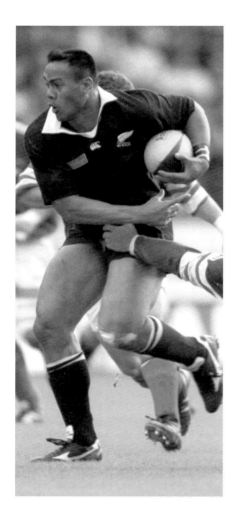

a Leeds hospital were to have their photo taken with him. Distinguished New Zealand rugby photographer Peter Bush said the mayhem after the 1996 Counties-Wellington national championship match as thousands of children closed in on Lomu was worse than Beatlemania.

Lomu is hot commercial property. He had endorsed Reebok worldwide and in New Zealand is closely associated with the McDonald's television advertising campaign. His first TV advertisement was for pizzas in Britain and featured England wing Tony Underwood and Underwood's mother. Stories and pictures of him appear in magazines in countries in which rugby is a minor sport at best. In April 1999, he signed a multi-million dollar contract with German sportswear company adidas.

His emergence coincided with the advent of professional rugby. When the New Zealand Rugby Union offered players professional contracts in 1995 there were various levels - provincial, Super 12, All Black and star. But the very top level comprised of just Jonah, acknowledgement that the big Tongan was so much more commercially valuable than any other player.

In spite of the fame and adulation, I've found Lomu a likeable, down-to-earth, modern young man. I had to smile in France in 1995 when he was the subject of a specially-requested interview by the French journalists. One of them asked him how he was enjoying his time in France. Lomu replied in his typical pseudo-American street kid rap language: "Sweet as, bro", which threw the team interpreter into paroxysms.

Lomu does all the things a celebrity in his position should. He signs countless autographs and is as accommodating as practicable with the fans. Considering the demands on his time, he is extremely good-natured. There's never a sign of big-headedness. He's had to live his life in a fishbowl. His engagement to a South African, their secret marriage in Auckland, then the one the parents attended in South Africa, and their subsequent separation, have all been huge stories. He is in demand for any range of tasks, from television commercials to judging the 1998 Miss World contest. He has been linked with league clubs in Australia and Britain and even with the Dallas Cowboys American football team.

I've found him to be bright - he speaks fluent Tongan, Samoan and English - and articulate. He has a particular interest in heavyweight boxing and will talk enthusiastically about the great fights between George Foreman, Muhammad Ali and Joe Frazier in the 1970s. Generally though, he's rather under-stated and relies heavily on his manager-mentor Phil Kingsley-Jones.

As a player, Lomu is far from rounded. He was dropped briefly from the New Zealand team in 1998 and though he quickly regained his place, he still does not have the range of skills of a Ron Jarden, Gerald Davies or David Campese. On the other hand, he brings incredible assets to his position. By his mere presence, he creates opportunities for his team-mates and he can score unlikely tries himself through strength and pace. Seldom is he brought down in a one-on-one tackle.

He played superbly at the 1998 Commonwealth Games sevens at Kuala Lumpur, being a vital figure in New Zealand's victories over Samoa and Fiji. We then saw another side of Lomu as he stripped off his shirt and performed the haka in front of the main stand. His pride in his country was obvious, as was his washboard rib cage, the result of hours of rigorous training. Lomu stayed on in Kuala Lumpur and was the biggest name in the Games village. Swimmers, athletes, ten pin bowlers, shooters and boxers swarmed around him. Such is the life of the century's great rugby superstar. **100**

BOY LOUW

What a Man

IT HAS ALWAYS SEEMED incongruous to me that some of South Africa's greatest players should be called 'Boy'. I suppose in the way we tag a quiet member of a team 'Rowdy' or a dark-haired player 'Snow', being called 'Boy' is a compliment of sorts. Certainly Boy de Villiers, Boy Morkel and Boy Louw were anything but boys on the field. They came from famous rugby families and were tough, skilled players in the developing years of Springbok rugby.

The most enduring reputation among the 'Boys' belongs to Boy Louw, who really was one of a kind, on and off the field. It's often been said that Louw was the greatest character in South African rugby history, and there is no disputing the quality of his rugby. In fact, when Springbok rugby followers pick their all-time XVs, Louw usually finds a place.

Danie Craven once confided that he could not recall Louw doing the wrong thing on the field: "Boy knew when to pass and when not to, and was a stickler for correct football, with an uncompromising will-to-win spirit."

Louw could hardly have helped being a rugby player. He was one of nine brothers, his uncle was a Springbok in 1891, and the sport was central to the family. The Louw brothers' beginnings in the game involved kicking around an old ball stuffed with cabbage leaves and corn stalks. One of Boy Louw's brothers, Fanie, played for the Springboks and Boy's twin, Japie, might have too, but died tragically in a swimming accident in 1936. The nine brothers reached senior club status, and six played at provincial level.

Louw attended Wellington High School and at 13 played his first organised rugby. He applied himself more seriously once he moved onto Paarl Boys High School. He had trouble playing for the school, not because of lack of ability but because he always looked over age. At Paarl, where he eventually captained the school First XV, he was fortunate to be coached by Western Province scrumhalf Philip Meyer.

In 1924 he made his debut for Western Province, and was chosen for the big game that year, against Ron Cove-Smith's British touring team. There weren't many tests back then and it wasn't until 1928 that Louw made his Springbok debut, playing the last two tests against Maurice Brownlie's touring All Blacks. That series was drawn, but after that the Springboks won every series Louw played.

He had undeniable stature. At 1.85m (6ft 1in) and 96kg (15st), he was big for those times. He was versatile, immovable and immensely strong, a

Matthys Michael Louw
Prop
Born: Wellington District, February 21, 1906
Died: Bellville, May 3, 1988
Test debut: South Africa v New Zealand, Port Elizabeth, August 18, 1928
Test career: 1928-28 (18 matches)
Test points: 3 (1 try)
* Held the South African record for most tests
* Played international rugby in five positions

Boy Louw, while he had an unusual turn of phrase, was a compelling speaker and Danie Craven invited him to talk to the Springbok team just before the first test against the All Blacks in 1949. Louw began by saying: "For the benefit of my English-speaking friends ... this is war! I know these New Zealanders; I played against their grandfathers. I want you to play hard, clean and fair. But always remember that if the circumstances of the game fit, it's easier to play against 14 of them than 15."

relentless competitor who combined the traditionally tough image of a forward with the thinking footballer. Louw could punt skilfully and pass or dummy effectively. He usually played at prop, but was comfortable anywhere in the pack. On the 1937 tour of New Zealand, he played 11 games - six at prop, three at No 8 and two at hooker.

Fearless and hard, he was a dominating force in any match he played. He was such a strong personality that he bowed to no-one, not even Bennie Osler, the dictator-genius of Springbok rugby around 1930. There are stories of Osler and Louw clashing during the Springboks' 1931-32 tour of Britain. Osler was captain, and the side's flyhalf, kicker and match-winner. The one person he never over-ruled was Louw. Danie Craven used to tell of how Osler called for the ball from a scrum during a test against Scotland that was being played in wet, windy conditions. "Hold and play with the forwards," Louw countermanded. Again Osler demanded that Craven pass. This time Louw whipped his head from the forming scrum and snapped, "***** you, Bennie. We're keeping it up front!" End of argument.

Another time he told a captain who had been endeavouring to show leadership qualities: "You make the speeches, I'll lead the pack!"

Louw's speech was legendary, full of malapropisms and witticisms, not all intentional. He tended to bastardise both the English and Afrikaans languages. He once ran past Springbok centre Johnny Bester, who had dropped the ball and then stood rooted to the spot, and snapped: "Hey, do you think you have bought this ground of plot?"

Then there was the occasion he scanned an ill-formed lineout and asked: "Why you stand so crooked? Can't you stand in a straight stripe?"

During the second test against New Zealand at Christchurch in 1937, Louw was concussed early in the second half. Worse, his concussion led to him giggling repeatedly, somewhat unnerving for both teams. He kept asking halfback Craven what was going on and what he should do. Finally Craven told him All Black prop Doug Dalton was coming through the lineouts. At the next lineout Louw stood beside Dalton simpering, then when play had moved on, lashed out at him with feet and hands flying. The referee, following the ball, missed the incident, but the effects on Dalton were obvious.

"Was that what you wanted, Danie?" giggled Louw.

"No, Boy, but it will have to do," Craven replied.

Louw always dispensed justice summarily and it was to him that his backs turned when they felt they had been victims of foul play. Louw's tactics might not have survived today's video scrutiny, but he was effective and swift.

Besides his test feats, Louw was an integral part of the champion Western Province teams of the inter-war years when the province dominated the Currie Cup competition.

It was appropriate that Louw was a member of the champion 1937 South African team to New Zealand. Louw was one of the tour selectors and after missing the first test through injury, played in the next two, which South Africa won to wrap up the series. However, critics felt that at 30 he was past his best, having slowed noticeably.

Back home he held his test spot for the 1938 series against Sam Walker's British Isles and was Craven's vice-captain. He retired after this series, won 2-1. For 11 years he had graced the test arena. Because test rugby was scarce in his time, Louw took part in only five series. His total of 18 tests (for 14 victories) stood as a South African record until Salty du Rand beat it in 1956.

Louw played his club rugby for Caledon, Paarl and Gardens and it was at Gardens, where he captained and later coached, that he moulded a great club pack. He was known by clubmates at Gardens as 'The Master'. Though rather offbeat off the field, once he had a rugby ball in his hand, he instinctively knew what to do. This showed not only in his own play, but also when he turned to coaching, administration and selecting. He involved himself in every area of the game. In 1939, just a season out of test rugby, he refereed the Currie Cup final between Western Province and Transvaal at Newlands.

During the war, he helped organise the services 'test' between the Kiwis and South Africa in 1945 and coached Basil Kenyon's Sixth Division team which became Middle East champion. The title does not sound particularly impressive, but the football involved some great players and was played with passion and commitment. At the end of 1945, Louw gave lectures on rugby at Paris University. Given his refreshing use of language, they would have been well worth attending.

Louw, a bank clerk, remained a big man in South African rugby and was assistant manager of the 1960-61 Springbok team to Britain.

When Louw died, Craven described him as 'probably the greatest player in his era'. From a man of Craven's experience and breadth of rugby knowledge, that was a supreme compliment. **100**

Boy Louw (centre) with Alfie van der Merwe (left) and Pony van der Westhuizen on the 1931-32 tour to Britain.

South African players whose test careers spanned more than 10 seasons:

13	Jackie Powell (1891-1903)
13	Barry Heatlie (1891-1903)
13	Naas Botha (1980-92)
13	Danie Gerber (1980-92)
12	Boy Morkel (1910-21)
12	Phil Mostert (1921-32)
12	Chris Koch (1949-60)
12	Hannes Marais (1963-74)
12	Jan Ellis (1965-76)
11	Gerry Brand (1928-38)
11	Boy Louw (1928-38)
11	Lofty Nel (1960-70)
11	Mannie Roux (1960-70)
11	Frik du Preez (1961-71)

CYRIL LOWE

Appearances are Deceptive

Cyril Nelson Lowe
Winger
Born: Holbeach, October 7, 1891
Died: Surrey, February 6, 1983
Test debut: England v South Africa, Twickenham, January 4, 1913
Test career: 1913-23 (25 matches)
Test points: 58 (18 tries, 1 drop goal)
* His 18 test tries was an England record for 67 years
* Held the England record for most test appearances when he retired
* The only England player to have gone 11 years without missing a test
* Set an England record with eight tries in the 1914 Five Nations Championship

CYRIL LOWE LOST HIS best years of international rugby to the first World War, yet still scored 18 tries for England, a record that endured until Rory Underwood beat it in 1990. What's more, the pint-sized Lowe achieved his record despite failing to score in each of the five matches in his first international season.

He was by all accounts an amazing player. He stood only 5ft 6in (1.67m) and weighed just 8st 10lb (54kg), but was a ferocious tackler and a right winger with a gift for seizing try-scoring chances. He could punt and drop-kick expertly and, unusually for a winger of his era, liked to involve himself in play by moving out of position.

Lowe was the son of a Lincolnshire clergyman. He attended Dulwich College, excelling at athletics, cricket, swimming, tennis, soccer and boxing. He never played rugby until he was 16, but once he took up the sport, he pursued it most vigorously and he captained Dulwich in 1911. Then it was on to Pembroke College at Cambridge University. Besides winning his rugby blue, he found time to claim the Cambridge 880 yards title in 1913.

'Kid' Lowe, as he was called because of his small stature, made his test debut in 1913 in an England side that was outplayed 9-3 by South Africa. He retained his spot as England brushed aside Wales, France, Ireland and Scotland. But though Lowe was a real speedster and a plucky defender, he certainly didn't *look* a rugby international. In fact, on January 29, 1913, *The Sportsman* ran a letter which asserted: 'I think it the utmost folly to persist in playing Lowe, as he is much too small for international games.'

By the time Lowe pulled out of test rugby a decade later, he had taught that letter-writer and other doubters not to judge a player by his size, explaining: "If you set your mind on something, and you enjoy doing it, then you can do anything." He went on to play 25 consecutive tests for England and held the record number of appearances for his country until Wavell Wakefield topped his mark.

He was in brilliant form in 1914, scoring two tries against Wales, three against France and three against Scotland. His total of eight is still an England record for tries in one Championship season. Of the two teams that took the field in that Scotland match, 14 of the players did not survive the first World War.

During the first war, Lowe greatly distinguished himself. He served

Some "little" players (physically) who made it to the top
They say rugby is a "big man's game", but here is a selection of prominent players of their time who defied the accepted rugby convention and shone in the test arena:

Brian Cox (Australia) 9 tests, 1952-57	1.62m (5ft 4in)	57.5kg (9st 3lb)
Jean Gachassin (France) 32 tests, 1961-69	1.62m (5ft 4in)	61kg (9st 7lb)
Tommy Gentles (S Africa) 6 tests, 1955-58	1.60m (5ft 3in)	62kg (9st 9lb)
Cyril Lowe (England) 25 tests, 1913-23	1.67m (5ft 6in)	54kg (8st 10lb)
Gordon McGhie (Australia) 2 tests, 1929-30	1.57m (5ft 2in)	57kg (9st 2lb)
Norman Mingay (Australia) 7 tests, 1920-23	1.62m (5ft 4in)	61kg (9st 7lb)
Alan ("Ponty") Reid (NZ) 5 tests, 1952-57	1.60m (5ft 3in)	60.5kg (9st 6lb)
Harold Snell (Australia) 3 tests, 1925-28	1.60m (5ft 3in)	63.5kg (10st)
Neil Wolfe (NZ) 6 tests, 1961-63	1.62m (5ft 4in)	67.5kg (10st 9lb)

initially in the Reserve Horse Transport, then volunteered for the Royal Flying Corps from 1916-18. He became a crack fighter pilot who won the Military Cross and the Distinguished Flying Cross, rising to the rank of Group Captain. He claimed to have shot down 30 German planes and was credited with nine. After the war he served for a time at RAF College, Cranwell and played for Blackheath, captaining the side in 1922.

Having earned nine caps before the war, he won another 16 afterwards and became part of one of England rugby's magic eras. In his six international seasons, England teams achieved the Grand Slam four times. He was in the losing side in only three of his 25 tests. Despite often being starved of ball by his centres, he kept up a wonderful ratio of tries, but the critics praised him, too, for his kicking ability and because he was such a willing and eager tackler, a featherweight who played like a heavyweight.

Lowe's records, though impressive, don't portray his appeal. Crowds loved the winger who inspired P G Wodehouse's poem *The Great Day*. Even the greatest players' reputations eventually get swallowed up in the mists of time, but for many decades Lowe was unhesitatingly labelled 'England's greatest winger'.

W J T Collins, in his *Rugby Recollections*, could hardly have been more praising, writing: 'He had all the gifts the ideal winger needs, all the qualities of mind and heart which lift a man above the crowd. All the skills of the complete footballer were his. He was the good little 'un who was superior to most of the good big 'uns. And there were days when he did two men's work in defence, using his speed unsparingly and cleverly to tackle men on the opposite wing and to rob dribbling forwards of the tries they would have scored but for his perversion and determination.'

E H D Sewell said Lowe possessed the two qualities that were inseparable from a great player - hands and pace - and in 1947 described him as the best winger England had produced.

Lowe remained closely involved with rugby, representing the RAF on the Rugby Football Union and being an England selector from 1934-38. "I wasn't very good at it," he once said. He lived to the grand old age of 91, one of the last links to a largely forgotten age of rugby. In 1981, two years before his death, he was honoured at the 100th University match. **100**

MICHAEL LYNAGH

Record-breaker

Michael Patrick Lynagh
Flyhalf

Born: Brisbane, October 25, 1963
Test debut: Australia v Fiji, Suva, June 9, 1984
Test career: 1984-95 (72 matches)
Test points: 911 (17 tries, 140 conversions, 177 penalties, 9 drop goals)

* The highest points-scorer in test rugby
* Has kicked the most penalties and conversions in test rugby
* Is Australia's second most capped player
* Lynagh and Nick Farr Jones were Australia's flyhalf/ scrumhalf in 47 tests, a world record
* Played tests against 17 countries, the record when he retired.

MICHAEL LYNAGH will enjoy enduring fame not only for his world record tally of test points, but also for his death-knell try against Ireland in the 1991 World Cup quarter-final. These days, that World Cup is recalled for Australia's semi-final and final triumphs over New Zealand and England. What's easily overlooked is that but for Lynagh's cool head in a time of crisis, the Wallabies would have been eliminated in the quarter-finals in Dublin.

The blond Queenslander had taken over the captaincy of Australia after Nick Farr-Jones had hobbled off with a wrenched knee. It was a torrid game, for the Irish, inspired by fierce home support, played way above themselves. Australia were clinging to a precarious 15-12 lead until Gordon Hamilton scored a try, and Ralph Keyes converted it.

Several years later, Lynagh recalled those critical few moments: "As soon as they scored, I asked the ref, 'How long?' He said, 'About four minutes after the conversion.' I called the guys together on the line and said, 'We've got to keep calm. Get down their end and we'll score, I promise.'" And so they did. Lynagh kicked off deep, the Irish made errors under pressure and suddenly, emerging from a scrap near the Irish line was none other than Lynagh to take the ball from David Campese and barge his way over.

Lynagh had been training a lifetime for that moment. Remaining unflustered, performing under pressure, turning opportunities into points … they'd been Lynagh hallmarks throughout his career. Lynagh exuded sports ability as a youngster, though few would have tipped rugby. As a schoolboy, he was a Queensland junior cricket rep. He played golf immaculately. His rugby league and soccer skills made him a standout. Then, when Michael was 15, his father, a psychologist, moved the family to Oregon for a year. Michael tried out gridiron and proved particularly adept at kicking.

Back in Brisbane, at St Joseph's Gregory Terrace College, he concentrated on rugby and was earmarked as a star in the making. I first saw him in Christchurch in 1982 when he was playing for Australia in an under-17 international. Already he'd toured Britain as a centre in the Australian schoolboys team. There were several big names on the field that day in Christchurch - Zinzan Brooke played at prop - but Lynagh stood out, even though his team went down 13-10. He had the stamp of class.

He was in the Queensland side at just 18 and travelled to Europe with the Wallabies late in 1983. His test debut came the following year, against Fiji at Suva. Though he preferred flyhalf, he was chosen for Australia at inside centre because rugby genius Mark Ella had a stranglehold on the flyhalf's jersey.

Lynagh toured Britain at the end of 1984 and became part of the famous Wallaby Grand Slam team. He appeared in every test, always at inside centre. He learned fast, from Paul McLean in Brisbane and Ella with the Wallabies. It is hard to imagine two better tutors for a young flyhalf. When Ella quit test football, Lynagh slipped easily into the flyhalf position, forming a lethal partnership with scrumhalf Farr-Jones - they would eventually appear in a world record 47 times in tandem.

Michael Lynagh's top points tallies in tests:

28	v Argentina, 1995	(2 tries, 3 conversions, 4 penalties)
24	v United States, 1990	(2 tries, 8 conversions)
24	v France, 1990	(6 conversions, 4 penalties)
23	v Canada, 1985	(7 conversions, 3 penalties)
23	v France, 1986	(1 conversion, 6 penalties, 1 drop goal)
23	v Argentina, 1986	(4 conversions, 5 penalties)
23	v Italy, 1988	(1 try, 8 conversions, 1 penalty)
23	v Wales, 1991	(2 tries, 6 conversions, 1 penalty)

Note: five of these performances were recorded at Brisbane.

Lynagh was humble, undemonstrative and calm. He was nicknamed 'Noddy' (for his habit of nodding during team talks), but there was nothing sleepy about his play. He was vital and alert. He scored in his first 59 tests, even the odd one early on when he wasn't the team kicker.

His career coincided with those of several other flyhalf greats, including Hugo Porta, Grant Fox and Rob Andrew. It was the All Black Fox against whom he often measured himself. They were of similar build - Lynagh was 1.78m (5ft 10in) and 80kg (12st 9lb) - but had different strengths. From my New Zealand viewpoint, I rate Fox the better place-kicker because he didn't suffer the odd form lapses as Lynagh did, though we are only talking degrees of perfection here. Both served their outside backs well and planned team tactics. But the Australian was a more willing and competent runner and a more decisive defender.

Lynagh played in three World Cups. In 1987 he suffered the demoralising experience of seeing the Wallabies eliminated by France in the semi-final

The world's leading test points-scorers:

911	Michael Lynagh	Australia	1984-95
767*	Neil Jenkins	Wales/British Isles	1991-99
733	Gavin Hastings	Scotland/British Isles	1986-95
687*	Diego Dominguez	Italy	1991-99
656	Hugo Porta	Argentina	1971-90
645	Grant Fox	New Zealand	1985-93
483	Stefano Bettarello	Italy	1979-88
428*	Andrew Mehrtens	New Zealand	1995-98
411*	Gareth Rees	Canada	1986-98
407	Rob Andrew	England/British Isles	1985-97

* still playing

after Serge Blanco scored a last-minute try. "I never felt worse. It was shattering," said Lynagh.

In 1991 there was the ultimate triumph. While Farr-Jones battled injury throughout the World Cup, Lynagh was rock solid. David Campese was the Australian star of that tournament, but Lynagh was the fulcrum of the backline.

He scored eight points in Australia's 16-6 win over New Zealand and another eight in the 12-6 win over England in the final. Lynagh's boot hurt England that day at Twickenham, not just in place-kicking, but in punting for length and the occasional chip kick for his centres and Campese to run on to.

After Farr-Jones stepped down as captain, Lynagh led Australia into the 1995 World Cup. He was unfortunate in his timing, for the great Wallaby machine was beginning to run down. Australia were edged out by England in the quarter-finals and Lynagh announced his retirement from test football.

As in everything, he was understated. He said he did not want to hang around until he wasn't wanted; far better to retire by choice. He had totalled a world record 911 points and set world records for test conversions (140) and penalties (177). Granted, some tests were against weak opposition, but Lynagh shone in the tough matches, too. He scored a record 24 points against France in 1990 and equalled that tally the same year against the United States. He reached 23 against Canada, Argentina, Italy and Wales and had highs of 20 against England, 19 against Ireland and 17 against New Zealand.

He set several Australian records for most points in a test, eventually reaching 28 against Argentina at Ballymore in 1995. Among his many test triumphs, he rates highest the Bledisloe Cup series victories over New Zealand in 1986 and 1992 and the 26-3 beating the Wallabies inflicted on South Africa at Cape Town in 1992, when the Springboks were returning to the test arena. There wasn't much in top rugby Lynagh didn't sample - he played tests against 17 countries, the record at the time of his retirement.

Lynagh excelled at other levels, too. He played 100 games and scored 1166 points for Queensland. He won three Brisbane club premierships with Queensland University and in 1993 was the central figure in Benetton Treviso's 27-19 win over Rovigo in the Italian club final. The Italian section of Lynagh's career was hugely important. He joined Benetton in 1991 and was feted like a superstar for several seasons. In addition, his wife, Isobella, is Italian.

After retiring from test football, Lynagh signed for the London club Saracens, linking with veterans Philippe Sella and Francois Pienaar. He bowed out of English rugby on a high, helping the Saracens beat Wasps 48-18 in the 1998 English Cup final.

Wallaby coach Bob Dwyer was often asked who was the better player, Ella or Lynagh. It was a real poser for Dwyer, who knew Ella from schoolboy days, and worked with Lynagh to win a World Cup title. Dwyer pointed out Ella's instinctive flair, but said Lynagh never stopped improving, until in the end he could smell a try as readily as Ella. He spoke about their running and ball-handling skills and finally summed up: "They both had beautiful skills, but Michael was the better kicker." Ella himself described Lynagh as 'the pivotal heart of the Wallabies for 10 years'.

Lynagh says his immediate goals do not involve coaching. He began a commercial property investment career in Australia and intends pursuing it while based in London. **100**

Michael Lynagh's magic moment. The match programme for the Australia v Ireland World Cup quarter-final in 1991, when Lynagh scored a last-gasp, match-winning try.

JO MASO

French Flair

JO MASO was one of my all-time favourites. When he toured New Zealand with the 1968 French team, he made a huge impression. He was so charismatic and talented and handsome that I used to cut out newspaper photos of him. Even in a backline that included players like Trillo, Dourthe and Villepreux, Maso still stood out, with his back flip passes, twinkling feet and deft kicking touches.

Maso epitomised the handsome Frenchman. He reminded me of Michel Jazy, the great French athlete of the 1960s, in that he invariably cut a stylish figure and seemed to prefer the finer things in life. Rugby followers flocked in their thousands to watch him play. With Maso, as with soccer star George Best, you got the best of both worlds - he was an exciting player and he oozed personality. He had star quality in abundance.

In 1995, while watching a New Zealand-France test at Paris, I saw Maso walk past, wearing the smartest suit from French haute-couteur. He was still the handsome man we'd seen in New Zealand all those years before and had on his arm the most beautiful woman imaginable. Some people try to cultivate style. Maso had it naturally.

As a player, Maso was a genius, blazing on attack and never one to shirk his defensive duties. Yet he was treated terribly by the French selectors. His career stretched from 1966-73. Of the 59 tests France played in that time, Maso appeared in just 25 of them.

Maso was the son of a rugby league international. He initially played league, learning the game in the Catalan town of Perpignan, where he finished his schooling. When in his teens, he switched to rugby union, though his father continued to be an influential figure in his football career.

New Zealanders first saw his skills when, as a 19-year-old, he played for South-East Selection against Wilson Whineray's All Blacks at Lyons in 1964. In those days he played as often at flyhalf as in the centres. Though he was always a quick-thinking, elusive flyhalf, he enjoyed the space and time that playing in the centres afforded.

Maso was 22 when he made his test debut in France's 21-0 win over Italy at Naples in 1966. He kept his place for the next test, when France beat Romania in Bucharest, then had an unhappy time against Scotland. Not only were France beaten 9-8, but Maso twisted his ankle and spent much of the match limping around at fullback.

Joseph Jean Maso
Centre/flyhalf
Born: Toulouse, December 27, 1944
Test debut: France v Italy, Naples, April 9, 1966
Test career: 1966-73 (25 matches)
Test points: 15 (4 tries)

Keith Quinn's ranking of the century's 10 greatest French players and personalities:

1. Jean-Pierre Rives
2. Serge Blanco
3. Jean Prat
4. Jo Maso
5. Philippe Sella
6. Michel Crauste
7. Benoit Dauga
8. Walter Spanghero
9. Pierre Albaladejo
10. Pierre Villepreux

He was dropped from the test side, which marked the beginning of his roller-coaster ride at international level. He missed France's next 10 tests before being recalled. In all he was dropped 10 times over the next seven years for reasons which defied explanation and seldom seemed related to rugby. He never had a full calendar year in the test side.

There were suggestions that the forwards who dominated French selection policies in those times did not like glamour backs basking in the spotlight. Some said the selectors were too intent on safety-first tactics. I think he suffered from being a creature of the Sixties. He grew his hair long and had an independent image. French rugby at the time was run by autocratic Albert Ferrasse, who once launched into Maso, declaring that 'long hair is for women'. There was talk that Maso spent too much time on and off the paddock worrying about his attire. It was strange: his own selectors judged him not up to the required standard, but opponents invariably targeted him as the danger player.

The person who seemed least affected was Maso. He played when chosen, shrugged his shoulders when he wasn't and did not allow such cavalier treatment to upset his happy-go-lucky nature. He was a charming person with a good command of English.

Maso played twice in France's Grand Slam year of 1968 and did enough to earn selection for the tour of New Zealand, where he really cemented his reputation with his midfield flair. He scored France's first points in New Zealand, a try against Marlborough, and played eight of the tour 12 matches, including all three tests. He was usually at centre, but proved an admirable flyhalf in the last test, in Auckland. The *New Zealand Rugby Almanack* remarked on his good tackling and fast, incisive running and described him as 'the best attacking player of his generation'.

There was a suspicion he would not enjoy the more physical brand of rugby, but he erased those doubts with his form in New Zealand, where he proved robust and brave enough to handle anything that was dished out. At 1.80m (5ft 11in) and 80kg (12st 9lb), he wasn't particularly big, but he was sturdy. The All Blacks were very wary of him. Colin Meads described him as 'all balance and deception' and went so far as to say he would have Maso in any world team of his 'at wing, centre, flyhalf … you name it'.

That tour should have launched Maso as a player of world stature and the obvious successor to the gifted Boniface brothers. Instead the capricious selectors ensured he played only sporadically for France. When he departed international rugby while still in his prime, he was acknowledged as a player with superb anticipation and vision, extremely light on his feet and with breathtaking acceleration. He had good hands and, like all the best centres, passed with split-second timing.

He had some great days. There was his sparkling performance against England in 1972 when France stormed home 37-12, scoring six tries, many set up by their prince of centres. A few months later, Maso was called into the French team for the second test of their Australian tour, at Brisbane, and showed coolness and steel in a crisis, scoring two tries in his team's 16-15 series-winning victory.

Perhaps the best indication of how he was perceived outside France was that he was selected along with Colin Meads, Bryan Williams, Frik du Preez, Greg Davis, Pierre Villepreux and other rugby luminaries for the President's Overseas team which played England at Twickenham as part of the RFU Centenary celebrations in 1971.

RUGBY FOOTBALL UNION

England

versus

President's Overseas
XV

1871   1871

TWICKENHAM
SATURDAY 17th APRIL 1971

OFFICIAL PROGRAMME 10p

Maso was not always appreciated at home, but was good enough to make the World XV for the Rugby Union Centenary matches in 1971.

Maso (dark jersey) releases one of his stylish passes for the World XV in England, 1971.

Even so, I felt he never quite fulfilled his vast potential. Perhaps if he'd played for a country that appreciated his class, he might have become one of rugby's superstars.

During the first part of his career, he played for Perpignan. He then switched to Narbonne, which caused problems, for the French rugby authorities decreed the transfer 'unjustified'. He was not granted the number one licence necessary to play in the club championship, so for a year Maso turned out in the Narbonne reserves. Even after the French selectors abandoned him, he continued to play outstanding rugby at club level and in 1974 helped Narbonne reach the national club final.

Maso was initially a wine and spirit merchant, then a men's fashion shop representative, before becoming a sales manager for a large sports goods company.

His gifts have not been lost to rugby, and recently he has managed the French national team, playing a pivotal role in helping France win the Grand Slam in 1997. **100**

WILLIE JOHN M^CBRIDE

He Took No Prisoners

William James McBride
Lock
Born: Toomebridge, June 6, 1940
Test debut: Ireland v England, Twickenham, February 10, 1962
Test career: 1962-75 (80 matches - 63 for Ireland, 17 for the British Isles)
Test points: 7 (2 tries)
* Held the world record for most test appearances
* Captained the 1974 Lions through South Africa unbeaten
* One of the First XV inducted into the International Rugby Hall of Fame in 1997
* Made a record five tours with the British Lions, since equalled by Mike Gibson

I HAVE CONTRASTING memories of Willie John McBride from the first test I commentated - New Zealand v the British Lions at Auckland in 1971. It was a radio broadcast and my commentary position was quite near ground-level. Early in the game McBride and his great rival, Colin Meads, became involved in a fist fight. There they were, these two giant men, both about 105kg (16st 7lb), swinging into each other and landing bone-crunching blows that could be heard in the stands. Both landed two or three haymakers that would have done credit to Mike Tyson.

Then at the end of the game, which was drawn, meaning the Lions had won a series in New Zealand for the first time, McBride and Meads walked off the field together. Meads, as All Black captain, was naturally disconsolate and McBride, who had locked against him in so many scrums over the years, tried to console him. It was a touching moment.

There is an awareness these days of the need to eradicate violence in rugby. But when McBride and Meads played, it was more acceptable - even expected - for a forward to stamp himself on the game and his opposition with some none-too-subtle physical activity that had little to do with rugby. In hindsight, some of it seems savage, but that was the game then and those players should not be judged by today's standards.

Though McBride was not the great runner or ball-handler of his locking rivals of the 1960s, Meads and Springbok Frik du Preez, he was critical to the Irish and Lions teams he represented. He was a reasonable lineout jumper, and excelled in rucks and mauls and at scrum time. More importantly, he brought to his rugby commitment and fire that was rarely seen in British forwards of his era. He never took a backward step.

McBride had a long career and, when he bowed out in 1975, held the world record with 80 test caps. He is recalled not just for his rugged, uncompromising play, but also for his captaincy of the 1974 Lions who toured South Africa unbeaten. Those Lions were a great side and they were led with spirit, wit and wisdom.

You'd have got long odds during McBride's school days on him becoming a rugby international. McBride did not play rugby until the end of 1957, in his fifth year at Ballymena Academy. Having lost his father when he was just four, young Willie John was busy enough helping run the family farm and contributing to feed a family of six children.

But once he took up rugby, as much to show the 'townies' that he wasn't the softie they thought, as for any desire to play the sport, McBride rose quickly through the ranks. He was nicknamed 'Shortie' or 'Wang' (slang for a bootlace - long and wiry), but at 1.90m (6ft 3in)brought obvious physical attributes to his play. He made the school First XV in that first season.

By 1960 he had switched from farming to banking and had joined Ballymena club. His first major game was for Ulster against South Africa and he was conclusively outplayed by that fine Springbok lock, Johann Claassen.

A year later, he was part of the Irish test side, making his debut at Twickenham in 1962. Until then, he had never seen an international match. England scored from the kick-off and went on to win 16-0. But, though Ireland were weak, McBride and his clubmate, prop Syd Millar, thrived and were selected for the Lions team to South Africa. McBride had already shown his grit by playing the last match of the season with a broken bone in his leg and was still in plaster just before departing for South Africa.

The next eight years were frustrating for McBride. He was in two Lions teams that were thumped by South Africa, and in the 1966 side that was thrashed 4-0 in New Zealand. Ireland had one or two good players, but neither the consistency nor the resolve to be Five Nations Championship contenders. McBride strove mightily, but it must have been disheartening playing in sides where not every forward had his strength or character, where some backs would not tackle and where coaching was non-existent. McBride always stood out, though. John Gainsford, the great Springbok forward, described him as 'mentally tough, physically hard and disciplined, ready to die on the field for victory'. It was said of McBride that for him every match was high noon.

McBride's time finally came in 1971, when the Lions toured New Zealand. He thrived under Doug Smith (manager), Carwyn James (coach) and John Dawes (captain) and stepped into the breach when senior forward Ray McLoughlin's injury ruled him out of most of the tour. As the pack leader, McBride proved an inspiration, instilling a resilience that was not evident in most previous Lions teams.

Back home, McBride took over from Tom Kiernan as Ireland captain, and in 1974 led Ireland to their first Five Nations Championship in 23 years. Then came the triumphant tour of South Africa. McBride and coach Syd Millar worked superbly and the Lions were dominant. McBride's catch-cry was: 'We take no prisoners.' It captured his attitude perfectly.

Again viewed from today's perspective, there were some unsavoury happenings. The '99' call the Lions instituted was effective but can hardly be condoned. It was a signal, to be used in times of emergency, for every forward to begin punching an opponent, the logic being that the referee could hardly send off the entire Lions forward pack. The first time the call was used was in the brutal third test at Port Elizabeth when McBride himself waded 20 yards through the opposition forwards, throwing lefts and rights with all his

Locks who have made the most test appearances:

80	Willie John McBride	(Ireland/British Isles)	1962-75
76*	Ian Jones	(New Zealand)	1990-98
62*	John Eales	(Australia)	1991-98
61*	Gareth Llewellyn	(Wales)	1989-98
61	Jean Condom	(France)	1982-90
58	Gary Whetton	(New Zealand)	1981-91
57	Wade Dooley	(England/British Isles)	1985-93
54	Olivier Roumat	(France)	1989-96
52	Donal Lenihan	(Ireland)	1981-92
52	Moss Keane	(Ireland/British Isles)	1974-84
50*	Mark Andrews	(South Africa)	1994-98
48	Colin Meads	(New Zealand)	1957-71
48	Alan Tomes	(Scotland)	1976-87

* still playing
Includes matches at lock

The determined run and steely look in the eye - a typical Willie John McBride image.

might. It was before this match that McBride delivered his famous team talk. Instead of the passion and fire of his usual pre-match speeches, he simply looked at each player and said: "Men, are we ready?"

McBride returned from that tour a hero, but a modest one. At a reunion 20 years later, he said to his team: "Thank you for making my hopes and dreams a reality."

He had one more season, his 13th, of international play, and scored his only test try for Ireland, in 1975 against France. He was by then a legend of Irish and British rugby, having gone on a record five Lions tours. Soon after his retirement, he became Irish coach.

Off the field, McBride, pipe in hand, was generally an affable figure, ready for a singalong. Unfortunately he did not often show the same good humour in 1983 when he managed the Lions in New Zealand. He was aloof and suspicious, and was dubbed 'Whinging Willie' because of his repeated complaints, particularly about refereeing. Only rarely did the old Willie John emerge. I recall him at Ashburton, smoking his pipe and drinking his Bush Mills, seeming very happy with the world, but more often a cloud hung over him. Perhaps his personality was more suited to being on the paddock, where by force of will he could shape a match, than to sitting in the stands leaving the outcome to others. **100**

IAN M^CLAUCHLAN

Mighty Mouse

IT IS A WONDER that Scottish prop Ian McLauchlan ever managed to play 51 test matches. He missed six years of international rugby because he was considered too small and was later dropped when at his peak because he was too old.

Despite the best efforts of the Scottish selectors, McLauchlan became a famous figure in world rugby, a prop who outplayed the best New Zealand and South Africa could offer and prospered in the most intimidating circumstances.

Though christened John, McLauchlan was known as Ian. During the 1971 Lions tour of New Zealand he was tagged 'Mighty Mouse', or simply 'Mouse' to those close to him. That tour launched him as a player of international stature. He arrived in New Zealand as second-string loosehead prop to Irishman Ray McLoughlin, but became one of the key figures in the Lions' test series victory.

McLauchlan had an impressive schoolboy rugby career at Ayr Academy, shining as a lock and loose forward, and was selected for Glasgow Schools four times. He moved on to Jordanhill College to study physical education and met Bill Dickinson, who became something of a mentor.

Dickinson, a far-sighted rugby thinker who later became Scotland coach, had a look at the determined forward with the big reputation and gave him some bad news. "He told me I wasn't fast or strong enough to play senior rugby, and advised me to take up weight training," recalled McLauchlan. "This was a shock since I had been the strongest boy at my school."

Desperate to prove himself, McLauchlan duly followed the weight training regime prescribed and put on 15.5 kg (34lb) in three months. He was soon in the Jordanhill College First XV and then the Glasgow District side. But it wasn't an easy path for him. He was dropped once for being too dirty and also drew the selectors' wrath for scoring too many tries and being too involved in passing movements.

Even so, at 20 he got his first Scottish trial, in 1962. Michael Campbell-Lamerton, the captain, thought he was a scrumhalf, a centre or even a wing, and couldn't believe the 1.75m (5ft 9in) man in front of him could be an international prop. "I was told that if I was two inches taller, I'd have worn the Scotland jersey straight away, but it took many more trials to convince the selectors that height isn't everything."

John McLauchlan
Prop
Born: Tarbolton, April 14, 1952
Test debut: Scotland v England, Twickenham, March 15, 1969
Test career: 1969-79 (51 matches - 43 for Scotland, 8 for the British Isles)
Test points: 3 (1 try)
* Captained Scotland a record 19 times

The match programme for McLauchlan's last match as Scotland captain, 1979.

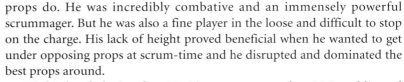

McLauchlan's debut for Scotland in 1969 (when he was a month shy of turning 27) came just in time, as he was by then pursuing skiing with some success. Once in the test side, McLauchlan proved a gem, and developed a public following in a way few

props do. He was incredibly combative and an immensely powerful scrummager. But he was also a fine player in the loose and difficult to stop on the charge. His lack of height proved beneficial when he wanted to get under opposing props at scrum-time and he disrupted and dominated the best props around.

His big break during the 1971 Lions tour came when McLoughlin and Sandy Carmichael, the two leading props, were both eliminated during a roughhouse match against Canterbury. This left McLauchlan and Sean Lynch as the No 1 test pair. How well they responded. McLauchlan gave tough All Black Neil Thimbleby a bath during the Hawkes Bay match and outplayed the considerably bigger Jazz Muller in the tests. He also scored the Lions' only try in the pivotal first test when he charged down a kick then pounced on the ball.

New Zealanders, unimpressed by his size, patronisingly altered his 'Mighty Mouse' nickname to 'Mickey Mouse', but the joke was on them and by the end of the tour, the All Blacks were conceding that the Scotsman was one fine player.

From there, McLauchlan's class shone through. He and Carmichael were a world-class pair of props for Scotland and in 1974 McLauchlan staggered the Springboks with his power and technique. He outplayed big-name props Johan Strauss and Hannes Marais and was part of a fantastic pack that laid the foundation for the unbeaten Lions team's glorious success.

He returned to New Zealand in 1975 as captain of Scotland, but saw his side hammered 24-0 in the farcical 'water polo' test at Eden Park. Back home, McLauchlan instilled fire and commitment into the Scotland side during the 1970s. His courage and determination were famous - he even played in the 1973 Calcutta Cup match after breaking a bone in his leg a fortnight earlier.

Then the murmurings began about his age. Staggeringly, after 32 internationals and four seasons as an inspiring captain, he was dropped for the test against England in 1977. Scotland were thrashed and McLauchlan was eventually recalled, though not as captain. He failed to make that year's Lions team to New Zealand.

McLauchlan's career received a jolt later when he was touring New Zealand with Jim Renwick and Andy Irvine in a Zingari-Richmond team. In a shameful incident, he was brutally stomped on during a game at Athletic Park and had his knee shattered, which put him out of rugby for many months.

Now McLauchlan had the stigma of being an 'old' player attached to him. Selectors felt they were being brave in picking him, though he was always effective. McLauchlan had the Scottish captaincy returned to him for the test against New Zealand in 1979, his 43rd for his country, but was then

The 'Mighty Mouse' looks somewhat stunned after scoring his only test try, for the British Isles v New Zealand, Dunedin, 1971.

dropped from the test team for good. Though he was 37 and slowing down, he felt he was still the best prop Scotland had and most outsiders would have agreed.

McLauchlan was a larger-than-life character who was a constant source of pride for Scottish rugby followers, but who sometimes crossed swords with authorities. Despite his wonderful career, and the fact that he'd captained Scotland to a record number of test wins, he was banned for a time when his autobiography was published.

After his retirement, McLauchlan, a teacher, became a keen marathon runner, but stayed close to rugby by writing about the game and then taking a role as a development officer for the Scotland Rugby Union. **100**

PAUL MᶜLEAN

One Third of the Queensland Rugby Trinity

Paul Edward McLean
Flyhalf
Born: Ipswich, November 12, 1953
Test debut: Australia v New Zealand, Sydney, May 25, 1974
Test career: 1974-82 (30 matches)
Test points: 260 (2 tries, 27 conversions, 62 penalties, 4 drop goals)
* Captained Australia in one test
* Was Australia's highest points-scorer in tests
* Became chairman of the Australian selectors in 1994

CONSIDERING HE WAS such an important figure in Wallaby rugby, Paul McLean received shoddy treatment from the Australian selectors. The gifted flyhalf was dropped several times during his nine-season test career and his position was claimed at various stages by Ken Wright, Tony Melrose, Michael Hawker and Mark Ella. Viewed from across the Tasman, it seemed he was often a victim of the inter-state rivalry between his own Queensland and the more dominant New South Wales.

It's not that the selectors didn't appreciate McLean's talents. He was used at fullback, centre and wing as they endeavoured to squeeze him into their side, but it was fairly cavalier treatment for one of the royal line of Australian flyhalves. Placing McLean on the wing or at fullback was a sad waste of talent.

Paul, one of seven members of the McLean family to represent Australia, attended St Joseph's College in Nudgee and Ipswich Christian Boys College. He shone in football and cricket and as a schoolboy had his kicking honed by league player Mick Cannon.

Brisbane's Brothers club grabbed his services eagerly when he turned up to training in 1972. He was to play in eight club finals for Brothers and help them win seven. By 1973, he was in the state side and showed his big-match temperament on his rep debut by earning his side a late draw against North Auckland with a drop goal.

McLean was part of what came to be called 'the Queensland Rugby Trinity' - 'God the Father' (Mark Loane), 'the Son' (Tony Shaw) and 'the Holy Spirit' (McLean). These three, plus coach Bob Templeton, helped turn rugby in Queensland into a major sport.

McLean's test career began against New Zealand at Sydney in 1974, the only test in which he played alongside his brother Jeff. In those days he was long-haired and had a rather detached air about him. Off the field he gave few clues as to his artistry and grace as a player. He flatted with Loane at St Leo's College at Queensland University. Jack Pollard, in his comprehensive *Australian Rugby: The Game and the Players* describes them as 'a couple of scruffs who, it was claimed, shared a pair of thongs as footwear. Loane persevered to become Dr Loane, McLean to gain a commerce degree'.

Over the years McLean had to battle not only fickle national selectors,

Paul McLean is the star member of one of rugby great family dynasties, seven members of the family having represented Australia. The line began with Douglas McLean just after the turn of the century, and continued through his three sons Doug, Bill and Jack. A fourth son, Bob, looked destined to reach the same level until cut down by injury. But Bob's two sons, Paul and Jeff, achieved national honours, as did Peter, a son of Bill. It's a formidable record, spanning nearly a century and 77 tests.

but a run of serious injuries. Twice in three years he had knee surgery and he also suffered a broken jaw, plus serious shoulder, wrist and finger injuries.

McLean toured Britain twice, in 1975-76 and 1981-82. On the first tour he set a Wallaby record with 154 points and was consistently brilliant. He was in poor kicking form on the second tour, though the critics praised his general play.

There were other highlights for McLean, including representing a World XV in South Africa in 1977, kicking 14 consecutive goals against Wales on its 1978 Australian tour, a breakthrough Bledisloe Cup victory over the All Blacks at Sydney in 1979 and the captaincy of Australia, on the tour of Fiji, in 1980.

Despite his self-effacing manner, the slender Queenslander became a contentious figure in rugby, never more so than in 1982. He was dropped for the first test against Scotland by new Australian selector Bob Dwyer, who hailed from Sydney's Randwick club. Dwyer chose Randwick brothers Glen and Mark Ella ahead of Queenslanders Roger Gould and McLean. Mark Ella was considered an instinctive, brilliant flyhalf; McLean safe and conservative. Dwyer opted for flair. The match, at Brisbane's Ballymore, was rather ugly as the Ellas were booed constantly and Australia lost 12-7.

Dwyer brought back McLean for the second test, which became an emotional occasion because McLean announced it would be his last international. He then proceeded to score a record 21 points as Australia pasted the Scots 33-9. So he departed the international scene, at the age of just 28, in a blaze of glory.

He was a skilled all-round player, 'a rugby thoroughbred' as Australian writer Bret Harris described him. Wallaby captain Andrew Slack said: "As a player's man, Paul McLean has no peer."

McLean really was a master craftsman. He was tactically astute, cool under pressure, had good hands and had a range of kicking skills. Bob Dwyer paid him this tribute in *The Winning Way*: 'McLean was a very fine rugby player and a very fine athlete. He had excellent hand skills and foot skills and was also a much faster runner than most people gave him credit for.'

In October 1982, I attended the Queensland Rugby Union's centenary match, staged in conjunction with the Brisbane Commonwealth Games. It turned out to be more like a testimonial match for McLean, for it was his 100th outing for Queensland. With typically pinpoint timing he scored his 1000th point for the state during it. There was little doubt he was Queensland's favourite son and he was given a memorable send-off.

The year after McLean retired, the Brothers club held a swept-up dinner in his honour. According to Pollard, during the evening he was compared to boxers Muhammad Ali and Les Darcy and marathon runner Robert de Castella. A priest with whom McLean shared an interest in a racehorse, said grace: "Lord, we thank you for the food and we thank you for the contribution Paul McLean has made to sport in Australia and the world." McLean answered typically: "It would be an understatement to say I am not embarrassed about this whole affair, but it is embarrassment of the nicest possible kind."

To understand McLean's impact on the Wallaby side, I should point out the next-highest Australian test points-scorer at that time was Arthur McGill, whose 21 tests produced 88 points. McLean's Australian record survived until Michael Lynagh passed it in 1987. This was particularly appropriate as McLean had played a large part in helping the young Lynagh learn the flyhalf craft. **100**

COLIN MEADS

New Zealand's Pinetree

IN A SENSE Colin Meads is owned by all of New Zealand. For the 15 seasons he played for the All Blacks, New Zealanders basked in the reflected glory. Meads epitomised the finest qualities of All Black rugby through its golden period of the 1960s. He was athletic, skilled, ferociously competitive and proud. He wasn't gregarious; on the field he was an unsmiling giant. But he was instantly recognised and immensely popular.

Today, nearly 30 years after his retirement, there is a flourishing Colin Meads Fan Club that meets annually on his birthday. Members wear the No 5 jersey, as Meads did, quote from their 'bible' (Meads' autobiography), drink from a 5oz glass and often telephone Meads. The club has branches from Dunedin to Wales. Sometimes Meads, who takes these things in the spirit they're intended, turns up to share a beer and a yarn with those celebrating. Many club members were not born when Meads retired. Such is his enduring fame in New Zealand, and further afield.

In my estimation he is the finest All Black forward. Even modern greats like Michael Jones and Sean Fitzpatrick lag behind. Meads was so driven, so devoted to the cause, that he seemed to muster supernatural powers. His team-mates included his brother Stan, Wilson Whineray, Kel Tremain, Ken Gray, Brian Lochore and Ian Kirkpatrick, but even in that exalted company Meads shone.

He played with the same intensity whether it was a club match or an international. Once when captaining his beloved King Country in a Ranfurly Shield challenge against Hawke's Bay, Kel Tremain, the Bay captain, asked the referee to count his players. "I think Meads has eaten one," Tremain quipped.

It was always so. In his early All Black days he and brother Stan were to oppose each other in King Country trials. They didn't speak for a week, got onto the park and punched the living daylights out of one other. Another trial was set for the following Saturday. Their mother wasn't having a repetition and told them before the game: "If you boys punch each other I will come onto the field and march you off holding both of you by the ear." Peace broke out.

Keith Lawrence, who became a respected test referee, recalls the time early in his career when he controlled a King Country match. "I was totally in awe of Meads. He was a legend. I called him Mr Meads at one stage."

Colin Earl Meads
Lock
Born: Cambridge, June 3, 1936
Test debut: New Zealand v Australia, Sydney, May 25, 1957
Test career: 1957-71 (55 matches)
Test points: 21 (7 tries)
* Played 55 tests, the New Zealand record until 1991
* Played 133 matches for New Zealand, still the record
* Played 361 first class matches, still the New Zealand record
* Colin and Stan Meads locked the New Zealand scrum together in 11 tests
* Was one of the First XV inducted into the International Rugby Hall of Fame in 1997

A fearsome sight - Colin Meads in full cry for the All Blacks.

Meads was born in the Waikato, schooled in Te Kuiti and then ran a King Country farm with Stan. Besides my deep admiration for his play, there is for me a personal relationship. When I meet Meads, we invariably first talk about life in the King Country. I feel I have known him forever because my family came from the same area. I lived in Bennydale, 20 miles south of Te Kuiti, where the Meads clan roamed. I can recall him playing on the Bennydale Domain. It was very early in his career, but already everyone in the district knew he was special. The wonderful thing about Meads is that he has never forgotten his roots, despite his fame.

Meads began a 19-season provincial career in 1955, the year he toured Australia and Ceylon with the New Zealand Colts. He made his test debut as a 20-year-old in 1957, touring Australia as a flanker. In the second test, he scored the first of his seven test tries while deputising on the wing for the injured Frank McMullen.

I watched him close up in 1959, when I was a ballboy at Athletic Park for the All Blacks-Lions test. He was still young, but he was a big name and was on his way. Over the next decade, he fronted up to Frik du Preez, Willie John McBride, Benoit Dauga and other giants and was not bettered by any of them.

Fred Allen, his All Black coach, described Meads as the ideal tourist, saying: "Meads' stupendously consistent form developed from his willingness to train - yet it could never be said of Colin that while on tour he made training such a fetish he was incapable of enjoying himself. Those weekend enjoyment sessions of his became a famous part of New Zealand rugby - but once he had had his fun, he resumed training as keenly as ever and kept his form as remarkably as ever."

As a player, Meads was way ahead of his time and would have thrived under modern conditions. He was fit and had hill country strength - legend has it that he carried a sheep under each arm while running over his farm.

When Don Clarke retired in 1964, we in New Zealand felt Meads became the dominant figure in world rugby. He was strong and fast, turning out at flanker and No 8 on occasion. With his distinctive style, he carried the ball in one of his huge paws. His ball skills were outstanding. Included in his 86 points for New Zealand is a conversion and he opened his rep rugby scoring account with a drop goal against Counties. He wasn't a great lineout jumper, but was so competitive he always held his own. What stood out was his unquenchable desire to be involved. He says: "I can remember saying I wanted to be not just an All Black, but a good All Black."

He was tough, and became involved in some punching incidents, as did many players of his day, but there was no kicking or gouging. I never felt with Meads it was gratuitous violence, so was disappointed that the British labelled him 'Dirty Meads' after he was ordered from the field against Scotland in 1967. That sending off, after an innocent-looking lunge towards the ball with his boot, was only the second time it had happened in a test. (Another New Zealander, Cyril Brownlie, was the first, in 1925.) New Zealanders regarded it as a nonsense.

Meads was vilified in Australia in 1968 when he ended Australian halfback Ken Catchpole's career by yanking him from a ruck and tearing Catchpole's groin muscle. Again I felt Meads had acted fairly and that the injury was accidental.

In 1966 he punched British Lion David Watkins and in 1969 he broke Welsh hooker Jeff Young's jaw. So he was certainly not lily-white. In fairness, he was often on the receiving end. The French kicked him brutally at Paris in 1967 and he played out the test with a huge bandage covering a wound in his head. In South Africa in 1970 his arm was broken by a kick by Eastern Transvaal forward Skip Henderson.

That injury was a tragedy. Meads was in sublime form, determined to help the All Blacks win their first series in South Africa. We were receiving black and white footage of him back in New Zealand and had never seen him look better. In the opening game, against Border, he showed all his athleticism and pace with a long, weaving run to the tryline. Then came the

"YOU'RE GOING UP THROUGH THE KING COUNTRY? WITH A NAME LIKE YOURS D'YOU THINK THAT'S WISE, MR. KELLEHER?"

Meads' ordering off at Murrayfield caused a furore in New Zealand (see headlines above), but Wellington cartoonist Nevile Lodge found humour in the situation.

One thing about Colin Meads: he was always available to play. Not only was he the New Zealand test record-holder when he retired, but he never shirked the midweek or minor games. His total of all rep matches played is hugely impressive, and given the shorter tours these days, may never be beaten.

New Zealanders who have played 100 games or more for their country:

133	Colin Meads (1957-71)
128	Sean Fitzpatrick (1986-97)
117	Andy Haden (1972-85)
113	Ian Kirkpatrick (1967-77)
113	Bryan Williams (1970-78)
102	Bruce Robertson (1972-81)
101	Gary Whetton (1981-91)
101*	Ian Jones (1989-98)
100	Zinzan Brooke (1987-97)

* still playing

broken arm. He returned for the last two tests of the series with his arm in a protective casing, but understandably was below his best.

Meads' test career ended in 1971 after he led the All Blacks to a 2-1 series defeat by a brilliant Lions side. It wasn't a year of riches for the All Blacks and Meads, at 35, was not the player he had been. But he was still better than any other New Zealand lock.

Since then, Meads has remained around rugby. His autobiography, *Colin Meads All Black*, sold 57,000 copies, the biggest selling New Zealand sports biography. He coached King Country, then moved onto the All Black selection panel in 1986. But he became embroiled in controversy when he coached the Cavaliers in South Africa. I wasn't impressed with his decision to be part of the Cavaliers. I remember the scene on the team's return when he appeared at a press conference in a brand new South African suit, not a Meads suit at all. It went against the grain. He received a 'severe reprimand' from the New Zealand union and was soon dropped from the All Black panel.

He eventually became a member of the New Zealand Rugby Union council and wielded enormous influence. Some of his fellow councillors seemed to cower away from him because of his reputation as a player. In 1994 he became All Black team manager, forming a partnership with coach Laurie Mains. It wasn't a successful era in the public relations sense.

Meads didn't trust the modern media and stories filtered back about him warning players not to talk to the media. An element of bitterness crept in and he clearly wasn't suited to the job. He often cut a lonely figure. He used to whistle a wordless tune and never quite looked comfortable in the spotlight, tending to keep his head down. Things worked a lot better at the 1995 World Cup, when Brian Lochore was appointed campaign manager to work alongside Meads. Through it all, Meads' pride in the All Black jersey was always evident. As Fergie McCormick said: "To Meads, the All Black jersey was like pure gold."

In 1995, the All Blacks toured France and played poorly to lose the first test. Meads, in one of his last acts as manager, ripped into the team at Nancy, reminding them about pride in the jersey. It was uncharacteristic of Meads, who generally left the motivational side of things to Mains, but it was mighty effective and inspired a superb second test All Black revival.

Through his many roles, Meads has remained a thoroughly good bloke. He loves rugby and if you can get him reminiscing late in the evening over a few drinks he is wonderful company with a fund of interesting stories. His voice gets ever deeper and his dark bushy eyebrows droop lower. In after-dinner speaking engagements, Meads is very modest and such is his presence that he is always well-received. He is at his best leaning on a table, with a jug of beer nearby and a chair available on which to rest a battle-weary leg.

During his career, Meads was regarded as an enormous player. His size - 1.93m (6ft 4in) and 102kg (16st 1lb) - wouldn't seem too big today for a lock, but even aged 60-plus, he still seems physically imposing.

Meads was known throughout the rugby world as 'Pinetree' ('Piney' to his mates, 'Tree' to those very close to him). It was a mark of his standing that his youngest son Glyn, an All Black trialist, was called 'Pinecone', and his daughter Rhonda, a New Zealand netball rep, was 'Pine Needle'.

Perhaps Lochore, his team-mate in so many battles, sums him up as well as anyone: "For a big man he had tremendous skills and real pace. He had terrific commitment to the game, both individually and as a team man. I think he is the greatest All Black that we have had." 🏉

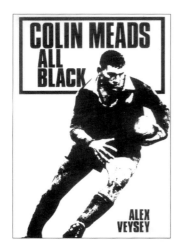

New Zealand's biggest-selling sports biography.

CLIFF MORGAN

Rugby's Ambassador to the World

IT DOES NOT DO JUSTICE to Cliff Morgan to talk of him in terms of tests played or matches won. True, he was one of the greatest to emerge from the Welsh flyhalf factory. But Cliff has always been a man of passion and humour, emotion and sentiment. He has been a fine rugby ambassador and once said of rugby, in a way that only he could: "I have never known a game with so much love."

His character comes through in his media work - he was for many years the BBC's head of outside broadcasts. I recall standing with him watching the Lions train at Eden Park before the fourth test in 1971. As the players were trooping from the field, some stopped by a group of severely disabled schoolboys in wheelchairs, wished them well, tousled their hair and handed out a few small souvenirs. I watched the scene and thought little more of it.

Cliff and I drove back into town and later Cliff filed his report. It began with: 'Today I saw a sight that made me cry …' This was a whole new method of reporting, putting sport into a much broader context, and he had a lot to teach in this regard.

As well as his humanity, Cliff has a mellifluous tone, a fluent, easy manner and perfect timing. He is as good a public speaker as he is a journalist. In 1997, when the World XV was voted into the International Rugby Hall of Fame at a swish function in London, they needed to elect a leader to reply on their behalf. There was little discussion. Willie John McBride, Colin Meads, Hugo Porta and the others turned as one and asked Cliff to speak for them, which he did in memorable fashion.

During my time as a broadcaster, Cliff has always been at and around sport. His BBC job took him well beyond rugby and he shone in his coverage of Olympics and Commonwealth Games. He has also been a writer and author.

As an interviewer on the BBC's popular *Sport on Four* programme, which was wound up in 1998, he invariably found a way to get a little more out of his subjects, whether they were rugby player Tony O'Reilly, soccer star George Best or cricketer Gary Sobers. He was a sympathetic interviewer, though on one much-discussed occasion he went after Charlie Francis, the coach of disgraced Canadian sprinter Ben Johnson. "I had his nuts," Morgan said later. He is never afraid to speak of his heroes, ranging from Muhammad Ali to Jesse Owens, and is unabashed in his praise of Nelson Mandela, describing

Clifford Isaac Morgan
Flyhalf
Born: Porth, April 7, 1930
Test debut: Wales v Ireland, March 10, 1951
Test career: 1951-58 (33 matches - 29 for Wales, 4 for British Isles)
Test points: 12 (4 tries)
* One of First XV inducted into International Rugby Hall of Fame in 1997
* For 38 years he held the record for most tests for Wales by a flyhalf

It is widely accepted that the try Gareth Edwards scored for the Barbarians against the All Blacks at Cardiff in 1973 is the 'Greatest Try' ever scored in a major match. To denigrate it in any way will probably be seen as a sacrilage, but the fact is that Edwards touched down in an end-of-tour festival game where free running was a priority way ahead of the rigours of true test match pressure.

So therefore under careful use of the word 'great', and bearing in mind some were match-winners or game-breakers, the following test match tries are listed as being among the very best ever scored:

Ted Morgan, Wales v New Zealand, Cardiff, 1905
Archibald Gracie, Scotland v Wales, Cardiff 1923
Prince Alexander Obolensky, England v New Zealand, Twickenham, 1936
Ken Jones, British Isles v New Zealand, Auckland, 1950
Jackie Kyle, Ireland v Wales, Cardiff, 1951.
Garth Jones, Australia v South Africa, Cape Town, 1953
Cliff Morgan, British Isles v South Africa, Johannesburg, 1955
Peter Jones, New Zealand v South Africa, Auckland, 1956
Peter Jackson, England v Australia, Twickenham, 1958
Jean Dupuy, France v New Zealand, Wellington, 1961
Richard Sharp, England v Scotland, Twickenham, 1963
Stuart Watkins, Wales v Scotland, Cardiff, 1966
Ian Kirkpatrick, New Zealand v British Isles, Christchurch, 1971
Phil Bennett, Wales v Scotland, Edinburgh, 1977
Hika Reid, New Zealand v Australia, Brisbane, 1980
John Kirwan, New Zealand v Italy, Auckland, 1987
Serge Blanco, France v Australia, Sydney, 1987
Noel Mannion, Ireland v Wales, Cardiff, 1988
Michael Lynagh, Australia v Ireland, Dublin, 1991
David Campese, Australia v New Zealand, Dublin, 1991
Jean-Luc Sadourny, France v New Zealand, Auckland, 1994
Gavin Hastings, Scotland v France, Paris, 1995
Jonah Lomu, New Zealand v England, Cape Town, 1995

him as 'one of the great men of the century'.

But it is as a rugby player that he comfortably earns his place in this collection. New Zealanders were sad when Morgan retired in 1958, so excluding himself from the 1959 Lions team to New Zealand. They were hoping to see in action the little wizard who did so much to help Cardiff and Wales inflict defeats on Bob Stuart's 1953-54 All Blacks, and who had an outstanding tour of South Africa in 1955.

Morgan was exhibiting unusual football skill by his mid-teens. A bout of pleurisy delayed his progress, but by 1950 he was ensconced in the Cardiff side and the following year made his debut for Wales against Ireland, marking another legendary flyhalf, Jackie Kyle.

Initially Morgan struggled at test level. Basil Kenyon's 1951-52 Springboks - especially the loose forward trio of Basie van Wyk, Hennie Muller and Stephen Fry - gave him a torrid time and Wales lost 6-3. There were whispers that perhaps Morgan wasn't up to it. But soon all doubters were silenced. Morgan had the skill and the cockiness to brush off a performance that might have had other players doubting.

Wales won the Grand Slam that season and one of the architects of the triumph was their 1.70m (5ft 7in) 76.5kg (12st) flyhalf. Film footage shows a dark, solidly-built, nimble player. Of his many attributes, his speed off the mark was what made him special. He was so quick he could outrun opposing tacklers, even in those days when the offside laws were framed in favour of the loose forwards. Morgan would take off diagonally, outrun the forwards, then arc around to straighten the attack. He tackled well and was a reasonable tactical kicker, but his speed was his most feared weapon.

Throughout the 1950s, Morgan was the Welsh kingpin. During the 1955 Lions tour, South Africans came to understand why British rugby experts rated him so highly. That tour is now sometimes referred to as 'Cliff Morgan's tour', amazing really when other stars in the British side included the incomparable Tony O'Reilly, Jeff Butterfield and Cecil Pedlow. South Africans, reared on the safety-first tactics of Bennie Osler and his clones, were amazed at Morgan's flair and versatility. The hard grounds suited the Welshman, who was able to display all his genius.

He scored a brilliant try during the first test at Ellis Park, lighting up a match (won 23-22 by the Lions) which is still a candidate for the title of 'best

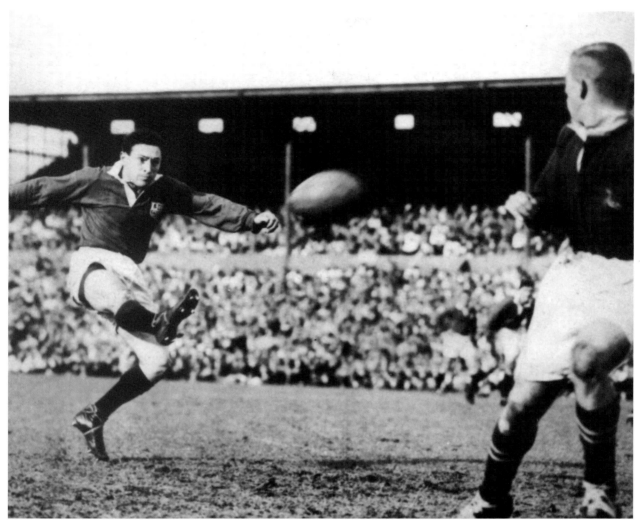

ever'. Early in the second spell Morgan received a pass from Dickie Jeeps, raced through the Springbok loose forwards and across the Springbok 25-yard line. Then he straightened up and outpaced the cover defence. Morgan captained the Lions to victory in the third test at Pretoria, which he nominates as his career highlight.

At home, Morgan led Wales to the Five Nations Championship in 1956, but surprisingly, in view of his enormous popularity, was not asked to captain the side again.

During his career Wales won four Five Nations Championships and a Grand Slam. Such was his impact that in 1955 he was offered by Wigan - and turned down - a hefty sum to turn to league. He was always closely marked, but his speed usually enabled him to escape trouble.

Morgan exuded character. He walked at a brisk pace, not slowed even by a stroke in 1972, had a ready sense of humour and unbounded energy. Perhaps the only thing he enjoyed more than to chat was to sing.

We in New Zealand have another reason to remember Cliff Morgan. He was the commentator when Gareth Edwards scored the wonderful try for the Barbarians against the All Blacks in 1973. It is the most replayed try in television rugby history and I cannot even estimate how many times I have heard Cliff say: "What a score!" as Edwards dives over the line. 💯

Cliff Morgan was never better than when he was in the British Isles team on tour in South Africa in 1955.

GERHARD MORKEL

The Prince of Fullbacks

Pieter Gerhard Morkel
Fullback
Born: Somerset West, October 15, 1888
Died: Somerset West, September 5, 1963
Test debut: South Africa v Scotland, Inverleith, November 23, 1912
Test career: 1912-21 (8 tests)
Test points: 16 (6 conversions, 1 drop goal)
* One of 10 Morkels, all related, to play for South Africa

GERHARD MORKEL WAS THE JEWEL in the first family of South African rugby. Ten Morkels have represented the Springboks, but it was Gerhard, the fullback who had everything, who put the family name in lights. Through the years he has so often been called 'the Prince of Fullbacks' that the expression has become a cliché. Yet the description is apt.

The sturdy 1.83m (6ft), 83kg (13st) Morkel was lauded wherever he played. Before the second World War, South Africa fielded such class fullbacks as Jackie Tindall and Gerry Brand, but always Morkel was the benchmark. He had the British critics in raptures when he toured with Billy Millar's 1912-13 Springboks. And when he travelled to New Zealand in 1921, he was nearly 33 and said to be past his best. Yet he was the star of the side.

Morkel was born into a Somerset West family which ate, breathed and talked rugby. At one stage 22 Morkels were playing high-level rugby in South Africa.

South African rugby has had some amazing families, names like de Villiers, Luyt, Louw, Pienaar and du Plessis that we recognise even today. But no family rivalled the Morkels. Ten boys of the same generation represented Western Province.

Gerhard was born with some advantages - the rugby ethos in his family, plenty of space on the sprawling family farm and natural ability, but no-one practised harder. As a boy he was hardly ever without a tennis ball in his hands. "My proficiency at handling the tennis ball made it easier for me to handle the rugby ball later," he once explained.

Even when an established player, he would organise groups of boys to pepper him with kicks during long practice sessions. He learned to screw kick for greater accuracy and distance. He became a renowned drop-kick artist. He was big for a fullback of his time and put his full weight into his punting, which was huge.

Morkel was not fast - he felt he was dreadfully slow - but his anticipation and positional play atoned for this weakness. He was a decisive tackler, preferring the barge tackle to snuff out opposing attacks. He would launch his tackle from a trademark crouch as the attack sped towards him.

He first played for Somerset West when was only 16, getting his first opportunity by pure chance. He happened to be at the train station when

When the strong South African team travelled to New Zealand in 1921 for the first test series between the two countries, it contained just two players who had played for the Springboks before the first World War. Fullback Gerhard Morkel played five tests during the Springboks' 1912-13 tour of the British Isles and France. His cousin, William Henry Morkel, known to all as "Boy", had played one test against a touring British Isles team in 1910, and all five on the 1912-13 tour. Both Morkels closed their test careers with the 1921 tour of New Zealand.

The five Morkels who toured New Zealand in 1921. Back row (left to right): Harry, Royal and Henry. Front row (left to right): Gerhard and Boy.

the team, about to depart, found they were a man short. Morkel's train fare was raised by a quick whiparound and he turned in such a fine performance he became a team regular.

Morkel made his Springbok debut on the 1912-13 tour of Britain and France. The team won all five internationals, the first Grand Slam, and the Morkels led the way. There were brothers Gerhard and Jackie (a penetrative midfield back), plus their cousin Boy (a brilliant forward), and goal-kicking front-rower Douggie.

While Gerhard didn't do much place-kicking - this task fell to Douggie - his play was a revelation. One writer said: 'He was around six foot tall and all wire and whipcord. I never saw him jib at the rough stuff or saw him so much as winded.'

E H D Sewell described Gerhard as 'well-nigh the perfect back at catching and kicking' and wrote: 'He was the best at kicking with either foot that I saw. His left was certainly as good as his right. As good a tackler as the next

man, he was a distance in front of nearly all of them as a punter.' Choosing a World XV from 1900-39, Sewell nominated both Gerhard and Douggie Morkel.

Morkel won special praise for his display against London. A reporter wrote that Morkel had 'gained for him a niche in the gallery of the world's greatest fullbacks'. His captain Millar described his fullback's play as 'daring to the point of recklessness'.

South Africa lost several stars during the first World War, including Jackie Morkel, and some others were a bit long in the tooth on the historic 1921 tour of Australia and New Zealand. The Springboks were captained by Theo Pienaar.

In a match in Australia, Morkel's deadly tackling so annoyed some spectators that afterwards he had to be smuggled to his hotel with the aid of his Australian opponents.

In New Zealand he played in nine of the last 14 matches, including all three tests. He was the key man, not just because with 42 points he was the leading points-scorer, but because he was the consummate fullback.

Perhaps his most vital attribute was his temperament, which was revealed during the second test at Auckland. Late in the match he received the ball near the touchline 50 metres from the New Zealand goal. He ran infield a few steps, then let fly with a drop kick and sent the ball high between the posts. The magnificent kick, worth four points, gave the Springboks a match-winning 9-5 lead, and was marked with the presentation to Morkel of a gold medal by the Auckland union. The kick so thrilled the crowd that some spectators ran onto the field and offered Morkel a drink. The Springbok fullback solemnly took a few sips from the proffered bottle and toasted the crowd.

The deciding third test was played in atrocious conditions at Athletic Park. The Springboks were said to be a fair weather team and the All Blacks were expected to dominate in the mud and rain. But Morkel, in his last test, handled the slimy ball immaculately. The match was drawn 0-0, so the series was split 1-1, an appropriate start to hostilities between two great rugby nations. Phil Mostert, the fine Springbok forward, recounted how the sound of the heavy wet ball could be heard repeatedly slapping into Morkel's hands, followed by an even louder thud as he thumped it into touch. "It was raining so heavily we could hardly see one another," Mostert remembered. "Gerhard was like a ghostly shadow somewhere at the back of us and he saved us from defeat."

Springbok hooker Tokkie Scholtz recorded 12 years later in *The History of South African Rugby*: 'Morkel excelled himself on a waterlogged field. I doubt whether those who saw the game consider even Nepia a better fullback. Gerhard never misfielded the slippery ball and his kicking to touch in the mud bordered on the miraculous.'

Though he quit test football after that tour, Morkel, always a model of fitness, played first league club rugby for another 10 years. In his 33 matches for South Africa, he scored 79 points.

Millar, his first test captain, said he was South Africa's finest fullback. New Zealand critics of the 1950s put him on the same elevated rung as Nepia, Bob Scott and Brand.

Morkel died at the age of 74, having taken particular pleasure in the play of his son Hannes, a relentless forward, who captained Western Province. **100**

GRAHAM MOURIE

Born Leader

GRAHAM MOURIE was one of the most significant people in New Zealand rugby history. As an openside flanker he played a style that was years ahead of its time. As a captain he was bracketed with Wilson Whineray at the top of the list of All Black skippers.

Mourie was a leader in other areas. In 1981 he elected not to play against the visiting Springboks, a stand that jeopardised his All Black captaincy and caused hostility towards him from some narrower-minded New Zealand rugby folk. When his autobiography *Graham Mourie - Captain* was published in 1982, Mourie stated that he was receiving book royalties and was declared a professional. Other players had blurred the line to preserve their amateur status, but Mourie had the integrity to be honest and, I believe, helped eventually have these archaic rugby laws rescinded. He was re-admitted to the rugby fold a decade later.

Finally, Mourie was a pivotal figure in the first World Cup, in New Zealand and Australia in 1987. His drive, planning and expertise helped transform a struggling organisational effort into a World Cup to be proud of.

So all up Mourie - 'Goss' to his mates - has made an immense contribution to rugby. Not bad for a Taranaki farmer who was equally happy sloshing around a paddock in his gumboots.

Mourie was leadership material from an early age. In the Taranaki coastal township of Opunake, he captained the local High School First XV at 15, then moved to New Plymouth Boys High School and represented Taranaki Secondary Schools in 1969-70.

While studying at Victoria University, he represented Wellington from 1972-74, including a brief Ranfurly Shield tenure, earned three All Black trials, and played for the national Colts, Juniors and Universities teams. He scored a try for the Juniors when they upset the All Blacks in 1973. In 1975, he returned to Taranaki and captained the Juniors against Romania, scoring two tries in a 10-10 draw.

Because he was injured when the trials were held, Mourie missed the 1976 All Black tour of South Africa. Instead he led an All Black B team unbeaten through South America, making his debut in Uruguay. Mourie and coach Jack Gleeson formed a partnership that was to serve New Zealand well. On his return, Gleeson said prophetically: "This young man has a great future as New Zealand captain."

Graham Neil Kenneth Mourie
Flanker
Born: September 8, 1952
Test debut: New Zealand v British Lions, Dunedin, July 30, 1977
Test career: 1977-82 (21 matches)
Test points: 16 (4 tries)
* Captained New Zealand in 19 of his 21 tests

Illustration courtesy of Murray Webb.

Keith Quinn's ranking of the century's 10 greatest New Zealand players and personalities:

1. George Nepia
2. Colin Meads
3. Michael Jones
4. Don Clarke
5. Jonah Lomu
6. Bob Scott
7. Wayne Shelford
8. Graham Mourie
9. Sid Going
10. Grant Fox

Mourie played the last two tests against the 1977 British Lions, covering himself in glory with a tackle that freed the ball for Lawrie Knight to score the series-clinching try. At the end of that year he took over the captaincy for the tour to France.

I admired Mourie's captaincy for many reasons. He was innovative, as he showed in France in 1977 when he and Gleeson devised tactics to combat the huge French forwards. After being hammered in the first test, Mourie decided to 'run the donkeys off their feet', so the All Blacks used short lineouts and quick kicks to keep the game moving at a hectic pace. The frazzled French went down 15-3.

Mourie played as hard as any player I've seen. Often he would finish a game with blood running down his face, for he was totally committed. But I never saw him flustered or resort to foul tactics. He sought desperately to win, but never at all costs. As captain, Mourie walked that fine line between players and team management. He was slightly aloof and sometimes it was difficult to know what he was thinking. But he was always interesting company and his players really enjoyed touring under him. His arrival was timely, for he was interested in history and foreign cultures and through his example the All Blacks began to move away from their previous boozy image.

As a captain, Mourie was intelligent, analytical and inspiring. He could switch tactics in mid-match and was able to lift a team-mate with a word or phrase. A recurring theme for Mourie was that players be honest with themselves. He encouraged personal responsibility, emphasising they must be able to look themselves in the mirror after a match and know they'd given 100 percent.

Mourie always had a sense of style and went out of his way to treat everyone fairly, even the touring media, which was virtually unheard of previously.

He led the 1978 All Blacks to a Grand Slam of victories in Britain. Most major matches were won in the dying minutes, testimony to Mourie's calming influence and the team's fitness. That All Black team contained stars like Andy Haden, Murray Mexted, Dave Loveridge, Bryan Williams and Bruce Robertson, but the dominant player was the dynamic, tireless Mourie, later named Player of the Year by the Rothmans yearbook.

The Grand Slam All Blacks lost just one match, to Munster. The New Zealanders entered the after-match function in single file singing 'Hi ho, hi ho, it's off to work we go …', taking their defeat in fine fashion. Again the captain's influence was significant.

Mourie led five New Zealand teams to Europe in as many years. In 1980, the All Blacks, invited to help Wales celebrate its rugby centenary, responded with a brilliant effort to win the test 23-3 in front of a packed, and stunned, Cardiff Arms crowd. Mourie scored the opening try and played superbly. Cliff Morgan commented: "I do not mind going to my maker because today I saw, from Graham Mourie, the greatest loose forward display the world could ever wish to see."

I recall an example of Mourie's rugby thinking from that game. With fulltime up, and New Zealand having cemented a commanding victory, the ball flew towards the sideline where Mourie leaned across to keep it in play. This epitomised his attitude - he encouraged continuity, used every moment and was always constructive.

He wasn't imposing physically - just 1.83m (6ft) tall and 89kg (13st 7lb). Nor was he especially fast - he did not have a high knee lift and scuttled

Programme for the Welsh Centenary match when Graham Mourie captained the All Blacks, 1980.

Graham Mourie, always constructive, initiates another All Black attack during the 1979 tour to Great Britain.

rather than sprinted. But he was so fit, the result of a gruelling training regime, that he was just as quick in the closing minutes, while others were slowing. His anticipation was uncanny, and he was a deadly tackler. His brand of non-stop rugby would fit in well today.

During some off-seasons he played for the University club in Paris and he thrived on the French lifestyle. His rival French test captain, Jean-Pierre Rives, became a particular friend - there were similarities in their make-up and approach to rugby.

In 1981, he was accused by some of treason for his stand on South Africa, but said: "I felt the South African situation was wrong morally. It was wrong for rugby and wrong for New Zealand." Despite some murmurs, even from team-mates, he later regained the captaincy.

Though he was declared a professional and retired in 1982, he unofficially helped John Hart coach the champion Auckland provincial side during the 1980s. Then he was employed by West Nally, the marketing body for the 1987 World Cup. Mourie and Eddie Tonks overhauled the organisation of the Cup, cracking the whip around New Zealand to get people moving and have the necessary details set in place.

During the final, at Eden Park, Mourie was not to be found up in the members' stand, but kitted out in an old tracksuit, down the end of the park ensuring the advertising signs were correctly placed. After the World Cup, he departed the corporate life and returned to his farm in Taranaki.

He remained an influential figure in New Zealand rugby and was named coach of an under-achieving Wellington team in 1998. He is tipped as a future All Black coach.

Mourie played 61 matches for New Zealand (figuring in just six losses) and scored 16 tries. If anything, he was a bigger star in Europe than at home, for he played 11 of his 21 tests in Europe and lost just one. **100**

HENNIE MULLER

The Greyhound of the Veldt

Hendrik Scholtz Vosloo Muller

Loose forward

Born: Witbank, March 26, 1922

Died: Cape Town: April 26, 1977

Test debut: South Africa v New Zealand, Cape Town, July 16, 1949

Test career: 1949-53 (13 matches)

Test points: 16 (3 tries, 2 conversions, 1 penalty)

* Captained South Africa in nine tests for eight wins
* Managed and coached the Springboks in the 1960s

HENNIE MULLER'S NAME is revered and cursed on cold New Zealand winter weeknights by thousands of players as coaches finish their training sessions with 'a few Hennie Mullers'. After a good session, they might get away with two or three; if things haven't gone well, perhaps they'll be required to run 10. The gut-busting length-of-the-field diagonal sprints were introduced to New Zealanders by Muller when he coached the 1965 Springboks and have formed a staple part of the rugby training since.

But Muller's name was cursed by New Zealanders long before he became Springbok coach. He was primarily responsible for South Africa's 4-0 series win over New Zealand in 1949, the All Blacks' lowest moment. Muller, a No 8 with the speed to match most wingers, wrought havoc on the New Zealand backline.

The All Blacks dismissed the man tagged 'the Greyhound of the Veldt' as a destructive player, but acknowledged that Muller, using the rules of his time, had out-thought and outplayed them. He would stand well off the back of the lineout, perhaps opposite the second-five, and stifle any attack.

Bob Scott wrote in his autobiography: 'I would unhesitatingly say that Muller was the greatest loose forward I have seen. He was the complete player and he more than anybody determined the result of the tests.'

Muller was at his peak in that series. Danie Craven described the 1.80m (5ft 11in), 85kg (13st) Muller as the fastest loose forward he'd seen and Bill Schreiner, a Springbok selector for 40 years, said Muller would have been chosen for South Africa as a winger if he hadn't become a No 8.

British fans saw him when the South Africans toured the United Kingdom in 1951-52. The Springbok captain, Basil Kenyon, was injured early, and Muller was saddled with the leadership responsibilities. He was also a stone heavier than previously, so the blinding pace was gone. Nevertheless, he was still a marvellous player and led a Springbok team that is regarded as one of the best combinations to visit Britain.

The South Africans lost just one minor game and swept the tests, thrashing Scotland by the unprecedented score of 44-0. It was a famous match and remained a world record defeat for 35 years. One Scottish supporter reportedly said in disgust: ' …and we were lucky to get nought!' At one stage Muller, feeling pity for the Scots, exhorted their captain and flyhalf Angus Cameron as he ran past: "Tell you forwards to get together."

Yet Muller's rise to international football was anything but easy. He was the youngest of five boys. While a toddler he lost his parents and was sent to an orphanage before being adopted by his uncle and aunt. He attended school at Ficksburg, Orange Free State and Wakkerstroom, Eastern Transvaal.

He first played rugby, in his school's under-13 side, as a winger. At just 14 he could run 100 yards in 10.5s, and turned out at fullback for the Wakkerstroom town senior Second XV. Until then, he'd played his rugby bare-footed - 'kaalvoet', as they say in Afrikaans.

Muller's ability was supplemented by toughness and strength, a result of his lifestyle. As a youngster he would lead oxen in the ploughing of fields day after day. Then, once he was 16, he worked in a gold mine in Boksburg. He had to fill and carry on his shoulders buckets filled with up to 70kg (just over 150lb) of mercury. Perhaps this contributed to the round-shouldered physique which became so well-known on the world's football fields. Later he worked as a rigger in the mine's mill section. Swinging the huge hammers was backbreaking, but developed the stamina and strength he showed as a player.

He played rugby for the mine's lower division teams as a winger, centre or flyhalf. Seeking promotion, he switched to the flank. Initially he still could not make the first team until many leading players went to the war. After a few matches, Jack Kipling, the team coach and a Transvaal forward, said: "Hennie, you'll never make a flanker. Try number eight." Muller was initially crushed by this observation, but later he blessed Kipling for his judgement. In his first season of senior rugby, he made the Transvaal side.

His progress was halted in 1948 when, playing Western Province at Ellis Park, his right leg was smashed in a terrible accident. The knee ligaments were badly torn. Normally this would have ended his career, but a revolutionary operation was performed. Recovery involved a three-month spell in hospital, six weeks in plaster and a month wearing a calliper. Finally, in February 1949, he resumed training. Who'd have believed that later that year he would demoralise the All Blacks and be regarded as the world's best No 8?

The series didn't begin well for the South Africans, some of whom had to be introduced

Hennie Muller leads the Springboks out for the Scotland test on the 1951-52 tour. South Africa won 44-0 to establish a test record.

Grand Slam captains

New Zealand, Australian and South African teams periodically aim to complete a Grand Slam of test victories over England, Ireland, Scotland and Wales during a northern tour. There have been some unusual near misses. The 1924 All Blacks could not organise a test against Scotland. The 1967 New Zealand side could not visit Ireland because of an outbreak of foot and mouth disease. A drawn match against Scotland cost the 1963 All Blacks a Grand Slam. In 1948, Wales denied Trevor Allan's Wallabies a Grand Slam by beating them 6-0. In 1998, South Africa fell to England at the final hurdle.

Captains who have led teams to Grand Slams in Britain and Ireland:
Fred Dobbin/Billy Millar

Doug Morkel	South Africa	1912-13
Bennie Osler	South Africa	1931-32
Hennie Muller	South Africa	1951-52
Avril Malan	South Africa	1960-61
Graham Mourie	New Zealand	1978
Andrew Slack	Australia	1984

Note: At the 1995 World Cup, New Zealand completed the traditional Grand Slam by beating Ireland, Wales, Scotland and England in turn.

in the dressing room before the first test at Cape Town. At halftime they trailed 11-3, but they fought their way through to a 15-11 victory and never looked back in the series.

The All Blacks criticised his spoiling tactics, a bit rich for a country which rejoiced in the wing forward play earlier in the century of Dave Gallaher and Cliff Porter. Even in South Africa debate raged: was Muller a rover or a spoiler, a marauder or a player who would kill rugby? A F Markotter, the wise old sage of South African rugby, damned him with faint praise, describing him as 'a deuce of a spoiler'.

I'm sure Muller was ahead of his time. All top teams now try to field a blindingly fast openside flanker to pressure opposing backs. Few do so as tellingly as did Muller.

He was so fast he could harass the scrumhalf and flyhalf, continue on through to the centres, and sometimes even the wing. He called it 'running the line dead'. With his car door ears, and wearing his trademark white kneeguard over a crepe bandage on that dodgy right knee, he was a frightening figure for his opposition. Muller was ruthless and fearless, had an abundance of energy and uncanny anticipation. It was a harrowing experience playing against him.

Because he was so fit and had an amazing work rate, there was never any let-up. But there was more to his game than just fearsome tackling. He had soft hands and could pick up the ball on the run, and was an able kicker - in tests he kicked two conversions and a penalty to go with his three tries.

In Britain, Muller formed a superb loose forward trio with Basie van Wyk and Stephen Fry. They upset emerging flyhalf genius Cliff Morgan in the Wales test, forcing him into hurried, unconvincing kicking that helped the Springboks score a narrow victory.

By the time John Solomon's Wallabies toured South Africa in 1953, Muller was slowing down. He'd dislocated a shoulder late in 1952 and had begun the 1953 season 9kg (20lb) overweight. It was touch and go if 'the Windhond', as he was called in South Africa, would make the test team.

The selectors kept faith in him and he led South Africa to a 3-1 series victory, then retired. His had been a short career, encompassing just 13 tests (12 victories). He'd also captained Transvaal to a Currie Cup triumph before transferring to Western Province.

Muller remained a legend in South Africa, his autobiography *Tot Siens to Test Rugby* running to three editions.

Though he had a killer instinct on the field, Muller was a soft-hearted and compassionate person with a stentorian guffaw. Danie Craven said of him: "He was finely strung and emotional, a strong man who, nevertheless could and did cry tears of sorrow and joy."

He turned to coaching, guiding Western Province with some success. He first managed, then coached the Springboks, but he had a disastrous Australasian tour in 1965, losing both tests in Australia and then three of the four in New Zealand.

Muller, who ran an outfitting business just outside Cape Town, died of a heart attack when he was only 55.

GEORGE NEPIA

New Zealand's Jewel

I'M OFTEN ASKED WHAT has been the proudest moment of my broadcasting career. Surprisingly, it hasn't been commentating an All Black rugby test victory or a New Zealand win at the Olympics. My proudest moment was a small incident that occurred at the St Helens ground in Swansea in 1982, just before the New Zealand Maori team played Swansea.

George Nepia, the famous All Black fullback of the 1920s, was at the ground that day, part of a tour group following the Maoris on their tour of Wales. He'd arrived unheralded in Wales six days earlier, had watched the Maoris at Cardiff, and had then travelled to Swansea.

I wanted to do a story on George returning to Wales after all those years and felt the St Helens ground was the appropriate place to interview him. It was on the St Helens ground that the 1924 'Invincibles', with George at fullback, had beaten Wales 19-0, to avenge the controversial defeat the 1905 Originals had suffered at the hands of Wales. "We beat them 19-0 - one point for every year that had passed since that 1905 defeat," George told me.

George said that while he really did not recognise the Arms Park in Cardiff, with the new grandstands and modernisation that had taken place, the memories flooded back when he walked inside the old ground at Swansea. It still had the strange oblong-shaped field, the ascending row of terraced houses surrounding the ground, the picket fence along the front of the grandstand.

It was a grey and bitterly cold day at Swansea. We set our cameras at halfway and I went to look for George. He was on the terrace behind the dead ball line with a group of supporters. He didn't want to come down. The ground was slippery, he was cold and the cameras were too far away. But some friends helped him down and he eventually agreed to do the interview. So I walked with George along the sideline towards halfway. He was wearing a heavy black overcoat down to his feet, a big scarf around his neck and a cloth cap. He was then 77 years old and had not been to Swansea since 1924.

Yet as we walked along people recognised him and began nudging each other, pointing and saying, 'That's him; that's George Nepia.' Like lightning, the news raced around that George Nepia, the famous All Black fullback, was back. Within seconds wave upon wave of applause echoed around the ground. It was the most incredible feeling. George realised what was happening and looked across at me and said, in that most endearing Maori manner, "Gee." George had tears in his eyes, and so did I. It was the most

George Nepia
Fullback
Born: Wairoa, April 25, 1905
Died: Ruatoria, August 27, 1986
Test debut: New Zealand v Ireland, Dublin, November 1, 1924
Test career: 9 (1924-30)
Test points: 5 (1 conversion, 1 penalty)
* Played all 32 matches on the 1924-25 'Invincibles' tour of Britain, France and North America
* Played one rugby league test for New Zealand
* First class career spanned 29 years (1921-50)
* At 45 years, 158 days, he was the oldest person to play first class rugby in New Zealand
* Was one of the First XV inducted into the International Rugby Hall of Fame in 1997

moving moment of my career.

The applause never stopped and became so great that while George was being interviewed, it was announced over the PA system that George Nepia was at the ground. He then walked out onto the field and was given a standing ovation by the 30,000 spectators. It went on and on and on as George turned and waved at the crowd. Most of the people at the ground would not have been born when he played in the 1924 test, yet his standing in the eyes of the Welsh was obvious.

George is often cited in New Zealand as our most loved rugby personality, and I would go along with that. You could sense his greatness when you were around him. He was not only an outstanding rugby player, but an outstanding New Zealander.

His start in international rugby was so amazing that fiction writers would baulk at writing such a story. He was the sturdy 19-year-old Maori boy who played at fullback in every match of the famous 'Invincibles' team's tour of Britain and France. He had virtually no experience at fullback before the tour but adapted so well that even today his legend endures.

George Nepia returns to Swansea 58 years after one of his greatest triumphs and is accorded a hero's welcome.

He was a key figure in Norman McKenzie's record-breaking Hawkes Bay Ranfurly Shield team of the 1920s and was still the best fullback in the country when he played in all four tests against the touring 1930 Great Britain team. He went close to winning selection for the 1935 All Black team to Britain and when he missed out, turned to rugby league, winning a Kiwis cap in 1937 and enjoying two fruitful years in the paid ranks in England. Nepia was too popular, too charismatic, to be shunned as others who switched to league were and he was readmitted to rugby union by dint of a special war amnesty.

When he eventually retired, he took up refereeing. He was always at or around rugby. Just four days before he died in 1986, he attended the New Zealand-Australia test at Dunedin. I recall him, looking rather frail, boarding the plane the next day and as we put our bags in the overhead locker, telling me how cold he was.

George's start in rugby came when he attended the Maori Agricultural College in Hastings and he came under the influence of American Elder Moser. With his gridiron background, Moser instilled into Nepia and his mates the secrets of tackling and torpedo kicking, both of which became

Spying on the opposition is certainly not a modern trend. George Nepia once told me of a spying mission undertaken by half a dozen of the 'Invincibles' during the 1924 tour.

"We were playing near London," he explained, "and on a rest day, a group of us took the train down to Cardiff, where we stood in the crowd and watched the Welsh trials. We wanted to remain as inconspicuous as possible, so we wore our overcoats and took the silver ferns off the front of our hats."

Nepia trademarks.

He was just a lad of 16 when he made his rep rugby debut, and got his break when playing in the Te Mori Rose Bowl match between Southern and Northern Maoris in Auckland. At the insistence of that great Maori identity Ned Parata, he played at fullback instead of his usual position of first five-eighth. He seldom played anywhere else again.

Though Nepia was a sure selection for 'Invincibles', he knew so little about fullback play that serious consideration was given to playing Mark Nicholls at fullback for the first few tour matches while Nepia learned his trade. In the end, Nepia was given his chance and responded magnificently.

He was 1.75m (5ft 9in), weighed 82.5kg (13st) and exuded solidity. His diving at the feet of onrushing forwards who used to dribble so much in those days, his fantastic punting, his uncompromisingly ferocious tackling and his courage made him a rugby sensation in a team of superstars. Though never a top place-kicker, he kicked 33 conversions and five penalties during the tour.

There is a famous piece of writing by Denzil Batchelor, the English sports journalist, which sums up beautifully the admiration Nepia drew. 'When I hear others debating who will play at fullback for the Kingdom of Heaven versus the rest,' wrote Batchelor, 'I turn to stone. It is not for me a question of whether Nepia was the best fullback in history. It is a question of which of the others is fit to loose the laces of his Cotton Oxford boots.'

Nepia was always extremely modest about his achievements. He said he would have been lost on the 1924 tour without Nicholls and downplayed the importance of his role in the unbeaten record: "Some matches they could have played without a fullback. They were such a brilliant team - a great pack of forwards and a brilliant set of backs."

As a Maori, he was ineligible for the 1928 All Black tour of South Africa, and after the 1930 season little was heard of him for some years as he struggled to eke out a living for his wife Huinga and four children on some rugged East Coast farmland during the Depression years.

Though he missed the 1935 team to Britain, he played very well that year for the New Zealand Maoris in Australia. Then it was onto league, and on the day the All Blacks lost the third test - and the series - against South Africa in 1937, he helped the Kiwis to an historic win over Australia.

He made his last first class rugby union appearance in 1950, aged 45 years, 158 days, a New Zealand record. He'd had the longest first class career in New Zealand rugby history and in that last match, his son, George junior, also played, the only instance in New Zealand rep rugby of father and son appearing on opposite sides.

After his retirement, he showed courage when he led the anti-South Africa tour marches through the late 1950s, two decades before public feeling turned that way. He maintained one of his greatest moments was in 1986 when he was made an honorary life vice-president of the South African Rugby Board, a mark of the respect in which he was held throughout the rugby world.

New Zealanders of a younger generation saw why Nepia was so special when he was the guest of a *This Is Your Life* programme in 1986. It drew a record audience and was repeated after he died later that year. One of the highlights of the programme was Nepia's beautiful rendition of the song *Under the Maori Moon.*

He was a friendly, kindly man, for whom nothing was too much trouble, and a player fit to take his place in any World XV. 🏉

George Nepia's status in New Zealand was confirmed when this stamp was issued in 1989.

GWYN NICHOLLS

Guardian of the Gate

Erith Gwyn Nicholls

Born: Westbury on Severn, June 13, 1874

Died: Dinas Powys, March 24, 1939

Test debut: Wales v Scotland, Cardiff, January 25, 1896

Test career: 1896-1906 (28 matches - 24 for Wales, 4 for a combined British side)

Test points: 19 (5 tries, 1 drop goal)

* In 1899 became the first Welsh player to tour overseas with a combined British side
* Captained Wales 10 times

Keith Quinn in front of the Gwyn Nicholls Memorial Gates at Cardiff, February 1999.

I AM REMINDED of how great a player Gwyn Nicholls must have been every time I walk through the gates named after him at the entrance to the Arms Park in Cardiff. When those gates were opened half a century ago, Nicholls was already dead and it was his great friend and Wales team-mate Rhys Gabe who did the honours on his behalf.

By the 1940s, Wales had already unearthed a string of legendary players. There had been all the greats from the first golden era of Welsh rugby, before the first World War. After that Wales had produced champions like Albert Jenkins, Cliff Jones, Wilfred Wooller, Vivian Jenkins, Haydn Tanner and Idwal Rees. But from this galaxy of stars, there was really only one candidate when it came to immortalising a player by naming the Arms Park gates after him - Nicholls, known throughout his career as 'the Prince of Centres'.

In all the literature about British rugby in the early years of this century, it seems impossible to find even a suggestion of criticism of Nicholls. Writers of the day, and fellow players, are absolutely unstinting in their praise of him.

For instance, the often crusty E H D Sewell in *Rugger the Man's Game* says Nicholls was unsurpassed by any player of his experience. 'On the field and off, Gwyn was an ideal player of the Man's Game. His was no sinecure post when he was captain of the Welsh XVs, which sometimes contained some pretty tough material. Gwyn ran the show like a Man, and was enormously popular with all his own team, not one of whom would ever stand for one word that there was ever a better centre, or comrade.'

W J T Collins, the prolific English writer, recounts in *Rugby Recollections* the manner in which Nicholls subordinated himself to his winger. 'His aim was to draw and hold the defence so that the way was open for his own winger. It was in the supreme gift of judgement that he was greatest. An all-round player with all the gifts, he could make a burst for the line with a gallop or a close swerve and was very difficult to stop; his fielding and screw-punting to touch were remarkable for quickness, accuracy and judgement; he was a good drop-kick; his tackling was of the best; and he had a masterly faculty for getting to the weak spot to strengthen defence … Gwyn Nicholls was the perfect centre - the greatest exponent of the game I have ever known.'

Rhys Gabe once wrote that Nicholls always stressed the importance of timely and accurate passing and credits Nicholls for the expression, 'A pass

not accepted cleanly is purely the fault of the giver.' This became the creed of the famous Welsh backline creed during Nicholls' career.

Players from the distant past face two problems when being judged so many years later. Either they are forgotten, or their deeds are so romanticised that they become ever more god-like as time marches on. Nicholls, even the best part of a century later, is in no danger of ever being forgotten, and his deeds do not need to be exaggerated. He had enough quality as a player and a human not to need the benefit of any embellishment.

J B G Thomas, when profiling Nicholls, compared his impact on Welsh sport to that of Trumper and Bradman in Australia, Dempsey in the United States, W G Grace and Jack Hobbs in England.

Nicholls, though born in Gloucestershire, grew up in Cardiff. He represented various Cardiff teams as a scrumhalf and a fullback, then broke into the strong Cardiff senior team in the 1893-94 season, playing mainly at centre.

He made an impact quickly, being capped for Wales against Scotland and Ireland in 1896 and achieved a personal ambition by playing alongside his hero, Arthur Gould, for one season. Gould had for years been the idol of Welsh rugby and normally it would be expected that a youngster like Nicholls would take some years to be accepted as his natural successor. But in an amazingly short time, Nicholls was acknowledged as a master. He was captain of Cardiff by 1898 and the following year excelled in Australia with a British team, playing in all four tests and being top try-scorer on tour.

In the years after Nicholls burst onto the scene, a wonderful Welsh backline built up. It is doubtful if Wales has ever fielded a more potent three-quarter

Gwyn Nicholls was just one of many stars of the first golden era of Welsh rugby. Wales won the Triple Crown six times from 1900-11, and shared another Championship with Ireland. After France joined the competition, Wales completed the first ever Grand Slam in 1908 and repeated the feat in 1909.

In 1905 they were the only team to beat Dave Gallaher's All Black side, and three years later they beat Australia 9-6.

Welshman are justifiably proud of the great backs of that era. Fullback Billy Bancroft, who made 33 consecutive test appearances, was there at the start, then gave way to the equally talented Bert Winfield. Bancroft's younger brother Jack took over from Winfield. On the wings, Wales boasted little Willie Llewellyn, who shot to fame by scoring four tries on debut, and Teddy Morgan, who scored the only try of that famous Wales-New Zealand test.

Other outstanding backs included Dicky Owen, who went on to play a record 35 times for Wales, Rhys Gabe, Nicholls' partner in the centres, Billy Trew, the wing/centre, Percy Bush, Tommy Vile, Reg Gibbs, Hopkin Maddock, and John Williams, who was to set a Welsh try-scoring record.

The forwards didn't have the same glamour, but Arthur Harding, Jehoida Hodges, George Boots, Bob Brice, George Hayward and hooker George Travers were all among the best players in Britain in their time.

line than Llewellyn, Nicholls, Gabe and Morgan. Nicholls, quick, astute and brave, was seldom bettered on the field but did have the occasional setback, such as a broken collarbone in 1903.

By the end of the 1904 season, Nicholls was talking retirement, but stayed to lead Wales to an immortal victory over New Zealand in 1905 - the battle of the disputed Deans 'try'. It was before this match that he gave the team talk which is still famous in Welsh rugby as the battle speech to end all battle speeches.

Nicholls told his troops: "Gather round, boys! The eyes of the rugby world are on Wales today, and it is up to us to prove that the Old Country is not quite barren of a team that is capable of giving New Zealand at least a hard fight. It has been suggested by some of the English papers that they come to Wales more or less stale; but as they played two English counties last week and won each match by 40 or 50 points, with half their best players resting for today's match, the staleness is not very apparent to me!

"We have already discussed tactics, so it remains only for me to appeal to you to be resolute in your tackling. You all know what they are like if given any latitude. They throw the ball about and their system of intensive backing-up makes them very dangerous, so there must be no hair-combing and every man with the ball must be put down, ball and all. You forwards already know what to do to get the loose head. Come on, let's get out!"

Nicholls played his last test against the 1906 Springboks at Swansea. He was not fully fit and Wales were beaten. However he rounded out his playing career gloriously a few days later when he led Cardiff to a 17-0 thrashing of the tourists in the mud of Cardiff Arms Park.

In 13 seasons for Cardiff, Nicholls scored just over 100 tries, though the true picture of his ability is the number of tries he made for those outside him. Soon after his retirement, he wrote his thoughts on rugby, including this telling statement: 'The modern game is essentially the merging of an individual in the team.'

He tried his hand at refereeing for a short while, then served on the Cardiff committee and finally became a member of the Welsh Rugby Union through the 1920s. He narrowly escaped death in 1923 when he made a courageous attempt to rescue a young girl from drowning at Weston-super-Mare. The incident affected him deeply. From then on, Nicholls, who was a laundry owner, suffered from nervous trouble and shunned the limelight. He was always a kindly and warmly-regarded man, but became increasingly introverted until his death at the age of 64.

TONY O'REILLY

Rugby, Beans and Business

TONY O'REILLY SAID IN 1956: "I have two ambitions. One is to qualify as a solicitor and the other is to play rugby football." The Irish winger succeeded in both spheres surely even beyond his most distant dreams.

He did indeed qualify as a solicitor, but that was only the start for O'Reilly the businessman. At a very young age, he was appointed Chief Executive of the Irish Dairy Produce Marketing Board. He was obviously headed for the very top of the business world and eventually became president of the Heinz empire, taking corporate America by storm. These days he is also a media tycoon with newspaper interests worldwide.

On the rugby field, his CV is no less impressive. He was a brilliant winger who, having just left school, and with only five senior club games for Old Belvedere under his belt, made his debut for Ireland. He had just turned 19 when he gained rugby immortality with his performances for the British Lions in South Africa in 1955. His 16 tries on the tour was a record for a tourist to the Republic.

It was the beginning of a glittering rugby career.

Yet through all his successes on and off the rugby field, O'Reilly has remained ever charming and approachable. He is as good a public speaker as I have heard and has a wonderful self-deprecating sense of humour.

When he toured New Zealand with the 1959 Lions team, rumour had it that he played with a comb tucked inside one of his socks. We ballboys used to debate whether we could see the comb. Thirty-five years later I was walking around the back of the main stand at Eden Park with him when a middle-aged chap with a glint in his eye approached O'Reilly and offered him a comb, saying it was one O'Reilly had discarded in 1959. O'Reilly loved the joke. Interviewing him one time, I asked him if he did indeed take a comb onto the field. He smiled. "It's never been clear until now, and I'll let that myth continue," he replied.

There are dozens of stories about O'Reilly, many of which he tells against himself. When, aged 33, he was recalled to the Ireland team in 1970 after a seven-year absence, during which his business career had flourished. He arrived at training in a chauffeur-driven Rolls Royce. That much of the story may be true. Whether, during the test match two days later, he went down in a tackle and really did hear someone in the crowd call out, 'And give him one for the chauffeur as well,' is a matter of conjecture.

Anthony Joseph Francis O'Reilly
Winger
Born: Dublin, May 7, 1936
Test debut: Ireland v France, Dublin, January 22, 1955
Test career: 1955-70 (39 matches - 29 for Ireland, 10 for the British Isles)
Test points: 33 (11 tries)
* Was one of the First XV inducted into the International Rugby Hall of Fame in 1997
* Set try-scoring records on both his tours for the British Lions, to South Africa in 1955 and New Zealand in 1959

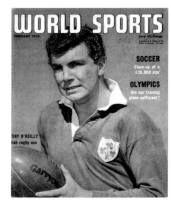

Tony O'Reilly's fame stretched well beyond merely rugby, even in the 1950s.

O'Reilly saved the evening during the New Zealand Rugby Football Union's 1992 centenary celebrations. There had been a succession of less than impressive speakers and those in attendance were fidgeting and twitching embarrassingly. O'Reilly rose and within three minutes had won over the audience. He sat down 15 minutes later to a standing ovation.

The 1955 tour of South Africa established O'Reilly as a great. He was young, strong, had pace to burn and on his way to his try-scoring record became a cult figure for the younger rugby followers. As Rupert Bates of the *Sunday Times* of London memorably wrote, he 'turned the toes of defenders and the heads of women with equal facility'. Though always an individual, and a colourful one at that, he impressed with his maturity and level-headedness for one so young.

O'Reilly was an outstanding sportsman at Belvedere College, excelling at cricket, tennis and soccer as well as rugby. He was so good that he skipped most junior sides and when just 18, was selected for the final Irish trial, only a month after his first senior club game. That was in January, 1955. Within three months he had played four tests for his country as a centre and been picked for the Lions. His meteoric rise can be seen in the inscription on the shield presented to him by Belvedere College: 'To Tony O'Reilly, who in the first year after leaving school was selected for Leinster, Ireland, the Barbarians and the British Lions.'

For the Lions he moved to the wing where his size - he was 1.88m (6ft 2in) and 93kg (14st 9lb) - power and eye for a try made him a sensation.

For several years O'Reilly was one of the giants of world rugby. He travelled to Canada in 1957 and South Africa in 1958 with Barbarians teams, and in 1959 was a member of Ronnie Dawson's Lions team to New Zealand. He and Peter Jackson were as good a pair of wingers as we have seen in New Zealand.

O'Reilly stood out not just because of his try-scoring prowess - 17 tries in 17 games - but because we did not see many wingers with flaming red hair, freckles and white skin running amok against the All Blacks.

He says his greatest thrill in rugby came on that tour when during the last test he scored his 17th try, to set a record for a player touring New Zealand. He accepted a pass from Andy Mulligan, the replacement halfback, beat the All Black defence and scored in the corner. The Lions won the test 9-6, but still lost, 3-1, a series in which they were sure they were the better side.

Mulligan and O'Reilly proved a big hit in New Zealand. With their Irish accents, story-telling ability, incessant mimicry and wit they became rugby's best known comedy double act. Using humour as their weapon, they were able to send up officials and other players without being offensive and were in great demand. They could be heard over aircraft intercoms, on sightseeing coaches, in aircraft lounges and on various local radio stations.

Oddly, while O'Reilly was proclaimed around the world as a rugby genius, he was not quite so universally accepted back in Ireland. He certainly played better on tour when he was made to train more assiduously and did not have any problems with excessive weight. And there were murmurs back home that he was not exactly devoted to the club scene. Eyebrows furrowed further when, having graduated as a solicitor and achieved a degree in civil law, his business took him to Leicester for some years.

O'Reilly played 22 consecutive tests for Ireland but in 1963, when he was aged just 25, he was left out of the test side. That seemed to be the end of his career. He wouldn't have been heart-broken. To him rugby had always been

there more for fun, whereas the world of commerce required his full attention. But of course, seven years later came his unlikely recall to international rugby.

Always stylish, always in control. Tony O'Reilly crosses for another try for the British Isles.

As the story goes, he was in London on business when injury deprived Ireland of a specialist wing, so he offered to help out (there was even an article written by him in the match programme). It's said that in the changing room beforehand, he confided to his skipper his fear that the England wing, a renowned speedster, would run around him. "Don't worry," came back his skipper's reply. "It won't take long."

Recalling that 1970 test many years later, he remarked on the difference in shapes, size and background of the Irishmen, saying they were 'united by the only thing that unites all Irishmen - which is Englishmen!'

O'Reilly often played at centre for Ireland, and liked the position. But in world rugby, he will always be remembered as a matchless left winger. **100**

BENNIE OSLER

The Little Master

Benjamin Louwrens Osler
Flyhalf
Born: Aliwal North, November 23, 1901
Died: Belville, April 23, 1960
Test debut: South Africa v British Isles, Durban, August 16, 1924
Test career: 1924-33 (17 matches)
Test points: 46 (2 tries, 6 conversions, 4 penalties, 4 drop goals)
* His 14 points in the first test v New Zealand in 1928 remained a South African record for 21 years
* Held the South African record for most test appearances
* Held the South African record for most test points

DESPITE THE CARPETING he took from some of the leading British critics of his day, there is little doubt that Bennie Osler was one of the three most important figures in the history of South African rugby, alongside August Frederick Markotter (Dr Mark) and Danie Craven.

Between the wars the bow-legged little - 1.72m (5ft 8in) and 74kg (11st 6lb) - flyhalf ushered the Springboks through major series against the British Isles, New Zealand and Australia without defeat. And in 1931-32, he led South Africa to a Grand Slam of test victories in Britain.

Osler, labelled an autocratic genius and a rugby wizard, became a benchmark player for Springboks who followed him. When the South Africans toured New Zealand in 1956 their team, and particularly their flyhalves, were still being measured on the unofficial 'Osler-scale'. He was the forerunner of other kicking Springboks flyhalves like Keith Oxlee, Gerald Bosch and Naas Botha.

No-one disputed that Osler was a match-winner. What rankled was his emphasis on kicking. He had mastery over a vast array of kicks - drop goals with either foot (worth four points in his day), huge punts, up-and-unders and chip kicks. Those who quibbled with his tactics felt he didn't play attractive rugby and starved his outside backs of possession.

The niggling criticism became a torrent through Britain in 1931-32 in what looks suspiciously like sour grapes. Leading rugby writers complained bitterly about South African tactics and vented most of their spleen on Osler. What probably hurt most was that South Africa won all four tests and lost only one of their 26 tour matches.

Not all Osler's opponents agreed with the British. Mark Nicholls, one of the shrewdest of All Blacks, was vice-captain of the 1928 New Zealand team to South Africa. He wrote: 'Bennie Osler is the best back I've ever seen. He is great because he dominates the game. He has a marvellous punt with either foot, getting height, direction and distance. He is a good drop and place-kicker. He boots the ball at such speed that once he gets the leather in his exceptionally safe hands, he may almost certainly be counted up on to make a clearance no matter how close the opposition.'

Osler's father was a lawyer and a keen rugby follower and his sons followed his footsteps (Bennie's younger brother Stanley was also a test player). Bennie,

Bennie Osler in control against the All Blacks, 1928.

freckle-faced and fair-haired, attended Wynberg and Rondebosch Boys High Schools, Western Province Preparatory School and then Kingswood College in Grahamstown.

Ironically, he was acclaimed at college for his running skills on the rugby field. He scored many tries, seldom kicked and was a good tackler. Blessed with twinkling feet, he used to delight spectators by gathering the ball on his own goal line, feinting to kick and then setting off of a solo corkscrew run to initiate an attack.

He established himself nationally while attending the University of Cape Town in the early 1920s. By 1922, aged only 20, he'd played his first game, at centre, for Western Province, which was a mighty force in South African rugby at the time and was to hold the Currie Cup virtually throughout Osler's career.

Because of his array of talents, Osler soon became a heavily-marked man and countered the extra attention with tactical kicking, though he always remained quick off the mark. He developed the technique of working the touchline, not giving his outside backs a run until they were near their opponents' line. Osler used to say he only kicked when his team won a slow heel or he received a bad pass, which induced wry comments about the poor quality of heeling and passing in Springbok rugby during his time. Some opponents, frustrated at his relentless kicking, would even chant ironically, 'Kick, Bennie, kick!' during the game.

In 1924 he appeared in all four tests against the touring Great Britain side, helping South Africa to three wins and a draw. Though he would be nervy and twitchy before a big game, once the whistle blew he always seemed in absolute control.

Osler, tagged 'Mr King of Rugby', was the pivotal figure in the 1928 series against Maurice Brownlie's All Blacks. He kicked 14 points (two drop goals, two penalties) in the Springboks' 17-0 first test win. The match came to be known as 'Osler's Match' and his points tally remained a South African record until Okey Geffin bettered it in 1949. Nicholls wrote after the first test: "Bennie Osler was the hero of the day. He rose nobly to the occasion, his kicking being magnificent, his tactics correct."

Osler plagued the All Blacks throughout the tour, helping South Africa win the third test and leading Western Province selections to two wins over the New Zealanders.

The team Osler led through Britain in 1931-32 contained some of South Africa's all-time greats. Besides Osler, there were Gerry Brand, Jackie Tindall, Danie Craven, Pierre de Villiers, Phil Mostert, Phil Nel, Boy Louw and several other legends. Osler was 30 and had lost some of his speed, but remained a master tactician. No-one could spot and probe the opposition's weaknesses better. The team's strength was its formidable forwards and Osler knew how to nurse them, carving off huge chunks of territory with his kicking.

He tended to have a sharp tongue on the field and was very fussy about the service he received from his scrumhalves, but came to appreciate the unique abilities of Pierre de Villiers and Danie Craven. Craven later related how every time he threw Osler a poor pass, his captain would shout out, 'Bliksem' - an Afrikaans swear word.

The British complaints about negative play must have sunk in and the drums began beating for a revision of Springbok tactics. Osler had intended to retire, but at the request of the selectors made himself available for the 1933 series at home against Australia. He lost the captaincy to Nel but held his test spot.

During the first test, Osler played his usual controlled, tactical game and South Africa won 17-3. But when Nel was injured before the second at Durban, and Osler was restored to the captaincy, he dramatically changed tactics and spun the ball at every opportunity, hardly kicking a ball. The result - a 21-6 win to Australia - probably only emphasised how right Osler had been all along. Sanity prevailed after this match. Nel resumed the captaincy, Osler returned to his kicking game, and the Springboks won the series 3-2. Osler rounded out his career at the top in style by dropping the winning goal to lead Western Province Town and Country to a 4-0 victory over the Wallabies.

Though Osler was a natural leader and enjoyed huge success at rugby, there was a certain sadness about his life. According to brother Stanley, his greatest regret was not being allowed to join the British Navy near the end of the first World War. Again according to Stanley, Bennie felt there was always something missing in his life because of this. He dabbled in law, became an insurance salesman and tried farming, but remained a depressed spirit.

During the second World War, he enlisted in the 2nd A-A Regiment of the Cape, was made a corporal, but refused further promotion. He contracted malaria and amoebic dysentery while serving in what was then Abyssinia. He was never able to shake off their effects and after years of ill-health died aged 58. 🔟

FRANCOIS PIENAAR

One Team, One Country

FRANCOIS PIENAAR'S test career lasted just four years, but the impression he made on world sport will last a lifetime. Pienaar led the Springboks into the 1995 World Cup on their home soil and was given the responsibility of drawing the various factions of South African society together after years of turmoil.

What a magnificent ambassador for the new South Africa proved to be. He became the third player to have the honour of hoisting the Webb Ellis Trophy aloft in triumph as the end of a World Cup. And the charismatic Pienaar proved the perfect Springbok captain when the role required not just a fine rugby player, but a visionary leader and a diplomat.

Pienaar was educated at Patriot School, Witbank. He was earmarked early as a leader - he captained South African schools in 1985 and then South Africa under-20. By 1989, at 22, he was in the Transvaal team, a raw-boned flanker with an imposing 1.93m (6ft 4in) 105kg (16st 7lb) physique.

South Africa returned to test rugby in 1992 and Pienaar was selected the following year. His first test, against France at Durban, resulted in a 20-20 draw. Remarkably Pienaar, aged 26, led the Springboks on debut, as had Basil Kenyon and Des van Jaarsveld before him. Pienaar was to pass Dawie de Villiers' record for most tests as Springbok captain. He was a natural leader who inspired his men by the ferocity and commitment of his play, and by appealing to their pride.

For Transvaal, Pienaar was equally successful. He led the province to the Currie Cup title in 1993 - their first triumph in 21 years - and 1994. In addition, Transvaal carried off the Super 10 title in 1993, going through pool play unbeaten and pipping Auckland 20-17 in the final at Johannesburg. In 1994, he steered Transvaal to a 24-21 win over England.

As a flanker, Pienaar was barely short of the highest class. He was aggressive and fast, had uncanny anticipation and was particularly skilled at claiming the loose ball. A concern with Pienaar was that he threw himself into the fray so willingly he tended to get knocked about. During the Springboks' 1994 tour of New Zealand, he suffered what appeared to be very severe concussion against Wellington. I didn't like what I saw that day. The South African management were at pains to have Pienaar leave the field under his own steam, though he was obviously in dire need of assistance. Perhaps they hoped they would then be able to claim he had not really been concussed.

Jacobus Francois Pienaar
Flanker
Born: Port Elizabeth, January 2, 1967
Test debut: South Africa v France, Durban, June 26, 1993
Test career: 1993-96 (29 matches)
Test points: 15 (3 tries)
* Captained South Africa in every test he played
* Held the South African record for most tests as captain (subsequently beaten by Gary Teichmann)

Francois Pienaar (centre) salutes the crowd after captaining South Africa to win the 1995 Rugby World Cup.

Pienaar returned (wearing headgear) in time for the second test, which seemed too soon.

There were other occasions when he suffered concussion and it seemed to be a problem that wasn't going to go away. Ironically his last test, against New Zealand at Cape Town in 1996, ended when he was stretchered off the field badly concussed.

The Springboks' early results under Pienaar were mixed as they strove to overcome their years without top rugby. There was a strong hint that he would be dropped in 1994, but he held on. When Kitch Christie became Springbok coach, Pienaar's job was far more secure. The two were firm friends and partners in a braai (barbecue) equipment business.

I was impressed with Pienaar's captaincy through New Zealand in 1994, even though he was leading a losing team. He was particularly obliging with the media and seemed to draw his team together well. He insisted they learn the words of *Nkose Sikelel' iAfrika* (God Bless Africa), the national anthem of the new South Africa.

What's more, with Pienaar, there was an air of sincerity. He was a blue-eyed, blond white South African, but seemed not only willing but eager to embrace post-apartheid South Africa unreservedly. His team called him 'Cappy' and there seemed genuine respect.

This shone through strongly during the 1995 World Cup. While he must have been under inordinate pressure, Pienaar handled himself magnificently throughout that testing period. He helped originate the team's 'One team, one country' theme, and was, as Dan Retief wrote, 'the handsome embodiment of South African rugby'.

No-one present will forget the final, not just the match, which went to extra time, but the emotion of the occasion. Before the game, South African President Nelson Mandela took the field wearing Pienaar's No 6 jersey, which brought an almighty roar from the crowd. The embrace of Pienaar and Mandela was clearly genuine, with heartfelt warmth on both sides. That moment had to be worth 10 points to the Springboks.

Two hours later, President Mandela was back on centre stage, handing Pienaar the World Cup trophy in a powerfully symbolic moment. While Pienaar held the trophy aloft, Mandela danced for joy on the podium. Pienaar made one of the unforgettable statements of world rugby when he was asked immediately after the presentation how it had been to have 65,000 South Africans cheering. "We did not have 65,000," he answered. "We had 43 million."

Only weeks later, Pienaar played a critical role in warding off the threat to traditional rugby authorities of the World Rugby Corporation. The last-minute refusal of Pienaar and his Transvaal team-mates to sign for WRC derailed the ambitious plan and paved the way for professional rugby in the form it now exists.

Pienaar always impressed as more than a rugby player. For instance, before the 1995 World Cup, he took the Springbok squad around Robben Island and visited the cell where Mandela spent 18 years. After the World Cup, he organised a free set of new adidas kit for the cash-strapped Romanian squad before they flew home.

Such was Pienaar's stature in South Africa then, it seemed unthinkable that a year later he would be out of the test team. His position began to look tenuous when coach Christie departed early in 1996. Then South Africa were beaten by New Zealand in Christchurch and Cape Town and Pienaar was so badly concussed that he missed the remaining three tests, Gary Teichmann taking over the captaincy. Even when Pienaar became available again, new Springbok coach Andre Markgraaff omitted him. The decision caused an outcry and Markgraaff received death threats.

Public reaction intensified when Transvaal, inspired by Pienaar, upset Northern Transvaal in the Currie Cup semi-finals. However, the fire died and Natal beat Transvaal in the final. Gradually it came to be accepted that the Pienaar reign was over.

At the beginning of 1997 Pienaar, resigned to having lost his Springbok place forever, signed for the London club Saracens, though he rang his friend Nelson Mandela first for approval. At Saracens they call Pienaar 'the man with the Midas touch'. Shortly after his arrival he was saddled with the responsibility of player-coach, but did such a good job that his team beat Wasps to win the 1998 Cup final and finished runner-up in the league. **⑩⑩**

Kitch Christie and Francois Pienaar had won 14 tests together - the South African record - as coach-captain of the Springboks when Christie stepped down in 1996, because of ill-health and because he began to feel agitation in rugby circles for Andre Markgraaff to replace him. Their mark has subsequently been beaten by the Nick Mallett-Gary Teichmann combination.

When Christie died shortly after, Pienaar said: "I first met Kitch Christie in 1991. I was an uncertain flank forward and an uncertain young man in many ways, but he took time to teach me about rugby, about life, about business, about people, about wisdom, about decency, about honesty. If I have achieved anything … it is due to Kitch Christie. He was like a father to me."

The match programme for South Africa's greatest victory - Rugby World Cup final, 1995.

CHERRY PILLMAN

The Icing on the Cake

Charles Henry Pillman
Loose forward
Born: Sidcup, January 2, 1890
Died: November 13, 1955
Test debut: England v Wales, January 15, 1910
Test career: 1910-14 (20 matches - 18 for England, 2 for the Lions).
Test points: 30 (8 tries, 3 conversions)
* Was a championship golfer
* One of the few players to have been selected in both the forwards and backs for tests.

IT'S NOT DIFFICULT, when reading about Cherry Pillman, to imagine him as the Zinzan Brooke of his era. Pillman was the outstanding England forward in the days before the first World War, and the same words of praise that were used to describe his play have in recent times been used to describe the dynamic All Black forward of the 1990s.

Pillman, christened Charles Henry but known to everyone as Cherry, was a wing forward, an anachronism these days. The British generally did not favour the wing forward, saying it was an obstructive position. In fact Bim Baxter, the British Isles team manager in New Zealand in 1930, went so far as to describe wing forwards as cheats.

However, there was never a suggestion that Pillman was anything but a constructive player. He was a forerunner of the modern openside flankers. But he was obviously more than a flanker. He could run like a hare, did most of the place-kicking duties for his teams and had safe hands. When critics seek to praise forwards, they often say they could play in the backs. Pillman not only could have played as a back but he did so, and produced one of the most extraordinary exhibitions of rugby imaginable.

It was the second test between Great Britain and South Africa at the Crusaders Ground, Port Elizabeth, in 1910. Pillman had missed the first test through injury and only just passed the fitness test for the second. His selection at flyhalf caused a stir among South African rugby critics who wondered how the 20-year-old Englishman would handle the unfamiliar role.

Apparently Pillman turned on an incredible display and Britain won, 8-3. Billy Millar, the Springbok captain, wrote later: 'My memories of this game are dwarfed by Pillman's brilliance. I confidently assert that if ever a man can be said to have won an international match through his own unorthodox and lone-handed efforts, it can be said of the inspired black-haired Pillman I played against on the Crusaders Ground.'

One report described Pillman as 'playing a game invented by himself'. Although listed as flyhalf, Pillman bobbed up anywhere from centre to wing to fullback, but still found time to lead one forward rush after another. His tackling demoralised the Springboks and he initiated both his team's tries, one with a perfectly-place tactical kick. He also put over a difficult conversion. Aside from peeling the oranges for halftime and blowing the fulltime whistle, there wasn't much else he could have done.

Though he undoubtedly reached his rugby peak on this glorious day, Pillman's class as a rugby player goes well beyond one sublime performance. He finished that British Isles tour as top points-scorer with 65 points. As a roving, utility player, he was impossible to keep out of the action.

Pillman attended Tonbridge School, where he shone in a variety of sports. He was from a sports-minded family. His younger brother Robert played one test for England in 1914 (replacing Cherry, who had broken his leg) and was killed two years later during the first World War. Both brothers were outstanding golfers, Cherry representing the South of England against the North.

England's 1913 Grand Slam team. Pillman is second from left, front row.

Playing for Blackheath and Kent, Pillman progressed so quickly through the rugby ranks that he was only a few days out of his teens when made his test debut in 1910, against Wales. He slipped easily into a classy England team that won the Five Nations Championship.

Thereafter Pillman was regarded as indispensable to the England side. Though he played at stand-off for Blackheath in the early part of his career, it was as a wing-forward that he gained international acclaim. E H D Sewell described him as 'not only a first class attacker, but a grand defender'. His speed was remarkable and he made it a point of personal pride to bring down the opposing wing.

During the war Pillman served as a Lieutenant in the 4th Dragoon Guards, and was awarded the Military Cross. He was a flour importer and during the second World War used his contacts for the national good, being appointed Area Flour Officer for the South-East Division. For many years he was a distinguished and highly respected member of the London stock exchange.

Like many true greats, he was a revolutionary and is credited with developing wing forward technique. Tragically, he broke his leg in 1914 while playing Scotland and never played top rugby again, though he maintained his interest in the game. It was Pillman, using his influence and stature, who was instrumental in getting Blackheath back on their feet when their ranks had been decimated by the first World War and he captained the team in 1919-20.

Pillman had a five-year international career. Reports of the time describe him as irrepressible and ubiquitous. He was tall and slender and played the game at great pace, using both flair and anticipation. When we think of Pillman, we should not think of a player who departed test rugby 85 years ago, but of a loose forward pioneer who paved the way for Hennie Muller, Kel Tremain, Jan Ellis, Jean-Pierre Rives, Simon Poidevin and … Zinzan Brooke. 💯

Cherry Pillman was but one of several brilliant players in the golden age of England rugby just before the first World War. England won the Five Nations Championship in 1910-12-13-14 and completed Grand Slams in the last two years.

The outstanding personality was Adrian Stoop, who represented his country from 1905-12, twice as captain. He was later a test selector and a member of the International Rugby Board. Stoop, a stalwart of the Harlequins club, was a deep thinker on rugby, especially backline play and his teams always played an innovative, attractive style.

Other leading backs during this period of riches for England included Dave Davies, Ronnie Poulton-Palmer, John Birkett (who held the England test appearance record for some years), William Johnston, Cyril Lowe and Francis Oakeley.

The big-name forwards, besides Pillman, were Leonard Brown, Robert Dibble, John Greenwood, Alfred Kewney, Jack King, Sidney Smart and Norman Wodehouse.

HUGO PORTA

Mr Ambassador

Hugo Porta
Flyhalf
Born: Buenos Aires, September 11, 1951
Test debut: Argentina v Chile, Montivideo, October 10, 1971
Test career: 1971-90 (66 matches)
Test points: 656 (12 tries, 91 conversions, 115 penalties, 28 drop goals)
* Had the world's longest test career
* One of the First XV inducted into the International Rugby Hall of Fame in 1997
* Holds the world record for most drop goals in tests

WHEN I THINK of the little wizard, Hugo Porta, I recall Argentina's test against the All Blacks at Dunedin in 1979. Within minutes, Porta drop-kicked 45-metre goals with both feet. I hadn't seen a player pot goals with impunity with either foot since Don Clarke. On that same tour, Porta headed a ball into touch soccer-style against Counties at Pukekohe.

Porta was a rugby genius and had many of the attributes of other greats, from Clarke to Philippe Sella and Barry John. To find so much ability in one player was astounding. For two decades, Porta wasn't just important to Argentinian rugby, he *was* Argentinian rugby. He was the test side's captain, tactical linchpin, points-scorer and inspiration.

Even playing for a rugby minnow, he made such an impression that he was one of the inaugural First XV voted into the International Rugby Hall of Fame in 1997. At that induction in London, Porta stood proudly alongside Gareth Edwards, Colin Meads and Serge Blanco, and not a person in the room begrudged him his place of honour. The recurring question is: if he did all that for soccer-mad Argentina, what would Porta have done if he'd been a New Zealander, Welshman or South African?

Porta could easily have gone to soccer. He was a soccer player until his teens and one of the top Argentine clubs, Boca Juniors, tried to sign him. Ironically, Porta became one of the first non-soccer sportsmen to receive recognition from the wider Argentinian community.

His soccer background, plus his natural talent, meant he could do things that were beyond most others. Punting, drop-kicking and kicking tactically with either foot came easily to him. I've watched him bounce a rugby ball from boot to boot, like soccer players do with their round ball.

Porta's reputation was set in 1973, when he toured Britain, but I first saw him play against England at Twickenham in 1978. The match was drawn 13-13, an indication that Argentina was a coming force, and Porta thrilled everyone with his flair and generalship.

He was thick-set for a flyhalf - 1.77m (nearly 5ft 10in) and 84kg (13st 2lb) - with a sturdy backside and thighs, and looked more like a hooker than a flyhalf. But he was an electrifying runner with sharp speed from a standing start and was capable of shifts of pace and direction that dazzled defenders. English journalist John Reason once wrote: 'Porta could play closer to an opponent without being tackled than a top matador working with a bull.' His build enabled him to run through tackles and helped him develop into a strong tackler himself.

Keith Quinn's rankings of the century's greatest Argentinian players and personalities:

1. Hugo Porta
2. Diego Cuesta Silva
3. Angel Guastella
4. Gabriel Travaglini
5. Fabian Turnes
6. Rafael Madero
7. Alejandro Iachetti
8. Lisandro Arbizu
9. Federico Mendez
10. Tomas Petersen

Porta, who attended De La Salle Monastery School in Buenos Aires, was initially a scrumhalf and in 1970 was included in the Argentine national training squad. After a series of injuries to the leading flyhalves, he was invited by Angel Guastella, the Argentina B coach, to switch positions for the 1971 South American championship. Porta, just 19, was on his way. Porta's test career was the longest in rugby history when he retired; it has recently been surpassed by Uruguay's Diego Ormaechea. Porta remains one of the select few to have played through three decades; he all but played through four.

Under the eye of Guastella who, he says, taught him everything about the game, Porta was a vital man in guiding Argentinian rugby through various styles. First there was the free-running approach of men like Guastella; later there was the change to hard scrummaging and kicking for the forwards. Porta was adept at both, and though he was a formidable kicker, the running game was his first love.

Porta, always so tidy and precise in dress, manner and style, captained Argentina and South America in nearly 50 tests after assuming the leadership against France in 1977 and was his country's skipper at the first World Cup, in 1987. He was 35, and part of a disappointing Argentina team, but still oozed class.

It was thought his last international appearances would be against Spain and Australia in late 1987. In those matches the team scored 86 points and the familiar figure in the No 10 jersey scored 54 of them.

Hugo Porta's points-scoring record in tests:
For various reasons, not the least being the reluctance worldwide of rugby reporters to regard Argentina as a significant world rugby power, the records of Hugo Porta lay unnoticed for years. It wasn't until after his retirement that his final totals were researched and finally given their rightful place in the rugby record of this century.

His test record for Argentina is:

	Pl	T	C	P	D	Total
v major IRB teams	48	4	47	95	23	464
v South American teams	10	7	37	6	3	126
For South America in South Africa	8	1	7	14	2	66
Total	66	12	91	115	28	656

Porta's top points hauls in tests:

26	v Paraguay, 1985	(13 conversions)
25	v Brazil, 1973	(2 tries, 7 conversions, 3 penalties)
23	v France, 1974	(1 conversion, 7 penalties)
23	v Uruguay, 1985	(7 conversions, 3 penalties)
23	v Chile, 1985	(1 try, 8 conversions, 1 penalty)
23	v Australia, 1987	(1 conversion, 5 penalties, 2 drop goals)
21*	v Sth Africa, 1982	(1 try, 1 conversion, 4 penalties, 1 drop goal)
21	v New Zealand, 1985	(4 penalties, 3 drop goals)
18	v France, 1977	(6 penalties)

* for South America

He duly retired from test rugby, but remained in demand for invitation teams around the world. In 1990 he made a comeback, aged nearly 39. Though he wasn't the force he had been, it was apparent Argentina would still be much stronger if he was in their side. He led his Banco Nacion club team to a shock victory over the England tourists and, at the request of new national coach Luis Gradin, captained Argentina to Britain. The fairytale didn't quite work out as his team lost all three tests. Unbelievably, Porta returned to the international arena in April, 1999, at the age of 47, playing 18 minutes for Argentina against a World XV. While the match is not regarded as an official test, it was still a remarkable effort to be playing top-level rugby alongside some players nearly 30 years his junior.

Porta played in many matches against non-traditional test nations, and represented South America eight times. His 656 points was the world test record until Australian Michael Lynagh topped him and he still holds the record for most drop goals. He is one of only three players - with Naas Botha and Jean-Patrick Lescarboura - to twice pot three goals in a test.

Selecting outstanding matches from his long career is a challenge, but some were classics. Against France in Buenos Aires in 1977, he kicked all 18 points to force an 18-18 draw. A newspaper headline read: *France 18, Porta 18*. For the South American Jaguars against South Africa at Bloemfontein, his 21 points piloted his team to a shock 21-12 win. He scored all 21 points - four penalties and three drop goals - when Argentina drew with New Zealand in 1985.

His highest test tallies were 26 and 25, against South American opposition. But he was equally prolific playing major rugby forces, scoring 23 against France in Buenos Aires in 1974 (a world record seven penalties and a conversion) and against Australia in Buenos Aires in 1987.

For eight or nine years, there wasn't a better flyhalf in the world according to those who knew best - his opposition. Welsh loose forward Mervyn Davies described Porta as the best flyhalf he encountered. All Black skipper Graham Mourie said he was unquestionably the finest flyhalf he played against …"He had balance and nous. He could transfer the ball in a trice from one hand to the other. Surely no other first-five can ever have had Hugo's instinctive vision, all-round ability or grace."

Michael Lynagh described the Argentinian as his 'most difficult opponent', saying: "He was hard even to get near. Hugo played like a matador and when he was going well, you could only keep doing your best, sit back and admire him through gritted teeth."

Porta is still an influential figure in Argentinian sport. His father encouraged him to pursue a law career and he studied at Buenos Aires University. Later he became a qualified architect. After retiring, he became the ambassador to South Africa in 1991 and then Argentina's Minister of Sport. With his charming personality and command of English, Porta has made a big success of his political career. But he had good training as a diplomat - for many years he was the Pumas' unofficial spokesman. **100**

Ambassador Porta in New Zealand visiting the Hall of Fame building, 1997.

JEAN PRAT

The Father of French Rugby

EVERY YEAR THOUSANDS of pilgrims descend on the town of Lourdes in the Pyrenees, for it was in a grotto there that the Virgin Mary appeared several times to a peasant girl named Bernadette Soubirous during the mid-19th century. The grotto waters are now said to have miraculous healing properties.

In a rugby sense, too, Lourdes marks the end of a pilgrimage, for that is where flanker Jean Prat, French rugby's first world figure, came from. Prat was the catalyst for the French rugby revolution after the second World War and is a legendary figure in France.

While touring France with the All Blacks one year, I detoured to visit Lourdes, and more particularly the *Winger* bar that for many years was run by brothers Jean and Maurice Prat. The bar, a short walk from the miracle grotto of Lourdes, reminded me of Jack Dempsey's New York restaurant in that it had become a meeting place for sports lovers.

Jean Prat was born on his father's farm within sight of the Lourdes Rugby Club he was to serve so well as a player and coach. His emergence in rugby coincided with the end of the second World War, and his first test, on New Year's Day, 1945, was against the British Army. The next year he lined up against Charlie Saxton's New Zealand Army side.

Prat, 21 when he played his first test, was a pivotal player in the new era of French rugby. The test against the British Army was France's first since 1940 and heralded the resumption of relations with the Home Unions after the rift that dated back to 1931.

At 1.78m (5ft 10in) and 85kg (13st 4lb), Prat wasn't especially imposing physically, but had rare ability. Not only was he quick (he was also a fine athlete) and eager, but he read a game superbly and had skills not expected of forwards of the time - on occasion he even turned out at centre. He was an excellent goal-kicker who possessed deadly drop-kicking ability. Prat became known by a variety of tags, among them 'Monsieur Rugby' and 'L'Extraordinaire'. He played a leading role in France's first wins in Wales, in 1948, and in England, in 1951.

He was the senior French player long before he became test captain in 1953. His first match as captain, against Scotland, resulted in an 11-5 victory in Paris. He went on to captain France in 16 tests before retiring in 1955. It was a glorious mini-reign: in that time France shared two Five Nations Championships titles (their first) and scored an historic test victory over the

Jean Prat
Flanker
Born: Lourdes, August 1, 1923
Test debut: France v British Army, Paris, January 1, 1945
Test career: 1945-55 (51 matches)
Test points: 145 (9 tries, 26 conversions, 17 penalties, 5 drop goals)
* Captained France to its first two Five Nations Championship titles
* His 51 caps was the French test record
* His 145 test points was the French record
* His 145 test points was for 43 years the world record for a forward
* His five drop goals is the world test record for a forward
* Played in 18 tests with his brother Maurice

Keith Quinn's list of forwards who kicked great goals in tests:

Zinzan Brooke (New Zealand) - loose forward who dropped three goals in tests.

Geoff Chapman (Australia) - flanker who kicked three penalties in the Wallabies' 9-9 draw with New Zealand in 1962.

W H Crawford (Scotland) - flanker who converted his own try and kicked a penalty in his team's 8-6 win over Wales in 1938.

Paul Descamps (France) - loose forward who, in his only test, against Scotland in 1911, kicked two conversions to help his team to a 16-15 win.

John Eales (Australia) - lock who kicked four penalties, including one in the last minute, to beat England at Twickenham in 1998.

Okey Geffin (South Africa) - the prop who broke the All Blacks' heart with his place-kicking during the 1949 series.

George Hastings (England) - prop who kicked a penalty to earn his team a 3-3 draw with Scotland in 1958.

Tiny Naude (South Africa) - the lock who handled most of the Springboks' goal-kicking duties during the mid-1960s.

Jean Prat (France) - flanker who dropped five goals in tests.

Gary Seear (New Zealand) - loose forward who rarely kicked in matches but booted a 45-metre penalty against France in 1977.

Neville Thornton (New Zealand) - All Black No 8 who kicked a penalty from halfway in the test against Australia at Sydney in 1947.

All Blacks. Against England in 1954, Prat sealed France's first Five Nations success by converting brother Maurice's try and adding a drop goal. Against Bob Stuart's All Blacks, his try late in the first half was the only score of the match.

Prat, who had foreshadowed greatness with his energetic play nearly a decade earlier against the Kiwis, certainly made his mark in the 3-0 win over the All Blacks. In his tour book, Terry McLean noted that Prat continually caught the eye and impressed with his speed and ability to harass the All Black inside backs. 'As the outstanding personality of post-war French rugby,' wrote McLean, 'Prat played a No 8 style game most efficiently and was particularly good at guarding the inside break and getting up to help [fellow loose forward Henri] Domec. He and Domec wrought the damage.'

Winston McCarthy wrote that Prat sorely embarrassed the All Black backline. McCarthy selected a team drawn from the All Blacks' opponents on that 1953-54 tour, so had the cream of England, Ireland, Wales, Scotland and France from which to choose. He named Prat to captain his side, paying tribute not only to his skills as a loose forward but also as a leader.

Prat's brother Maurice, five years his junior, made his test debut in 1951 as a centre and eventually played 31 times for France. He scored six test tries and, in fact, Jean raised his 100th point at test level when converting Maurice's try against Ireland in 1954.

When Jean Prat retired, he had set all sorts of records - including most tests for France and most test points by a Frenchman. His 145 points in tests was not beaten by a forward until Wallaby John Eales topped it in 1998.

Through an 11-season career, Prat missed only three tests, against Ireland in 1951, when he was ill, and two in Argentina in 1954 when he was unavailable to tour. Prat captained Lourdes to six French club final wins in 10 years (on three other occasions they were runners-up), the last three as player-coach after he'd retired from international rugby.

He was an inspirational leader whose passion and drive spread throughout his team. So dominant a personality was Prat that in 1955, during a heated match against England at Twickenham, a team-mate finding himself in possession, tossed the ball to his captain, shouting: "See what you can do with it." Prat responded with a drop goal.

Prat remained involved in rugby, turning to coaching and against guiding Lourdes to the French championship in 1960. He was assistant manager of the French side to South Africa in 1964. His book *Melee Ouverte* was published in 1968. He was a refreshing rugby thinker and was a fan of the peel off the back of the lineout, a move he refined with notable success. He was fortunate that during his time in the French team, he played with some outstanding loose forwards, among them Domec, Michel Celaya and Guy Basquet.

Besides his famous bar at Lourdes, Prat occupied himself in several ways. Initially he was a woodcutter. Once he achieved rugby fame, he ran a cafe and later a club on the Cote d'Azur. He was always in demand as a coach, and not just in France.

Prat was much honoured at home, among his most significant awards being the French Rugby Federation gold medal, awarded in 1959, and the Legion of Honour. **100**

Jean Prat lining up a drop goal attempt. He landed five in his test career.

JEAN-PIERRE RIVES

Captain Courageous

Jean-Pierre Rives
Flanker
Born: Toulouse, December 31, 1952
Test debut: France v England, Twickenham, February 1, 1975
Test career: 1975-84 (59 matches)
Test points: 20 (5 tries)
* Rives' 34 tests as captain was the world record when he retired
* He holds the record for the most test appearances by a French flanker
* One of the First XV inducted into the International Rugby Hall of Fame in 1997

IT IS IMPOSSIBLE to separate Jean-Pierre Rives the person from Jean-Pierre Rives the rugby player. With his John Lennon glasses and long flaxen hair, Rives looked like a combination of pop star and student. Off the field, he was a warm, charming person with a nonchalant attitude towards life. But put him in a pair of rugby boots and he was a terror. He had a will of steel and was the most selfless and courageous of flankers.

He was so dominant that his time as French captain, from 1978-84, is known as the Rives era. Even today he is one of the most influential people in French rugby.

Rives, whose father was an air force officer in Morocco and the Ivory Coast, was a good student, specialising in medicine and law. He showed ability in several sports, but always shone at rugby, representing France at schoolboy, junior, university and under-23 levels. In 1971, aged 19, he played for France B.

He made his test debut in 1975, when France hammered England 27-20. Rives was a revelation. His marauding display in his second test, against Scotland, is still recalled by those who saw it. Compared to some international forwards he was little more than a midget - 1.78m (5ft 10in) and 82kg (12st 12lb) - but he played with unbending, relentless fury. Rives didn't look a natural runner, with his shuffling scamper and hunched shoulders, but was lightning fast and terrorised opposing inside backs. He tackled with an all-enveloping, driving style that left no room for debate.

Eleven of Rives' first 13 tests resulted in wins. Even early on, he revealed exceptional positional sense and was staggeringly consistent, always looking to be creative. He was part of a brilliant loose forward trio that played 18 tests together. His fellow flanker was Toulouse clubmate Jean-Claude Skrela and the No 8 was Jean-Pierre Bastiat.

For several years, some named Rives as the world's best open-side flanker. Though he missed many matches through injury, including the 1975 tour of South Africa and the 1977 and 1981 home series against New Zealand, he always came back stronger than ever. This was well illustrated in Sydney in 1981 when he returned for the second test, having sat out the first six days earlier with a badly dislocated shoulder. Rives took the field only after half a dozen pain-killing injections and with his shoulder heavily strapped. He was in agony throughout, but ran and tackled as fearlessly as ever.

My strongest image of Rives is of him trooping off the field at the end of a match, blond hair matted with mud, blood streaming down his face. He disregarded flying boots and stray punches, his sole goal being to make life miserable for the opposition.

Rives was part of the French side that achieved the Grand Slam in 1977 and led them to another in 1981. In 1983 France shared the Five Nations Championship with Ireland. He seemed set to bow out on a high note in 1984, but France played poorly in their Five Nations decider with Scotland at Murrayfield and were beaten 21-12.

Perhaps the greatest single victory of his career came in New Zealand in 1979. He enjoyed playing the All Blacks, and particularly pitting his skills against his counterpart Graham Mourie. At Auckland on July 14 - Bastille Day - he led France to a magnificent 24-19 victory, the French scoring four tries to two. Rives had a brilliant tour of New Zealand, playing in seven of the eight tour games, and left a lasting impression.

Mourie and Rives had much in common. They were both top flankers, and inspiring, resourceful captains. They could be part of their team, yet still stand apart slightly. And for both, there was more to life than rugby. Mourie summed it up like this: "I respected him for his playing ability and approach to the game. He was also able to command the same respect off the field for his approach to the life rugby had created for him. He was balanced in many ways. To me, his greatest strength as a player was his courage, his complete commitment and the belief that trying hard was sometimes enough."

Rives was an inspiring captain, but it undersells him to pass off his leadership as merely inspirational. He was most astute, with excellent tactical vision and the ability to alter plans during a match. Rives did much to re-introduce the free-flowing style of rugby in France, bringing his own brand of dash and verve to the game.

Skrela, who knew his game better than anyone, once said: "He was a phenomenon, quite unlike any other player in France, or indeed the world at that time. He was so fast, so courageous. There will never be another quite like him."

After helping Toulouse reach one national club final, in 1980, Rives later represented the Paris-based Racing Club de France. He was invited several times to play for the Barbarians in Britain and was so taken with the concept that he was instrumental in setting up the French Barbarians in 1979.

Rives was adored in France, receiving truckloads of fan mail. He was known as 'the Golden Boy' and even 'the Blond Angel', but was never affected by the adulation.

After retiring, Rives remained a flamboyant personality and a headliner in French society. His autobiography *A Modern Corinthian* not only gave an insight into his attitude to rugby, but also his Bohemian lifestyle. He had originally been a court clerk, then worked in public relations for the Pernod company. For a time he ran a restaurant in Toulouse, then was an advisor to the Mayor of Cannes. He also acted in several films. But overriding everything was his passion for sculpting. He based himself in Paris to dedicate himself to his work as a sculptor in metal, his works being exhibited widely. These days, again because of his sculpting, he divides his time between France and California. 🏉

JEAN-LUC SADOURNY

The Try from the End of the World

FRENCH FULLBACK Jean-Luc Sadourny will be forever recalled for scoring a brilliant, series-winning try against the All Blacks at Eden Park in 1994. Given the circumstances, I have not seen a better try. It is one thing to throw the ball about with careless abandon in a Barbarians game, or an early-season exhibition, but another to contrive a magical try in the dying moment of a grimly-contested test match.

Philippe Saint-Andre's French team, which won just two matches in the 1994 Five Nations Championship and then lost to Canada, arrived in New Zealand at a low ebb. Their spirits plunged further when they were beaten by North Harbour. But, typically French, they cast aside the form book with a resounding 22-8 win in the first test. There followed another mid-week loss, to a mediocre Hawkes Bay combination. So by the second test at Auckland, the French were under extreme pressure as they endeavoured to seal an unlikely series victory against a wounded All Black side.

It was a hard-fought test, and the All Blacks looked likely to eke out a win as they clung to a 20-16 lead into injury time. Then came what Saint-Andre later described as "a try from the end of the world".

All Black first-five Stephen Bachop kicked long towards the French corner flag, but failed to find touch. Saint-Andre took the ball and launched an audacious last-gasp counter-attack. Setting off behind his own posts, the French captain shrugged off three tacklers, then linked with scrumhalf Guy Accoceberry who, in turn, passed to charging prop Laurent Benezech. Lanky winger Emile N'Tamack took it next, surging into the All Black half. Then Laurent Cabannes took over, changing directing to allow Sadourny to sprint for the line. An abiding memory of this breathtaking movement is of the All Blacks' new teenaged wing sensation, Jonah Lomu, being twisted and turned as he doubled back, trying to halt an attack that simply would not be stopped.

Finally Sadourny dived across the line for what is often described as the greatest try scored on Eden Park. The ball had passed through nine pairs of hands in a glorious movement that combined pace, passing skills, vision and improvisation - "a true image of French rugby," said Saint-Andre.

That try was pivotal in Sadourny's career. He became the toast of the nation and finally established himself as a worthy successor to Serge Blanco. It is never easy in sport to succeed a legend and Sadourny was one of four fullbacks who scrapped for the test spot after Blanco finally closed his

Jean-Luc Sadourny
Fullback
Born: Toulouse, August 26, 1966
Test debut: France v Wales, Cardiff, September 4, 1991
Test career: 1991-98 (64 matches)
Test points: 81 (14 tries, 4 drop goals)

Programme for the match made famous by 'the try from the end of the world' - New Zealand v France, Auckland, 1994.

Jean-Luc Sadourny goes high for a catch for France against England at the 1995 Rugby World Cup. Another counter-attack to follow?

244

wonderful test career in 1991. He had to see off the challenges of Stephane Ougier, Sebastien Viars and Jean-Baptiste Lafond before confirming himself as the No 1 fullback. After that try from the end of the world, the doubters were silenced and Sadourny became accepted for what he was: a brilliant running fullback, full of flair and verve.

Sadourny, born and educated in Toulouse, earned a reputation as a speedy wing/fullback with the Colomiers club on the outskirts of his home town. He was first seen in Britain in 1991 in a France B team that played its Scottish and English equivalents. He played superbly in the Scottish match at Hughenden, scoring a try, but suffered concussion in the 10-6 win over England B at Bristol.

He was promoted into the full French team for the tour of the United States in 1991 and scored two tries against USA B. Soon after came his test debut against Wales. It was a special occasion, for the night match was staged to celebrate the introduction of floodlights at Cardiff Arms Park and France played gloriously to win 22-9. When Blanco was forced to leave the field injured 10 minutes from the end, out trotted 24-year-old Sadourny. The first impressions of the 1.86 (6ft 1in), 86.5kg (13st 9lb) fullback were of his pace. He looked sharp in everything he did, and it appeared France had uncovered a worthy successor to Blanco. And so it transpired, but only after Sadourny had repelled a succession of challengers for the No 15 test jersey. He was Blanco's understudy during the 1991 World Cup, and got onto the field against Canada - as a replacement for Philippe Sella at centre.

His next appearance at test level was at Paris against England as a 55th-minute replacement for injured captain Sella. But it wasn't a happy Five Nations debut for him. After nine minutes he was involved in a head-on collision with team-mate Alain Penaud attempting a scissors movement, and left the field looking decidedly groggy.

On the 1992 tour of Argentina, Sadourny began as second-string fullback to Ougier, but during the first test in Buenos Aires turned out as a replacement. Though Sadourny kept his place for the home series against South Africa, he had the mortification of seeing Viars and Lafond leapfrog him early in 1993. So it wasn't really until the tour of South Africa in 1993, followed by his outstanding play through the 1994 Five Nations Championship and the tour of New Zealand afterwards, that Sadourny was assured of his test spot.

Since then he has become one of the greats of world rugby. His first test try was against Ireland in 1992. After that tries came regularly and on occasion he could chip in with a handy drop goal. In 1995 he scored five tries, including two against Italy. But though played in five matches at the World Cup, he went tryless and endured the misery of being involved in France's narrow elimination by South Africa in the semi-finals.

Sadourny, nicknamed 'Bilou', struck a golden patch during the 1998 Five Nations Championship, with his most memorable exhibition coming against Wales at Wembley. The fullback scored two early tries and France romped away to a dazzling 51-0 victory.

Though he had all the prerequisite fullback skills, it was Sadourny's pace, nimbleness and balance - as befitting a person who lists classical dancing as a hobby - that appealed to me. His speed and desire to be involved in backline movements made him a constant threat, especially on the hard grounds of South Africa. Like many great players, Sadourny was an innovator. From my observation, he was the first player at international level to tap the ball to himself after taking a mark. This is a standard ploy now, but Sadourny deserves credit for his ingenuity in thinking of this quick counter-attack tactic. ●●●

Over the years there has been nothing more thrilling in rugby than seeing a crowd rise and roar at a sweeping French rugby team playing at their best. I have mentioned that the Jean-Luc Sadourny try for France against the All Blacks at Auckland in 1994 was the greatest I have personally ever seen. As a New Zealander speaking English that day I hope people saw it as appropriate for me (as the TV commentator) to switch to schoolboy French to shout "magnifique!" as an ultimate compliment when Sadourny dived over.

But there have been many other 'superbe' French tries. My list here is of some I remember fondly, from the excitement of seeing them scored live or watching them on TV:

Jean Dupuy,
France v New Zealand, Wellington, 1961 (second test)
Jean Trillo,
France v New Zealand, Auckland, 1968 (third test)
Jean-Luc Averous,
France v New Zealand, Auckland 1979 (second test)
Philippe Sella,
France v England, Twickenham, 1987
Serge Blanco,
France v Australia, Sydney, 1987
(World Cup semi-final)
Serge Blanco,
France v Australia, Sydney, 1990 (third test)
Jean-Luc Sadourny,
France v New Zealand, Auckland 1994 (second test)

BOB SCOTT

Ponsonby's Barefoot Boy

I CANNOT THINK of a better advertisement for New Zealand rugby than Bob Scott. Not only was Scott a superb fullback who was decades ahead of his time, but he is an unfailingly enthusiastic supporter of rugby and the most genial personality imaginable.

By the time I saw him play, in 1954, he was nearing the end of his career, but his class was obvious. He had moved from Auckland to Petone to set up a menswear business. Such was his appeal that within hours of the announcement that he was moving south, the Petone Recreation Ground was sold out for the season. I don't know whether Bob was superstitious, but he played the entire season in a pair of faded black shorts which, it was said, he'd worn on his most recent All Black tour.

His play was a revelation. At 1.79m (5ft 10in) and 81kg (12st 11lb), he was perfectly proportioned. He never seemed hurried, he had tremendous balance and body positioning and he could evade on-rushing players by all sorts of feints and dodges. Sometimes he would let the ball bounce off his knee when it was kicked through to him. It sounds ridiculously risky, but he virtually never came unstuck because of his uncanny feel for a rugby ball. He had a massive spiral kick with either foot and, for his time, was generally an excellent place-kicker. When he kicked for goal he would finish his action with his right arm behind his back. My mates and I spent months imitating our hero in our backyard games.

Scott remained a tremendous drawcard at any level. When Petone made the Wellington club final in 1955, 25,000 people turned up to watch, a massive number for a non-rep game. And at club level, he was totally dominant. In fact, the flow of the game would be interrupted because often even when pressing forward, the Petone players would win possession and then throw the ball way back to their fullback so that he could set up the attack with his distinctive flair.

I have no doubt that Scott, playing as he did in the years after the second World War, would not look out of place even in today's speeded-up game in which the fullback is such a vital attacking weapon. I have seen films of Scott playing in All Black matches in Britain and South Africa and his skill is undeniable.

Until Scott's arrival, New Zealanders (and many others around the rugby world) chose George Nepia as the greatest fullback ever. But Nepia himself

Robert William Henry Scott
Fullback
Born: Wellington, February 6, 1921
Test debut: New Zealand v Australia, Dunedin, September 14, 1946
Test career: 1946-54 (17 tests)
Test points: 74 (16 conversions, 12 penalties, 2 drop goals)
* His 840 first class points was a New Zealand record at the time
* Was also a rep softballer

What, no boots!

Bob Scott had another, unique, string to his bow. He would give goal-kicking demonstrations with his bare feet, a thought to make some of today's top kickers cringe, especially as he was not an in-step kicker. Bob could kick 'em over from halfway, no problem at all, and people came from miles to see him do it. A famous photograph showing him kicking for goal without his boots was taken at practice in England before the 1953-54 tour, and became a curiosity around Britain.

I saw Bob kick barefooted several times, the most memorable occasion being during a charity match in Wellington in 1966. He was appearing along with the great Don Clarke. Both were successful from halfway, but Bob Scott wowed the crowd because he was raising the flags consistently with effortless barefooted shots.

was emphatic he never saw a player to touch Scott. And Don Clarke, Scott's successor as All Black fullback, echoed those views.

Like many true geniuses of sport - including cricketers Victor Trumper and Don Bradman - Scott was never coached. Yet he exhibited the same mastery of rugby skills as Joe Davis did in billiards and Rod Laver in tennis.

He was born in Wellington, but grew up in Auckland during the Depression years and suffered extreme poverty. Sport was the making of him. Often he did not have shoes to wear to school, but when it came to sport, he was more than a match for his peers. By the time the second World War began, he was regarded as a brilliant rugby union, league and soccer player, all of which he played competitively to a high level. He also represented Auckland at softball and later became a fine golfer and lawn bowler.

At the end of the war, Scott was chosen in Charlie Saxton's famous Kiwis Army side, though he had to tussle mightily with the brilliant Herb Cook for the No 1 fullback's role.

When Cook switched to league, Scott had the All Black position to himself and enjoyed some triumphant years. In Australia in 1947 his goal-kicking was sublimely good - he hardly missed a place kick on the entire tour - and he totalled 72 points in six matches, including 15 in the second test. Two years later in South Africa, he played as well as ever, but suffered severe kicking woes and in a low-scoring series was unable to land critical goals which might have turned defeat into victory.

He blamed himself for the 4-0 series defeat, yet his captain Fred Allen and his team-mates laughed off the suggestion, saying it was Scott's ability that had kept the All Blacks in with a chance. The Springboks themselves rated Scott supreme. Hennie Muller, the legendary loose forward, called him 'the greatest footballer I've ever played against, in any position'.

Scott and his wife Irene were still struggling financially in 1950 - they didn't own their first car until 1957 - and he retired to concentrate on business. But after pleading from the national selectors, he made a comeback for the 1953-54 British tour. It was one long triumph for Scott, who was feted wherever he went and turned on a string of breath-taking displays, the peak being the Barbarians match at Cardiff, won 19-5 by the All Blacks. Scott's entries into the line and his linking with his forwards that day foreshadowed by decades the development of fullback play, and he was chaired from the field.

He retired again, yet when he was 35, was once more asked to return to international rugby, to take on the 1956 Springboks. "I felt fit enough," he said, "but I was worried the pressure of the situation might affect my kicking. Eventually I turned down the invitation, but I regarded it as the biggest compliment of my career."

I have no doubt he would have been fit enough. As late as 1961, Scott was still playing in rep charity matches where his poise and matchless skills had hardly faded. I've seen Bob around rugby ever since I've been commentating, and he has always exuded fitness and strength. To call his handshake firm does not do it justice.

Rugby experts from Winston McCarthy to Charlie Saxton and Fred Allen shook their heads in wonder at his skills. In New Zealand at least, he has continued to be a benchmark fullback and surely, for a player in his prime half a century ago, there can be no finer tribute than that. 🏉

PHILIPPE SELLA

First to the Century

THE ALL BLACKS aren't renowned for bringing joy to their opposition, but they certainly did at Lancaster Park, Christchurch, on June 26, 1994. France scored only their second victory in 15 tests against New Zealand away from home and did it in style, with a comprehensive 22-8 victory.

It was an appropriate way for the French to celebrate the 100th test appearance of their revered centre, Philippe Sella. "This historic victory for my 100th cap, with a score I never imagined - that's one of my really great, great memories," said an emotional Sella.

With the rugby calendar expanding markedly, it was apparent that one day players would reach the magic century. How fitting that someone of Sella's stature should be first. He was the complete centre - tigerish on defence, a selfless servant and a brilliant individualist. Perhaps his major contribution to the French cause was the coolness and organisation he brought to a backline that oozed flair but required a calming influence.

Sella was groomed for test honours from relatively early. As a boy, he played amateur rugby league in Clairac, then had a couple of seasons of rugby with Valance d'Agen. Once he switched to the Agen club, he progressed rapidly. Blessed with a natural hardness and fitness that was the product of his rural upbringing, he represented his national schools, junior and universities teams before being called into the test side in 1982 to play Romania at Bucharest. It was literally a forgettable experience, for Sella was concussed and had to spent a night in hospital. Only later did the 20-year-old learn France had suffered a surprise 13-9 defeat.

He held his test spot but was moved to the wing. Ironically, in 1982 Serge Blanco, having served his apprenticeship on the wing, was finally given an extended run at fullback. Sella replaced him on the wing, where he was to play six times (once he also turned out at fullback) before he established himself at centre.

His value to France cannot be overstated. In 1984 he scored Five Nations Championship tries against Scotland, Ireland and Wales. Two years later, he scored in every Five Nations match, becoming only the fourth player, after Carston Catcheside of England (1924), Arthur Wallace of Scotland (1925) and Patrick Esteve of France (1983) to do so. Gregor Townsend matched this feat in 1999.

Some of his tries were brilliant solo efforts. One came during France's

Philippe Sella
Centre
Born: Clairac, February 14, 1962
Test debut: France v Romania, Bucharest, October 31, 1982
Test career: 1982-95 (111 matches)
Test points: 125 (30 tries)
* Holds the world record for most test caps
* Scored a try in each of France's Five Nations Championship matches in 1986
* His 29 test tries as a centre, is the world record

Players with the most test caps:

111	Philippe Sella (France)	1982-95
101	David Campese (Australia)	1982-96
93	Serge Blanco (France)	1980-91
92	Sean Fitzpatrick (New Zealand)	1986-97
91	Rory Underwood (England/British Isles)	1984-96
81	Mike Gibson (Ireland/British Isles)	1964-79
80	Willie John McBride (Ireland/British Isles)	1962-75
79	Ieuan Evans (Wales/British Isles)	1987-98
77	Adrian Lungu (Romania)	1980-92
76	Rob Andrew (England/British Isles)	1985-97
76*	Ian Jones (New Zealand)	1990-98

* still playing

1987 Grand Slam triumph in the pivotal match against England at Twickenham. Sella intercepted a pass to Rob Andrew and set off on a weaving 65m run, during which he taunted the would-be tacklers with surges of pace and side-steps. This was France's only Grand Slam during Sella's career, though he was part of six Five Nations champion combinations.

Sella could create space, either for himself to burst through and breach the advantage line, or for his wingers or the lightning fast Blanco, coming in as the extra man. He was stockily built - 1.81m (just over 5ft 11in) tall and 84kg (13st 2lb) - and was an excellent defender who delighted in pulling off big tackles. His presence added immense solidity to the French midfield.

Recalling his 14-season test career, Sella nominated France's thrilling 1987 World Cup semi-final win over Australia as the most exciting moment. "For the occasion, the suspense, the beauty of the game ... that was really the greatest match," he said.

He played in three World Cups. In 1987 France excelled in reaching the final and in 1991 they lost a foul-tempered quarter-final to England, though Sella distinguished himself in the pool match against Fiji with two dazzling tries. For the 1995 World Cup, the French backs caused a stir when, in a show of unity, they shaved their heads before the tournament. France gained a measure of revenge when, after being shaded by South Africa in the semi-finals, they gave England a beating in the third place play-off. This was Sella's 111th and last test.

With his dark, lank hair, distinctive Roman nose and imposing presence, Sella graced the test stage so long that the French team seemed incomplete without him. He departed while still a force, even if he was 33, and would have still justified a test place.

Instead, he signed for the wealthy London club Saracens, one of the club's golden oldies, along with Michael Lynagh and Francois Pienaar. Deep into his 30s, Sella continued to reveal the timing and all-round skills that made him so respected.

It seems strange such a level-headed player did not captain France more. He led his country only five times, through the 1992 Five Nations campaign and against Romania in 1993. Perhaps the selectors sought a more obviously exuberant leader, though there was no doubting Sella's commitment to the French cause.

There were two low points in Sella's career. In 1992 he was dropped briefly, and missed France's tour of Argentina. A worse moment occurred at Elms Park, Ontario in May, 1994 when Sella, in his 99th test, was ordered from the field during France's shock 18-16 defeat by Canada. The Frenchman, who had an impeccable behaviour record, was banished for a punch few people besides the South African referee Ian Rogers thought he threw. In fact, the punch was reported to Rogers by a linesman. Sella was suspended for one match.

Sella was never overly demonstrative. When he announced his test retirement, on December 19, 1995 at a press conference in the famous Parisian

France v New Zealand, Christchurch 1994. Philippe Sella becomes the first rugby player to appear in 100 tests.

Two fine centres: Philippe Sella evades Frank Bunce, France v North Harbour, 1994.

cafe *Le Procope*, he was the picture of control. Only once did he betray his emotion - when he spoke of one of his most treasured moments in rugby.

It happened in Whangarei, New Zealand in 1994 when the French team met a group of Maori schoolchildren. "I will never forget those children," he said. "It was our first training run in New Zealand and I was in the depths of despair. I had never been sent off in my life. Those kids stood on the sideline and sang to us. Their songs touched my soul and gave me the strength to overcome my depression. It was a unique moment which made me stronger and more resilient."

Sella departed test rugby with many records, besides the big one, for most appearances. At one point he had played 45 consecutive tests. He is France's most capped centre (104) and his 30 test tries, 29 (the world record) as a centre, gives him membership of the exclusive 30-plus club. The records, even the magic 111, never became all-consuming. As he said: "I never thought of setting or breaking a record. Perhaps that's why I got them. But records are made to be broken, and I'm sure some day mine will be."

On the domestic scene, Sella was a stalwart member of the Agen club side, helping it to four national finals, of which two were won.

Before he became a professional player, Sella, who attended the Bordeaux Sports University, was a PE teacher, then was employed in sales and marketing for clothing company Lee Cooper. Eventually he set up his own company, Sella Communications, which expanded into Britain and other parts of Europe. He was awarded the gold medal for Youth and Sport. ⦿

WAISALE SEREVI

Sevens Supremo

IT'S EASY TO RECALL the first time I saw Waisale Serevi in action - the Hong Kong sevens tournament in 1990, when Fiji cut a swathe through the draw, beating New Zealand 22-10 in the final. Sevens football could have been invented with the Fijians in mind. With their athletic, high-stepping running, ball skills and dynamism, they are wonderfully suited to the abbreviated brand of rugby. But for all their brilliance, the Fijians have still needed a stabilising influence, someone to direct the play. Over the past decade that man has been Serevi.

The world sevens circuit has expanded dramatically through the 1990s, taking in tournaments in such distant places as Dubai, Tokyo, Paris, Punte del Este and Jerusalem. The major rugby nations now take the game seriously, naming specialist sevens squads. But while any one of a dozen players could lay claim to being the best test player at any given time, Serevi stands supreme in sevens, even in the face of the increasing focus on that arm of rugby.

Back in 1990, when he was only 19, Serevi looked the complete player, with plenty of time to do his bidding. Even in the frenetic hurly-burly of sevens, Serevi is a serene figure. He is calm and composed, and concentrates hard, his face seldom betraying emotion. I was on the judging panel at the 1990 tournament, along with Ian Robertson, Roger Uttley and Naas Botha, and we had little debate before voting Serevi Player of the Tournament. He is so good at sevens that he could be accorded a similar honour in nearly every tournament he plays. At Kuala Lumpur in 1998, he all but guided Fiji to victory in the Commonwealth Games sevens final against New Zealand.

Though powerful beyond his size, Serevi is not a big man - just 1.7m (5ft 7in) and 70kg (11st). He is very light and nimble on his feet. His breadth of vision is incredible. When all options seem cut off, he can contrive an attacking move out of nothing. Often he will quietly feed his team-mates and set up play, then suddenly he'll explode into action. He can turn a game in an instant, which is why he is so dangerous. He has the sleight of hand of a magician and the confidence to try virtually anything. He can stand an opponent still with just a flicker of his eyes or a slight body shimmy.

Besides his outstanding general play, Serevi is a useful place-kicker with a style honed for sevens rugby. He takes no run-up, but merely places the ball, then snaps it through the crossbar in a jiffy.

Waisale Serevi Tikoisolomoni
Flyhalf
Born: Suva, May 20, 1969
Test debut: Fiji v Scotland, Edinburgh, October 28, 1989
Test career: 1989-98 (23 matches)
Test points: 123 (3 tries, 22 conversions, 19 penalties, 3 drop goals)
* Captained Fiji to victory in the World Cup sevens tournament in 1997
* Has been in 6 Fijian teams that have won the Hong Kong sevens.
* Won a silver medal at the 1998 Commonwealth Games sevens.

In 1998, Scotland, on tour in Australia, were scheduled to play a one-off match against Fiji in Suva. Scotland expected to win, of course, and in fact flew over only 22 players from their touring base in Australia, the rest of the group travelling on to Melbourne.

But in the steaming humidity of Suva, the Scots found they were really up against it. Derrick Lee opened with four penalties and Scotland led 12-8 at one point. Then Fiji surged ahead to lead 13-12 at halftime. Fifteen minutes into the second spell, the determined Fijians had their noses in front, 20-19. Then Fiji coach Brad Johnstone played his master stroke. He brought on Waisale Serevi and within 10 minutes, Fiji led 44-19. Serevi proved an inspiration. He created a try and converted it, then added two more conversions and a penalty.

The match ended 51-26 in Fiji's favour, their first win over a Five Nations team. The Scots limped out of the country with much-increased respect for Fijian rugby, and Serevi in particular.

Surprisingly, he has not proved as big a force in the 15-man game, where he usually plays at flyhalf, though his preferred position is fullback. His defence is sometimes suspect and in the more structured form of the game, he does not get the same opportunities to dominate. He has not held down a regular test spot through the 1990s, partly because his global commitments to sevens rugby have often forced his unavailability.

In 1997-98, Fiji coach Brad Johnstone sometimes adopted the policy of using him as a second-half substitute for flyhalf Nicky Little. Serevi's biggest contribution in test rugby came near the end of 1998 when Fiji played above themselves in the Oceania zone of the World Cup qualifying competition. Against strong rivals Samoa, Serevi changed the complexion of the game as soon as he got onto the field in the second half. His two conversions and a penalty swung the match Fiji's way and they scored a come-from-behind 26-18 victory. He landed two conversions, four penalties and a drop goal in Fiji's 32-15 win over Tonga and even in the 66-20 mauling by Australia, he scored a try and kicked four goals, giving test rugby a taste of his sevens magic.

Serevi, who grew up in Suva, first played rugby at the age of 10, and proved a natural. He represented the Rewa union in 1987 and the following year was promoted to the Fiji B side. He has been playing for Fiji, at sevens and test level, since 1989 and has been in winning Fijian sevens teams in places like Sydney, Gala and Sicily, though Hong Kong remains his spiritual home. Fiji has won the Hong Kong sevens title six times during Serevi's career, and he has been their outstanding player.

Before Serevi toured France with the Fiji side in 1990, BBC commentator Ian Robertson, who'd seen him in Hong Kong, described him as one of the world's outstanding players. Robertson said Serevi had 'wonderful hands, a lovely jig, superb acceleration off the mark and the ability to really get a backline going'. Such extravagant praise of a newcomer to international rugby has been more than justified over the years.

The highpoint of Serevi's career came in 1997 when he captained Fiji to a 24-21 victory over South Africa in the World Cup sevens final in Hong Kong. When Serevi's side returned home with the Melrose Cup, they were feted as celebrities and a two-day national holiday was declared.

In Suva, Serevi is treated like a living god. Even 1998 US Open golf champion Vijay Singh is a distant second in the popularity stakes. "It is too much sometimes," says Serevi. "People see me and want to talk to me. Sometimes I have to hide in my car to get away from them."

Former Wallaby coach Bob Dwyer, an astute judge of a player, sought Serevi's services for the Leicester Tigers for more than a year, but was initially thwarted by the Fijian's contract to a Japanese club. In 1997, Dwyer finally managed to recruit him and has made the most of his talent, playing him at fullback and scrumhalf. "Serevi is a real livewire and reminds me of a pinball, bouncing about all over the place," says Dwyer. "When a great player like him becomes available, you move heaven and earth to grab him."

Serevi's wife Kara is an army officer in the United Nations peace-keeping force. **100**

WAYNE SHELFORD

Warrior Spirit

WAYNE SHELFORD was the living embodiment of 'mana', the beautiful and evocative Maori word that might best be described as stature, presence or charisma. He epitomised the famous warrior spirit the Maoris showed during the Maori Wars of the 1860s, bringing those qualities of courage, dynamism and fire to his rugby.

There have been loose forwards with a wider range of skills than Shelford, and captains who delivered their team talks more fluently. But by his passion and commitment, Shelford turned himself into a great No 8 and a leader who inspired by example. The All Blacks never lost a test when Shelford was captain.

Shelford, known to most as 'Buck', resurrected the haka, which All Black teams had only dabbled with for decades. When Shelford did the haka he really was a Maori warrior issuing a challenge. This led to a famous nose-to-nose confrontation with Irishman Willie Anderson at Lansdowne Road in 1989.

But it would be wrong to describe Shelford as the pride of just the Maori population. He developed a massive following and became a New Zealand folk hero. When he was sensationally dumped from the test side in 1990, 'Bring Back Buck' signs sprang up everywhere. He remained the people's champion and there continued to be calls for his recall even when it was obvious he did not figure in the All Black selectors' plans.

Shelford was born in Rotorua and represented the Western Heights High School First XV and Bay of Plenty Schools before moving to Auckland. Though he played for the New Zealand Colts in 1978, his decision to join the Navy on leaving school slowed his rugby rise. It did, however, instil in him outstanding discipline.

He made his Auckland debut in 1982, and in 1985 moved to the fledging North Harbour province as captain. He became the public face of North Harbour rugby and was such a commanding figure at rep level that locals called him 'God'.

Shelford made his All Black debut in 1985, not in South Africa as originally planned but on the substitute tour of Argentina. In 1986 he was one of the rebel Cavaliers who defied their national union and toured South Africa, which cost him his Navy career. His rise to the top coincided with the retirement of incumbent No 8, Murray Mexted.

Wayne Thomas Shelford
No 8
Born: Rotorua, December 13, 1957
Test debut: New Zealand v France, Toulouse, November 8, 1986
Test career: 1986-90 (22 matches)
Test points: 20 (5 tries)
* Captained New Zealand in 14 tests for 13 wins and a draw
* Captained New Zealand in 33 matches without defeat

Wayne Shelford (centre), who inspired All Black teams with his captaqincy as well as reviving the Maori haka challenge.

By 1987, Shelford was a first-choice All Black and an integral member of the World Cup side. His driving play off the back of the scrum was a key factor in the All Black domination during that tournament. He played five of the six matches, and his ferocious charges had the opposition continually stretched.

Then Shelford led an All Black side to Japan, handling the captaincy well. I was impressed when at a function in Tokyo he thanked his hosts in Japanese, which went down wonderfully with the locals.

From 1985-87, he was a New Zealand sevens representative, twice being in sides that won the annual Hong Kong tournament. Shelford wasn't as quick as some, but his crunching tackling made him a feared sevens player.

He captained the All Blacks through a golden era, and did so despite not having a great coach or manager for much of that time. There was talk that he was undermined by the powerful Auckland contingent in the All Blacks, but I never saw any sign of that. His seniority, forceful personality and playing ability made him a natural captain. Shelford led the All Blacks unbeaten to Japan, Australia, Canada, Wales and Ireland.

I never felt he was a great speaker. If you wrote down his words, they did not seem particularly deep. However when delivered with Shelford's intensity and passion, they became compelling.

He preferred to lead by example. In hindsight, some of his actions seem somewhat brutal, but he was a player of his time. He delivered a copybook punch to knock out petulant Welshman Huw Richards in the 1987 World Cup semi-final. Richards had the mortification of coming to and finding he had been ordered from the field, for referee Kerry Fitzgerald realised the difference between rough justice and rough injustice, deciding Richards had been the trouble-maker. Once, when captaining the New Zealand Maoris against a Pyrenees Selection in France, he led his team from the field because he wanted an interpreter to explain his frustrations to the referee.

With his tremendous leg and thigh strength, Shelfiord's driving over the advantage line from scrums and rucks was superb and he became the All Black 'momentum man'. With his low centre of gravity, he was very difficult to bring down. At 1.89m (6ft 2in) and 104kg (16st 5lb), he was solid though not tall for a loose forward and because he was so fit and had good anticipation, he was an ideal support player. He was always eager to commit his body and his tackling was chilling. Shelford was at his best when the game hung on a knife edge - he was that rare breed who could turn a match by his own performance.

His courage was legendary. Few players have been better able to shrug off pain. The most often-cited example occurred in the second test against France, at Nantes, in 1986. He lost three teeth and was concussed and it was not until he was in the shower afterwards that he discovered he had a severe gash in his scrotum. That story has grown in the telling; these days legend has it that Shelford discovered his testicles virtually rolling down the road!

Against the Barbarians in 1989, Shelford was labouring with a neck injury when giant Welshman Phil Davies crashed towards him. He made a feeble attempt to tackle, then instinct took over. He turned, chased and made the tackle, worsening the injury to such an extent that he subsequently had to leave the field.

He played in France during the New Zealand off-season, and sometimes on his return did not have his usual zing. In 1989, there were suggestions he was struggling to hold his place in the side. But his form on the end-of-year tour of Wales and Ireland was magnificent.

By 1990, though, he was past his best and Zinzan Brooke was pushing for the All Black No 8 spot. At the trial at Wanganui, Shelford looked underweight and below full fitness. He was only mediocre in the two tests that followed against Scotland. I suggested in a televised comment that the All Black pack needed a reshuffle, 'and if that means dropping the captain, so be it'. Coach Alex Wyllie did indeed drop Shelford, which started a national controversy. Wyllie tried to soften the blow by saying Shelford was carrying an injury, but Shelford was having none of it. He stated that he was not injured, and described himself as 'disappointed, bloody disappointed'. His axing left him bitter and over the years he has taken some unfortunate public swipes at those he felt were responsible.

Rugby purists suggested Shelford didn't have the power or speed of his best years and was not getting out wide any more. The public pointed to his unbeaten record as New Zealand skipper and asked what more he could do. Towering over the debate was the admiration New Zealanders had for Shelford. Though he battled to regain his test spot, he never got closer than leading a New Zealand B team in 1991. He became player-coach of the English club Northampton and did a fine job.

In 1998, Shelford became the North Harbour provincial coach and was a qualified success. Some wondered if Shelford had the technical expertise, but no-one doubted his commitment and he produced a raw spark that had been missing in the side.

Besides his coaching, Shelford dabbled briefly with television commentary and maintained a high profile with TV commercials for the Accident Compensation Corporation and public speaking engagements. 🏉

Players who captained New Zealand in most tests:			Won	Drew	Lost
51	Sean Fitzpatrick	1992-97	39	1	11
30	Wilson Whineray	1958-65	22	3	5
19	Graham Mourie	1977-82	15	0	4
18	Brian Lochore	1966-70	15	0	3
17	Andy Dalton	1981-85	15	0	2
15	Gary Whetton	1990-91	12	0	3
14	Wayne Shelford	1988-90	13	1	0
11	David Kirk	1986-87	9	0	2
10	Andy Leslie	1974-76	6	1	3
9	Ian Kirkpatrick	1972-73	6	1	2

FERGUS SLATTERY

Ireland's Finest Flanker

John Fergus Slattery
Flanker
Born: Dublin, February 12, 1949
Test debut: Ireland v South Africa, Dublin, January 10, 1970
Test career: 1970-84 (65 matches - 61 for Ireland, 4 for the British Isles)
Test points: 12 (3 tries)
* Captained Ireland 17 times
* Shares the title of world's most capped flanker with Peter Winterbottom
* Has played more games as flanker for one country than any other player

WITH HIS CHARMING MANNER, wit and appealing Irish lilt, Fergus Slattery is a popular speaker who has graced rugby functions all around the world. One speech of his that I felt was particularly well-received was in Singapore in 1997, when he was a special guest at the banquet the night before China made its international rugby debut.

But there's one way to bring a frown to Fergus' normally sunny countenance - mention his 'try that wasn't' for the Lions against South Africa in 1974. It was at Ellis Park, the last test of that historic tour and the Lions were shooting for an unprecedented 4-0 series whitewash. In the last moments of the game, Slattery drove over the line and, according to him, scored the try which would have broken the 13-13 deadlock. Referee Max Baise ruled no try and the test was drawn. A quarter of a century later, Slattery still goes through agony when he recalls that moment.

The try would have been a fitting end to the series. The brilliant Lions team merited a 4-0 series victory and Slattery would have been a deserving hero, for on that tour he played the best rugby of his long, distinguished career.

Slattery was a model openside flanker. He wasn't especially big - 1.85m (6ft 1in) and about 92kg (14st 7lb) - but was ever industrious. He was fast, read a game superbly and was a renowned support player. He would harry an opposing backline mercilessly. Phil Bennett said he would rather play against anyone than Slattery because the Irishman was forever running at him. Always an assiduous trainer, Slattery was able to see out a match at maximum efficiency so as others slowed he became more dominant. His blond-haired good looks, allied to the quality of his play, made Slattery an institution in Irish rugby, long before he captained the national team to a series win in Australia.

In his early years at Blackrock College, Slattery was torn between rugby and soccer so compromised: he played both. This meant two or three games of football on weekends, plus up to four nights' training each week, but that suited him just fine.

He attended University College in Dublin and gained a commerce degree. By the time he was 21, he was an established member of the test team. He made his debut in torrid circumstances, at Lansdowne Road against South Africa on the Springboks' protest-plagued 1969-70 tour. The match resulted in an 8-8 draw. Some said the rugby in such circumstances - with barbed wire ringing the ground and no spectators permitted behind the goal-posts - was unenjoyable, but Slattery thrived on the test match atmosphere.

He was a junior member of John Dawes' great 1971 Lions team to New Zealand. Though unable to break into the test side, he looked and listened, calling the tour 'a terrific theatre of education'.

By the time his countryman Willie John McBride led the Lions to South Africa in 1974, Slattery was the equal of any flanker in the world, and he had a sensational series. Hannes Marais, the Springbok captain, later said: "The best of the Lions back row forwards was Fergus Slattery, who, given much more freedom than our own committed loose forwards, created havoc among our backs."

But the South African trip also marked a turning point in Slattery's career. He seemed rather stale afterwards and following an uninspiring home season, was dropped from the Irish side in 1976.

When he returned from the wilderness, he revealed fresh purpose. By 1979 he was the test captain, though only after several others had been found wanting, and he led Ireland to a stunning 2-0 series win in Australia.

New Zealanders didn't see the best of Slattery. He didn't enjoy long tours and opted out of touring New Zealand with the 1976 Irish team and the 1977 Lions. But he did play memorably for Ireland in the 10-10 draw at Lansdowne Road in 1973, and for the Barbarians shortly after when they beat New Zealand 23-11 in a thrilling match. Slattery scored a try in that game. He was also in the 1974 Barbarians side that drew 13-13 with Andy Leslie's All Blacks. In 1976 he turned out, along with fellow Irishman Tom Grace, in Johannesburg for the Quagga-Barbarians against the All Blacks. This was the match in which the All Blacks trailed 31-9 well into the second half, then climbed back to win 32-31 in injury time.

Slattery was a part of some famous back-row combinations. For Ireland, he, Willie Duggan and John O'Driscoll played together 19 times. For the 1974 Lions, Slattery, Roger Uttley and Mervyn Davies were a formidable trio. Throughout it all, 'Slats', as he was known, was a tireless, unflinching servant of Irish rugby.

There was still one more tribute paid to his rugby genius many years after his retirement. In March, 1999 the British magazine *Rugby World* published a list of the all-time greatest flankers and ranked Slattery second, behind Michael Jones.

A leading commercial real estate agent and auctioneer by profession - perhaps it was this experience that paved the way for his public speaking exploits - Slattery has remained involved with rugby and I've spotted him on occasion doing television commentaries. He still looks very fit, having taken to hockey after his rugby days. **100**

Players who have appeared at flanker the most times for Ireland:		
61	Fergus Slattery	1970-84
41	Noel Murphy Jnr	1958-69
28	James McCarthy	1948-55
25	David Corkery	1994-98
24	Stewart McKinney	1972-78
24	John O'Driscoll	1978-84
23	James McKay	1947-52

IAN SMITH

The Flying Scotsman

Ian Scott Smith

Winger

Born: Melbourne, October 31, 1903

Died: Edinburgh, September 18, 1972

Test debut: Scotland v Wales, February 2, 1924

Test career: 1924-33 (34 matches - 32 for Scotland, 2 for the British Isles)

Test points: 72 (24 tries)

* Scored three tries on his test debut
* Twice scored four tries in a match during the 1925 Five Nations season
* Held the world test try-scoring record for 54 years

IAN SMITH HAD ONE of the plainest and most common of names, but there was nothing plain or common about his rugby. For ten seasons, Smith, steaming down the right wing, ran in tries for Scotland. He was an integral part of Scotland rugby's greatest era and, during his last season, had the rather rare distinction for a winger of captaining his country.

Earlier, the odds on Smith playing international rugby for Scotland would have been extremely long. He was born in Melbourne, Australia, but both his parents were Scottish - his middle name was Scott - and they returned to their homeland when he was three.

After learning the rudiments of rugby union at Edinburgh's Cargilfield Prep School, he was sent to school at Winchester. There was no serious rugby at Winchester, only a local offshoot of the game called 'Winchester Rules', and Smith spent more time playing soccer, at which he excelled. In fact, he was obviously talented at most sports. He'd won the cup for the best all-round athlete at Cargilfield school and at Winchester was a member of the cricket First XI, the soccer First XI, the rugby seven and was a school racquets and swimming rep. As an athlete he won every school running title from 100 yards to the mile, which suggests not only speed but stamina.

It wasn't until he moved to Oxford in 1922 that he really took to rugby. He won his blue for rugby in 1923, scoring a try to help the Dark Blues win the annual match against Cambridge 21-14, but also excelled in several other sports at Oxford, particularly athletics.

Within two months he was in the test team - one of four famous Oxford products who graced the Scottish backline during the 1920s. The four - Smith, Phil Macpherson, Johnnie Wallace and George Aitken - were high-class players who came to be linked in the public mind, rather like Kershaw and Davies of England, Welshmen Tanner and Davies, Springboks Ellis and Greyling, Farr-Jones and Lynagh of Australia, the New Zealand wing combination of Batty and Williams and All Black locks Ian Jones and Robin Brooke.

Amazingly, three of Scotland's four Oxford men were born outside Britain. Smith was born in Melbourne, Aitken in Westport, New Zealand, Wallace in Sydney and only Macpherson in Scotland. Aitken captained New Zealand in two test matches against the 1921 Springboks, then moved to Scotland, for whom he subsequently played a further eight internationals. Wallace captained the famous 1927-28 Waratahs on their tour of Britain and by the finish of his illustrious career had played nine tests for Scotland and eight for Australia.

Ian Smith (right) with the three other brilliant Scottish three-quarters of the 1920s: from left Johnny Wallace, George Aitken and Phil Macpherson.

MacPherson, a beautiful jinking runner, became a superb attacking centre who played 26 tests and captained Scotland in some of their glory seasons.

Smith's test debut was against Wales in 1924. He was 20, 1.83m (6ft) tall and 73.5kg (11st 8lb). He had big shoes to fill, as Scotland's winger in 1923 had been Eric Liddell, who gained fame by winning the Olympic 400m gold medal in 1924. That victory was immortalised in the film *Chariots of Fire*.

Wales didn't have to wait long to sample the brilliance of Scotland's new winger. Smith had a dream debut, scoring three tries and sharing in a 35-10 win, an almost unprecedented margin in those days. Afterwards his opposing Welsh winger asked for Smith to be pointed out to him, saying he had not had the opportunity of identifying the wonder winger during the match!

Smith always made a point of emphasising how indebted he was to his centre, Macpherson, and it is true that Macpherson set up many tries with his beautifully-timed service to his wingers. But Smith himself had a tremendous ability to seize a half-opportunity. One contemporary writer

At least 50 Smiths have played test rugby. Scotland leads the way with 14, followed by England 9, New Zealand and Australia 8, South Africa 6, Ireland 4 and Wales 1. Among the best known Smiths have been:

Arthur Smith (Scotland/British Isles)	1955-62
Brian Smith (Australia/Ireland)	1987-91
George Smith (New Zealand)	1905
Ian Smith (Scotland/British Isles)	1924-33
John Smith (England)	1950
Johnny Smith (New Zealand)	1946-49
Nelie Smith (South Africa)	1963-65
Steve Smith (England/British Isles)	1973-83
Wayne Smith (New Zealand)	1980-85

Of course, this list takes no account of the various players named Smyth who have made their mark, or off-shoots of the name Smith such as Ronald Cove-Smith of England, who captained the 1924 British Isles team to South Africa.

Wingers who have captained their country in the most tests:

34	Philippe Saint-Andre (France)	1990-98
17	Arthur Smith (Scotland/British Isles)	1955-62
12	Adolphe Jaureguy (France)	1920-31
10	George Stephenson (Ireland)	1920-30
10	Christian Darrouy (France)	1957-67

Other notable wingers who have captained their countries, besides Ian Smith, include:

1	Edgar Mobbs (England)	1909-10
4*	Arthur Wallace (Australia)	1921-28
3	Rowe Harding (Wales)	1923-28
8	Tom Grace (Ireland)	1972-78

* later scored 11 tries for Scotland

summed him up: "A long-striding flier on the right wing and a sure scorer whenever there was a real chance of a try."

The Scotsman toured South Africa with the 1924 Great Britain side and began with a hiss and a roar, including a much-praised fifty-metre try against Transvaal. However injuries curtailed his effectiveness later in the trip, but Rowe Harding, a fine winger who represented Wales and toured South Africa with Smith, remembered him as a first class winger, saying: "Smith had the speed and strength of leg of an ostrich. Many wingers are easily stopped, or once stopped rarely come again, but Smith was stopped only by the most devastating tackle."

Smith bounced back to his best at home the following season. There were four tries in the second half of the test against France at Inverleith in 1925, which produced a comical after-match conversation. One of the French players, impressed with Smith's speed, asked him his track time for the 100 metres. Smith did not hear the question properly and thought he was being asked how many tries he had scored, so answered, "Four or five, I believe." At this the astonished Frenchman reeled away, murmuring to himself, "Mon dieu!" Smith was known as 'the Flying Scotsman' and the French knew why after his reply.

In Scotland's next match, against Wales at Swansea, Smith bagged another four. He actually scored six successive tries for Scotland, a test record which has never been matched. Smith remains the only player to have scored four tries in successive tests. His partnership with Macpherson had Welsh old-timers shaking their heads and wondering if they'd ever seen better.

While 1925 was Scotland's greatest year - they ran away with the Triple Crown and the Five Nations Championship - Smith was to enjoy many glorious days over the next few seasons. By the end of the 1920s, he had played in four Scotland teams that won or shared the Five Nations Championship.

The wheels began to fall off for Scotland in 1930-31. Then in 1932 they lost to the touring South African side and finished with the wooden spoon in the Five Nations Championship. The veterans who had served Scotland so well had either retired or were past their best.

There was talk of Smith being dropped, but the selectors showed faith in him. Not only was he retained, but he was promoted to the captaincy and Scotland scored a Five Nations Championship/Triple Crown double for the first time in eight years. Smith's leadership, even from the wing, was inspiring and the Scottish side became noted for its enthusiasm and spirit. Eight of the test team made their debuts that season, so the string of victories was unexpected. Smith himself began the season well, scoring his team's first try, against Wales at Swansea.

When Smith retired, after a crucial victory, he had played 32 times for Scotland - the second highest number - and made two appearances for the British Isles. At the time of his retirement he was the world's highest test try-scorer and his tally was beaten only in 1987 by Australian David Campese.

Like most truly great players, Smith brought something new to his position. He could kick and tackle effectively and reports repeatedly mention his stamina. But he is recalled as perhaps the first winger to make a habit of leaving his side of the field and sprinting to the far corner to cut off an opponent. By using his speed in this manner, he saved any number of tries. **100**

WALTER SPANGHERO

Big Hands, Huge Heart

IT TOOK AN ACT OF physical courage to shake hands with Walter Spanghero, who was reputed to have the biggest mitts in world rugby. He would smile his cheery smile and offer a vast paw. You wondered what would be left when he released your hand from his grip. If shaking hands was a challenge, matching the big French forward on the field must have been truly formidable.

As a lock or loose forward, he was a mainstay of the French pack for nearly a decade from 1964, and had engrossing battles with the greats such as South Africans Frik du Preez, Jan Ellis, Tommy Bedford and Piet Greyling, Irishman Willie John McBride and All Blacks Brian Lochore, Kel Tremain and Ian Kirkpatrick.

If he'd played for New Zealand, Wales or South Africa, where rugby is cherished, he'd have been a national hero. But, as with others from his country, such as brilliant centre Jo Maso, Spanghero had a less-than-cosy relationship with the French selectors. He was repeatedly omitted from the test side, sometimes for five or six matches on the trot. So while he played 51 tests during his 10-season career, he missed another 19 in that time.

Though Spanghero's family was of Italian Tyrol stock, he grew up in Narbonne, in the Languedoc region of southern France, where his father was a farmer.

He rose to international rugby prominence when, aged just 20, he was a late inclusion in the French team for the 1964 short tour of South Africa. He forced his way into the test lineup for the one international, at Springs, locking the scrum with Benoit Dauga. France scored an upset 8-6 win and Spanghero and Dauga established a locking partnership that was to serve France for 15 tests. South African writers were lavish in their praise of Spanghero, calling him 'the fastest 15-stone forward in the world'.

He had a second tour there in 1967, playing all four tests and impressing the South African critics when matched against the talented loose forward trio of Ellis, Greyling and Bedford.

Back home he helped France to their first Grand Slam, in 1968, so his reputation was well-established by the time he tangled with the All Blacks. His first joust with New Zealand was at Paris in 1967, when the All Blacks won a rough, ugly match 21-15. Spanghero was outstanding, stretching his opposite, All Black captain Brian Lochore, to the limit.

Walter Spanghero
Lock/loose forward
Born: Parra-sur-l'Hers, December 21, 1943
Test debut: France v South Africa, Springs, July 25, 1964
Test career: 1964-73 (51 matches)
Test points: 10 (3 tries)
* Walter and Claude Spanghero were the first brothers to lock the French test scrum
* Captained France 11 times in tests

New Zealanders knew very little about French rugby players until the tours to New Zealand began in 1961. But from that time (and with the advent of worldwide television coverage) the country was soon impressed with the consistent quality France's lock forwards. 'Hard Men' they were called, capable of 'fronting up' to the physical confrontations which were part of the game in the 1960s and early 1970s, but which are being slowly eliminated because of the advent of video disciplinary committees. Here are some of the hard men of the 'Walter Spanghero era' of French rugby:

Jean Pierre Bastiat
Christian Carrere
Elie Cester
Michel Crauste
Benoit Dauga
Bernard Dutin
Alain Esteve
Andre Herrero
Alain Plantefol
Claude Spanghero
Walter Spanghero

Earlier in his career Spanghero played mainly at lock, but by the late 1960s he was more often a No 8 and occasionally a flanker, and he filled that role superbly on France's 1968 tour of New Zealand, even when pitted against Lochore, Tremain and Kirkpatrick. He was a mobile, ball-handling forward long before it became fashionable. Many a time he rescued a lost cause with his brilliant corner-flagging. Known as 'Le Monstre de Narbonne', Spanghero once said, 'Rugby is all about heart,' which is exactly how he played.

The *New Zealand Rugby Almanack* said he had all the attributes which made a good player a great one. 'He could match the speed of his backs, could handle the ball like a champion and could fill in the No 8, lock or flank positions without deterioration to his form,' the *Almanack* noted. Spanghero also impressed because, unlike some of his team-mates, he did not bother trying to rough up or niggle opposition. He played hard and could be physically intimidating because of his frightening commitment, but was always scrupulously fair. Off the field he was, as Colin Meads described him, 'that most docile, delightful man'. One writer summed him up by saying he had an abundance of the three Hs - heart, head and hands.

While Spanghero, 1.85m (6ft 1in) and 100kg (15st 10lb), was not particularly tall, he had massive legs and thighs and was immensely strong. He also had ample courage, as he showed in Australia on the way home after the New Zealand tour. Spanghero was targeted by some aggressively-minded Australian forwards. He had his nose broken in the Queensland match but carried on regardless, assisting in a 31-11 win. In the test at Sydney shortly after, Spanghero was again in the thick of the action. He scored a try and played superbly, but Australia sneaked home 11-10.

At that stage it seemed Spanghero would become an inspiring test captain. He did lead France once, to an 8-8 draw against Wales in 1969, but in typically dramatic French fashion, there were many paths to be walked before he became the regular captain.

Spanghero withdrew briefly from the French side in 1969, expressing dissatisfaction with the attitude of some players. In 1970 he wrote a book, *Rugby au Coeur*, and criticised several French test selections, including his old locking partner Dauga. He was never afraid to express his opinions on rugby or, as a confirmed right-winger, politics.

His book put him offside with the establishment and he retired, just before he was dropped, so it was said. Yet by November, 1970 he was back in the test side against Romania at Bucharest. Early the next year he locked the scrum against England with his younger brother Claude, the first French brothers to achieve this distinction. The Spangheros were to play seven tests together.

Walter Spanghero continued to be chosen sporadically, but it wasn't until 1972, after France had lost five and drawn three of their last 10 matches, that the selectors turned to him, perhaps in desperation. To do so, they had to drop the great Dauga as the two men had fallen out so badly they could not be chosen in the same side.

In his first test back at the helm, he led France to an astonishing 37-12 trouncing of England in the last test played at the Colombes Stadium. Suddenly he had gone from persona non grata to 'Walter the Magnificent'. He then captained France to a series win in Australia and led France to a 13-6 victory over Kirkpatrick's All Blacks in Paris in 1973. The 1973 Five Nations Championship resulted in the only quintuple tie in the competition's history, so in next to no time Spanghero had drastically altered France's fortunes. In all, Spanghero led France 11 times, for six wins, two draws and three losses,

Walter Spanghero dominating proceedings for France on their 1968 tour of New Zealand.

which in the context of the shambles he inherited, represented a fruitful haul.

Spanghero came from a prominent rugby-playing family dynasty. His brother Claude eventually played 22 tests and two other brothers were also prominent players. One, Jean-Marie, joined Walter and Claude in the Narbonne team which narrowly lost the French club championship final to Beziers in 1974. At times, four Spanghero brothers turned out for Narbonne, in what was then called 'half a ton of Spangheros!' Walter Spanghero finished his career playing for club teams in Toulouse and Bramaise.

He busied himself in a range of ways. Initially he worked on his father's farm, before turning to banking, then insurance. Now, among other business enterprises, he runs car rental companies in Toulouse and Narbonne. He has been awarded the French Order of Merit and the gold medal for youth and sport.

Spanghero's has remained a famous rugby name. Around Narbonne, he is absolutely revered and his name was recalled in Cardiff when Spanghero's Bar opened directly opposite the Arms Park. **100**

HAYDN TANNER

The Consummate Scrumhalf

Haydn Tanner
Scrumhalf
Born: Penclawdd, January 9, 1917
Test debut: Wales v New Zealand, December 21, 1935
Test career: 1935-49 (26 matches - 25 for Wales, 1 for British Isles)
Test points: 0
* Led Wales in 12 tests
* His 14 seasons equalled the record for the longest test career span for Wales

HAYDN TANNER WAS PARTLY responsible for one of the most enduring of rugby quotes. Tanner and his cousin, Willie Davies, pupils at Gowerton Grammar School, turned on some magical rugby to pilot Swansea to a shock 11-3 victory over the 1935 All Blacks. New Zealand captain Jack Manchester begged reporters later: "Say what you like about this result, but just don't tell New Zealand we were beaten by a couple of schoolboys."

Tanner at scrumhalf and Davies at flyhalf were a revelation, playing with maturity well beyond their years. While Davies was to become an international player of quality, Tanner had real star quality. I've spoken to several members of that 1935-36 All Black team who vowed Tanner was the best scrumhalf they ever saw.

Wales has produced many brilliant scrumhalves, but the best three are said to be Dicky Owen, Tanner and Gareth Edwards. Tanner was great for many reasons, but a significant factor is that during his time, Wales were not a particularly formidable side. Owen and Edwards were key men in the golden eras of Welsh rugby. Tanner, though, was not in a Welsh side that won even a Triple Crown. It says much that he maintained his standard despite less than top-level support.

Tanner was everything to Welsh rugby ... a brilliant schoolboy player, a senior member of the side, Welsh captain and a legend while still playing. Half a century after his retirement, his name is still revered.

From the age of 12, Tanner and Davies played and practised together at Gowerton Country School. There they came under the influence of sports master Bill Bowen and by 1934, aged 17, were playing senior rep rugby. They were, of course, Welsh schoolboy internationals and attracted immense publicity.

There was much debate about whether Tanner should play for Llanelli or Swansea. He had two outings for Llanelli, but then the village and his family got into the act. After that he played for Swansea.

Came the All Blacks and local rugby experts knew that despite their youth, Tanner and Davies were vital if Swansea were to have any chance. It required a deputation from the Swansea club to Mr Bowen before the teacher relented and allowed his boys to play.

Neither lad showed any sense of being overawed. They mesmerised the All Blacks and the famous St Helen's Ground has never been witness to more joyous scenes as the locals outplayed the visitors.

After his mature showing for Swansea, pressure mounted for Tanner to be picked for the test against the All Blacks. True, Wales needed a big, mobile scrumhalf with a long pass, but would a promising career be ruined if Tanner was thrown in too soon? The selectors opted for youth and chose Tanner to partner flyhalf Cliff Jones. The result: a never-to-be-forgotten 13-12 Welsh victory. Just 18, Tanner had been in two sides that had beaten the All Blacks. Many great players have waited a whole career and never known that feeling.

Tanner was never dropped from the Welsh side. He missed only one test, through injury, in the next 15 years, his career straddling the second World War. Always he drew fulsome praise. For example, the 1936-37 *Rugby Football Annual* noted: 'Tanner was so cool and accurate that he nearly always seemed to have plenty of time to send a glorious stomach-high low-trajectory pass to his partner. Game in tight corners, a kicker who could place the ball within a yard or two of where he intended, Tanner was a model for all.'

Tanner played 13 of his 25 tests before the second World War. He was tall for a scrumhalf, and at 91kg (14st), solidly-built with very strong forearms. He was lightning fast in getting the ball into the hands of his flyhalf, giving his backlines a significant advantage.

In an era when grounds were not well-drained, Tanner won a reputation for being able to clear his pass no matter how heavy the ball or the footing. Using the old leather ball which was often slippery or caked in mud and operating when offside rules made things a lot more difficult for the attacking side, he never let his backline down.

Cliff Jones, Wales' great flyhalf, played his best rugby outside Tanner and wrote in his book *Rugby Football*: 'I refuse to believe that there is, or ever has been, or ever will be, a better passer of the ball from the base of the scrum. Flight, direction, speed and consistency are all there; it is done in one motion.'

Tanner had all the other necessary accoutrements of the top-class scrumhalf. He was a dominant, influential personality, he was strong and resilient, tackled and handled well, was mobile and could make devastating solo runs, being noted for his muscular breaks around the fringes. With his body crouched forward characteristically, he would surprise defenders by feigning to pass, then breaking on his own. With his low centre of gravity and his strength, it was no easy task stopping him. He didn't kick a lot, preferring to feed his backline, but did have a good drop kick.

The lowest moment of his career was on the 1938 British Isles tour of

Haydn Tanner passing, back in the days when scrumhalves wore jersey No 7.

South Africa. Tanner was the third scrumhalf in Sam Walker's team and was really only a bit-part player because the side already included two international scrumhalf-flyhalf pairings. He did make the second test side, but the Lions were well beaten 19-3 and he was dropped.

During the war Tanner played regularly for the Welsh Guards, the Army and the Welsh Services XV. He particularly enjoyed playing alongside several rugby league stars in 'mixed' wartime football. As the war drew to an end, Tanner played in eight services internationals, including four Victory Internationals in which he captained Wales.

When test football resumed, Tanner, turning out for Cardiff, was a giant figure. In shades of his 1935 exploits against New Zealand, he captained Cardiff and the Barbarians to wins over the 1947 Wallabies. His game for the Barbarians was perhaps the finest of his career.

His final test was against France in 1949, by which time his test career had reached record lengths. When he walked off the field at Stade Colombes it was fitting that Monsieur Auriol, the French President, called Tanner to his box to thank him for the great rugby he had produced and the delight he had given to so many spectators.

Tanner remained in touch with rugby as a journalist, and, living in London, built a successful business life as an industrial executive.

The four players who appeared for Wales before and after the second World War:

Howard Davies (Swansea, Llanelli)	1939-47, 6 tests
Les Manfield (Mountain Ash, Cardiff)	1939-48, 7 tests
Haydn Tanner (Swansea, Cardiff)	1935-49, 25 tests
'Bunner' Travers (Newport)	1937-49, 12 tests

Tanner's 25 tests spanned the second World War. The top Welsh cap winners prior to 1940 were:

35	Dicky Owen	1901-12
33	Billy Bancroft	1890-1901
29	Billy Trew	1900-13
27	Arthur ('Monkey') Gould	1885-97
27	Wickham Powell	1926-35
25	George ('Twyber') Travers	1903-11

JOHN THORNETT

Integrity and Inspiration

JOHN THORNETT, ONE OF THREE BROTHERS who excelled at sport, epitomised all that is good in rugby. He was an outstanding forward - strong, resourceful and versatile. He was an inspiring captain who was always immensely popular. And for him rugby was only ever a game, to be played hard and enjoyed, not to be abused.

Along with Ken Catchpole, Thornett helped lead the revival in Australian rugby in the 1960s that set the platform for the Wallabies to win the 1991 World Cup.

The aspect of Thornett's rugby which stands out for me was his versatility. He was 1.83m (6ft) tall and his weight during his career ranged between 90.5kg (14st 3lb) and 100kg (15st 10lb). He played as a flanker in 17 of his 37 tests, as a lock in a handful more and as a prop in the rest. Yet at school he began on the wing and played at centre when he first attended Sydney University, in 1952. I remember him as a burly, fair-haired forward with good ball-handling skills, but whose real strengths were his ability to scrummage and to tidy up loose ball. There was a sort of gentlemanly calm about him. He spoke modestly but had undeniable presence, which is what made him such an outstanding captain.

Thornett excelled in several sports, including swimming and water polo, at Sydney Boys High School. He captained the school First XV and was elected captain of the school, an early indication of his leadership skills.

In 1955, he forced his way into the state rugby team and then toured New Zealand with the Wallabies, playing all three tests. He was a flanker in those days and his anticipation and temperament drew praise.

It was the start of a test career that was to span 13 years, though not all of them were glory days for Australian rugby.

There was a disappointing tour of Britain in 1957-58 when ill-discipline was rife and the Australians lost all five tests. Thornett, though he contracted hepatitis early on, fought back to play in all but one test.

Even more sobering was the tour of South Africa in 1961. Thornett later wrote in his book *This World of Rugby*: 'We were absolutely overwhelmed. I have never had such a feeling of helplessness on a football field as wave after wave of Springbok players poured through our defences. It was my first test as a front rower and we were pushed back so fast in some scrums that even when we won the ball, [halfback Ken] Catchpole had to dive to escape being

John Edward Thornett
Flanker/lock/prop
Born: March 30, 1935
Test debut: Australia v New Zealand, Wellington, August 20, 1955
Test career: 1955-67 (37 tests)
Test points: 3 (1 try)
*   Played in nine tests with his brother Dick
*   Captained Australia in 16 tests
*   Was a champion swimmer

John Thornett is carried off the field after leading Australia to a test series win over South Africa in 1965.

trampled by our own scrum, which seemed almost to be running back. The scrums were like South African charges and near the end, with my shoulders red raw from the pounding my opposite number had given me, I kept telling myself there couldn't be many more scrums. I had a tremendous relief as the final whistle went because it meant South Africa couldn't score any more - the only time I felt like that.'

From the ashes of that shattering 28-3 defeat arose in the Aussies a will to never again be canon-fodder to other rugby nations.

In 1962, when the Wallabies toured New Zealand, Thornett was captain. At 27, he had the absolute respect of his team and was boosted by the presence of his younger brother Dick, with whom he locked the scrums. The All Blacks won the series 2-0 but the Australians hinted at their potential. The first test was drawn 9-9 only after New Zealand fullback Don Clarke kicked a last-second penalty. The second test was a grim 3-0 victory for the All Blacks. Thornett was a low-key captain and explained modestly: "I was not a great tactician, and always let Ken Catchpole organise the backs."

The following year was one of Thornett's best. After beating England 18-9 at home, the Australians headed for South Africa reasonably optimistic, despite the bath they'd received there two years earlier.

The Springboks won the first test 14-3 but the Australians bounced back to win the next two 9-5 and 11-9, sensational stuff as the South Africans had not lost consecutive tests at home for 67 years. The series was eventually drawn 2-2. Thornett became a household name in South Africa. Ian Dieham wrote in *Giants in Green and Gold*: 'The 1963 Wallabies were ably led by John Thornett. South Africans loved the big fellow, who proved one of the most popular captains ever to visit.'

The highlight for Thornett of the 1964 series in New Zealand was the Wallabies' 20-5 triumph in the last test, at Athletic Park. Even more impressively, the next season he led the Wallabies to two straight wins at home over the Springboks and Australia's first series defeat of South Africa. Thornett was carried shoulder high after the second test, at Sydney.

Thornett's form slipped after this tour, but he played on until the 1966-67 tour of Britain. It wasn't a happy finale. He contracted impetigo from a rival prop at Leicester and when he returned to the fray, he struggled for form. He was left with the uncomfortable decision of having to cast the deciding vote against himself for the test team throughout Britain, though he did return for the international against France. There was no fairytale end. France beat the Wallabies 20-14.

It was not an easy tour, for Wallaby hooker Ross Cullen was sent home early after an ear-biting incident. Some felt the penalty was too severe, but Thornett, with memories of the unruly tour of Britain 10 years earlier, felt there was no choice.

After retiring, Thornett has remained a loyal servant of rugby, though he has not been afraid to speak out against on occasion. He graduated in engineering from Sydney University and became a successful businessman in Sydney, before returning to the country to farm and to run a small company.

Rugby left its mark on him - he has unmistakable cauliflower ears and has had two hip operations. But by any reckoning, Thornett had a wonderful career. He played nearly 120 times for Australia, made eight Wallaby tours, four as captain, and is one of the historic figures in Australian rugby. ⬤

There was a rare occurrence in the Eden Park test in 1962 when both teams had a set of brothers locking their scrum - Dick and John Thornett for Australia, Colin and Stan Meads for New Zealand.

The Thornetts are one of Australia's most famous sports families. Brothers John, Dick and Ken were all brilliant sportsmen. John played 37 tests for the Wallabies was also a champion swimmer. Dick, five years his junior, was a rare triple international. He played 11 tests in two years for the Wallabies, represented Australia at the 1960 Rome Olympics as a water polo player and at 23 turned to league, touring Britain and France with the 1963-64 Kangaroos and going on to play 167 first grade games for Parramatta. Ken, the middle brother, was a superb fullback who did not represent Australia at rugby simply because he switched to league so early. He played league for Leeds and then, from 1962-71, for Parramatta. He won 12 caps for the Kangaroos. After his retirement, a grandstand at the Parramatta Stadium was dedicated to him.

CYRIL TOWERS

The Spiritual Father of Australian Rugby

Cyril Henry Thomas Towers
Centre
Born: Mansfield, Victoria, July 30, 1906
Died: Sydney, June 8, 1985
Test debut: Australia (New South Wales) v New Zealand, July 10, 1926
Test career: 1926-37 (19 tests)
Test points: 27 (8 tries, 1 penalty)
* Captained Australia in 2 tests
* In 1993, his test career was posthumously extended by a further 10 matches when New South Wales' internationals of the 1920s were upgraded

NOW AND THEN, a player has such an influence on a country's rugby that its effects can be seen not for years, but for decades. Carwyn James certainly had such an effect on Welsh rugby, and in New Zealand Vic Cavanagh filled a similar role. So it was with Cyril Towers and Australian rugby. But whereas Cavanagh did not play international level and James had only two tests for Wales, Towers was a brilliant player whom many still say was the best Wallaby centre ever.

Towers was a stalwart of Sydney's Randwick club and it was through this link that he proved such an influence. In the 1960s, he imbued in a young Randwick flanker named Bob Dwyer the principles of the running game. Dwyer went on to coach teams that included Randwick stars like the Ella brothers, Simon Poidevin and David Campese. It would be simplistic to say that Towers was a key to Dwyer's Wallabies winning the 1991 World Cup, but his influence was there in the back play.

The outspoken and at times irascible Towers was years ahead of his time in rugby terms. He didn't have the easiest of childhoods. His father died at Gallipoli before Cyril turned 10 and the family moved about. In Victoria, Cyril grew up with Aussie Rules the dominant brand of football. But from Melbourne, the family shifted to Roma, in Queensland and then onto Sydney. Teachers like Oates Taylor (at Randwick Boys High) and Arthur Hennessey (at Waverley Christian Brothers) coached him as a footballer, though they were merely moulding ability that was already present.

For a time cricket was Towers' first sports love. But that changed in 1924 when he joined Randwick, donned the famed myrtle green jumper and got caught up in the club's running game, then being developed by scrumhalf Wally Meagher. In July 1924, he had played in the curtain-raiser to the New Zealand-New South Wales game, then sat on the sideline transfixed by the play of All Black backs Bert Cooke and George Nepia.

Two years later he was chosen for New South Wales and helped the state beat the All Blacks 26-20, marking the great Cooke. Towers became one of the stars of the New South Wales side (in the 1920s, this was actually the Australian side and the state team's internationals have since been reclassified as tests). His great tour was the 1927-28 Waratahs trip to Europe. He played brilliantly throughout, scoring 15 tries. There was one particularly remarkable effort against France when he scored after a swerving length-of-the-field run, and was surprised to be kissed on both cheeks by his opposing number.

He formed a famous partnership with Syd King in the midfield and thrilled the British with his speed, ability to sidestep, uncompromising defence and wonderful rugby brain. He was the thinking man's centre and had that splendid combination of speed and toughness that is the preserve of only the very best.

The opposition began to target Towers. The 1929 All Blacks roughed him up so much that he had to leave the field during the first test with a broken nose, but he returned for the third test to help Australia sweep the series 3-0.

Towers' uncanny ability to read a game was best revealed in 1930 when Australia beat the British Lions. With Australia leading 6-5 in the dying moments, a desperate Lions attack seemed sure to produce a try, until Towers left his opponent, sprinted for the corner flag and tackled Ivor Jones into touch just before the British winger could dot down.

Besides being a brilliant rugby player, Towers could be outspoken and dogmatic and became unpopular with some officials. Still, his omission from the Australian team to tour South Africa in 1933 was staggering, and was the result of a rift with Wallaby team manager Dr Wally Matthews. The decision left Towers hurt and very bitter.

Certainly Towers was never afraid to venture an opinion. Max Howell and Lingyu Xie in *Wallaby Greats* relate some of Towers' favourites: "If he got a bright idea on rugby, it would die from solitary confinement," he said of one Wallaby coach. He would say of people he did not respect: "Anyone who takes him for a fool is no mug." And: "He's not such a bad bloke, but he doesn't weigh much." Or, of a selector he didn't like: "He's a little like the Chinese. If you can't be wise, be mysterious."

Always fiercely individual, Towers travelled to Europe in 1936, bought a

bicycle and arrived in Berlin in time for the Olympics, where he trained with legendary American sprinter Jesse Owens.

Through the 1930s, Towers continued to be a shining figure in rugby. He captained New South Wales to a 17-6 win over the 1937 Springboks, then scored a try and kicked a conversion in Australia's 9-5 loss in the first test. Towers played in all three tests in the series, though he had to leave the field injured in the third. It was to be the last of his 19 tests.

He captained The Rest against Australia in the final trial in 1939 for the Wallaby team to Britain. Though the Rest won 48-3 and Towers was game's dominant figure, he was omitted. Dr Matthews, still the manager, felt Towers was 'too strong a personality'.

In 1940, aged 34, Towers retired from rep rugby, saying he was tired of the union's 'petty muddling and stupid administration'. He accused the executive of playing favourites and ignoring ability. "It's far more important to go down to headquarters and pat a few people on the back than it is to play brilliant football," he told the *Daily Telegraph*. He and Bill Cerutti had become the first two players to appear 50 times for New South Wales and Australia. Towers at the time of his retirement held the state points and tries records.

Towers continued to appear at club level for several more years, eventually playing a record 233 games for Randwick. He also enjoyed a second rugby career, as a commentator for the ABC. In his early days he commentated in the manner of Australia's famous cricket commentators, covering matches overseas while sitting in a Sydney Studio and reconstructing play from a flow of cables. Through the 1950s he became a tremendously popular radio commentator.

He was never shy about advising youngsters down at the Randwick clubrooms about where they were going wrong. "No matter how many points we had won by, Cyril would always tell us we were no good," Bob Dwyer recalled in his book *The Winning Way*. "I often found myself talking to him about technique and tactics and he started telling me about the backline game he had played thirty years or more before. At first I regarded what he was saying as the ramblings of an old footballer, but … the logic of what he was saying gradually seeped into my thinking because one day, probably about 1975, I grasped it. Suddenly it was obvious that Cyril's concept of backline play was right. As soon as I accepted that fact it opened up a different world of analysis for me. At once there was a new scope for moving and manipulating opposition defences. The challenge was to get the opposition to react the way you wanted them to, as if they were puppets on a string."

Dwyer also commented wryly on Towers' personality: "Cyril was one of those teachers who preferred to tell his pupils what to do, rather to than to explain to them why they should do it." But for those willing to listen, Towers' passion for the running game and his understanding of how it should be acquired offered lessons more valuable than were to be found in most coaching books. He involved himself in the science of angles and timing and, as Norman Tasker once wrote, 'made the running game a living, breathing philosophy'.

Towers and his wife Rita had four children, Tom and Tim, both useful club footballers, Lyn and Margariete. Lyn married Wallaby Ray Prosser and Margariete married Wallaby Jake Howard. One of their sons is Wallaby back Pat Howard. The line continues. **⟨100⟩**

RORY UNDERWOOD

The Flying Winger

RORY UNDERWOOD'S feat of scoring 49 tries in his 85 test appearances for England defied belief. The dynamic winger played international rugby for 13 seasons and it is fair to say that during much of that time England's game plans centred around a kicking flyhalf rather than sweeping backline movements. After four years of test rugby, Underwood had scored just four tries. Often he was little more than a spectator.

But, given a sniff of a chance, the man could score tries. While he had the speed and awareness to convert an overlap on halfway into a try under the posts, he was at his best in those last two metres before the tryline, the aptly-named 'zone of pain'. I've not see a winger better at wriggling through a bunch of cover-defenders and muscling his way over just inside the corner flag when all options seemed closed. He was strong, determined and resourceful, and the tiniest gap was enough for him.

The try of his I most vividly recall was for the Lions against the All Blacks at Athletic Park in 1993. He was given the ball about 50 metres out and put his foot on the accelerator, side-stepping and fending off a succession of would-be tacklers to score in the corner. It was a breathtaking effort that set up an emphatic Lions victory.

Underwood was one of the most interesting rugby figures of his era for many reasons. He was one of two brothers who played on the wing for England. In fact, when Rory returned to test rugby in 1992 after a short-lived retirement, he replaced his younger brother Tony. When the Underwoods played their first test together, in 1993, they became the first pair of brothers to turn out for England for 55 years.

The brothers' father, who died in 1982, was English; their mother Malaysian. Rory spent the early part of his childhood in Malaysia and Tony was born in Ipoh, Malaysia. As a schoolboy in Malaysia, Rory's prowess was acknowledged in a teacher's report which said, 'Very good at sport. Doesn't know when to stop, though.'

From his mid-teens Rory seemed headed for England honours. He swam and played cricket for Barnard Castle School in Durham, where his long-time England team-mate Rob Andrew was also a pupil, but he really shone at rugby. He played initially for Middlesborough, and helped Yorkshire reach the 1983 English county final against Gloucester.

He rose quickly through the England Colts, under-23 and national B team ranks before making his test debut against Ireland in 1984, taking over

Rory Underwood
Winger
Born: Middlesborough, June 19, 1963
Test debut: England v Ireland, February 18, 1984
Test career: 1984-96 (91 matches - 85 for England, 6 for the British Isles)
Test points: 210 (50 tries)
* His 50 test tries placed him second to David Campese (64) on world lists
* Holds England test records for tries (49) and appearances (85)
* His 91 tests (including Lions matches), is a British record
* Scored 5 tries for England against Fiji at Twickenham in 1989
* Brothers Rory and Tony Underwood, both wingers, played 19 tests together

from Mike Slemen on one wing. A couple of months previously he'd bagged a brace of tries for Leicester against the Barbarians and from then it was only a matter of time until he received his England call-up.

He was a dashing player, befitting his occupation as a fighter pilot in the Royal Air Force. When asked about the lure of the RAF, he said that he liked to fly, but that being a commercial pilot would not be challenging. "I didn't want to be driving a bus. My job is dynamic. In certain situations, such as when you are close to another aircraft, flying at speed, the adrenalin is pumping." The RAF posted Underwood to the Midlands and after that he was a Leicester club man.

Underwood, 1.76m (5ft 9in) and 84kg (14st), played in the first three World Cups and was always a must selection for England. There were weaknesses in his game - he wasn't a formidable tackler, was only adequate as a kicker and was sometimes criticised for lapses in concentration - but he had the priceless asset of being able to score tries. He had good acceleration and could sustain his speed over long distances, while his upper body strength enabled him to ride tackles and force his way across the tryline.

He drew attention, too, because of the antics up in the stands of his vociferous mother Annie. British television seemed fascinated by her. Each time one of her sons touched the ball, the cameras would zoom in on her and she could usually be relied upon to provide good entertainment - 'incredibly vehement' was how Rory described her.

Mrs Underwood must have been in convulsions watching Tony, especially, during the 1995 World Cup. When England met New Zealand in the semi-final at Cape Town, Tony had the unenviable task of marking big Jonah Lomu in full flight, and not surprisingly he emerged from the contest battered and beaten, as did all Lomu's opponents during that tournament until James Small held him in check in the final. The confrontation had a happy sequel for Tony and Mrs Underwood, though, as they subsequently appeared in a popular pizza television commercial with Lomu.

Rory Underwood had some memorable highs in rugby. He was in three Grand Slam-winning England combinations and contributed to four Five Nations triumphs. He was a member of the Lions side which won the series in Australia in 1989 and scored wins over New Zealand for both the Lions and England in 1993. His four tries helped England reach the 1991 World Cup final.

All the time, there were tries and more tries. As French star Jo Maso once said of Underwood: "From the moment he gets the ball, he has only one idea in his head, and that is to score." By the time he finally called it a day, Underwood's 50 test tries placed him second only to Wallaby David Campese.

Perhaps his greatest day was against Fiji in 1989 when, playing on the right wing for a change, his five tries equalled Dan Lambert's England record, set against France way back in 1907. He had another big day at Twickenham in 1988 when his two tries pushed England to a record 28-19 win over Australia. Underwood scored a dazzling try at Murrayfield in 1992 when his 50-metre sprint to the line stunned the partisan Scottish crowd and set England up for a runaway 25-7 win.

It is a measure of Underwood's consistency and brilliance that he is both England's most capped player and record try-scorer. He was the first England player to win 50 caps. His 91 tests, including his Lions appearances, place him well ahead of any other British player. Remarkably, the tally would have been much higher if his RAF commitments hadn't forced him to miss several major tours, including to South Africa in 1984, New Zealand in 1985, and to Argentina in 1990. **100**

Notable examples of brothers in test rugby

Five brothers:
Manu, Elisi, Kapa, Viliame and Fe'ao Vunipola of Tonga.

Four brothers:
Rino, Nello, Bruno and Ivan Francescato of Italy.
Hans, Andre, Mats and Peter Marcker of the Netherlands.
George, William, Walter and Robert Nelson of Scotland.

Prominent twin brothers in test rugby:
Glen and Mark Ella of Australia
Gary and Alan Whetton of New Zealand
Jim and Finlay Calder of Scotland
Jim and Stuart Boyce of Australia
Juan and Pedro Lanza of Argentina
Marcello and Massimo Cuttitta of Italy

Prominent brothers who were wingers:
Rory and Tony Underwood of England
Jim and Stuart Boyce of Australia
Fred and Kawhena Woodman of New Zealand

An example of what can be achieved by brothers in modern rugby:
Steve, Rob and John Gordon of New Zealand have each represented a different country: Steve - New Zealand; Rob - New Zealand and Japan; John - Hong Kong.

JOOST VAN DER WESTHUIZEN

The Eyes of a Gun-slinger

Joost Heystek van der Westhuizen

Scrumhalf

Born: Pretoria, February 20, 1971

Test debut: South Africa v Argentina, Buenos Aires, November 6, 1993

Test career: 1993-98 (50 matches)

Test points: 125 (25 tries)

* Holds the South African test record with 25 tries
* The first South African back to reach 50 test appearances

HOW DOES THE SAYING GO … the face of a choir boy, the eyes of a gun-slinger. That's Joost van der Westhuizen, the most capped back in Springbok history and his country's leading test try-scorer. Van der Westhuizen, with his blue eyes and open face, looks like every mother-in-law's dream. But on closer inspection, the lack of emotion is chilling. He is a feisty, tungsten-tough competitor who thrives on the cut and thrust of test rugby.

At 1.86m (6ft 1in) and 84kg (13st 2lb), the Northern Transvaal star is big for a scrumhalf and uses his size well. He is aggressive and explosive, and his speed off the mark is unmatched by modern scrumhalves - in 1994 he even played 50 minutes of a test against England as a winger, replacing the injured Chester Williams.

He was born in Pretoria and has stuck to the city and to Northern Transvaal. During Craven Week in 1988, aged just 17, he hinted that he was more than just another promising player. He went on to represent his province at under-20 level from 1989-91 and the following year was promoted into the full Northern Transvaal side. Things happened quickly for him. Within 18 months of playing lower grade football for the Pretoria club, he had been pulled into the 1993 Springbok side for the tour of Australia.

Back in those early years, his play was rather ragged. The dynamism and audacity were there, but his passing was inaccurate and his option-taking erratic.

Touring Australia, he couldn't tip Robert du Preez from the test spot, but bagged 11 tries in six matches. His most spectacular effort was a four-try haul on debut, against Western Australia at Perth.

Shortly after, he beat Johan Roux for the test berth on the tour of Argentina and celebrated by scoring tries in both tests. The Pumas struggled to combat his strong running and discovered van der Westhuizen had the strength to consistently break the advantage line. Perhaps he derived some of his agility and ball skills from his other sports passion, korfball (similar to netball), at which he has also represented his country.

For the next year or so, van der Westhuizen battled with the more orthodox Roux for the test scrumhalf position. His cause wasn't helped by the Springbok selectors' propensity for change. Not only could they not settle on a No 1 scrumhalf, but Joel Stransky, Henry Honiball and Hennie le Roux all jostled for the flyhalf role. In his first three tests, van der Westhuizen played

with three different flyhalves.

After being Roux's understudy on the 1994 tour of New Zealand, van der Westhuizen grabbed his chance on the tour of Scotland and Wales. The Scots had no answer to his in-your-face aggression and he ran rampant, scoring two tries in a 34-10 win.

Van der Westhuizen had an outstanding World Cup campaign, giving flyhalf Stransky a joyride. Though he didn't score a try in the tournament, his defence was superb, especially in the final against New Zealand. Jonah Lomu had struck fear into opposing defences, but van der Westhuizen made it his personal mission to hound the big All Black wing and bring him down before he could get up a full head of steam. Van der Westhuizen played a major role in marshalling the Springboks and had a tough, even battle with his Graeme Bachop, his All Black counterpart.

It became obvious as extra time ticked away that South Africa would try to steal the match with a drop goal. My television co-commentator, John Hart, became increasingly agitated, emphasising the need to counter the expected drop goal attempt. He stressed it was imperative for someone stop the pass at its source - van der Westhuizen - rather than running at Stransky, explaining that the speed of the ball always beats the speed of the man. But

Leading South African test try-scorers:

25* Joost van der Westhuizen (93-98)
20* James Small (1992-97)
19 Danie Gerber (1980-92)
18* Pieter Rossouw (1997-98)
13* Chester Williams (1993-98)
12 Gerrie Germishuys (1974-81)
12 Ray Mordt (1980-84)
10* Andre Joubert (1989-97)
10* Percy Montgomery (1997-98)
 9* Mark Andrews (1994-98)
 9* Stefan Terblanche (1998)
* still playing

van der Westhuizen was able to get his pass away, Stransky duly dropped the goal and a few minutes later Francois Pienaar was holding aloft the Webb Ellis Trophy.

Since 1995 van der Westhuizen has justified South African claims that he is the world's best scrumhalf. His strong running, defence and eye for the try are his outstanding traits. The dazzling try he scored in the 24-12 win over England in 1995 brought the Twickenham crowd to its feet. Rather like New Zealander Sid Going of an earlier generation, he can force his way to the tryline because of his strength, but he is bigger than Going and more aggressive. Despite the attention defences pay him, he has still managed a string of tries for Northern Transvaal and South Africa.

In 1996, he fought to regain the scrumhalf position from Roux. After swapping with Roux during the Tri-Nations series, he missed selection for the first test against New Zealand at Durban. However, he replaced Roux a few minutes before the end of the test, then scored a try at Pretoria the following week. A pair of tries in South Africa's consolation victory at Johannesburg took him clear of the challenge from Roux.

In Europe late in 1997, van der Westhuizen was injured in the dying moments of the test against France at Lyon and missed the rest of the tour, conceding his test spot to Werner Swanepoel of Griqualand West. There was talk of Swanepoel remaining the test scrumhalf, but coach Nick Mallett showed his faith in van der Westhuizen by re-selecting him when he was again available. That faith has more than been repaid.

He had a huge year in 1998. An early highlight came in the Cape Town mud against England when he charged down a kick and ran through to score his 20th test try, equalling James Small's South African record. Van der Westhuizen gave the All Blacks plenty of headaches, too. There was his darting 20m run to score against New Zealand at Durban when the All Blacks were shut out of the Tri-Nations with four straight losses. Earlier, at Wellington, he made a quick, short run by the posts and had the whole of the New Zealand defence chasing him. Then he cleverly in-passed to Peter Rossouw, who scored under the posts.

During the Springboks' end-of-year tour of Britain in 1998, van der Westhuizen had the honour of leading the side onto the field against England at Twickenham in his 50th test, the second South African after lock Mark Andrews to reach that mark. During the tour, he scored tries in three of the four internationals, including a brilliant 25m run to dive in under the posts against Wales at Wembley.

Van der Westhuizen has been just as successful in other arenas, too. He is a brilliant sevens player and was captain of the South African team which finished second to Fiji in the 1997 World Cup. He has played consistently well for the Blue Bulls in the Super 12 competition and in 1998 led Northern Transvaal to victory over Western Province in the Currie Cup final at Pretoria's Loftus Versfeld Stadium.

With his good looks and star quality, van der Westhuizen had been a magnetic personality in the Springbok team through much of the 1990s. Because of the introduction of professional rugby, he has been able to resist some huge rugby league offers and the former student now lists his occupation as rugby player.

Naturally, 1999 - World Cup year - shaped as crucial in van der Westhuizen's career, but a serious knee injury, sustained in the United Kingdom at the end of 1998, set him back by some months. **100**

INVESTEC

THE INVESTEC
INTERNATIONAL

ENGLAND
versus
SOUTH AFRICA

Kick-off 2.30pm

ENGLAND UNDER 21
v
SOUTH AFRICA UNDER 21

Kick-off 11.45 a.m.

TWICKENHAM
5th December 1998

OFFICIAL PROGRAMME
£3.00

The match programme marking 50 test appearances by Joost van der Westhuizen.

PIERRE VILLEPREUX

Simply Superbe

FRENCHMAN Pierre Villepreux's name is associated with great rugby deeds all around the world, but New Zealanders recall him for one magic moment during the second test against the All Blacks at Wellington in 1968.

Half an hour into the match, with the score still 0-0, France were awarded a penalty eight metres inside their half and 15 metres from the right hand touchline. French captain Marcel Puget called for his fullback, Villepreux, to kick for goal. There were titters among Athletic Park's 48,000 spectators as Villepreux lined up his 70-metre attempt, from north to south, with a moderate wind at his back. Television commentator Doc Williams, understandably sceptical, remarked that it would require a miracle to kick the goal from that distance. Then Villepreux ran in on the curve and his instep struck the ball without any particular force, but with perfect timing. The ball went on and on, clearing the crossbar with height to spare. The crowd's laughter turned to cheering and Villepreux had etched his name into All Black folklore.

In a way it does Villepreux an injustice to focus on that mammoth kick, for he was much more than just a magnificent long-range place-kicker. He was certainly one of the dashing backs of that fine French touring team. New Zealanders warmed to his panache and spirit of adventure. For about four years, from 1968-71, Villepreux was arguably the world's best fullback. He had vision, daring, timing and the skill to enter a backline at the critical moment. The Frenchman was one of the bridges between the era of the safety-first kick-into-touch fullback and the modern running fullback like Andy Irvine, J P R Williams and France's own Serge Blanco.

Pierre Villepreux went to school at Brive, then attended Toulouse University. He started his career with his local Brive club, whom he helped reach the national club final in 1965. Shortly after, he began his long association with Toulouse, playing one club final with them, in 1969.

Villepreux made his test debut in 1967 when France walloped Italy 60-13, scoring 11 tries. Guy Camberabero did the place-kicking that day, but Villepreux impressed with his intuitive running. Even so, he struggled to cement a test spot in the face of opposition from Claude Lacaze and, when he wasn't turning out at flyhalf, Jean Gachassin. In South Africa in 1967, Lacaze got three tests, Villepreux one.

Back home, Villepreux played against New Zealand, finishing the match

Pierre Villepreux
Fullback
Born: Pompadour, July 5, 1943
Test debut: France v Italy, Toulon, March 26, 1967
Test career: 1967-72 (34 matches)
Test points: 163 (2 tries, 29 conversions, 32 penalties, 1 drop goal)
* His 5 conversions against England in 1972 was a French record
* Was an extremely successful coach of the Toulouse club in the 1980s and 90s

with two broken ribs after falling to the ground to stop an All Black forward rush. Lacaze was then chosen for three of the four matches during France's triumphant 1968 Grand Slam season. Both toured New Zealand a few months later, but Villepreux was fullback in all three tests. The following season he had to see off the challenge of Henri Magois before finally establishing himself as the first-choice fullback. In 1971 he had one test as captain, against Wales, during the troubled period when those two mighty forwards, Benoit Dauga and Walter Spanghero, were locked in their struggle for power.

The fullback bowed out of international rugby after the 1972 tour of Australia. He played right up to his best form in the second test at Brisbane, which France won 16-15 to sew up the closely-fought series. Through his six seasons at the top, he played 34 tests, scoring 163 points, including two tries.

Villepreux was an innovative, dashing player. Few fullbacks have had his array of trick passes and handling skills. At 1.80m (5ft 11in) and 82kg (12st 12lb), he was big and strong enough to make an impact bursting into the line and was a marvellous counter-attacker. He didn't always do the place-kicking for France, but had some wonderful days with the boot.

Always a free spirit and an independent thinker, Villepreux proved an endearing personality when he spent some time in New Zealand, playing social rugby, including several outings for the strong Ponsonby club in Auckland.

When he retired, Villepreux turned to coaching with extraordinary success, instilling in every team he coached his concept of attacking 15-man rugby. He transformed Toulouse into the glamour team in France. Under the passionate Villepreux, Toulouse reached the club final in 1980, and won the title in 1985-86-89. Through the 1990s they were even more dominant. winning five titles on the trot, by which time Villepreux had just about qualified to receive the keys to the city.

Villepreux, a physical education instructor by profession, had coaching success in other areas, too. In the mid-1970s, he spent four productive seasons helping lift the standard of rugby in Tahiti. Then in 1978 he took over as Italian coach, and guided the test side to 10 wins before standing down in 1981. Later the English seconded him to assist with their backs. Rob Andrew described working with the Frenchman as 'an exhilarating adventure, a magical blend of continuous support and Gallic improvisation'.

The big puzzle was why French rugby authorities were reluctant to enlist Villepreux to help their own test side. There were suggestions he had fallen out of favour with key French officials. Finally in 1997 his claims could be ignored no longer and he was appointed as coach Jean-Claude Skrela's assistant. **100**

WAVELL WAKEFIELD

The One and Only 'Wakers'

WAVELL WAKEFIELD would have exuded class drinking a cup of tea. I met him at Twickenham in the 1970s when he was an old man and he still had an undeniable stature that set him apart. Nigel Starmer-Smith introduced me to him and while we chatted briefly, quite a group gathered around, with those of senior years hailing him and pointing out who he was to younger people.

Wakefield was one of the most important figures in the history of rugby. He was a great player, an innovative and successful captain during England's glory era of the 1920s and a respected administrator and writer. By the time I met him, he was an elder statesman of rugby, a symbol of wise counsel for the game and its future. His success in sport mirrored the rest of his life. After his playing career, he entered Parliament, was knighted and then became Lord Wakefield of Kendal. I suppose his New Zealand equivalent has been Wilson Whineray, the successful All Black captain of the 1960s who became a leading figure in the business world and was knighted in 1998.

Though 'Wakers', as he was affectionately known, was involved in many strands of rugby, he is included here purely for his deeds as a player. Many rugby historians rank him at least the equal of any forward in the first half of this century.

As is often the case with great players, he revolutionised his position. Though he sometimes played at lock, it was as a loose forward that he really shone. He was an innovative thinker who, while captaining Cambridge University, the Harlequins, Leicester, Middlesex and England, insisted on each forward undertaking a specific role, rather than plodding together from set piece to set piece as had previously been the style. And under Wakefield, England's back row combinations became the first in Britain to work as a unit. Until the 1920s, British forwards had tended to be subservient, merely winning the ball for their backs, but under Wakefield, they began to play more constructively and to exhibit unsuspected skills.

Wakefield played for England 31 times from 1920-27 and though he did not become captain until Dave Davies' retirement in 1924, he was a pivotal figure even before then as leader of the pack.

As a youngster, he played soccer, but he turned to rugby while attending Sedbergh School near the Lakes District. Even as a teenager, his skills were astonishing - he could handle like a back (remembering that in those days

William Wavell Wakefield
Loose forward/lock
Born: Beckenham, March 10, 1898
Died: Kendal, August 12, 1983
Test debut: England v Wales, Swansea, January 17, 1920
Test career: 1920-27 (31 matches)
Test points: 18 (6 tries)
* His 31 tests was the England record for 46 years
* Served on the International Rugby Board for seven years
* A Member of Parliament from 1935-63
* He was a representative athlete and cricketer and a champion pilot
* Was knighted in 1944 and became Lord Wakefield in 1963

Rugby Knights

There have been dozens of cricket knights, but as far as I can ascertain, only two people have been knighted exclusively for their services to rugby. The first was William Ramsay, an administrator from the 1920s until his death in 1973. He was a key figure in the launch of the Middlesex sevens tournament, and was later treasurer of the Rugby Football Union for 20 years, besides twice being the Union's president. For three years he served on the International Rugby Board. The other rugby figure honoured with a knighthood is former England lock Peter Yarranton, the driving force behind the organisation of the 1991 World Cup.

Many other prominent rugby figures have been knighted, sometimes partly because of their contribution to rugby and sometimes for totally unrelated reasons. Such people include Wilson Whineray, Harcourt Caughey, Terry McLean and Vincent Meredith (New Zealand), Nicholas Shehadie and Ernest Dunlop (Australia), John Megan (Ireland), Louis Greig (Scotland), Carl Aarvold, William Milton, Percy Royds and Basil Hill (England). Two Fijians, Ratu Penaia Ganilau and Ratu George Cakabau were knighted and later both became Governors-General of their country.

At least two well-known test players were elevated to the peerage, Wavell Wakefield and John Bannerman, who played 37 tests for Scotland in the 1920s. Both became strongly involved in politics after their rugby playing days were over.

forwards did not generally display the range of skills we see now), dribble, tackle and sprint. Added to these talents were his huge energy and fire. At 16 he was not only his school's rugby team captain, but was head of the school.

Wakefield served in the Royal Naval Air Force and the Air Force during the latter stages of the first World War. In 1919 he played for the Air Force in the inter-services league matches and he remained a strong supporter of service rugby. He retired from the service in 1923, by which time he was a Flight-Lieutenant.

By the time he attended Cambridge University in late 1921, he was already a complete player. He'd first played for England against Wales at Swansea in 1920, an inauspicious debut as England were well beaten. But England were on the brink of a wonderful era. Cyril Kershaw joined the England side for the next test, against Ireland, and with Dave Davies, Tom Voyce, Cyril Lowe, Ronald Cove-Smith and others either in the side or about to come on board, England were suddenly a top-class team.

Wakefield had some priceless attributes as a player. At 1.83m (6ft) tall and 88.5kg (14st), he was sturdily built, but was blessed with exceptional speed as well as strength and stamina. He was fast enough to have been his school 440 yards champion and in fact did play for England on the wing at times when injury forced a rejig of responsibilities. He had the dynamism and workrate to inspire any team. Like any good loose forward he could sniff a try and ran with his head low in a charging, bullocking manner that was hard to stop. He once described rugby as 'a friendly, controlled war' and his play certainly epitomised that description.

He played his first 21 internationals consecutively, winning 17 and drawing one. In his eight seasons of test rugby, England won three Grand Slams. He captained England 13 times and it is a mark of his stature that in spite of his famous team-mates, those years have come to be known in English rugby as 'the Wakefield Era'. As a captain, Wakefield emphasised team talks and preparation. He kept meticulous record books that detailed results and opponents' strengths and weaknesses.

Though Wakefield bowed out of international rugby in 1927, he continued at club level. Having guided Leicester for several years, he then turned out for Middlesex and led them to their first county championship, in 1929.

When his playing days were completed, he became a member of the Rugby Football Union, rising to the presidency in 1950. He served as a delegate on the IRB from 1954-1961.

But rugby was only part of his life. He was a representative athlete, played cricket for the MCC, skied competitively and was president of the national water skiing and sub-acqua diving clubs. In 1924 he won the first air race for reserve officers. He had a pleasantly serious personality and was a good public speaker with a rather husky voice. It was not surprising that he was courted by political parties and in 1935 he became a Conservative Party MP for Swindon. In 1945, he switched constituencies and was elected MP for St Marleybone in London, a seat he held until 1963.

Initially he was a pilot during the second World War. Then he was made director of the Air Training Corps. Wakefield was knighted in 1944 and became Lord Wakefield in 1963.

He always retained his sense of humour. In 1930, he campaigned in his book *Rugger* for a curb on kicking into touch as a means of closing up games, saying the tactic robbed rugby of its fun. Nearly 40 years later the kick-into-touch rules were finally changed. Wakefield's wry comment was: "That's about the length of time it takes to get a law changed in rugby football."

Keith Quinn's rankings of the century's 10 greatest English players and personalities:
1 Wavell Wakefield
2 Dave Davies
3 Bill Beaumont
4 Will Carling
5 Cyril Lowe
6 Cherry Pillman
7 Jeremy Guscott
8 Rory Underwood
9 Rob Andrew
10 Peter Jackson

Former All Black first five-eighth Earle Kirton was based in England through much of the 1970s and got to know Wavell Wakefield, or Lord Wakefield as he was then, reasonably well. Kirton retains vivid memories of Wakefield's personal magnetism and stature.

"Some of the parties he held at his home in Knightsbridge were glittering social occasions," Kirton recalls. "I knew him mainly through the Harlequins club, where he was a major figure. He was wealthy, but certainly did not spend his money too freely. There was a litmus test for judging how well you'd played. If Lord Wakefield bought you a half-pint, you knew he felt you'd acquitted yourself with distinction."

BILLY WALLACE

Carbine Wins Again

William Joseph Wallace
Fullback/winger
Born: Wellington, August 2, 1878
Died: Wellington, March 2, 1972
Test debut: New Zealand v Australia, Sydney, August 15, 1903
Test career: 1903-08 (11 tests)
Test points: 53 (5 tries, 12 conversions, 2 penalties, 2 goals from a mark)
* Played test rugby in three positions
* His 379 points in the All Black jersey was a record for 50 years until bettered by Don Clarke
* Scored 28 points against Devonshire in 1905, an All Black record until 1951
* Scored 230 points on the 1905-06 All Black tour of Britain and France, still a record for such a tour, and added a further 16 in Canada on the way home

BILLY WALLACE REMAINS ONE of the most special people in New Zealand rugby history. Not only was he a wonderful player, and a member of the famous 1905 'Original' All Blacks, but he lived to the grand old age of 93 and for many years was a bridge between New Zealand rugby at the turn of the century and of more modern times.

He was still alive and well when I became a trainee broadcaster in 1967 and I have one particular memory of him. In 1967, I went to a match at Athletic Park with Dave Henderson, a friend of mine. At the aftermatch function, we spotted Billy and went across to have a chat with him. We were only 21 and he was 88, but he talked to us for ages. Then it was time to go. He was living then with his daughter in Tawa, about 20 miles away, and we offered him a ride, which he gladly accepted. As we were driving through Wellington, he piped up: "Boys, don't you think we should stop for a drink?" So we stopped at the Grand Hotel.

Not surprisingly, our conversation turned to the famous Wales-New Zealand test of 1905 and the disputed Deans 'try'. Though he'd been asked about the incident countless times previously, Billy was as passionate as ever. He was emphatic Bob Deans had scored that day and that New Zealand had been robbed of at least a draw in the test. I recall him using the condensation that had rubbed onto the table from under the beer glasses to sketch out for us where the key players were in the movement that led to Deans going over the line. It was a classic case of a legendary story being passed on.

Until his death in 1972 (he'd been the oldest living All Black for some years), Billy was a clear thinker on rugby and New Zealanders were very proud of him. He was certainly sprightly, even as an old man. In Wellington in 1966, I watched him kick off in a testimonial fund-raising match for a boy who had been killed in a club game. He was 87 at the time and looked as if he was kicking off in an All Black trial.

In scanning the records and reading of the rugby that Wallace played, it is obvious he was a player ahead of his time. He is recognised as the father of All Black fullbacks, but played rep rugby in every backline position and on the big tour of Britain and France, made most of his test appearances as a winger.

Wallace is famous for many reasons besides his astonishing points-scoring records. He was a member of the first test team New Zealand fielded, against

Billy Wallace was one of many outstanding players in the 1905-06 'Original' New Zealand team to Britain and France. The team is regarded with special affection by New Zealanders. It played 35 matches (including two in North America on the return journey) and won 34, scoring 976 points and conceding just 59. But it was the game it lost that is most talked about. Wales beat the All Blacks 3-0 at Cardiff, though the New Zealand team claimed that centre Bob Deans scored a try which referee John Devan Dallas, some distance away at the time, wrongly disallowed.

The 'Originals' contained some of the greatest names in New Zealand rugby history. They were captained by Dave Gallaher, a magnificent loose forward who ran foul of British referees because he adopted the controversial wing forward position. Other stars whose names live on in New Zealand rugby history included Billy Stead, the vice-captain; Jimmy Hunter, who scored 44 tries on tour; George Smith, the brilliant winger who was also a champion jockey, athlete and rugby league player; Freddie Roberts, the incomparable halfback and Charlie Seeling, the brilliant flanker.

Australia at Sydney in August, 1903. He became New Zealand Rugby Union executive member during the 1930s and managed the 1932 All Blacks to Australia. And in 1937, he was pulled in as backline coach of the New Zealand team against South Africa.

Here truly was a legend. He made two particularly significant contributions to New Zealand rugby - he introduced the art of the running fullback and he lifted goal-kicking to unprecedented levels.

Because of his speed and flair, he was an adventurous fullback who thought nothing of entering the backline, beating a couple of players and scoring. On his big tour of Britain, he scored 27 tries. In New Zealand terms

The early days of headgear

There was one particularly distinctive aspect of Billy Wallace's appearance when he played his rugby - he liked to wear a cap on a sunny day. This seems very logical and given that some rugby players these days wear headgear or headbands to protect their ears, the question might well be asked: why do modern players not do what Wallace did and wear a cap to shade their eyes from the sun? If it was knocked off in general play it would be only a matter of picking it up and putting it back on. Wallace became so skilful that on one famous occasion he apparently held his hat on with one hand as he raced in to score, while carrying the ball in the other!

At Cambourne, in the second match of the 1905-06 tour, Wallace scored a sensational try while wearing a hat, only to have it initially disallowed because the referee thought he was a spectator.

Another distinctive aspect of Wallace's attire was that he sometimes played wearing pink socks. They were originally white, but when thrown in the wash with other touring laundry, including red garments, the white changed to pink - permanently!

it is easy to see how far ahead of his time he was. After his retirement, the fullback's role reverted to a more orthodox defensive one for the next 40 years. Thus players such as George Nepia became experts on defence but played lesser roles on attacks. Wallace was really the player who preceded Bob Scott and all the modern running fullbacks.

As a kicker, too, Wallace was unique in his time. A century ago, there weren't the quality balls and boots of today and kickers could not build the equivalent of a golfer's tee for themselves. Ground drainage was a thing of the distant future and fields were often heavy and muddy. Despite these handicaps, Wallace was a good kicker. He became the first New Zealander to total 500 first class points and when chronic knee problems curtailed his rep career in 1908, he'd scored 527 points, another mark which stood for decades, from 112 first class matches, 51 of them for New Zealand.

He had exceptional speed - he was second fastest behind sprint champion George Smith of the 'Originals' - and a gift for keen analysis, which was why he was a tour selector that year. For his Poneke club, for Wellington, whom he helped to win the Ranfurly Shield in 1904, and for New Zealand, his was always one of the first names written down, though often his position was not finalised until the rest of the team had been sorted out.

Wallace, a Wellingtonian through and through, was inspired to take up rugby when just a street urchin kicking an old jam tin through town. He saw famous Englishman Andrew Stoddart's 1888 team arrive in an impressive carriage and followed them to the Basin Reserve to watch his first game of rugby.

Surprisingly, Wallace suffered some terrible injuries. He was sturdily built for the time - 1.73m (5ft 8in) and 76kg (12st) - but on various occasions played with a broken nose, broken ribs and a broken jaw. He broke his leg in 1898, dislocated his shoulder in 1899 and badly sprained his ankle in 1900. In 1905 a broken collarbone all but cost him a place in the team to Britain. It required a split-decision vote by the selectors before he was allowed to sail.

Though Wallace was nicknamed 'Carbine' after the famous racehorse, some of his team-mates called him 'Kill Danger'. That name had its origins at Hartlepool when, as he was running back to take a ball, lock Bill Cunningham called out 'Nil danger, Billy'. Cunningham's words were misheard by reporters and a nickname was born.

Wallace was a blacksmith by trade and his influence was seen in the play of Mark Nicholls, one of the masterminds in the 1924 'Invincibles'. The young Nicholls would stop by Wallace's work and Wallace would be ever eager to discuss rugby and perhaps scratch a diagram in the dust to explain a point.

In 1930, Cynic, the *Sydney Referee's* rugby correspondent had held the job for 45 years. He wrote of great fullbacks he had seen and spoke of Nepia, Billy Warbrick, Frank McMillen, Alexander Ross and South Africans Marsburg, Joubert and Burmeister. Of Wallace he said: 'No more perfect fullback can be conceived. He was five foot eight inches and well timbered on top to taper nicely in the limbs. He was very high class in fielding either in the air or on the ground at the feet of dribbling forwards. He had a beautiful line kick, both for distance and direction, and was extremely quick in getting rid of the ball at close quarters. He could kick with either foot, though his best was his right. Wallace was a very fast and tricky runner of the dodgy variety, with a good swerve. To my mind he ranks in advance of every other fullback I have seen.' **100**

BLEDDYN WILLIAMS

A Partner for Life

BLEDDYN WILLIAMS AND JACK MATTHEWS - their names fit together like Gareth Edwards and Barry John, or Haydn Tanner and Willie Davies. The friendship of Bleddyn Williams and Jack Matthews has been one of the most enduring and warming in British rugby.

They made their test debuts together, toured with the Lions together, and provided the midfield quality in a grand Welsh rugby era. Since their retirement, they've attended countless rugby games together, big and small. I last saw them at the International Rugby Hall of Fame dinner in London in 1997, and guess what - they were sitting together!

While Matthews, a hard-tackling inside centre, was a very fine footballer, Williams was the rugby genius of the pair. He was that rare case in sport: a schoolboy prodigy who went on to fulfil his potential. Besides his indisputable skills as a footballer, he had other qualities. He was utterly selfless and loved rugby with a passion.

Bleddyn Llewellyn Williams (another fine Welsh name, that one) was one of 12 children. All eight boys went on to play rugby for Cardiff and two, Bleddyn and Lloyd, played for Wales. Asked once how he produced so many fine rugby players, Bleddyn's father said: "Plenty of beef stew and rugby conversation."

By his early teens Bleddyn seemed destined for the top. At eight he was the Taff's Well junior school scrumhalf. At Rydal School, he played at flyhalf. In 1937 he was fullback for Welsh schools against England schools. When the second World War erupted, he was the big-name schoolboy rugby player in Wales. In one match, for the Public Schools against Welsh Secondary Schools, his two late tries drew banner headlines.

In 1942, he joined the RAF on leaving Rydal and for several years played good rugby for the RAF and Welsh Services. He played in seven Victory Internationals, three Services Internationals and captained Wales against the Kiwis Army side.

But it wasn't until 1947, at the age of 24, that he finally made his test debut, at flyhalf against England. Others also playing their first test that day included Matthews, Billy Cleaver and Ken Jones. Wales lost 9-6, but went on to share the Championship. Williams reverted to centre for his next test against Scotland, scored a brilliant try in the opening minutes and was suddenly wearing the mantle of Wilf Wooller.

Bleddyn Llewellyn Williams
Centre
Born: Taff's Well, February 22, 1923
Test debut: Wales v England, Cardiff, January 18, 1947
Test career: 1947-55 (27 matches - 22 for Wales, 5 for British Isles)
Test points: 24 points (8 tries)
* Scored a record 185 tries for Cardiff
* Captained Wales 5 times for 5 wins

His combination with Matthews became famous. Matthews, stocky and fast, liked to take the ball at top speed and Williams, with his gift for timing, got the most out of his fellow centre. As Wooller wrote: 'If I were forced to choose one player who made the ball do the maximum of attacking work by simply giving a pass from the right position and at the right moment, I would certainly choose Bleddyn Williams as my prototype. He had an uncanny knack of timing.'

He was the ideal centre, strongly built - 1.78m (5ft 10in) and 83kg (13st) - and hard to stop. He was a fast runner with a long stride, and possessed a trademark sidestep that left many defenders grasping only air. Though a prolific try-scorer, Williams was a team player in the real sense, and his wingers had a picnic. In fact, Williams was occasionally chided for passing when he might have scored himself.

He attained national fame during the 1947-48 season when he ran in a record 41 tries for Cardiff. He needed three in the final game, against Gloucester, for the record and turned in a non-stop, 100mph performance, grabbing the vital third try just before the end. That season, too, Williams was a key figure in three victories over the Wallabies - for Cardiff, Wales and the Barbarians.

In 1950 Williams was appointed Welsh captain, but there began a sequence of injuries that blighted his rugby from then on. He hurt his knee, attempted to come back too soon, and missed the entire international season. This was to be the story of the rest of his career. He loved playing rugby and seldom allowed himself enough recovery time after an injury, so often played when not fit.

He was vice-captain of the 1950 British Isles tour of Australia and New Zealand and one of the stars of a superb backline that also boasted Ken Jones, Matthews and Jackie Kyle. The Lions lost a hard-fought series in New Zealand 3-0 with one drawn, but Williams enhanced his reputation. New Zealanders admired his pace, handling, power and straight running. When Karl Mullen missed three tests through injury, Williams stepped in as Lions captain.

Perhaps because of staleness, Williams' form became more erratic afterwards, though he played well against the brilliant 1951-52 Springbok side. Cardiff and Wales both lost unluckily to the South Africans, but atoned for the defeats with famous victories over Bob Stuart's 1953-54 All Blacks.

Williams plotted carefully for Cardiff's match with the All Blacks. He reckoned if his pack could hold the New Zealand forwards and if lethal fullback Bob Scott could be contained, Cardiff could win. Before the game, he said to his forwards: "It's up to you. Give me just two-fifths of the ball and we'll win this match." The forwards responded and Williams was as good as his word. Cardiff won 8-3 and Williams was chaired from the field. "That result, and being hoisted on the broad shoulders of my good friend Stan Bowes at the close of the match, was my proudest moment," he said years later.

Shortly after, he captained Wales to a rather fortuitous 13-8 win over the All Blacks, when Clem Thomas' cross-kick bounced kindly for winger Ken Jones, who galloped away for the match-winning try. Who could have guessed that Wales would not beat New Zealand again this century?

By then, New Zealanders had seen more than enough of Williams. He'd played five times against the Kiwis, toured New Zealand with the Lions and now engineered two wins over the All Blacks. Radio commentator Winston McCarthy, who saw all those matches, later wrote glowingly of Williams' footwork, speed and intelligence. In the modern vernacular, Williams had great 'vision'.

After 1954, he was not the same force. He was controversially omitted from the 1955 Lions team to South Africa because of a much-criticised youth selection policy and played his last game for Wales against England in 1955.

Following his retirement, Williams, a company director and steelworks official, maintained his links with rugby by writing incisively for the *Sunday People*. **100**

Bleddyn Williams during one of the hundreds of games he played for the Cardiff club.

Bryan Williams heads towards the posts to score against Australia at Wellington, 1972. The over-keen photographer (left), who had tried to get close to the action, got closer than he intended!

BRYAN WILLIAMS

First Samoan Superstar

I LIKE TO THINK I PLAYED a small part in making Bryan Williams' 100th game for New Zealand a memorable occasion. It was in 1978 and at that stage only two players - Colin Meads and Ian Kirkpatrick - had reached their All Black century.

When the All Blacks departed for their end-of-year tour of Britain, Williams was perched on 99. On the plane trip from New Zealand, television producer Gavin Service and I approached All Black coach Jack Gleeson and offered him this suggestion: the first match, against Cambridge, would not be televised live. The second, against Cardiff, a grander occasion, would be. Why not save Williams' 100th match for Cardiff? Gleeson gave us a wry look and said he might get back to us.

We never heard any more from him, but Williams did indeed miss the Cambridge game. The publicity about his century built up and he was given the honour of leading the All Blacks onto the field against Cardiff after a presentation by the club in front of the main stand - a fitting tribute to a hugely popular servant of New Zealand rugby.

Williams' career had both impact and longevity. He was the 19-year-old part-Samoan who had South African crowds in raptures in 1970, and he went on to build a fabulous career spanning nine seasons of test football and 15 for Auckland.

After some early flirting with rugby league, Williams - 'BG' to his fans - made the Mt Albert Grammar School First XV at 14, the Ponsonby club senior team at 16, the Auckland Colts at 17 and the Auckland rep side at 18. He started as a second five-eighth/centre, like his older brother Ken, who was an All Black trialist. But he played nearly all his international rugby on the wing, which was definitely his best position.

These days, Williams doesn't look all that imposing. He is 1.78m (5ft 10in) and in his rugby prime weighed 89kg (14st). Back in the 1970s, he seemed massive. He had the huge thighs typical of a Samoan and bristled with power and dynamism.

It is hard to imagine any winger playing better than did Williams on that 1970 tour of South Africa, when his form was truly amazing. The first time he was passed the ball on his All Black debut, he scored a try. He ended the tour with 14 tries in 13 games, but that does not tell whole story of his genius. He exasperated opponents with his powerful running, side-stepping, strong

Bryan George Williams
Winger
Born: Auckland, October 3, 1950
Test debut: New Zealand v South Africa, Pretoria, July 25, 1970
Test career: 1970-78 (38 matches)
Test points: 71 (10 tries, 2 conversions, 9 penalties, 1 drop goal)
* In 1978 he became the third player - and first back - to reach 100 games for the All Blacks
* His 66 tries for New Zealand was the record until passed by John Kirwan in 1994

At least 65 players named Williams have appeared in test rugby. Not surprisingly, Wales leads the way with 46, followed by England 7, South Africa 5, Australia 4 and New Zealand 3.

The best-known players named Williams have been:

Bleddyn Williams (Wales/British Isles)	1947-55
Bryan Williams (New Zealand)	1970-78
Chester Williams (South Africa)	1993-98*
Denzil Williams (Wales/British Isles)	1963-71
John Williams (South Africa)	1971-76
John 'JJ' Williams (Wales/British Isles)	1973-79
John 'JPR' Williams (Wales/British Isles)	1969-81
Rhys Williams (Wales/British Isles)	1954-60

* still playing

fend and flair. Veterans like Brian Lochore, Colin Meads and Fergie McCormick had never seen anything like him. McCormick later said of him, in a reference to a popular television show of the time, "He's a bloody six million dollar man."

In the first test, Williams scored the All Blacks' only try, a typical 40-metre effort past and through the defence after a Sid Going blindside break. His greatest try was against Eastern Province. After a pass went behind him, he stopped and heeled it in soccer fashion between two opponents, picked it up and beat three other defenders before racing away to score between the posts. Television commentator Doc Williams shouted, "They'll never stop him" when he had three men to beat! In the final test, he scored another try, evading two players in the in-goal area to score under the bar.

A favourite photograph is of the teenaged Williams at home in his lounge surrounded by thousands of letters and cards from fans around the world. "My mother and I attempted to answer them all," he said, "but there was such a mountain we never got halfway. The response was amazing."

Though Williams was never again quite the player we saw in that flickering black and white film from South Africa, he remained a top winger, capable of turning half-opportunities into tries. Except for the All Blacks' 1973 internal tour, Williams held his All Black spot until his retirement, though he was dropped for the New Zealand-Ireland test in 1978 and came on as a replacement during the game. For several years he formed a brilliant partnership with mercurial winger Grant Batty. Both were tough and combative and they combined superbly.

Williams scored 12 tries on the 1972 internal tour, one in each of the three tests against Australia in 1972 and played sensationally in the 1975 test against Scotland on Eden Park. The ground was flooded that day - it has since been dubbed 'the water polo test' - but Williams' strength overcame the conditions and he scored two fine tries.

Back in South Africa in 1976, Williams broke Jimmy Hunter's 68-year-old record of 49 tries for New Zealand. He went on to push the mark to 66.

In Toulouse in 1977, Williams suffered a gruesome injury during the first test against France. After contributing a try and a penalty, he dislocated a hip and was invalided home. Watching him being carried onto the plane by stretcher, it was hard to believe we would see Williams in international rugby again. Yet he was back within six months and played against Australia at home in 1978, marking his return with a typically barging try. "I felt that my career wasn't over; I didn't want it to end on that note, so I fought really hard to get back," he said.

His final tour was to Britain in 1978 when he was the senior pro in Graham Mourie's Grand Slam team. After showing fine form when he replaced Brian Ford during the Ireland test, he kept his test spot. His tour ended on a high when he scored a try against the Barbarians, giving him 401 points for the All Blacks.

When he retired, his 113 appearances for New Zealand and 38 tests were All Black records for a back.

Williams kicked some mammoth penalty goals. One that stands out was his 55-metre effort in the third test at Newlands in 1976. However, he was never happy being the No 1 kicker, preferring to be called up to have the odd long-range attempt.

He continued playing for Auckland until 1982 and once he had lost some pace, he turned out at fullback and did an excellent job. During Williams' career, he helped Auckland win the Ranfurly Shield four times and in 1982 he was a key member of the province's first national championship-winning team, playing 10 games. In his final match for Auckland, against Wellington, he scored a try.

He has gone on to become a respected coach. He was player-coach of leading Auckland club side Ponsonby from 1975 and in 1987 became Auckland coach Maurice Trapp's assistant.

Williams, a lawyer, has devoted himself to Samoan rugby. He was the team's technical adviser when they performed so well at the 1991 World Cup and in 1996 became their coach. He is a very determined person, which comes through in his tireless and outspoken advocacy of Samoan rugby.

He has been a significant figure for another reason. In 1970 Williams was one of four dark-skinned players - with Sid Going, Buff Milner and Blair Furlong - to tour South Africa, a sign that the poisonous apartheid system was beginning to be broken down. I believe that the class and popularity of Island players in New Zealand rugby has helped eradicate a strain of racism in our society. When I was growing up, a number of derogatory terms were used to describe Island people. Such language has now largely disappeared, partly because of the influence of respected players like Williams and his successors, including Michael Jones, Inga Tuigamala and Jonah Lomu, in New Zealand society. **100**

The last try scored by Bryan Williams for the All Blacks, against the Barbarians Club in 1978.

CHESTER WILLIAMS

The Black Pearl

Chester Mornay Williams
Winger
Born: Paarl, August 8, 1970
Test debut: South Africa v Argentina, Buenos Aires, November 13, 1993
Test career: 1993-98 (18 matches)
Test points: 65 (13 tries)
* Set South African record with four tries in a test against West Samoa in 1995.
* Captained South Africa to the quarter-finals of the 1998 Commonwealth Games sevens tournament in Kuala Lumpur.

FRANCOIS PIENAAR might have held the Webb Ellis Trophy aloft at the end of the 1995 World Cup, but another of the darlings of South African rugby that year was winger Chester Williams. In the lead-up to the World Cup, organisers used the popular Williams' face to promote the tournament, with the slogan 'The Waiting's Over'.

He is a pivotal player in Springbok rugby history. He wasn't the first black player to represent South Africa. Others, notably Errol Tobias, had worn Springbok jersey with honour. But Williams' arrival coincided with South Africa's re-admission to the international arena. The reprehensible system of apartheid had been broken down and the world sought a sign that South Africa was choosing its teams without reference to skin colour.

In those circumstances, Williams was a treasure. Nicknamed 'the Black Pearl', he was a dynamic winger with nimble footwork and speed to burn. Though not very big - 1.74m and 80kg - he was a devastating tackler. There was no question of his test selection being a sop, for he and James Small formed a world class pair of wingers.

As the rugby world talked about 'the Rainbow Nation' and Pienaar memorably spoke of playing for 43 million people, Williams became the embodiment of this new spirit. He was perfect for South Africa at that time. He wasn't aggressively black, and there wasn't a hint of arrogance in his quiet, under-stated manner. He was a devout Christian who shied away from becoming enmeshed in the politics of colour.

After the World Cup pre-publicity revolving around him, there was a public relations disaster when he was forced to withdraw injured on the eve of the tournament. But, like all good fairytales, the story ended happily. He returned to the side when Pieter Hendriks was suspended for foul play early in the World Cup and marked his comeback match with four tries against Western Samoa at Johannesburg.

Williams was born into a rugby family. On his father's side, his uncle Avril was involved to a high level in South African rugby, his father Wilfred and uncle Adam played for the Proteas and another uncle, Randall, toured Wales with a South African schools team.

Chester caught the public eye in 1988, when he was 17. His play at centre for the Western Province League team during Craven Week at Port Elizabeth showed the benefits of expert tuition by former Springbok Ian Kirkpatrick.

It's been 15 long years of exile since South Africa last played in the world arena. It is with great pride, therefore, that South African Airways welcomes 15 great sporting nations to our beautiful land for this, the third Rugby World Cup, as we rejoice in the Springboks re-entry onto the international rugby scene. Because good things come to those who wait ...

WE'VE WAITED LONG ENOUGH.

SAA
SOUTH AFRICAN AIRWAYS
OFFICIAL AIRLINE FOR

RUGBY WORLD CUP 1995

The promotional advertising surrounding the 1995 Rugby World Cup strongly featured the image of Chester Williams.

Keith Quinn's ranking of the century's most admired test rugby players, using the 'Three Ps' criteria - presentation, popularity and personality (in other words, the world's 'best loved' players):

1. Cliff Morgan
2. Gareth Edwards
3. George Nepia
4. Jo Maso
5. Serge Blanco
6. Jean-Pierre Rives
7. Tony O'Reilly
8. David Campese
9. Waisale Serevi
10. Chester Williams

(With apologies to Mike Gibson, Andy Irvine, Jackie Kyle, Michael Jones and Mark Ella)

That year he was chosen for a mixed-race national schoolboy team which played at Free State Stadium in Bloemfontein.

On leaving Klein Nederburgh School in Paarl, Williams joined the Navy, which gave him the opportunity to play and practise. It wasn't until 1995 when he became the Western Province union's development officer that he changed his career path.

As South Africa was slowly untangling itself from its apartheid system, Williams' rugby flourished. In 1991 he was chosen by Western Province. He had a good tour of Australia and New Zealand for the province in early 1993, until against Canterbury he scored a try and was then sent from the field for a late tackle. This was a surprise, for Williams had never run foul of referees previously and has had an exemplary record since.

Shortly after, Williams toured Australia with the Springboks, scoring a try in his first outing, on Perth's famous WACA ground. He didn't break into the test side on the tour, but played seven matches and contributed seven tries, including a hat-trick against Victoria.

Later in 1993 came his test debut, when he was pulled into the Springbok team for the second test against Argentina at Buenos Aires after regular left winger Jacques Olivier withdrew with the flu. Williams scored a try in South Africa's 52-23 victory and never looked back.

In 1994, he played in all seven of South Africa's tests, scoring four tries. His play matured quickly. His pace and uncompromising tackling were still his trademarks, but I was always impressed by his workrate. No sooner had he made a big tackle than he'd be on his feet again, looking for more action. Naas Botha suggested Williams was as good as David Campese, an indication of the impact the balding Western Province player had made. He played all three tests on the tour of New Zealand, but his team struggled and he didn't get many attacking opportunities. At the end of the year he gave the British a taste of his class, scoring tries against Scotland and Wales. His try near the end of a rugged test against Wales set Cardiff Arms Park alight and took the Springboks to a narrow victory.

His four-try virtuoso performance in the ultra-physical World Cup match against Western Samoa and his faultless play in the final against New Zealand were the highlights of his 1995. He brought the curtain down on the year with a pair of tries against England at Twickenham. In 16 tests he had scored 13 tries, a remarkable ratio.

But after that his career became increasingly affected by injury. He damaged his right knee early in 1996 in a match against Canterbury and it took him nearly two years to regain mobility and fitness.

He made a successful return in 1998, scoring two tries for the Western Stormers against the Otago Highlanders in his Super 12 comeback. He helped Western Province reach the Currie Cup final, which they lost to the Blue Bulls (formerly Northern Transvaal) and played another two tests, as a replacement. He continued to be a force in sevens rugby, at which he first represented his country in 1993. Williams captained South Africa at the 1998 Commonwealth Games sevens tournament at Kuala Lumpur. **100**

JOHN 'JPR' WILLIAMS

Rugby Buccaneer

I HAVE MANY MEMORIES of JPR Williams. He was the young fullback who fought valiantly in an outclassed Welsh side in New Zealand in 1969. He was the player who dropped his only goal in tests from 40 metres to earn the Lions a draw in the fourth test at Eden Park in 1971, denying the All Blacks a share of the series and breaking New Zealanders' hearts. In the same match, Williams conceded hulking All Black prop Jazz Muller four stone and barged him into touch.

Williams scored a fine try for the Barbarians against Ian Kirkpatrick's All Blacks in 1973. And he made a comeback for the 1980 Centenary test, Wales against New Zealand, at Cardiff Arms Park. He proved in that match that class is permanent, making a bone-shattering tackle on Murray Mexted and denying Stu Wilson, Nicky Allen and Bernie Fraser tries with three superb tackles.

But my over-riding memory of JPR occurred when the All Blacks played Bridgend in 1978. He was the victim of a disgusting piece of stomping by John Ashworth and was left with a huge gash in his cheek. He could easily have lost an eye.

I recall Williams at the press conference afterwards, dabbing his face to stem the flow of blood. At the after-match dinner, Bridgend's club president, Dr Peter Williams (JPR's father) made a speech condemning the incident.

New Zealanders did not come out of the business well. Up in the commentary box, I saw what had happened and labelled it a disgrace. There wasn't the same emphasis on eliminating foul play in the 1970s and my comments were not well-received back home. All Black coach and manager Jack Gleeson and Russell Thomas refused to view videotapes of the incident, a head-in-the-sand attitude that did neither any credit. There was no apology from the All Black camp, though in a curious sidelight, two Fleet Street tabloid journalists got together and invented an apology, then created headlines out of it.

Feelings ran so high that when the All Blacks met the Barbarians at Cardiff Arms Park later in the week, rival captains Graham Mourie and Derek

John Peter Rhys Williams
Fullback
Born: Cardiff, March 2, 1949
Test debut: Wales v Scotland, Edinburgh, February 1, 1969
Test career: 1969-81 (63 matches - 55 for Wales, 8 for the British Isles)
Test points: 39 (6 tries, 2 conversions, 3 penalties, 1 drop goal)
* Held the Welsh record of 55 tests when he retired
* Was the world's most capped fullback when he retired
* Was in eight Welsh teams that won or shared the Five Nations Championship
* Was one of the First XV inducted into the International Rugby Hall of Fame in 1997
* Was a junior Wimbledon tennis champion

Quinnell chose to publicly shake hands before the game to try to ease the tension.

What really inflamed feelings was that status of the victim. Williams is one of rugby's gems, a fullback who had everything.

There was no area where he was deficient. He had a long career, yet it is impossible to say when he was at his peak because he was always a superlative player. He had a combative temperament, incredible courage, was rock solid under the high ball, had excellent ball retention, knew how to run into the backline with maximum effect and could kick well. The hallmark of his play, though, was aggressive defence. His philosophy was that the harder he went in, the less likely he was to get hurt. He was a shade over 1.83m (6ft) tall and weighed nearly 89kg (14st), the perfect build for a player who thrived on physical confrontation. Even when the Lions had a brilliant player like Andy Irvine available, Williams was indisputably the first-choice fullback.

Williams - he was called JPR, or Japes, to distinguish him from the other John Williams (JJ) in the Welsh team - played on the wing at Laleston Primary School, but when he moved to Bridgend Grammar School at 11, he was stationed at fullback.

His rugby flourished at Millfield in Somerset, a noted nursery of sports talent. Williams was a Welsh schoolboys rep and played for Bridgend at just 18. He says his most cherished rugby memory is of being selected to represent Wales under-15 against England in 1963, and still has the red jersey on his wall to prove it. Williams' medical studies took him to St Mary's at Paddington and he joined the exciting London Welsh side.

Despite his promise as a rugby player, tennis nearly grabbed him. He was so good at tennis that in 1966 he won Junior Wimbledon, beating future Davis Cupper David Lloyd in the final. Soon after, he beat top pros Sandy Mayer and Dick Stockton. Eventually he plumped for rugby because he felt it would leave him more spare time than would a career as a tennis pro. His tennis experience was valuable, though. "Tennis taught me to watch the ball all the time, which is especially important when forwards are bearing down on you and you have to take a high kick," he said.

Williams was a running fullback even before rule changes encouraged such adventure. He was an exciting player but never neglected the defensive duties of his role. The man was so tough and committed that in Sydney in 1978 he even played as a flanker, making him one of the few players to play test rugby as both a forward and a back.

He toured Argentina with a Welsh second selection in 1968 and the following year made his test debut against Scotland at Murrayfield. Wales won 17-3 and went on to claim the Five Nations crown. Williams never looked back.

What a career followed! It is hard to think of an honour he didn't achieve. He was a star player in the two greatest Lions teams, to New Zealand in 1971 and to South Africa in 1974. During his career Wales won or shared eight Five Nations Championships, won the Triple Crown six times, and achieved the Grand Slam three times. He played England 11 times and never lost, and

Most capped fullbacks:		
81	Serge Blanco (France)	1980-91
67	Gavin Hastings (Scotland/British Isles)	1986-95
64*	Jean-Luc Sadourny (France)	1991-98
62	John "JPR" Williams (Wales/British Isles)	1969-81
59	Tom Kiernan (Ireland/British Isles)	1960-73
55**	Andy Irvine (Scotland/British Isles)	1972-82
41	Luigi Troiani (Italy)	1985-95
37	Paul Thorburn (Wales)	1985-91
34*	Andre Joubert (South Africa)	1989-97
33	Jonathan Webb (England)	1987-93

* still playing
** includes one appearance when Irvine switched from wing to fullback in mid-match.

JPR was never far from the thoughts of Welsh supporters.

scored five of his six test tries against them. In 1979 Williams captained Wales to the Five Nations Championship and the Triple Crown, and led Bridgend to victory over Pontypridd in the Schweppes final.

Williams retired in 1979, but was persuaded to return for the Welsh centenary match, and showed he had lost none of his bravery or resolution. His last test was against Scotland at Murrayfield in 1981. In his 55 tests for Wales, Williams was on the winning side 37 times. In the 55 tests Wales played before JPR's arrival, they used eight other fullbacks.

He was a clever footballer. Barry John said: 'The subtle things he got up to were not always appreciated by spectators, but for such a big man he had considerable grace and his part in the golden era of Welsh rugby needs to be underlined.'

Williams was not the fastest of runners, certainly nowhere near the pace of an Irvine or a Christian Cullen. But he had a distinctive shuffling style, with minimal knee-lift, somewhat like Graham Mourie. He got the most out of his running because he always knew exactly when to enter the line, whether to create an overlap or to act as a decoy.

He was not a long punter - he never screw-kicked - but rarely missed touch. Playing with Barry John and Phil Bennett, he was not often required as a test place-kicker, though he kicked usefully at club level.

They loved him in Wales. There he was, a rugby buccaneer, patrolling the back, socks often around his ankles, medieval sideboards and a Beatles haircut. But he was no showman. International rugby was a serious business to him. What a comfort he must have been to his team-mates. Willie John McBride says that in South Africa in 1974 he did not drop one ball on the entire tour.

Off the field, he is pleasant if serious company. He is consultant orthopaedic surgeon at the Princess of Wales Hospital in Bridgend, a working class town in southern Wales, and is honorary doctor for the Welsh Rugby Union. His daughters, Lauren and Annie, have represented Wales at hockey. JPR himself still plays lower-grade rugby. 🏉

JEFF WILSON

The Midas Touch

FEW PEOPLE ARE BLESSED with anything like Jeff Wilson's sports ability. Not only was he a New Zealand rugby and cricket representative while still a teenager, but he was a champion junior athlete. Yet he says his best game was basketball!

Wilson attracted national headlines while at Cargill High School in Invercargill. In a First XV match against James Hargest High School he totalled 66 points, scoring nine tries and kicking 15 conversions. He was in the New Zealand Secondary Schools side for two years and in 1992 scored a brilliant try at the Sydney Football Stadium against Australia Schoolboys. While at college, he played seven games for the Southland.

Even as a youngster, he had pace, flair and a formidable array of skills. His rugby future seemed assured … if cricket didn't claim him first.

He made his first class cricket debut at 18 and in 1993 was selected in the New Zealand one-day team for the home series against Australia. He pulled off a blinding catch in one match, bowled with aggression throughout and showed his temperament by scoring the winning runs in the international at Hamilton. As he ran off the field waving his bat to the crowd, it was clear New Zealand had a new sports sensation. One writer cheerfully called him 'the deep South's best gift to New Zealand since the Bluff oyster'.

But in these days of longer seasons, he was forced to specialise and opted for rugby. While New Zealand cricket officials lament his loss, it was the right decision. He was better at rugby and the game has offered him immense opportunities.

In 1993 Wilson moved to Dunedin to attend Teachers College and get first division rugby experience with Otago. He made the All Blacks' end-of-year tour of Britain, taking the right wing spot that had belonged to John Kirwan for a decade.

Wilson scored two tries in his first outing for New Zealand, against South-East Division at Twickenham, and went one better on his test debut against Scotland at Murrayfield, scoring three tries and dazzling the Scots with his footwork. His last try, in the closing moments, was near the sideline. All Black skipper Sean Fitzpatrick threw him the ball, so Wilson calmly slotted the conversion, which meant the All Blacks had reached 50 points against Scotland for the first time. He was the first All Black in 80 years to score three tries in his first test.

Jeffrey William Wilson
Winger/fullback
Born: Invercargill, October 24, 1973
Test debut: New Zealand v Scotland, Edinburgh, November 20, 1993
Test career: 1993-98 (42 matches)
Test points: 151 (28 tries, 1 conversion, 3 penalties)
* Is second to John Kirwan (35) on the list of All Black try-scorers
* Has played four one-day cricket internationals for New Zealand
* Scored hat-trick of tries on test debut v Scotland in 1993
* Scored five tries v Fiji at Albany in 1997

But Wilson thudded back to earth the following week against England. All Black coach Laurie Mains erred by asking too much of the youngster. He wanted him to score the tries, made him place-kicker, and had him taking the kick-offs and dropouts. Wilson had a poor kicking game and the All Blacks tumbled to defeat.

It was the first of three reverses in what has otherwise been a career of rare achievement. Against Australia at Sydney in 1994, Wilson had the chance to cap a stirring All Black second half comeback when he dived for the try that would have won the match. But the ball was knocked from his hands by a flying tackle by Wallaby halfback George Gregan. An hour later, when I was making my way to the marquee where the official after-match function was to be held, Wilson's despair was still evident. All the players were inside except the tearful Wilson, who was slumped in the foyer, with Michael Jones at his side trying to console him.

The biggest disappointment of Wilson's career was the 1995 World Cup final when he left the field early and the All Blacks lost to South Africa in extra time. Since then, some All Blacks have claimed their form was affected by deliberate food poisoning, a charge I tend to treat sceptically. Wilson at that time suffered from "trauma-induced migraine", which produced double vision, and had previously forced him from the field, so his premature departure from Ellis Park was to me no proof that the team was under-performing through illness. As he has got older, Wilson's problems with this disorder seem to have eased.

Counter-balancing these low moments, Wilson has produced some glorious highlights. New Zealand fans nominate his play for Otago in a first division match against Wellington at Athletic Park in 1997 as an example of almost perfect rugby. Wilson, playing at fullback, scored just one try in a 32-27 win, but his penetration on attack and his commitment on defence were decisive.

He has had three tests at fullback for the All Blacks, all in 1995. The arrival of Christian Cullen has given the All Blacks a world class fullback and Wilson has stayed on the wing. But he continues to often play at fullback for Otago and if Cullen is injured or loses form, the All Blacks would not lose by replacing him with Wilson.

There has been some memorable slow-motion footage of Wilson steaming up the right-hand sideline, his blond hair bouncing and his brilliant footwork there for all to see. He must be a nightmare to mark. Not only does he have startling acceleration and pace, but his range of skills enables him to cope with any situation. He has a strong sidestep, and because he is solidly-built at 1.81m (5ft 11in) and 90kg (14st 2lb), he can muscle his way across the line in close-quarter situations. But where Wilson has it over many top wingers is his kicking. He has mastered the chip-kick and has an effective high centring kick. He seldom runs out of options or dies with the ball. I admire him for his vision and style.

Over the years his defence has steadily improved and I like his aggression. He won't be trampled over by anyone. These qualities, coupled with the way he goes looking for work, make Wilson one of the greatest players I've seen. He is one of the senior players in the All Black side. Though Jonah Lomu on the left wing gets more publicity, Wilson is the strategist who is involved in planning moves.

Though he has scored tries everywhere, Wilson has made the Auckland's Albany Stadium a favourite. In 1997 he scored five tries against Fiji there in

Jeff Wilson's test debut, New Zealand v Scotland, 1993. He scored three tries in this match.

1997 and another five when captaining the New Zealand Academy against Ireland A.

In New Zealand he has been criticised for showboating after scoring tries. Wilson is certainly aware of the close-up television camera and on occasion performs for it, gesturing and making facial expressions. But I've never had a problem with this. He doesn't go too far and adds colour to the game.

Wilson has been nicknamed Goldie, a reference to his hair colour and the fact that on the field everything he touches turns to gold. There was one occasion when his locks were less than golden. After New Zealand had beaten South Africa in Cape Town in 1996, he joined Christian Cullen - a staunch member of the crew cut club brigade - in having his head shaved. There must have been something in their high-spirited action for in the next test at Durban they scored brilliant tries in the same corner.

He is good to deal with, and considering the demands on his time, readily accessible by the media. He showed his colours in 1995 when he and Josh Kronfeld became the first All Blacks to break ranks and sign professional contracts with the New Zealand union. Other players were holding out, using the rival World Rugby Corporation's offers as leverage, but once Wilson and Kronfeld signed, they started an avalanche. There was some residual ill-feeling and Zinzan Brooke was quoted later as saying he'd 'like to get Jeff Wilson at the bottom of a ruck'. The way I saw it, Wilson and Kronfeld had shown more class than many of their team-mates. **100**

Jeff Wilson, who made his test debut in 1993, is among the youngest of the 100 players profiled in this book. The temptation is to look about the rugby world and try to identify the future greats, those players who would demand inclusion in such a collection if it was written a few years later.

Among the players who have emerged since the 1995 World Cup:

Tom Bowman (Australia), lock
Thomas Castaignede (France), flyhalf
Christian Cullen (New Zealand), fullback
Ben Evans (Wales), prop
Nathan Grey (Australia), centre
Steve Hanley (England), winger
Eric Miller (Ireland), No 8
Scott Murray (Scotland), lock
Anton Oliver (New Zealand), hooker
Jeremy Paul (Australia), hooker
Breyton Paulse (South Africa) winger
Bobby Skinstad (South Africa), loose forward
Chris Whitaker (Australia), scrumhalf
Jonny Wilkinson (England), centre
Jamie Williams (England), wing/fullback
Royce Willis (New Zealand), lock
Chris Wyatt (Wales), lock

CURRENT WORLD RECORDS

Eligibility for inclusion as a world record:

*   Any genuine international or test match between two countries where at least one of the teams awarded caps (or test status) to its players, and the country is a member of the IRFB.

*   Any match in the Rugby World Cup finals tournaments of 1987, 1991 or 1995.

*   Any match played in a Rugby World Cup qualifying or elimination tournament.

*   Any officially-sanctioned matches like the Asian, Pan American, Latin Cup or Pan Pacific Championships.

*   Matches involving the British Isles and South America (in the early 1980s) are also included.

Note: These records are for 15-a-side games only.

Part One
World records by teams

Highest score in a test match
164 by Hong Kong v Singapore, Kuala Lumpur, 1994 (Rugby World Cup Asian qualifying tournament)

Biggest winning margin in a test match
151 by Hong Kong v Singapore, Kuala Lumpur, 1994 (final score 164-13)

Most tries in a test match
26 by Hong Kong v Singapore, Kuala Lumpur, 1994

Most conversions in a test match
20 by New Zealand v Japan, Bloemfontein, 1995

Most penalty goals kicked in a test match
9 by Japan v Tonga, Tokyo, 1999
8 by Canada v Scotland, St John's, 1991
8 by Wales v Canada, Cardiff, 1993
8 by Italy v Romania, Bucharest, 1994
8 by Argentina v Canada, Buenos Aires, 1995
8 by Scotland v Tonga, Pretoria 1995
8 by France v Ireland, Durban, 1995
8 by Ireland v Italy, Dublin, 1997

Most drop goals by one team in a test match
There are 14 instances of three dropped goals in a test match by a team (11 are by individual players, see individual records.) The other three instances of three dropped goals in a test are by a team. They are:
New Zealand v France, Christchurch, 1986 (2 players were involved)
Fiji v Romania, Brive, 1991 (2 players were involved)
France v New Zealand, Christchurch, 1994 (2 players were involved)

Most drop goals by both teams in a test match
6 by New Zealand and France, Christchurch, 1986

Most consecutive test matches unbeaten
23 by New Zealand between 1987 and 1990

Longest winning streak in test matches
17 by New Zealand between 1965 and 1969
17 by South Africa between 1997 and 1998

Highest drawn score in a test match
26-26 England v New Zealand, Twickenham 1997

Part Two
World records by individual players

Most test matches
111 by Philippe Sella, France, 1982-95

Most test matches at fullback
81 by Serge Blanco, France, 1980-94

Most test matches as a winger
91 by Rory Underwood, England and British Isles, 1984-96 (85 for England and 6 for British Isles)

Most test matches at centre (either inside or outside centre and including matches in the position called second five-eighths)
104 by Philippe Sella, France, 1982-95

Most test matches at flyhalf (or first five-eighth)
75 by Rob Andrew, England and British Isles, 1985-97 (70 for England, 5 for British Isles)

Most test matches at scrumhalf (or halfback)
63 by Gareth Edwards, Wales and British Isles, 1967-78 (53 for Wales, 10 for British Isles)
Note: The most tests at scrumhalf for one country is 62 by Nick Farr-Jones, Australia, 1984-94

Most test matches by a forward (any position)
92 by Sean Fitzpatrick, hooker, New Zealand, 1986-97

Most test matches at No 8 forward
53 by Dean Richards, England and British Isles, 1986-96 (47 for England, 6 for British Isles)

Most test matches at flanker
65 by Fergus Slattery, Ireland and British Isles, 1970-84 (61 for Ireland, 4 for British Isles)
65 by Peter Winterbottom, England and British Isles, 1982-93 (58 for England, 7 for British Isles)

Most test matches at lock
80 by Willie John McBride, Ireland and British Isles, 1962-75 (63 for Ireland, 17 for British Isles)

Most test matches at prop
74* by Jason Leonard, England and British Isles, 1990-99 (71 for England, 3 for British Isles)
* still playing

Most test matches at hooker
92 by Sean Fitzpatrick, New Zealand, 1986-97

Most consecutive test matches (any position)
63 by Sean Fitzpatrick, hooker, for New Zealand, 1986-95

Most test matches as captain
59 by Will Carling for England, 1988-96

Part Three
Scoring by individuals

Most points in all test matches
911 by Michael Lynagh, Australia, 1984-95 (in 72 tests)

Most points in one test match
50 by Ashley Billington, Hong Kong v Singapore, Kuala Lumpur, 1994 (10 tries)

Most points in a test match by a player on test debut
45 by Simon Culhane, New Zealand v Japan, Bloemfontein, 1995

Most tries in all test matches
64 by David Campese, Australia, 1982-96

Most tries in one test match
10 by Ashley Billington, Hong Kong v Singapore, Kuala Lumpur, 1994

Most tries in a test match by a player on test debut
5 by Daniel Lambert, England v France, Richmond, 1907

Most conversions in all test matches
140 by Michael Lynagh, Australia, 1984-95

Most conversions in one test match
20 by Simon Culhane, New Zealand v Japan, Bloemfontein, 1995

Most penalties in all test matches
177 by Michael Lynagh, Australia, 1984-95
177* by Neil Jenkins, Wales/British Isles, 1991-99
* still playing

Most penalties in one test match
9 by Keiji Hirose, Japan v Tonga, Tokyo, 1999
8 by Mark Wyatt, Canada v Scotland, St John's, 1991
8 by Neil Jenkins, Wales v Canada, Cardiff, 1993
8 by Diego Dominguez, Italy v Romania, Bucharest , 1994
8 by Santiago Meson, Argentina v Canada, Buenos Aires, 1995
8 by Gavin Hastings, Scotland v Tonga, Pretoria, 1995
8 by Thierry Lacroix, France v Ireland, Durban, 1995
8 by Paul Burke, Ireland v Italy, Dublin, 1997

Most drop goals in all test matches
28 by Hugo Porta, Argentina and South America, 1971-90

Most drop goals in one test match
3 by Pierre Albaladejo, France v Ireland, Paris 1960
3 by Phil Hawthorne, Australia v England, Twickenham 1967
3 by Hugo Porta, Argentina v Australia, Buenos Aires, 1979
3 by Naas Botha, South Africa v South America, Durban 1980
3 by Naas Botha, South Africa v Ireland, Durban 1981
3 by Jean-Patrick Lescarboura, France v England, Twickenham, 1985
3 by Hugo Porta, Argentina v New Zealand, Buenos Aires, 1985
3 by Jean-Patrick Lescarboura, France v New Zealand, Christchurch, 1986
3 by Didier Camberabero, France v Australia, Sydney 1990
3 by Opeti Turuva, Fiji v Western Samoa, Nadi, 1994
3 by Neculai Nichitean, Romania v France, Bucharest, 1995

Longest span as a test player
21* years, Diego Ormaechea, Uruguay, 1979-99
20 years, Hugo Porta, Argentina, 1971-90
* still playing

Longest gap between test matches
13 years and 2 months, 1908-21, Ned Hughes, New Zealand

Oldest player to play in a test match
40 years and 123 days, Ned Hughes, New Zealand, 1921

Youngest player to play in a test match
17 years and 36 days, Ninian Finlay, Scotland 1875
17 years and 36 days, Charles Reid, Scotland 1881

Bibliography

The author gratefully acknowledges the authors and publishers of the following books:

Australian Rugby - the Game and the Players, Jack Pollard, Ironbark, 1994

Beegee, Bob Howitt, Rugby Press, 1981

Blacked Out, Richard Becht, Ross Land and Ross Setford, Meadowset Graphics and Photopacific, 1991

Broadcasting with the Kiwis, Winston McCarthy, Sporting Publications, 1947

Centenary History of the Rugby Football Union, Uel Titley and Ross McWhirter, The Rugby Football Union, 1970

Centenary: 100 Years of All Black Rugby, Rod Chester and Neville McMillan, Moa Publications, 1984

Colin Meads All Black, Alex Veysey, Collins, 1974

Complete Book of Rugby, The, Richard Bath, SevenOaks, 1997

Complete Who's Who of International Rugby, The, Terry Godwin, Blandford Press, 1987

Courage Book of Sporting Heroes 1884-1984, The, Chris Rhys, Stanley Paul, 1984

Days Without Sunset, Denzil Batchelor, Eyre and Spottiswoode, 1949

Encyclopedia of New Zealand Rugby, The, Rod Chester, Neville McMillan and Ron Palenski, Hodder Moa Beckett, 1998

Encyclopedia of Rugby Union, The, Donald Sommerville, Aurum Press, 1997

Encyclopedia of World Rugby, The, Keith Quinn, Shoal Bay Press, 1991

Encyclopedie Francaise, Pierre Lafond and Jean-Pierre Bodis, Editions Dehedin, 1989

Famous Flankers, Joseph Romanos, Rugby Press, 1990

Famous Fullbacks, Joseph Romanos, Rugby Press, 1989

Fergie, Alex Veysey, Whitcoulls, 1976

Fourth All Blacks, The, John Hayhurst, Longmans, 1954

Fronting Up: The Sean Fitzpatrick Story, Steven O'Meagher, Hodder Moa Beckett, 1994

Game Goes On, The, H B T Wakelam, Arthur Backer Ltd, 1936

Game the Goal: The Grant Fox Story, The, Alex Veysey, Rugby Press, 1992

Gareth Edwards' 100 Great Rugby Players, Gareth Edwards, Queen Anne Press, 1987

Giants in Green and Gold, Ian Diehm, Boolarong, 1994

Giants of Irish Rugby, John Scally, Mainstream Publishing, 1996

Giants of South African Rugby, A C Parker, AH and AW Reed, 1956

Graham Mourie: Captain, Graham Mourie, Moa, 1982

Great Number Tens, The, Frank Keating, Partridge Press, 1993

Great Rugby Players, David Norrie, Hamlyn, 1980

Guinness International Who's Who of Sport, The, Peter Matthews, Guinness, 1993

Haka! The All Blacks Story, Winston McCarthy, Pelham Books, 1968

History of South African Rugby Football, The, Ivor Difford, Specialty Press, 1933

How the Lions Won, Terry O'Connor, Collins, 1975

Ian Jones Unlocked, Bob Howitt, Celebrity Books, 1998

International Rugby Championship 1883-1983, The, Terry Godwin, Collins Willow, 1984

John Kirwan's Rugby World, John Kirwan (editor), Rugby Press, 1987

Listen, It's a Goal!, Winston McCarthy, Pelham Books, 1973

Love of Rugby, The, Peter Walker, Octopus, 1980

Kirwan: Running on Instinct, Paul Thomas, Moa, 1992

Lions 77, Keith Quinn, Methuen, 1977

Lochore, Alex Veysey, Gary Caffell and Ron Palenski, Hodder Moa Beckett, 1996

Marauding Maroons, Bret Harris, Horwitz, 1979

Men in Black, Rod Chester and Neville McMillan, Moa Publications, several editions

Men in Green, Sean Diffley, Stanley Paul, 1974

Mud in Your Eye, Chris Laidlaw, Howard Timmins, 1973

New Zealand Barbarians Rugby Book, The, Murray Reid, J M McGregor, 1980

On The Ball, Gordon Slatter, Whitcombe and Tombs, 1970

Our National Game, Ron Palenski, Moa Beckett, 1992

Oxford Companion to Sports and Games, The, John Arlott, Paladin, 1977

Phoenix Book of International Rugby Records, The, John Griffiths, Phoenix House, 1987

Portrait of Scottish Rugby, A, Allan Massie, Polygon, undated

Round the World with the All Blacks 1953-54, Winston McCarthy, Sporting Publications, 1954

Rugby Companion, The, Wallace Reyburn, Hutchinson, 1969

Rugby Football, D R Gent, George Allen and Unwin, 1922

Rugby Football, Cliff Jones, Pitman and Sons, 1937

Rugby Football Today, E H D Sewell, John Murray, 1931

Rugby in My Time, Winston McCarthy, A H and A W Reed, 1958

Rugby in South Africa: A History 1861-1998, Paul Dobson, South African Rugby Board, 1998

Rugby on Attack, Ron Jarden, Whitcombe and Tombs, 1961

Rugby Recollections, W J T Collins, R H Johns, 1948

Rugby - The Great Ones, Cliff Morgan (editor), Pelham Books, 1970

Rugby '98, Paolo Pacitti and Francesco Volpe, Gruppo Tipografico Editoriale, 1997

Rugger: The Man's Game, E H D Sewell, Hollis and Carter, 1947

Rugger, W W Wakefield and H Marshall, Longmans, 1930

South Africa's Greatest Springboks, J Sacks, Sporting Publications, 1938

Springbok and Silverfern, Reg Sweet, AH and AW Reed, 1960

Springbok Saga, Chris Greyvenstein, Don Nelson and Toyota (South Africa) Ltd, 1981

Springboks 1891-1970, The, A C Parker, Cassell, 1970

This World of Rugby, John Thornett, Murray, 1967

Visitors: the History of International Rugby teams in New Zealand, The, Rod Chester and Neville McMillan, Moa Publications, 1990

Wallaby Greats, Max Howell and Lingyu Xie, Rugby Publishing, 1996

Who's Who of International Rugby, David Emery (editor), Queen Anne Press, 1984

Winning Way, The, Bob Dwyer, Rugby Press, 1992

With the All Blacks in Springbokland, 1928, Mark Nicholls, L F Watkins, 1928

World of Rugby, The, Wallace Reyburn, Elek Books, 1967

World of Rugby: A History of Rugby Union Football, The, John Reason and Carwyn James, BBC, 1979

Wounded Pride, A, Keith Quinn, Methuen, 1983

30 Super Springboks, Paul Dobson, Human and Rousseau, 1995

100 Great Rugby Characters, Joseph Romanos, Grant Harding and Murray Webb, Rugby Press, 1991

All the books of Terry McLean, published by AH and AW Reed, Hutchinson and Hodder and Stoughton, between 1954 and 1990

All the books of J B G Thomas, published by Pelham and Stanley Paul, between 1954 and 1985

Annual editions of the following publications: *New Zealand Rugby Almanack*, 1935-98; *Rothmans Rugby Union Yearbook*, 1972-90; *The Save and Prosper Rugby Union Who's Who,* various editions; *John Wisden's Rugby Football Almanack,* various editions.

The following periodicals: *Rugby News*, New Zealand; *Rugby News*, Great Britain; *Rugby World and Post*, Great Britain; *The Game*, Great Britain; *Sports Digest*, New Zealand.

The author also wishes to acknowledge the many newspapers and international match programmes he drew on for information.